Hertfordshire Children
War and Peace, 1914–1

£2

Also by David Parker

John Newsom: A Hertfordshire educationist

Hertfordshire Children in War and Peace, 1914–1939

David Parker

HERTFORDSHIRE PUBLICATIONS
an imprint of the
University of Hertfordshire Press

First published in Great Britain in 2007 by
Hertfordshire Publications
an imprint of the
University of Hertfordshire Press
Learning and Information Services
University of Hertfordshire
College Lane
Hatfield
Hertfordshire AL10 9AB

Hertfordshire Publications, an imprint of the University of Hertfordshire Press,
is published on behalf of the Hertfordshire Association for Local History

British Library Cataloguing in Publication Data
A catalogue record for this book is available from the British Library

ISBN 978-1-905313-40-2

Design by Geoff Green Book Design, CB24 4RA
Cover design by John Robertshaw, AL5 2JB
Printed in Great Britain by Hobbs the Printers Ltd, SO40 3WX

To Pamela – again and always

Contents

Illustrations

Every effort has been made to contact copyright holders in order to seek permission to reproduce images. Where it has been impossible to trace copyright holders, the publishers would be pleased to hear from them.

Abbreviations

CTA	County Teachers' Association
HMI	His Majesty's Inspectors
KC	King's Counsel
KCB	Knight Commander of the Bath
LEA	Local Education Authority
MP	Member of Parliament
NFU	National Farmers' Union
NSPCC	National Society for the Prevention of Cruelty to Children
NUT	National Union of Teachers
PE	Physical Education
PT	Physical Training
RAMC	Royal Army Medical Corps
RSPCA	Royal Society for the Prevention of Cruelty to Animals
SRC	Schools Reorganisation Committee
VAD	Voluntary Aid Detachment
VC	Victoria Cross
YMCA	Young Men's Christian Association

CHAPTER ONE

Introduction

T HERE WERE SCENES of wild excitement in Trafalgar Square and Whitehall as Big Ben struck 11pm on 4 August 1914. The British ultimatum to Germany to withdraw from Belgium had expired unanswered. War was imminent, and the war, it was assumed, would be brief and glorious. Germany's threat to British trade and European peace would end in the Kaiser's total humiliation – probably by the coming Christmas.

Such hopes were soon dashed. Within weeks the conflict had pitched Britain, France, Italy, Russia and Serbia against Germany, Austria–Hungary and Turkey, and the dashing cavalry charges had been replaced by slogging matches in seas of dust and mud. Vast armies, millions strong, fought across the valleys and villages of north-east France and south-west Belgium, the endless forests and plains of Russia and Poland, the snow-capped mountains and passes of Austria, Italy and the Balkans, and the rocky Gallipoli peninsula in Turkey.

During the autumn of 1914 many thousands of Britons from all walks of life volunteered to serve King and country. They came from a nation full of inequalities and internal tensions. The divisions were all too obvious. Across numerous landed estates a hierarchy of outdoor and indoor employees, from estate managers to grooms and from housekeepers to scullery maids, perpetuated a closely ordered and paternalistic rural society. In the ever-expanding towns the nation's industrial and commercial wealth displayed itself as much in the slum dwellings and rows of narrow-fronted terraces and their tenants as in the block-like factories, belching chimneys and neo-Classical and neo-Gothic town halls.

The decade before the war had seen the state take a few more steps to succour the needy through the provision of school meals to the desperately poor, a basic pension to those consistently employed in jobs carrying low wages, and unemployment benefit to those in areas of cyclical employment such as shipbuilding and the construction industry. The huge opposition to such initiatives, and the

1

host of conditions surrounding them, accentuated rather than allayed social divisions. Many thought state intervention had gone far too far, but many others asserted it still had far to go.

Just before the war, between 1909 and 1911, immense tensions were created by the prolonged and bitter dispute between the Conservative opposition, especially in the House of Lords, and the Liberal government, which sought to introduce super-tax on high salaries and death duties on major estates to help pay for welfare reforms. At the same time the trades unions were beginning to flex their collective muscles, and a series of major strikes occurred in cotton factories, coal mines, docks and railways between 1910 and 1914. The social commentator C.F.G. Masterman had considerable evidence to support his claim that, for all the charitable giving, the rich despised the working classes while the middle classes feared them.[1] Nevertheless, in 1914 all classes donned their uniforms, and fought, died or somehow survived.

After four years of mutual attrition the defeated German and Austro-Hungarian empires were destroyed, and Imperial Russia, Britain's ally, had been torn apart by violent internal revolution. Great Britain and its empire emerged victorious, but far from unscathed. Nearly three-quarters of a million British servicemen had died, and many thousands more had been physically injured and mentally scarred. Husbands, fathers, sons and brothers had endured the horrors of war on land, on sea, or in the air; wives, mothers, daughters and sisters had endured the trials of waiting and managing alone. A generation lived out its life with memories of screeching shells, bleeding bodies and sudden death. Materially, the country's long-standing trading patterns in the Far East and Latin America had been disrupted, with many markets seized by the United States and Japan. In addition, the United States, not Great Britain, had become the world's major creditor, and acquired huge influence as a result.

This book explores the aspirations and anxieties of people living in Hertfordshire during a particularly tumultuous quarter of a century. It looks at wartime events and peacetime developments, many of them controversial, through the eyes of a cross section of local society. In particular, it examines the lives of ordinary families, and especially their children, and the attitudes shown towards them by local landowners, farmers, factory owners, magistrates, clergy, teachers, county councillors and county officials.

The story starts with the outbreak of one world war in 1914, continues through twenty years of uneasy peace, and concludes with the outbreak of another world war in 1939. It sets local trends and experiences within wider national political, economic and social contexts, and examines the similarities and differences between what went on in Hertfordshire and elsewhere in the country. It reveals a county of striking contrasts; much changed over these eventful twenty-five years, but much did not. New ideas and expectations as well as thousands of new families arrived on the scene, but at the same time many old practices and assumptions, and many old families, continued to hold political as well as social sway.

The book argues that, alongside Hertfordshire's rapid expansion and rising prosperity, developments in agriculture, education and public health remained firmly in the hands of those who strove to preserve the social hierarchy, and to ensure that the next generation were carefully nurtured in habits, attitudes and skills appropriate to the pre-ordained places in life that were assumed to be theirs. The chambers of the county council and its major committees, notably agriculture and education, consistently resounded with debates and decisions to this effect.

Absolute economy in public expenditure was always a major ambition, yet it is clear that many local initiatives were voted into being in full knowledge of the considerable extra cost. Irrespective of the swings in the economic and political fortunes of the nation as a whole, Hertfordshire County Council remained remarkably consistent in the educational and social welfare policies it chose to pursue – and also those it did not. For example, its determined preservation of all-age (5–14) village schools after 1918, and its continual investment in gardening, handicraft, domestic subjects and physical education in the elementary schools was in striking contrast to its steadfast refusal to increase the proportion of pupils from those schools allowed to enter the prestigious secondary schools as scholarship holders or to create opportunities for older village children to attend urban schools.

This essentially utilitarian and patrician view of schooling, so characteristic of Victorian times, had taken firm hold in 1914, when everything to do with elementary education had been subordinated to the needs of the war effort. Attendances plummeted unchecked as hundreds of children worked in farms, factories and shops, while those in school were used to promote the war effort at every opportunity, not least by the intensive cultivation of 'war gardens' and the production of thousands of garments and other goods for the Red Cross and army. So extreme was Hertfordshire's encouragement of child labour that the Board of Education, which usually reflected the government's tacit acceptance of wartime exigencies, was moved to remonstrate.

Nevertheless, throughout the period the county council remained high in popular esteem as a prudent, yet also progressive, public body providing an ever-increasing range of facilities and opportunities to families fortunate enough to live within its borders. In retrospect, many of its decisions appear distinctly reactionary, but that was far from how most people viewed developments at the time.

The book draws on many contemporary sources. There were headteachers writing in logbooks, speaking at teachers' meetings, addressing conferences and contributing to education committee debates. There were school inspectors compiling reports on the work, standards and problems of individual schools, submitting memoranda to Board of Education officials and dispatching advisory papers to the county council. There were the county medical officer and his district assistants sending carefully argued recommendations to the Local Education Authority (LEA), and the specialist 'organisers' appointed by the LEA recording developments in school gardening, physical education, practical instruction and domestic science. The hopes and fears of Church of England and Nonconformist clergy were extremely well represented in numerous newspaper reports, editorials, articles and correspondence. The large number of aristocratic landowners and gentlemen farmers living in Hertfordshire also had little trouble in getting their views into print in a county where their wealth and status still commanded considerable respect. Local newspapers devoted regular columns to rural affairs, and the agricultural lobby was particularly well represented on county committees. Conversely, as the urban population rapidly expanded the views of commercial and industrial employers, chambers of trade, and even trades unions, increasingly found their way into newspapers and also into the briefing papers sent to county committees by their officers. The agendas and minutes of the county council and its committees survive in numerous leather-bound volumes, and these are complemented by local newspapers which customarily sent reporters to these meetings to ensure readers could enjoy not only the editor's critical reflections but also reasonably verbatim accounts of the discussions themselves. There are also the memories of older inhabitants regarding their childhood experiences during and after the First World War, which were taped during Stevenage Museum's Oral History Project in the mid-1980s.

For access to all these sources of information I am grateful to the staff of the British Library Newspaper Library, the Public Record Office at the National Archives in Kew, the Department of Education and Skills Library, London University Institute of Education Library, Stevenage Museum, the First Garden City Heritage Museum in Letchworth, and especially Hertfordshire Archives and

Local Studies in Hertford itself where particular thanks are given to Diana Vanderson. I appreciate, too, the permission readily given by Mr Stephen Ruff, Hertford Museum, Stevenage Museum, the First Garden City Heritage Museum and Hertfordshire Archives and Local Studies to use illustrations in their possession, and by *History of Education, History of Education Quarterly, Journal of Vocational Education and Training, Journal of Educational Administration and History*, and *European Journal of Research in Physical Education* to use material I had incorporated into articles they published. My thanks also are given to Ben and Chris Lee for their invaluable help in reproducing many of the illustrations.

All sources of evidence of the past must be treated with caution. The things people said and wrote were said and written in particular contexts and to or for particular audiences, and bias is usually present. Far from being a problem, this makes the evidence more telling and the story more interesting. For example, Hertfordshire newspapers of the period were either staunchly Conservative or Liberal in sympathy, and the stance of their reports and editorials is illuminating. Following major trends in public opinion, they tended to fawn upon the aristocracy, abhor rises in public expenditure, dismiss the views of trades unions, and treat the hierarchy of expensive public schools, prestigious grammar schools and free elementary schools as an immutable buttress of the social order.

As a rule, county councillors were not inclined to be in the vanguard of costly and possibly unsettling reform, but they could be cajoled by government grants and persuaded by public opinion, and rural issues were treated with a particular sympathy that often overrode the general desire for economy. In addition, the growing number of professional experts – the medical officers and the county 'organisers' – lost no opportunity to extend their influence. Their reports invariably confirm the worth of previous initiatives while revealing yet more areas for investment.

Equally illuminating are the teachers' perceptions of their roles, and the ways in which they were treated by those in authority over them. As we shall see, the lives of elementary school headteachers were strictly circumscribed by government and LEA regulations, and they rarely forgot that their logbook entries were open to scrutiny, and critical comment, by His Majesty's Inspectors (HMI), school managers and county officials. Nevertheless, they had a voice at county education meetings, where three teacher representatives had full membership, and the annual conferences organised by the County Teachers' Association (CTA) received press coverage. However, it was the headteachers of the secondary schools, largely the preserve of fee-paying families, who probably represented the social and educational divide in its most striking form. Their sense of superiority knew no bounds, and included a powerful and freely expressed bias against most of the elementary schoolchildren who entered their portals as 'free place' scholarship holders. Caught up in the turmoil of war, and the uncertain political, economic and social climate of the decades that followed, the schools fought their own battles for their 'place in the sun.'

The book falls into two parts. Chapters Two to Six are devoted to the First World War, and Chapters Seven to Eleven to the 1920s and 1930s, although the argument is made that the experiences of war contributed much towards subsequent social, economic and educational policies and practices. Many themes in the first part are therefore picked up again in the second.

CHAPTER TWO

Hertfordshire in 1914

O LD PHOTOGRAPHS OF HERTFORDSHIRE at the turn of the twentieth century give the impression of a county still slumbering in rural isolation, with dozens of peaceful villages surrounding a scattering of ancient towns largely devoted to agricultural markets and industries, and a few steam-powered factories nestling by canals and railways. The frozen images do not lie, but they do not portray the whole truth. They may suggest a time when the pace of life was slower and less stressful, the roads quieter and safer, and families and communities more ordered and closer-knit, but the monochrome image belies a far more complex picture of agricultural decay, rural stagnation, urban expansion, industrial growth and social tension. The county, in common with most shire counties surrounding London, was experiencing unprecedented social and economic changes. The pace of these changes was accelerating, and Hertfordshire went to war in 1914 wrestling with the stresses brought about by the lingering decline of long-established rural communities and the endless construction of new urban estates housing as many families commuting to London each day as worked for local employers.

As early as 1746 a visitor to Hertfordshire noted the lure of London. There is 'little or no manufacture in the Shire', he observed, but it 'is full of Maltsters, Millers, Dealers in Corn'. The county would have remained a rural backwater, he concluded, but for London, which rendered its market towns 'a great Thorough-Fare' for 'the sale of Wheat and Barley, and all sorts of grain.'[1] Fifty years later the Grand Junction Canal, in the west of the county, and the widening of the rivers Lea and Stort, in the east, were facilitating the passage of bulk goods to and from the capital, and another fifty years on main railway lines were beginning to radiate from London throughout Hertfordshire, bringing cheaper and quicker transport in their wake. As the twentieth century dawned the quickening pace of communications and building meant that while the north and east of Hertfordshire were still largely rural, the south and west were buffeted by the ever-expanding and easily accessible metropolis. By 1914 the council chambers and committee rooms, newspaper columns and speakers' platforms, resounded with arguments about the awesome nature of the changes afflicting the county, and the social and economic problems they posed for the inhabitants. The arguments continued to rage during and after the war.

In 1914 east Hertfordshire was mainly arable, and mixed farms dominated the north. The old market towns of Baldock, Hitchin, Royston, Bishop's Stortford, Ware, Hertford and Stevenage formed a rough circle, and although each one had regular, if not particularly rapid, rail communication with London, the cross-country routes by rail and road were so inadequate that some county council committees met in Holborn, rather than Hertford or St Albans, and continued to do so until 1939. The Great Northern Railway's slow branch line to Baldock and Royston gave sufficient ease of access to London to stimulate farming, but was far too time-consuming to encourage daily commuting. The Northern and Eastern line to Broxbourne and Bishop's Stortford opened in the 1840s, and twenty years later a branch line wound its way through the countryside to Buntingford, but the slowness of the trains coupled with the inconvenient siting of the original terminus at Stratford meant the towns failed to expand as the railway directors had hoped.[2]

In the south-east the extensive Broxbourne Woods area possessed ancient scattered villages but was mainly conspicuous by its division into several large privately owned parkland estates. By 1914, though, the main roads and railways skirting the forest were encouraging the rapid growth of Lea valley towns such as Hoddesdon, Cheshunt and Waltham Cross. Intensive potato growing and market gardening for London were already dominating the area.[3] The fast Great Northern Railway loop from London to Hertford was promoting new suburban estates in and around Cuffley.[4]

Central and south-west Hertfordshire had a very mixed society of old established rural estates, new intensive market gardens and encroaching commuter development. Originally most of the land in this area had been owned by the Abbey of St Albans, with numerous small hamlets servicing this powerful and highly centralised religious institution with rents and produce. After the dissolution of the monasteries by King Henry VIII, St Albans continued to be the dominant market town. The last third of the nineteenth century saw the whole of this area of scattered farms and villages pierced by several main railway lines linking London with the Midlands, the north of England and Scotland. Villages in the

Lea valley greenhouses, c.1927 (HALS)

south, such as London Colney, Radlett and Elstree, developed rapidly in the wake of the construction of the Midland Railway out of St Pancras. The Great Northern Railway opened up Barnet in the 1870s, and the Metropolitan Railway reached the future residential suburbs of Rickmansworth and Chorleywood in 1887.[5] This southern part of the county witnessed the greatest influx of population and industry prior to the First World War.

Watford, by far the largest town in the county in 1914, exemplified this development. In 1838, the year the London and Birmingham Railway station opened, its population was below 3,000. As the old town estates were sold, in particular the Earl of Essex's Cassiobury Park in 1897, so the villas, terrace houses, shops and factories proliferated, until the population stood at nearly 30,000 in 1901 and over 40,000 in 1911. The breweries perpetuated the town's traditional trade, but by 1914 they had been joined by printers, food processors, machine- and tool-makers and numerous small firms manufacturing parts for motor vehicles. An unusually vigorous local Board of Health had ensured the burgeoning town had adequate roads, sewers and water supplies, and a determined publicly elected local School Board, established in 1883, had embarked upon a continuous programme of school building.[6]

Watford still had its share of overcrowded and ill-serviced houses, but major slum districts were more evident in the ancient city of St Albans and old market towns such as Hitchin. After the war the appalling conditions lingering in the poorest parts of these towns came to the fore in official reports and numerous newspaper articles.[7] In Hitchin nearly 200 decaying houses were crowded into five notorious acres in the town's centre, and equally appalling unsanitary and vermin-ridden ghettoes existed in St Albans.[8]

A few miles from Hitchin, Ebenezer Howard was pioneering a different sort of town. The source of much contemporary misunderstanding, suspicion and downright hostility, Letchworth Garden City represented different things to different groups. To some it was a curiosity, the abode of mystics and dreamers out of touch with reality; to others it was a den haunted by radical freethinkers only too ready to contaminate the rest of society. To Howard, though, it was to be a virtually self-contained city in a garden with well-laid-out houses, factories and services surrounded by, and integrated with, extensive countryside and farms. It was not to be confused with a city of gardens or suburbia. The Garden City Association gave effect to his fundamental belief that 'the satisfactory solution of almost every other social problem is dependent on the satisfactory solution of the housing problem'. Its aim was nothing less than the prevention of the evils of overcrowded towns and the wasting depopulation of the countryside.[9] Having purchased a site not far from a main railway and roads at agricultural prices, a limited liability company converted much of it to housing and industrial plots at higher, but still attractive, rates, and utilised the profits after paying modest dividends to provide communal facilities.

Letchworth started in green fields in 1904 and, although suffering from a lack of capital and high borrowing over the next decade, the sheer energy of the early pioneers created a core of access roads, a range of modest but modern houses, two small schools, and attracted the first factories.[10] By 1913 C.B. Purdom, a leading enthusiast and planner, was contrasting Letchworth with other ancient towns with obvious pride and pity:

> In Garden City there are no slums; there are, therefore, no slum children. There are none of those conditions which reduce the vitality of the child and make town life a curse to the race.[11]

As early as 1905 the pioneers had opened a co-educational and non-sectarian elementary school in rudimentary premises. This was later taken over by the LEA and rebuilt in modern premises with extra facilities paid for by the Garden City Company. Unusually for the time, it had a central hall and generous space for recreation, and, even more unusually, it remained a mixed school in which the sexes actually mixed. Letchworth's schools, Purdom claimed, were 'as near being models of what schools should be as education authorities will let them', and in due course HMI noted their liberal regime and wide curriculum with approval.[12]

Not surprisingly, a noted Hitchin historian, Reginald Hine, later recalled the loathing displayed by his ancient town towards its newly born neighbour's constant preening, self-advertisement and success. Hitchin was led by a Quaker-dominated council, which steadfastly resisted all social change and public expenditure, and many in the town detested 'the cocksure dexterity of these new-fangled strangers who undertook to build a city in a single generation'. 'We called them dreamers', Hine said, 'and hoped that the dawn might come and shatter all their dreams.' Ruefully he admitted that 'we concentrated our eyes in disgust upon their sandals and forgot to notice that these men had heads.'[13] Ironically, for all its oddities in the eyes of outside observers, the isolation that characterised Letchworth before 1914 transformed itself into active integration into county affairs after 1918. The growing business acumen and financial support that accompanied the utopian vision and pioneering energy of Letchworth were to provide Hertfordshire not only with numerous modern industries and an innovative example of civic planning but also with well-publicised, if not always completely welcome, ideas on social welfare provision and modern approaches to education.

Occupations across the county, like the population and its housing, were a mixture of old and new. Traditional industries retaining merely a vestige of their former significance were straw plaiting, hat-making, woodware carving, and brick- and tile-making, but paper-making and printing expanded with new mass production techniques, and malting grew along with brewing to keep pace with both local and London demands.[14] Agriculture remained the greatest single employer, with London its greatest market. In 1911, 15.2 per cent of the male population in Hertfordshire –17,920 men – worked on farms or market gardens, well above the national average of 8.3 per cent. However, if the Rural Districts are aggregated separately the county figure of 27.1 per cent falls below the national one of 29.5 per cent, illustrating both the overall importance of agriculture locally and the relative diversity of employment. The comparable figures for 1901 offer further evidence of the changes taking place. Then the number of local men engaged in agriculture had been considerably higher – 17.1 per cent compared with the national average of 8.8 per cent – and the county figure for Rural Districts – 30.6 per cent – had exactly matched the national average.[15]

Remote from coal and iron deposits, the heightened industrial expansion of

Paper mills on the river Gade and Grand Junction Canal, c.1927 (HALS)

the eighteenth and nineteenth centuries had largely bypassed Hertfordshire. Only in the final decade of the nineteenth century did expanding firms in central London, faced with high costs for alternative sites, follow the movement of population to the new suburbs and beyond. The county now afforded ease of communication with London and the Midlands, and provided a cheap pool of labour, and the moderately priced land carried attractively low rates.[16] One major industrial employer, however, had arrived long before. In the nineteenth century the old paper mills along the banks of the river Gade had been substantially modernised and extended, and by 1914 the factories of John Dickinson at Apsley, Croxley Green and Hemel Hempstead were the largest in the country, employing 3,000 people and contributing much to the rapid growth and prosperity of these former villages.[17]

The new industries were varied. Numerous small workshops and larger factories supported the motor industry, several bulk chemical and clothing manufacturers arrived, a mass-produced brush manufacturer finally crippled the local cottage industry, and a number of large-scale printers and publishers established headquarters in St Albans and the new Garden City at Letchworth.[18] Not surprisingly, by 1914 the building trade had become the second-largest occupational group.[19]

The county's population rose by 47,203 between 1901 and 1911 to a total of 311,284, of whom 21,391 were the net gain from immigration, principally from London.[20] Mobility was high – only 53.7 per cent of the population had been born in the county.[21] All Hertfordshire towns grew to a greater or lesser extent between 1901 and 1911, but this was in marked contrast to rural areas. Villages near main line stations, such as Digswell, near Welwyn, and North Mimms, near Hatfield, and villages near expanding towns, such as Sandridge, near St Albans, were major but isolated growth points in the otherwise static or declining rural districts.[22] In general, the more isolated the village the greater the decline, with only those few on the more accessible cross-country routes showing signs of maintaining population levels.

The middle years of the nineteenth century had seen the peak of village expansion and agrarian prosperity. These were followed by decline, as farmers' profits and labourers' wages fell. Among many examples, the Chiltern village of Great Gaddesden declined from a population of 1,161 in 1851 to 752 in 1911; Ayot St Lawrence, in central Hertfordshire, fell from 151 in 1871 to 130 in 1911; Weston, in the north, fell from 1,196 in 1861 to 834 in 1911; and Braughing, in the east, declined equally steeply from 1,358 in 1841 to 949 in 1911.[23] In 1911 62.4 per cent of Hertfordshire's population lived in Urban Districts, 37.6 per cent in Rural Districts.[24] Urban employment was now bringing the attraction of higher wages, shorter hours and cleaner work, with the towns also providing more facilities, services and entertainment. Already, by 1895, industrial competition around Watford had obliged local farmers to pay summer wages of 15s a week, compared with the 11s at Royston in the far north-east. In addition, the rapid improvement in long-distance rail transport caused Hertfordshire farmers to lose the great advantage proximity to London had previously given them as corn producers. An increasing acreage was dropping back to permanent grass – 38 per cent of the cultivated area in 1905, compared with 26 per cent in 1870.[25]

Serving this varied and mobile population was a varied pattern of schools. The educational writers Wilfrid Carr and Anthony Hartnett accurately summarised mid-nineteenth-century attitudes when they wrote that:

> in a society which had adopted a form of democracy that placed such heavy emphasis on individual freedom, minimal state intervention and a *laissez-faire* market economy, the division of society into a wealthy capital-owning class and a poor labouring class, each requiring very different kinds of education, seemed obvious and natural.[26]

By the end of the century, they added, the distinction between elementary educa-tion for the masses, and secondary, often called grammar school, education for the few:

> was not perceived as a distinction between two levels of education but as a social distinction reflecting the belief that only children of the upper and middle classes could benefit from an education which went beyond the rudiments of elementary provision.[27]

Their analysis perfectly matched the assumptions, policies and practice prevail-ing in Hertfordshire in 1914.

A range of public, private and secondary grammar schools existed within the county. The most prestigious, and costly, public schools attracted families from across the nation, and indeed abroad, while the plethora of private schools ranged widely in size, reputation and fees and tended to have purely local appeal.[28] A number of secondary schools were scattered across the county, and their locations in places such as Barnet, Berkhamsted, Bishop's Stortford, Hert-ford, Hitchin, St Albans, Stevenage and Watford owed far more to historic chance than to county-wide planning. They received public grants to supplement their fee income, and their intake included a number of publicly financed elementary school pupils whose successful entry depended upon a rigorous scholarship examination at about the age of eleven. The overall percentage of Hertfordshire elementary school pupils entering secondary schools was never published, but calculations based upon various school returns suggest it was no higher than 4 per cent.[29]

Some elementary schools were provided and maintained wholly by county and borough councils acting as Local Education Authorities (LEAs), while others – the majority in Hertfordshire in 1914 – were 'voluntary' schools founded by the Anglican, Roman Catholic and various Nonconformist churches. The borough of Hemel Hempstead had asserted its right under the terms of the 1902 Education Act to become its own authority for elementary education, but everywhere else the county council was the LEA. Thirty members of the county education com-mittee were county councillors or aldermen, and twenty-two were appointed from outside, including three elementary school headmasters nominated by local branches of the National Union of Teachers (NUT).

Overall, there were enough elementary school places in Hertfordshire in 1914, but rural depopulation meant that many village schools had empty desks while some urban schools were overcrowded. The 64 council elementary schools could accommodate 23,249 pupils, although the average on roll for the academic year 1913–14 was only 17,020. The 194 voluntary schools – 185 of them Church of England foundations, 7 Roman Catholic and 2 Nonconformist – had 33,592 places, with 25,936 on roll. By 1914 Hemel Hempstead had built 4 schools to complement the existing 4 voluntary ones. The 8 schools possessed 2,052 places, and in the summer of 1914 they had 1,747 on roll.[30]

Staffing all these schools was becoming increasingly difficult. Salaries were poor, most classes were large and many of the older Victorian buildings were in poor condition. There were several grades of elementary school teachers, and Hertfordshire relied heavily on the lower, and less-well-paid, ones. There were 152 male and 217 female college-trained Certificated teachers, a further 113 men and 275 women, originally untrained, whose Certificate had been gained by part-time study and subsequent examination success, together with 75 men and 403 women accorded the much-inferior Uncertificated status. Uncertificated teachers had had a sound secondary school education, but might or might not be working towards their Certificate. Still employed in the county were 250 Supplementary teachers, without secondary schooling or any form of training, who had been reprieved recently from intended oblivion by the Liberal government's Board of Education under pressure from LEAs beset by a dearth of qualified staff. Their qualifications were minimal – they needed to be vaccinated and over eighteen years of age. The teaching force was completed by two male and seven female monitors.[31]

The elementary schools had been a source of controversy in the nineteenth century, and they remained so in the early decades of the twentieth. For all the voluntary efforts over the past 100 years by Anglicans, Roman Catholics and Nonconformists to build and maintain schools, and with an elementary education rate that had reached eleven pence in the pound by 1911, many county councillors believed, like local newspaper editors, that they were reflecting the opinion of the vast majority of ratepayers in publicly condemning the soaring expense as unjustified because the curriculum had expanded far too much and the standard of teaching was far too poor.[32] Most county councillors perpetuated the Victorian view that elementary schools were founded to give children from working-class families enough religious education, and skills in reading, writing and arithmetic, to become God-fearing and conscientious workers in factories, farms, offices and shops, and the host of upper- and middle-class homes requiring servants.

If the children were particularly lucky their basic education would be supplemented with utilitarian lessons in gardening and handicraft for the boys, and

Boys' class at Letchmore School, Stevenage, c.1910. A typical classroom and posed
photograph of the period (Stevenage Museum)

needlework for the girls. Hostility towards the schools as costly yet inefficient and
often inappropriate instruments of working-class education was steadily mounting, but it did so in the face of consistent pressure from the Board of Education,
HMI and school medical officers to modernise buildings, extend facilities, introduce new subjects, train more teachers and expand the school health service.
Nevertheless, by 1914 Hertfordshire County Council and education committee
were steadfast in their resistance to further expense, particularly on expanding
the curriculum.

School attendances were high. In 1913–14 the figure of 91.5 per cent for the
average attendance of the average number on roll was marginally better than
other metropolitan counties such as Kent (88.8 per cent) and Essex (91 per cent),
and marginally poorer than the neighbouring shires of Buckingham (91.6 per
cent), Bedford (91.7 per cent) and Cambridge (93.9 per cent). Hemel Hempstead's
figure of 91.5 per cent exceeded nearly all the boroughs in neighbouring counties.[33]

Great efforts were made to maintain high pupil attendance figures, as the
government grants hinged on it. The well-publicised termly attendance
returns to the LEA, the frequent education committee debates on any downward
trends, and the annual awards to children with unsullied attendance records over
several years made headteachers feel that their professional reputation was
directly related to achieving the minimum degree of absenteeism. Several factors

conspired to frustrate this ambition. Epidemics were common. Scarlet fever, whooping cough, mumps, chicken pox and diphtheria closed 105 Hertfordshire schools, nearly 40 per cent, for a week or more in 1913.[34] In 1910 the Board of Education had ignored the LEA's request for Article 101 of the Elementary Code, the so-called 'epidemic grant', to be reinstated. This would have compensated the LEA for the loss of attendance grant when schools were closed in attempts to limit infection.[35] In addition, boys as young as ten were regularly absent working for farmers or shopkeepers, and older girls frequently proved too useful at home cleaning, washing, running errands and caring for younger siblings to be sent to school.[36] More often than not, prosecution failed to discourage parents of persistent absentees, as magistrates, frequently employers themselves, displayed obvious sympathy with the defendants' excuses.[37] Headteachers tried to bolster their personal influence over pupils and their families with the lure of additional prizes and the threat of attendance officers. This practice was so prevalent that in 1913 medical officers filed complaints against two Hertfordshire teachers for exerting undue pressure upon manifestly sick pupils, including those with highly contagious ringworm.[38]

The inadequacies in buildings and staff were constantly being brought to the LEA's attention. For several years the county school medical officer, Dr Francis Fremantle, had criticised many older schools which were without running water supplies or adequate heating, lighting and ventilation. Gravel yards made playtime dangerous and drill difficult, and contributed to blocked gullies and filthy floors. Remedial action was slow, and reluctantly undertaken. Some teachers and school managers, Fremantle complained, still disdained the services of a school nurse, scorned the scrubbing of floors, and remained ignorant of the benefits of fresh air and exercise.[39]

E.N. Wix, His Majesty's Inspector of Schools, also found much to criticise. In a Bishop's Stortford infants' school he witnessed 'much friction and consequent inattention where 4 classes are taught in one unpartitioned room.' Improvements had been long delayed here, as they had been at Puckeridge, where HMI saw 'no prospect' of a separate classroom for the older pupils.[40] The same was true of Hitchin, where Wix blamed poor results directly on the 'filthy' and 'dingy' room that comprised St Andrew's School.[41] For two years Eastwick had waited for the ancient infants' 'gallery' of fixed staged seating to be removed, and for the rough stones of the play area to be crushed and rolled.[42] At Wareside, parish furniture was piled in the hall that was used as the schoolroom.[43] Utter condemnation was reached at Wallington, where not only the walls, roof, earth closets and urinals

but also the curriculum and the monitress (an older pupil working as an unqualified teacher) needed urgent attention on peril of loss of government grant.[44] In
July 1914, F.S. Marvin succeeded Wix and continued the assault on managers and
the LEA.

Schools such as these, all old Church of England foundations, were suffering
from far more defects and inadequacies than those maintained by the county
council. The Reverend Basil Reay, the Diocesan Inspector, was well aware of the
reason, and the remedy:

> Our Church Schools have done, and are doing, their best to carry out what the
> Board of Education demands from them ... But if our schools are to hold their
> own, Churchpeople must be ready to do more than they have done in the past.[45]

By the end of 1914 thirty-six Anglican parishes in Hertfordshire had received
notice 'of more or less serious requirements' from the Board of Education. The
total needed was £11,666, and the Diocesan Board of Finance had £2,500 available for school repair grants.[46] Reay gave clear warning that voluntary contributions would have to make up the deficit.

Although Reay had praise for many teachers, he found fault with many
others. Younger teachers, he said, were often 'severely handicapped through
inadequate training'. He opposed the cramming that persisted in most schools,
and he feared the effect of those teachers 'who are not only ignorant, but are
apparently unconscious that they are ignorant'. It was 'very difficult for us, or for
the head teachers to convince them that they are so'.[47] Such anxieties over buildings and staff were widely reported in county newspapers, contributing to the distinctly sullen concern over the state of elementary education. Few were satisfied
with it, but few wanted to spend yet more money on it.[48]

The educational problems of the early twentieth century were more than fifty
years old, and they reflected the social, political and religious controversies of the
times. In 1870 W.E. Forster, the Vice-President of the Committee of Council in
W.E. Gladstone's Liberal administration, had introduced an Education Bill which
created a 'dual system' of education in England and Wales for children of the
working classes. Both Forster and Gladstone had recognised the strengths and
weaknesses of the provision of schools through voluntary efforts, largely by the
Church of England and Nonconformists, that had hitherto prevailed. Local initiatives had raised large sums of money, but they had led to very patchy coverage
nationally – not least because the major purse-holders in some parishes had no
wish to educate their future youthful employees. As a result of the multiplicity of

influences, some districts had overcrowded schools, some had no schools at all, and others had half-empty mutually antagonistic Church of England and Non-conformist schools within earshot of each other.[49]

Although these voluntary schools, once they had been approved, were supported by Treasury grants and their standards regularly inspected, the government was not responsible for any national or local planning. The gaps in the provision tended to be filled on an *ad hoc* basis by small private schools making small daily charges for children to attend lessons when they could be spared from work or household chores. Known contemptuously as 'dame' schools, although in fact they were run by a cross section of society, these often ephemeral, and certainly uninspected, establishments raised considerable fears among the middle classes. The possibility that the teaching of literacy and numeracy might be inadequate was far outweighed by the thought that they might be contaminating children with completely inappropriate religious and political dogmas. The Education Act of 1870 therefore aimed 'to fill the gaps', where voluntary efforts were missing, with schools proposed by directly elected local School Boards, built and maintained through the rates as well as taxes, and subject to state inspection.

From now on the state largely determined where and when new grant-aided schools were built, and it committed itself to maintaining religious teaching devoid of any distinctive denominational 'catechism or formulary' in all Board schools. Religious teaching in the voluntary schools, though, remained firmly in the hands of the denomination largely funding them. Immediately prior to the 1870 Act taking effect there was a massive burst of fund-raising by Anglican and Nonconformist congregations to fill as many gaps as possible, and this was followed by a prolonged investment in school building by many new School Boards. One way or another the necessary schools were built, as Forster had hoped, but the sectarian bitterness between the churches, and the rivalry between church and Board schools in heavily populated urban areas over the recruitment of pupils, never went away. Watford School Board was particularly assiduous in providing the ever-growing residential estates with fine new school buildings, which voluntary efforts could not hope to match.

As the nineteenth century closed, Anglican anxieties mounted at the growing superiority of rate-supported school buildings and their own substantial difficulties in raising funds from supporters – many of whom, of course, were also ratepayers. By the 1890s the controversy over the possibility of rate-aid for church schools had become acute, especially with the Conservative administration of the third Marquis of Salisbury (1895–1902) so openly receptive to Anglican pressure.

In an atmosphere of bitter antagonism the 1902 Education Act swept away the School Boards and placed the vast majority of publicly supported elementary and secondary schools under the control of county councils, the new LEAs. As a sop, larger county boroughs were allowed to retain responsibility for elementary schools. Although Hemel Hempstead took this option, Watford and St Albans decided upon incorporation within the county LEA. Under the Act, the cost of running church schools as well as council schools would be met from both local rates and government grants. In return for the continuing right to provide denominational religious instruction, voluntary schools were obliged to provide the school buildings, keep them in good repair, and make such improvements as 'reasonably required' by the LEA.

The determined Nonconformist opposition to what its adherents believed to be the self-evident misuse of public money stemmed largely from their failure to preserve their own schools. The bitter rivalry between Anglicans and Nonconformists in the nineteenth century spilled over into the new century with undiminished venom. Gradually, however, most Nonconformist congregations found the financial burden too great to bear and handed over their schools to the county council. Forty-four Nonconformist schools had been established in Hertfordshire during the nineteenth century, the earliest in 1811 and a few more each decade until the 1860s, with the last one opening in 1884. By 1897 only fourteen survived as Nonconformist schools, and by 1914 just two struggled on in increasingly unsatisfactory buildings in Hitchin and Hoddesdon.[50]

This collapse meant the end of extensive Nonconformist control, but not the end of strong Nonconformist opposition to state and county council investment in the surviving Church of England establishments. Despite the vehement, and occasionally violent, opposition to the 1902 Act in operation, even the sympathetic Liberal administration of Sir Henry Campbell-Bannerman (1905–8) failed to turn back the legislative clock. The massive Conservative majority in the House of Lords ensured the consistent defeat of Liberal bills, but it also guaranteed that the fires of sectarian antipathies remained unextinguished and that the major political parties were clearly identified with one side or the other. The 1902 Act governed education up to the end of the First World War, but the flames it fanned were to burn brightly in Hertfordshire up to the outbreak of the next war, twenty years later.

As many historians remind us, change can be rarely explained simply.[51] Growing state intervention in social and educational affairs in the later nineteenth and early twentieth centuries was accompanied by agonies of doubt even among the politicians who were promoting the reforms. This was especially true in 1902. Deep suspicions of the creation of an autocratic state with ever-rising taxation, the twin fears of diminishing local responsibility and soaring rates, and the desperate desire to preserve the voluntary agencies striving to ameliorate the lot of ordinary people all conspired to ensure that some sort of balance was retained between the educational actions and financial investment of the churches and the state. For all the sound and fury of the debate, few in 1902 or long afterwards advocated exclusive state control of schools or envisaged schools without some form of religious, and overtly Christian, education. The years between 1902 and 1914 were tense, as the new LEAs assumed control and dealt with a host of religious, administrative, and political controversies and misunderstandings. In later life Sir John Lovell Pank, the first chairman of Hertfordshire's education committee, acknowledged that by far the most difficult initial problem he faced had been the bitter post-1902 religious antipathies.[52]

Powerful vested interests on the county council and education committee go a long way to explain their decisions. For all the urban expansion in south and south-west Hertfordshire, in 1914 landowners and farmers remained the dominant force in county policymaking. Many of the fifty-four county councillors were highly regarded local figures who were rarely, if ever, challenged at elections. The vote was restricted to the heads of households who paid rates, and county councillors themselves exercised the additional privilege of electing eighteen aldermen to sit on the council and its committees. Each county councillor served for three years and each alderman for six years, and they could be re-elected for further terms.[53]

Chairmen of the county council were influential figures. In 1914 this was the Rt Hon Sir Thomas Halsey, who had inherited the Gaddesden family estate. He had been elected to the position soon after the Liberal landslide victory in the general election of January 1906 ended his thirty-year reign as a Conservative MP for local constituencies, and he was to be re-elected annually until 1920.[54] In common with his predecessors as chair, Earl Cowper (1899–1901) and Sir John Evans (1901–5), Halsey was from an old established family with a tradition of patronage well known in the locality. During the nineteenth century the Cowper, Evans and Halsey families had all founded and endowed elementary schools in and around their estates.

Possibly by accident, but probably by design, the personal political allegiance of chairmen at this time alternated between Liberal and Conservative. This served to emphasise the claims of members to be non-partisan – they called themselves

The Right Honourable Sir Thomas Halsey   Sir John Lovell Pank (HALS)
Bt (HALS)

Independent – when determining county policies. Certainly, national party politics never overtly intruded into contemporary debates, although the vicissitudes of the 1902 Education Act strained the generally clubbish nature of the full council. The chairmen of the education committee were powerful figures in their own right, and also alternated between Conservative and Liberal, although abiding by their Independent status as local office-holders. John Pank gave up the business he had entered as an orphan and eventually risen to head soon after he was elected chairman of the newly created education committee in 1903. A lifelong Conservative, devoted Anglican and vocal advocate of public parsimony, Pank remained proud that after 'tremendous fights' he had gained the confidence of the powerful Nonconformist caucus of members and their mainly, if not exclusively, Liberal affiliations.[55] By 1914 Pank had long established a personal ascendancy over the education committee which lasted until his death, full of honours, including a knighthood, in 1923.

Pank was a determined advocate of local autonomy, and applied this creed to the provision of new school buildings, extensions and major refurbishments. Local education sub-committees monitored local needs and put forward ideas for future developments. These sub-committees comprised nominated rather than elected members drawn from parish and district councils and the churches, and also included others well known for their interest in, although not necessarily their enthusiasm for, education. The county council's policy of adding the major part of its share of the capital cost of major new works to the rates of the parishes and districts benefiting from these improvements ensured that due caution characterised most sub-committees' debates.

In 1914, and long afterwards, the farming interest on the county council and its education and agricultural committees was preserved by a powerful group of long-serving councillors. Many came from well-established families. They were respected as squires in their villages, and most were Justices of the Peace (JPs). They included W.A. Fordham of Ashwell, A.J. Bowlby of Gilston Park, H.W. Hall of Benington and Edmund Barnard from Sawbridgeworth. Colonel Abel Smith of Woodhall Park, Hertford, represented another particularly notable county family. A number of other county councillors and aldermen came from the ranks of the nobility.[56] The Hatfield estate of the Cecil family was the venue for major county shows, and the fourth Marquis of Salisbury was a frequent and forceful speaker in the council chamber, usually urging savage economies in public expenditure while at the same time contributing handsomely but privately to local Anglican school refurbishment funds. In common with other county magnates, the marquis had been elected alderman as a matter of course on inheriting his title in 1903. In a rare interview in 1920 he remembered with pride the pre-war voluntary efforts which had preserved many Anglican schools, and the county council's recognition of the value to the nation, and to local ratepayers, of those efforts. He recalled:

> We were able to show that we could build schools on a voluntary basis much cheaper than the suggested schools for the county, and the argument was that the county ought to be able to do the same as we did. A good many said our schools were not first-rate; but I think by the pressure that was brought to bear, we kept the price of the County Council school buildings down to some extent.[57]

As Lord David Cecil remarked, his father's Conservatism was 'against the new kind and very much in favour of the old: feudal, paternal, traditional'.[58] In no way did these attributes diminish his popularity and prestige. His son's comment could have been applied equally well to many other county councillors and aldermen, irrespective of whether they were aristocrats, knights or commoners.

Large estates, with farms let to tenants influential locally in their own right, were also owned by the Earl of Verulam around St Albans and the Earl of Lytton at Knebworth. Verulam was assiduous in attending meetings of the county

The fourth Marquis of Salisbury (HALS)   The Honourable A.T. Holland-Hibbert
                                            (HALS)

council and education and agricultural committees. Lytton was an unusual Conservative, like Salisbury, but more because of his passionate commitment to free
trade, female suffrage, the arts and social welfare than a veneration of tradition.
A county alderman for several years until 1913 he, too, devoted much time to local
affairs, his estates and a range of local philanthropic activities.[59] Other noble
houses had fewer acres but still commanded considerable respect in county
affairs. The Honourable Arthur Holland-Hibbert, twin brother of Viscount
Knutsford, had been a county alderman since 1889. Owner of the Munden estate,
he was chairman of the North London Railway Company and the Commercial
Union Insurance Company, and a noted pig breeder. He was also an aggressive
and volatile Gladstonian Liberal as totally committed as Salisbury to extreme
public parsimony and the virtues of private charity. For many years he was an
active chair of the county branches of the Red Cross, National Society for the Prevention of Cruelty to Children (NSPCC) and, during the war, the Voluntary Aid
Detachment (VAD).[60]

  The Earl of Clarendon inherited his title in 1914, and immediately became a
county alderman. He, too, attended council meetings regularly and was a noted
benefactor of rapidly expanding Watford, remembered as 'a great aristocrat,
who was also a great and kindly gentleman'.[61] Viscount Enfield, JP and city

Sir Charles Longmore (Hertford Museum)

stockbroker, who later succeeded as Earl of Strafford and owner of Wrotham Park, near Barnet, had been an assiduous county alderman since 1901. Several county councillors and aldermen were baronets or knights, including Rear Admiral Sir Thomas Fellowes of Stevenage, Sir Richard Cooper of Boxmoor and Sir William Church of Hatfield.[62] Another county councillor in 1914 was Dennis Herbert, who was to be elected Conservative MP for Watford in 1918.

Many of these figures – lords, knights and commoners – loom large in the controversies and developments that faced Hertfordshire during the war and afterwards. One other personality, a county official, merits attention, not least because of the light he throws upon local policies and practice at this time. Sir Charles Longmore was a trusted public servant who acquired not only immense official authority and personal prestige but also an assured social position exceeded only by the most aristocratic aldermen. Originally a solicitor in the family firm, he succeeded his grandfather as County Treasurer in 1878 and became the first Clerk of the County Council in 1894.

Well-acquainted with senior civil servants, elected president of the Law

Society, and created a Knight Commander of the Bath (KCB) in 1911, Longmore was as honoured a guest at speech days and the opening of schools as the chairs of the county council and education committee.[63] A.J. Hallidie, the chief education officer since 1903, was a member of Longmore's staff, and remained little more than a senior clerk.

In 1914 the county had one foot tentatively in the twentieth century and the other firmly in the nineteenth. Indeed, attitudes probably a century apart separated the remote villages and new urban estates. Urban and industrial growth was accelerating, London threatened to overwhelm the county and, as Sir Charles Longmore realised, much was expected of the county council in terms of improved services and efficient administrative machinery. In place was a county council largely dominated by patrician attitudes, rural interests and parsimonious policies, with few contested elections and, with the marked exception of Longmore himself, a scattering of council officers who made little or no contribution to policymaking. It is an irony that the coming world war, dominated by modern technology, witnessing a vast sacrifice of life and ending with widely publicised promises of major social reform, should actually lead to so few benefits for most families. Instead, it was to hasten the creation of local social and educational policies which sounded highly progressive and child-centred but actually harked back to the nineteenth century in their aims and the attitudes of their creators.

The elementary schools, working in this tense pre-war atmosphere, were also under continuous and probably confusing assault by a plethora of new ideas on education paraded by social reformers, medical practitioners, moralists, scientists, naturalists and the English disciples of radical thinkers such as Johann Herbart, Friedrich Froebal and, latterly, Maria Montessori, who saw the developing child rather than the academic subject to be taught as the focus of a teacher's life.[64] Hertfordshire LEA and teachers met these ideas with responses ranging from great enthusiasm to apathy and downright hostility. HMI reports from just prior to the war reveal that a handful of schools were pointing the reformers' way, but the vast majority had still to follow.

The subject of arithmetic epitomised local reactions to most new ideas. In 1912 a Board of Education circular praised those schools experimenting with schemes involving practical work and problem-solving. They were rejecting the age-old assumption that arithmetic was 'an abstract and self-contained science' made up of a collection of rules taught one by one, and concerned 'almost exclusively with figures, not often with words and almost hardly ever with actual things'.[65] Although HMI Wix and Marvin were enthusiastic about the changes, there were few innovators in Hertfordshire. The graded exercises incorporating simple problems used at Waterford, the 'practical arithmetic' at Cowper Boys' School in Hertford, and the 'household arithmetic' undertaken by the older girls in Royston met with HMI's approval, but elsewhere methods appeared unenlightened and standards poor. The 'mere dogmatic teaching of the rules' which daunted pupils at Priory Park, St Albans, and the 'very mechanical' arithmetic at Wallington reflected HMI's general findings in the county.[66] It did not help that in the summer of 1914 the chief education officer confirmed that the LEA would not be supplying weights and measures to schools.[67]

In 1911 the Board asserted that reading, silent or aloud, should always be with understanding, hopefully with enjoyment and eventually with appreciation. The following year a circular urged the establishment of school libraries, the stimulation of classroom discussion, the selection of shorter poems and extracts for committal to memory, and the introduction of lessons devoted to children writing from their own experiences.[68] Few Hertfordshire schools had absorbed such ideas by 1914. The well-mannered mastery of speech, the result of the 'free and confident' oral work at Great Wymondley, was exceptional.[69] Wix and Marvin could only condemn the 'want of self-reliant effort and of freedom and distinctness of speech' in Puckeridge, the 'utter lack of confidence in response' at Wyddial, and the 'unintelligent' approaches to reading, mechanically taught oral subjects and excessive silent reading at Clothall.[70]

History had grown rapidly in status since the 1890s, due partly to the impact of British imperialist writers and partly to the minor publishing boom following the appearance in England in 1897 of John Adams's vastly popular work, *The Herbartian Psychology Applied to Education*. The early nineteenth-century German philosopher and educationist Johann Herbart had argued that the purpose of education was the formation of moral character, with History and Literature being particularly valuable in achieving this aim. Stories of human endeavour and adventure, not mere facts and dates, would help inculcate 'right' attitudes in children, such as fairness, cooperation, sympathy, perseverance and respect for law and authority. Nearly a century later, early twentieth-century educators could not fault this assertion.[71]

In 1905 the Board of Education's *Handbook of Suggestions* noted with patriotic fervour that the growth of Empire 'ought to form a stirring theme full of interest to every young citizen'. *Suggestions on History* was published during the rising tension across Europe in 1914. The emphasis lay upon British and Imperial history, but it included a firm if rather patronising caution:

When dealing with the story of our Empire [the teacher] will have abundant
opportunity to bring home to his class the fact that in learning British history
they are learning a part of the larger whole, and that their sympathy and respect
are due to other nations and races, with whom, whether as enemies, allies or
traders, Englishmen have had and still have so many dealings.[72]

Drama, pageants, models, visits and the study of first-hand contemporary
accounts were all encouraged.[73] Although Wix and Marvin criticised teachers'
attempts to impart too many facts too soon to young children, they did note the
introduction of new ideas at Royston and Buckland.[74] At Anstey, too, dramatised
history stories proved popular, and in May 1914 the children at Wareside had special lessons on Westminster Abbey, the Houses of Parliament and Buckingham
Palace in preparation for a rare educational visit to London.[75]

Geography featured little in HMI's reports on Hertfordshire schools immediately prior to the war, but the few comments were highly critical of the antiquated
rote memory approach to learning about British towns, industries, rivers and
hills.[76] The 1905 *Handbook of Suggestions* highlighted the importance of first-hand
local knowledge, together with an understanding of maps, types of climate, contrasting ways of life overseas and the impact of geography upon historical developments. These factors were re-emphasised early in 1914 in *Suggestions on
Geography* – just in time to achieve an unexpected prominence alongside the massive resurgence of interest in History during that traumatic autumn.[77]

Physical training (PT) was another subject where association with national
interests could easily influence school syllabuses and teaching approaches. Until
1892 military drill constituted the sole exercise in elementary schools. In that year
basic gymnastic exercises were permitted, but they were not eligible for government grants until 1895. In 1899 the war against the Boers in South Africa led to an
army recruitment drive, and the alarming percentage of applicants rejected as
unfit, combined with a series of embarrassing military defeats, led to a demand
for greater physical fitness and a martial spirit in the nation's youth.[78] The Board
felt military drill would inculcate both, and back it came into fashion. The pen-
dulum continued to swing, however, and the Board's 1909 *Handbook* was dominated by the physical and moral benefits of organised games and apparatus
exercises. Elementary schools were urged to introduce football, cricket and athletics – the last two, if not the first, formerly the prerogative of the socially superior and vastly better-equipped grammar and public schools.

Hertfordshire LEA was unimpressed. By 1914 there were a few PT courses for
teachers, but HMI urged greater efforts in vain. Inspectors found many teachers

with inadequate knowledge of the 1909 *Handbook*. Most children did not even remove collars and coats before exercise. Dr Fremantle reported that only half the schools held a daily PT lesson, let alone the twice-daily sessions recommended by HMI.[79] Organised games were often hamstrung by severely restricted indoor and outdoor space.[80] Hardly any elementary schools possessed fields, and access usually depended on the goodwill of farmers. Wheathampstead was unusually fortunate, as the Earl of Cavan, soon to achieve fame as a successful general during the war, donated a community football ground. 'I am a firm believer in the value of games,' he explained, 'as a training not only for a soldier's life but for life in general.'[81] As part of the overall PT syllabus, teachers were expected to inculcate habits of temperance and hygiene in their pupils. In practice, Fremantle observed, the impact was severely offset by teachers' inexperience in handling the subjects and the 'very variable degree of interest'.[82]

In one major curriculum area Hertfordshire did make significant headway. By 1914 schemes for 'handwork' for younger children and 'practical instruction' for older pupils had been introduced, and a continuing investment made in the necessary equipment, specialist teachers and local centres. Behind the initiatives there was a gnawing anxiety that education should play a greater part in maintaining the country's industrial and commercial strength. Perceptive observers had been aware that Great Britain's economic 'greatness' had been under assault from both Germany and the USA for a quarter of a century or more, and they loudly publicised the fact. The implications for the next generation were clear. Mass education should ensure the masses were in a fit state, both physically and mentally, to contribute as much as possible to the preservation of national supremacy.[83] R.B. Haldane, a notable imperialist, politician and philosopher, argued forcefully in *Education and Empire*, published in 1902, that on education 'depends our position as the leading commercial nation of the world, aye, and also the empire'.[84] The influential social and political scientist Herbert Spencer optimistically proclaimed that poverty could be eliminated by the rational application of science to the whole range of human affairs. Education, he asserted, was a powerful weapon in the worldwide industrial and commercial struggle, and undoubtedly the basis for instilling the knowledge and beliefs necessary for national regeneration.[85] Sir Philip Magnus, a well-known and respected proponent of practical and technical instruction, consistently condemned the exclusively literary diet and dull cramming of elementary children, deeming it manifestly unsuited 'to the practical needs of artisan life'.[86] All these demands came not as part of an educational theory, but as a response to a national need.

Manual instruction, science, nature study and drawing were all involved in serving this end, and all received official recognition by 1914.

In 1900 boys over the age of twelve could earn grants for manual instruction, a directive revealing, significantly, that such training was seen as a contribution to industry rather than education. Hertfordshire's first Handicraft organiser, R.R. Bunn, was appointed in 1913, along with a second organiser for gardening. Based in St Albans, they began to provide courses to improve teachers' own knowledge and skills, and to run more advanced classes for older children who walked to their centre from nearby schools. A year later HMI Marvin persuaded the LEA to authorise the instructors to visit individual schools throughout the county to promote their subjects. The consequent need for an assistant at the St Albans centre was agreed, despite the open hostility of several education committee members towards the extension of 'officialdom' at the whim of a transient HMI.[87]

Hertfordshire schools embraced practical subjects with enthusiasm. By 1913–14, 2 schools and 13 local centres were providing handicraft lessons, 46 schools and 36 centres gave cookery lessons, 5 centres were set up for laundry-work, and gardening classes were held in 43 schools and 2 centres.[88] Out of every 1,000 pupils on roll, 19 earned the gardening grant compared with the national average of 21, but 39 gained the handicraft grant and 99 gained the domestic subjects grant, against the average of 20 and 58 nationally.[89] The first Letchworth Handwork Exhibition was held in July 1914, attracting entries as far away as Barnet, Bushey and Hertford.[90] A few details survive, revealing that boys from Hitchin displayed 'Brushwork, Pastel Drawing, Memory and Imaginative Studies, Pen and Ink Sketches and Cardboard Modelling'.[91]

Despite all the anxieties over agriculture and rural depopulation, there was little evidence in the county of schools fostering the visits and walks, observations and recordings, nature calendars and wildlife collections advocated in the Board's 1908 *Suggestions on Rural Education* and its follow-up circular three years later.[92] Gardening, though, was a different matter. It was seen as vocational training. In March 1914 Hertford education sub-committee was particularly interested to learn from each headteacher 'What proportion of the boys who have received instruction in Day School Gardening ... are now earning their livings as gardeners or gardeners' assistants?' The replies showed that the commercial greenhouses in the Lea valley, the Hatfield estate of the Marquis of Salisbury and the Knebworth estate of the Earl of Lytton took on as gardeners' assistants or apprentices a substantial minority, and some years the majority, of boys leaving the local elementary schools. Fully imbued with the prevailing assumptions, the headteacher at

Sarrat confessed that 'Our difficulty at times is to supply the demand for gardening lads.'[93] Seventy years later several Stevenage residents clearly recalled that while most 'poor' girls entered domestic service most boys became local estate gardeners, glasshouse workers or farm labourers.[94] It was the generally accepted thing to do. HMI encouraged gardening, but viewed the initiative differently. At Royston, Wix was gratified to observe a rare example of subject integration and mutual enrichment. Here, he recorded, 'The gardening is well connected with Nature Study, Drawing and Manual Instruction', and he urged the school to establish further links with reading, English composition and arithmetic.[95]

In the early twentieth century the elementary schools, and the children they taught, were being shepherded into line by the vested interests controlling their affairs. There were those who favoured a narrow diet of basic literacy and numeracy laced with plentiful religious and moral directives, while others advocated a curriculum which was broader in content and more practical in approach. Despite the relative liberality of the latter group, both parties were far more absorbed with the preservation of social order, the promotion of industrial output and the maintenance of Empire than the provision of educational opportunities which remotely matched those of the middle classes, who could afford to pay, sometimes heavily, for their children's schooling, to working-class children. The evolution of a national pattern of schools ranging from the most expensive and socially exclusive major public schools through the ranks of the less costly and less prestigious minor public schools and grammar schools to the mass of local schools provided free of charge seemed immutable in its reflection and preservation of the prevailing social hierarchy.

CHAPTER THREE

The direct effects of military conflict

T HROUGHOUT MOST OF JULY 1914 summer activities in Hertfordshire – fetes, outings and shows – continued as usual, affected only by the
uncertain weather. The Tsar of Russia's brother attended the annual
Knebworth Flower Show on 22 July, and an unusually large crowd visited the
county agricultural show in the grounds of Hatfield House on 30 July.[1] A few days
later, however, the roads were suddenly and strangely quiet. Newspapers
reported that Tring Show was 'shorn of much of its customary attractiveness' by
the 'war cloud', and popular Bank Holiday events such as horse races, fairs and
sports fixtures were blighted by mobilisation and the subsequent dislocation of
railway timetables.[2] Early in August shops across the county began to run out of
goods as transport was commandeered by the army. Most areas reported sharp
price rises. Sudden orders hit bakers and grocers as panic-stricken families accentuated shortages with unusually high demands. Protestors in Hitchin attacked
shops suspected of profiteering.[3]

Families soon began to feel the effects of mobilisation. In the first week of
August 980 men of the 1st Hertfordshire Regiment marched in column through
Hertford on their way to France. The *Hertfordshire Mercury* thoroughly approved
the 'animated and martial appearance of the town' and a fortnight later it noted
proudly that the Marquis of Salisbury and Viscount Hampden, the Lord Lieutenant, had left the county to head their regiments, and the Earl of Cavan was to
command a brigade.[4]

Men departed, but new troops arrived. Thousands passed through Hertfordshire on their way to embarkation, and thousands more stayed to train in the
rolling countryside. Headed by bands and accompanied by endless wagons, the
soldiers were cheered by residents and noisily followed by children. Khaki socks
and shirts were soon hanging from the windows of houses, halls and schools.[5]
Very swiftly Hertfordshire had become a vast military base and training camp for
the expeditionary force across the Channel.

The 23rd London Regiment arrives in Hatfield, 1914 (HALS)

The processions, the bands, and the washing heralded over four years of disruption to families and schools, years which brought not only unprecedented pressures upon daily routines in homes and classrooms but also renewed controversy over the nation's health, social welfare reform and the very purpose of schools. It was not long before the pain of war followed the pageantry. Towards the end of August 200 horses stampeded from Great Havers Farm towards Much Hadham and Sawbridgeworth, injuring themselves and wrecking property; early in September local families passed refreshments to 144 wounded soldiers when their train halted at Bishop's Stortford station; and in mid-November one of the first public memorial services was held in Braughing for a officer killed a month earlier in France.[6]

Few headteachers recorded the outbreak of war on 4 August, as it occurred during the summer holidays, but the military implications soon became obvious and unsettling for pupils and teachers alike. As the schools embarked on a new academic year, everyone involved in their affairs was caught completely by surprise by the demands on staff, facilities and resources. Everything to do with elementary education was subordinated to the efficient billeting and movement of thousands of men under arms. As soon as war broke out county councillors were only too willing to place all county property at the disposal of the military authorities and leave local communities to face the consequences. This attitude barely

Army camp on Royston Heath, 1914 (HALS)

changed throughout the war. Buildings could be requisitioned as required by the army, again without thought for the consequences. Schools were assaulted by a literal invasion of troops, and by children frequently distracted, sometimes distraught and occasionally delinquent because of the wartime conditions at home, the news and the fear of news from abroad, and the sights and sounds of military operations around them. The LEA, school managers and teachers had to cope as best they could with disruptions great and small, short-lived and long-term, occasionally heralded but frequently sudden, in circumstances completely without precedent. And all of them remained controlled by inflexible rules governing every moment of their professional lives.

Many rural and urban homes were invaded. During the first autumn of war local newspapers asserted that 100,000 billets were acquired across Hertfordshire for troops in transit or training. By early 1915 at least 25,000 men, and often many thousands more, were stationed at any one time across the county, mainly concentrated around Watford, Berkhamsted, St Albans and Bishop's Stortford.[7] Infantry, cavalry and artillery battalions, and multitudes of animals, wagons, limbers and guns, became common sights. Initially the soldiers were received enthusiastically. They were cheered, offered sweets and cigarettes, and welcomed into homes.[8]

Gradually, however, the constant billeting and frequent change of personnel

Local families accompany a troop of soldiers in St Albans, c.1914 (HALS)

took its toll, unsettling families at home and in school. A local autobiography recalls childhood astonishment that non-commissioned officers scouting in Hoddesdon 'found accommodation for the men when all the cottages seemed to be overflowing with big families as it was'.[9] As early as November 1914 a Sawbridgeworth headteacher recorded pupils being unusually tired, anxious and distracted.[10]

Although county newspapers continued to praise the smoothness of the billeting operations, the good behaviour of the troops and the generosity of householders, the long-term pressures inevitably led to family disagreements with the soldiers, and sometimes letters of complaint to their officers and, occasionally, letters of public protest to local editors. In 1916 Berkhamsted became deeply divided on the issues. The local newspaper published letters and commentaries on the pernicious effects of billeting upon the town's families, but it did so alongside other correspondence and articles criticising as deeply unpatriotic those complaining in times of national emergency.[11] There is no doubt that some householders felt victimised. One asked:

> Do the ... authorities make it clear to the new men what they are to expect for the
> princely sum of 2s 11d? I think not, otherwise we should not find them from the

Troops at the ford, Much Hadham (S. Ruff)

first day invading our sitting rooms and assembling there at the tea hour. On the contrary, it looks as if they were actually initiated into these predatory manners.[12]

The financial remuneration was for the weekly provision of a bed only, and the War Office expected no meals to be served to billeted soldiers. Many poorer labouring families were happy to receive the billeting allowance to help offset the depleted family income if the major wage-earner had enlisted.[13] They needed to make a profit. Some made the soldiers pay for meals, and for extras such as candles and fires, but they did so to the disgust of middle-class correspondents who had no hesitation in equating such mean-spirited householders with the profiteering dealers in provisions.[14] A bitter rejoinder came from one householder who compared the ill-rewarded householder, bludgeoned by public opinion into sullen silence, with the local tradesmen in receipt of the soldiers' custom when 'patriotism does not dictate that the shopkeeper should give something for nothing.'[15] The early enthusiasm for the troops had set a precedent regarding hospitality that became difficult to sustain economically and emotionally.

Initially headteachers were tolerant of the presence of troops, and patriotic fervour prevailed. One afternoon in November 1914 20,000 men marched through the village of Much Hadham. The school managers immediately granted a half-day's holiday for the school rather than compete with the noisy attraction. The headmaster also found it a deeply impressive event, and he was moved to write an unusually emotional passage in the school logbook:

Such an Educational sight will not very soon be forgotten. It will be something the children can or will be able to recall in the great future. It was an opportunity too, when the villagers showed to advantage in the way of practical Kindness to the soldiers, by their readiness to do anything in their power to assist, and by giving them hot coffee, and cocoa, water for horses, biscuits and cigarettes. All this was done right thro' the village from one end to the other. A noble sight! Many were the expressions of gratitude one heard from these brave and good fellows. 'God Speed' we say to them.[16]

Camp life and, especially, military pageantry proved irresistible to children but increasingly annoying to teachers. As pupils' attendances governed the Treasury grant to the schools the registration regulations were strict, and registers could be scrutinised without notice by managers, LEA officers and HMI. Unless an official holiday was granted, teachers had to record attendances and fulfil the timetable – whatever the sights and sounds outside. Not surprisingly, teachers often lost the wartime conflict of interests for children's attention. On 17 November 1914 the headmistress at Wareside complained that:

Owing to a large number of soldiers passing through the village at dinnertime, and late into the afternoon, it was impossible to hold the afternoon session today.[17]

The managers of Sandridge School wisely gave a half-day holiday on 6 October 1914 when the renowned soldier, Field Marshal Earl Roberts VC, the hero of many well-publicised stories about the defence of the Empire in India, Afghanistan and South Africa, held 'a grand review' at the close of extensive local manoeuvres.[18] On 11 January 1916 the schools in Sawbridgeworth equally wisely closed when Princess Louise, Duchess of Argyll, inspected troops encamped nearby.[19] The school at neighbouring High Wych stayed open, but lost most of its pupils.[20] On 19 February 1915, 20 out of the 84 boys on roll at Much Hadham ignored school and walked five miles to Bishop's Stortford to watch King George V inspect an array of 25,000 men before they marched to London.[21] The managers and headmaster probably believed the spectacle was far enough away to deter truants. During the war the average attendance at this school fell by more than 10 per cent due, the headmaster stated, to the lure of troops on manoeuvres, the opportunity to earn money by casual jobs in the camps and the increased incidence of illness the army brought to the area.[22]

With or without permission children sought the sight of soldiers, and often their company. In addition to the mass troop movements, the deliberate noise and colourful pageantry of recruiting campaigns attracted children as well as

Troops under canvas in the grounds of Moor Place, Much Hadham (S. Ruff)

volunteers.[23] The regimental bands sought out the smallest villages. Teachers resorted to various stratagems to maintain high attendance figures. On occasion the register was marked and closed earlier or later than usual – usually by a quarter or half an hour – to allow troop movements to be witnessed and still record a reasonably full class.[24] Playtime was curtailed to make up the time. Arrival after registration led to the cane and detention at Wareside, where:

> eleven boys followed a band of soldiers this afternoon, and came into school too late for their marks. Each boy received two strokes of the cane and then remained after school to do the lesson he had missed.[25]

At the same school the teacher felt obliged to fetch all the pupils away from an army balloon that had descended nearby just before the start of the afternoon session.[26]

An aeroplane was a rare, exciting and disruptive sight, and their pilots possessed almost celebrity status. At Gilston, 25 out of the 30 pupils were missing:

> owing to an aeroplane coming down 2 fields away. I explained the principles of register marking and school grants to them and the rule of the code as to 2 hours instruction daily, of which they had missed ten minutes. They willingly forewent 10 minutes of their playtime.[27]

The two hours of instruction daily was a logbook entry error. The regulations demanded a minimum of two hours each morning and afternoon. At Wareside and Much Hadham children also ignored the demands of school to flock around newly arrived planes and their pilots.[28] In Hoddesdon the whole school was forced to wait until playtime to be led by the headmaster to admire the machine that had landed nearby during a lesson.[29] At Ashwell 'rich and poor, young and old' turned out to watch the squire's son, a Royal Flying Corps officer, land in a field to visit his parents and old school. After the visit pupils had the privilege of turning his aeroplane round ready for take-off.[30]

As far as a school's reaction to such events was concerned, forewarned was – probably – forearmed. Holidays seem to have been given freely for large parades, and for the pilot's homecoming at Ashwell. Then teachers and pupils enjoyed the spectacle without anxiety and fear of recrimination. At other times timetables were easily wrecked, pupils unsettled and teachers deeply frustrated.

Modern machines of war brought danger as well as excitement. At Royston an army dispatch rider collided with a young girl wandering in a lane during play-time, and children suffered similar fates near St Albans and rural Barkway.[31] Hitherto rural roads had been the preserve of horses, carts and pedestrians, and schools had little need to fence and gate playgrounds. Shortly before the end of the war two children played truant to dig up dandelion roots in the fields near Norton. The roots possessed cathartic and diuretic properties, and money could be earned by selling them to pharmaceutical companies. A Royal Flying Corps pilot landed unofficially to pick up a colleague living nearby and as he took off the aeroplane struck the children, killing one and seriously injuring the other. The subsequent inquiry attracted great publicity, largely because people found it hard to believe the pilot's claim that he failed to report the accident because he had not seen, felt or heard the impact.[32]

Military requisition of schools took place at short notice. The occupation was usually for an unknown length of time and was totally disruptive. Just as classes had been planned for the long-awaited new Technical School in Hitchin, its open-ing was delayed for a year due to intermittent occupation by troops.[33] Few occu-pations were as shortlived as the one resulting in a compulsory holiday in Bengeo in November 1914 when 'soldiers passing through the Town occupied School all night and remained until after 10 o'clock this morning'.[34] Few, too, were received with as much equanimity as at Ashwell where unannounced manoeuvres around the village in the summer of 1915 necessitated soldiers billeting each night in the school and the establishment of company headquarters in the adjacent Technical Room. Here the inconvenience was elevated by the particularly jingoistic head-master to the status of a proud, even privileged, contribution to the war effort.

Certainly the children enjoyed the frenetic activity which had invaded the north Hertfordshire countryside:

> A number of telegraph and telephone wires were laid and carried to the villages round about, and the incessant arrival and departure of motor cycle despatch riders gave to the village a very busy aspect ... much excitement has been caused especially among the juvenile population.[35]

Demands by the army in and around Bishop's Stortford during the autumn of 1914 disorganised several schools. In November one headmaster was instructed to vacate his school by midday, and the occupation lasted a month.[36] The sudden occupation of the town's Technical School terminated its use as a cookery and handicraft centre for local children.[37] At Braughing, attempts to share the small school building with troops using it as their local headquarters proved entirely unsatisfactory, with class routines 'entirely disorganised' and work 'almost impossible'.[38] Lessons in Sawbridgeworth were disturbed by the frequent training sessions held by non-commissioned officers in the school's playground and drill shed. Here the disruption to timetables and lessons went on throughout the war, as new troops continually replaced those sent overseas.[39]

During the summer holiday of 1914 troops occupied ten schools in St Albans, and showed no sign of vacating them in the week before term was due to start. Patriotism did not stifle parental protests, but they were directed against the city council rather than the troops. In response, the clerk could only plead that no arrangements had been made to meet the emergency because officials had to negotiate on the spot with billeting officers as units arrived.[40] Eventually, rooms in large private houses were made available for dispossessed classes from the prestigious High School but no elementary school received such offers of help. The proposal to use churches and chapels to house elementary schools was steadfastly resisted by a majority of city councillors on the grounds of likely cost, and there is no evidence that any Anglican incumbent or Nonconformist minister volunteered the use of a building.[41] A month after the term opened hurried arrangements were made to crowd the elementary schoolchildren into five schools partly vacated by the troops. The dispossessed Priory Park School met in three rooms at Hatfield Road School, with wretched results. In December the Priory Park logbook recorded that two classes were still packed into each draughty room, with children and teachers suffering constant colds.[42] During the summer of 1915 the troops went under canvas, and the schools returned to normal. They were requisitioned again in the autumn, and the chronic overcrowding in shared schools was repeated for another winter.[43]

In contrast, Hemel Hempstead's education committee consistently opposed the army's use of its prerogative to requisition schools. In August 1914 all public and many private buildings in the borough had been commandeered, and the borough clerk and surveyor failed to persuade the army to vacate the schools, or at least some rooms, before the new term started. The local newspaper backed the borough council. In a fiery report it asserted that an army officer terminated a brief meeting with borough officials outside the final school to be requisitioned with the contemptuous comment that 'it was a very nice little school, just painted up, which we propose to take.' By the afternoon an army mobile kitchen had been installed in the playground. The surveyor found the army had occupied all the well-maintained property, leaving for the children's use a scattering of derelict workshops and halls without toilets.[44]

The borough's education committee discussed every expedient but had to accept that no alternative space was available, and that they had insufficient teachers to take responsibility for classes scattered all over the neighbourhood. No-one had any idea how long the troops would be in the schools, or whether the army would pay compensation to offset the cost of hiring other premises. In desperation the committee dispatched a delegation to the War Office and Board of Education to argue that there were sufficient billets in private houses for most of the soldiers lodged in the schools. Faced with the indefinite loss of all premises, the fear of a reduced grant, the cost of temporary accommodation, and showing a growing hostility towards the commanding officer's intransigence, the committee's debates were free from the patriotic utterances and consideration for the troops so prevalent elsewhere in the opening weeks of the war.[45]

Elementary education in Hemel Hempstead would have been brought to a complete standstill but for the committee's vehement protest. It secured the reluctant evacuation of four schools, and the Board instructed HMI Marvin to assist in the identification of alternative premises and, if necessary, in the reorganisation of education in the borough. The army still occupied the rooms of seven departments – infants, juniors and seniors – but their classes were gradually dispersed among the borough's Sunday School rooms and Congregational, Baptist and Salem chapels rejected by the army. In their usual, or unusual, buildings, all the schools opened on time.[46] During a belated inspection Marvin expressed satisfaction with all the hurried arrangements except for the ventilation in two of the chapels. He had little real choice.[47]

Marvin urged the repair of broken windows in some of the chapels but the borough council was reluctant to bear the cost unless the children were to be there for a long time. The army could not, or would not, give a date for the final evacuation. Anger at the military authorities intensified, one education committee member publicly complaining that 'they walk in and do as they like and then walk out again without anyone knowing.'[48] As winter approached, the children were still working in the inappropriately furnished and inadequately ventilated and heated chapels. The borough had received no advice from the Board regarding the financial repercussions of requisition and hiring alternative premises.

In late November 1914 Marvin brought the crisis to a head, probably deliberately, by withdrawing his approval for one of the Sunday School rooms. This threatened Boxmoor Council School with a substantial loss of grant if it failed to open for the absolute minimum of 400 morning and afternoon sessions. Confusion reigned in the borough education committee until one radical member, H.F. Hebert, carried the day with a vigorous attack on the army. In the face of public opinion he argued that the future of elementary education was far more important than the temporary comfort of the troops. The soldiers should utilise the chapels, he argued: 'they were not half so important as the schools.' He ridiculed the current rumours of a German invasion. He denied that the committee had the slightest responsibility towards the army and, in direct criticism of some members' divided loyalties, he noted that their anxieties over the soldiers' welfare were far from being reciprocated – indeed, he added, 'it was pretty clear if they turned the whole of the children into the streets the local military would not help them.' He condemned the lowly place currently accorded elementary education, and he included his colleagues in the condemnation. The habit of regular attendance, he asserted, so laboriously but successfully inculcated before the war, was under dire threat through the borough's capitulation to the thoughtless actions of the military authorities.[49]

Perhaps shamed by Hebert, the committee embraced his arguments and protested once more to the Board. The reply took several weeks to arrive, and was unsympathetic. It accepted the commanding officer's assurance that his division's billets were overcrowded and the schools were essential. The children continued to endure the chapels and halls, and their trustees increased the charges.[50]

Not counting occupations for a night or so, at least seventeen elementary schools in Hertfordshire were commandeered totally, and another five in part, for long periods of a term or more, usually in winter. All twenty-two were large urban schools, each with between 200 and 350 pupils on roll, and their problems often meant disruption for yet more schools in the neighbourhood. The small Technical Schools in Hitchin and Bishop's Stortford can be added to this list. They had few, if any, full-time students at this time, but their occupation dislocated their range of part-time programmes. Throughout England 705 elementary schools had been occupied wholly or in part by troops by 1 November 1914 – and these figures included occupations for just one night – with 178 remaining occupied by April 1915.[51] Representing over 10 per cent of the 1915 figure, Hertfordshire had more than its fair share of long-term disruption.

The Board of Education's annual report for 1913–14 adopted an emollient and patriotic tone. Understandably, the promotion of national unity was uppermost in mind. The billeting officers, although not Hertfordshire's teachers and local authority officials, would have approved the statement that:

> The requirements of the military authorities have been made with much consideration for the trouble they inevitably entailed upon the schools, and we have reason to believe that our efforts to assist both parties in their difficulties have been appreciated by the War Council.

There was little local evidence to substantiate the Board's claim that:

> the owners of public and private buildings have also in many places shown great liberality in placing them at the disposal of the Local Authorities for temporary use as schools,

and any agreement of local teachers and officials would have been tinged with bitterness at the comforting conclusion that:

> temporary arrangements have usually been found possible and local authorities, managers and teachers have co-operated in reducing to a minimum the effects of the disruption.[52]

Only in February 1915 were the requisitioning and compensation procedures agreed between the Board of Education and the War Office. The War Office accepted liability for the cost of schools renting temporary premises, moving into them and fitting them up for educational purposes. It would also pay for any damage to school premises and equipment, the costs of schools moving back into the buildings, and the restoration of the hired premises to their original use.[53]

Once this was known, Marvin took full charge of the situation when the army required the use of four large elementary schools in Watford in October 1915. He organised a shift system of schooling unique in the county. The details were swiftly formulated and agreed between Marvin, the chief education officer and the single group of managers who held responsibility for all Watford's council elementary schools and handicraft centres. Four schools not required by the army became the hosts for two shifts of children from eight schools. Teachers and children from one school carried out the day's work in an extended morning session from 8.30am until midday, and were followed between 1pm and 4.30pm by staff and pupils from another school. The morning and afternoon sessions alternated on a monthly basis between the host and the dispossessed school. Marvin told the managers that teachers could be asked to occupy their 'spare' half days with clerical work for local recruiting committees, meeting parties of their schoolchildren for organised games, rambles or visits to places of interest, assisting teachers at other schools, and visiting colleagues to observe different methods of work.[54]

The initial Watford shifts lasted throughout the autumn, winter and spring of 1915–16.[55] In January 1916 three more schools had to be handed over to the army, and the shift system was extended to include these and two new host schools.[56] Thirteen out of the twenty-three elementary schools in Watford were now disrupted, involving a total of 3,184 children.[57]

After a summer spent under canvas, the army requisitioned the same seven schools for the autumn and winter of 1916–17.[58] Although bound to surrender the premises, the managers and county council were openly hostile to the proposal after the damage done to the buildings during the previous occupation. Other worries were the likely overwhelming of the schools' sanitary systems and the dangers to public health.[59] Watford contained some poor areas, and the shift system there could well have contributed to the complaints reaching the Board 'from parents in poorer districts at the increased wear and tear of children's boots and clothes, and the trouble involved in looking after the younger children, when kept at home on wet days.'[60]

Marvin made allowances for the problems imposed by the shifts, but expected much, perhaps too much, from the teachers. Most could not emulate Alexandra Council School where, despite the shifts and the enlistment of all the male assistants, the headmaster and his staff of female war supply teachers had maintained 'a high standard of efficiency'. Pupils here continued to gain a disproportionately high number of scholarships to the selective Higher Elementary and secondary grammar schools.[61] In contrast, at Parkgate Road Boys' School Marvin found the long single session 'a severe tax on little children', and noted that teachers needed 'to relieve and diversify the work as much as possible'. The school's standards had declined as staff fell ill, with the abnormal working conditions held partly to blame.[62] At Callow Land Boys' School the shifts had led to increased homework, which pleased Marvin, but in December 1917 he judged the general performance of pupils to have dropped 'fully a standard below the normal for their age'.[63]

The shift system operated in other LEAs, and overall it met with a mixed response. In May 1916 the influential *Times Educational Supplement* reported that the time given to physical training, practical arithmetic, English, and drawing was seriously curtailed.[64] The Board of Education had to agree but, making a virtue out of necessity, it also claimed that 'to some extent ... the system has the quality of its defects: by curtailing instruction it concentrates the efforts of teachers and scholars on essential matters.'[65] It sounded close to an admission that much of an ordinary whole schoolday was less than essential, a view long held by many county councillors. HMI generally, though, confirmed that many children spent much of their free mornings or afternoons with their teachers on open-air studies, organised games and visits.[66] Notwithstanding HMI's conclusions, the *Times Educational Supplement* asserted that the most serious drawback was the tempting opportunities the short schoolday gave for both child labour and juvenile delinquency.[67] With considerable justification, both issues absorbed much time in parliamentary and county council debates and a great deal of space in national and local newspapers during the war.[68]

As hundreds of miles of German, French and British trenches were dug across Belgium, France and Alsace, and the casualties of the vast war of attrition mounted, contingency plans were invoked in the spring of 1915 to convert selected schools into emergency reception hospitals and convalescent homes. The children's home in Much Hadham, specialising in epileptic cases, became a convalescent home for sixty soldiers. Local donations of extra furniture and materials were immediately forthcoming, and the children were quickly boarded out in the neighbourhood.[69]

In Royston, Queen's Road School became a military hospital, and the classes were dispersed among neighbouring schools, a disused Nonconformist school and a floor hastily cleared in the town hall. The curriculum and the timetable needed hurried and drastic revision to contend with the split sites and the loss of the cookery and handicraft centres, which became the hospital kitchen and store. On occasion the town hall had to be evacuated due to the inadequate heating system or rehearsals for patriotic concerts. The school remained in use as a hospital until May 1919, and Marvin praised the energy and imagination of the headmaster in making the best of such a disruptive situation. The children utilised the town hall gardens for lessons and recreation, they undertook drill exercises on the squire's lawn, they turned spare land into an intensive 'war garden', and the staff and pupils regularly collected vegetables and other goods for the hospital itself.[70] The commandant of the VAD wrote an open letter to

The children's home at Much Hadham, converted into a military convalescent home
(S. Ruff)

the local newspaper thanking the numerous volunteer workers and donors of
equipment who turned 'what was a bare building into a well-equipped Soldiers'
Hospital ready for the reception of wounded warriors', but made no mention of
the teachers and children who had swiftly moved out the furniture, equipment
and themselves in order to provide that 'bare building'.[71]

Perhaps the strangest event of all took place in Ashwell. At first, the managers
of Merchant Taylors' Boys' School approved the building's use as a convalescent
hospital on condition that the LEA found suitable temporary accommodation for
the pupils. The LEA, however, saw this moment as the opportunity to close the
school permanently and house all the village children more economically in the
girls' and infants' school. It was badly mistaken, though, in claiming that local
feeling supported amalgamation. A wealthy school manager offered spare rooms
in his mansion for use as the hospital, and a well-orchestrated public campaign
was launched to save the school. Its leaders included the rector, the squire and
County Alderman the Honourable Holland-Hibbert. Their campaign concentrated upon celebrating the Merchant Taylors' Company's historic and continuing generosity to the school, and condemning the LEA's ill-informed and
ill-judged intervention. In public meetings the rector added a host of personal
assumptions. He claimed mixed schools tended to make boys effeminate, while

Queen's Road School, Royston, converted into a military hospital (HALS)

the Merchant Taylors' boys 'had proved by their manliness in going in such large numbers to fight in our defence that they had the right grit in them.' In defiance or ignorance of the regulations he argued that attendance figures in the school were low solely because many older children were working on local farms to offset the shortage of adults. He was confident that once 'normal times' returned the figures would show that the number of boys could not be accommodated in the other building. The campaigners' influence, if not the validity of their arguments, was overwhelming and the school stayed open.[72]

The county council and education committee subordinated the elementary schools to the needs of the war in other ways, and they did so with little regret. Patriotism and parsimony went hand in hand, and the war provided the opportunity for cutbacks to be presented to ratepayers as a personal and public virtue. To mounting criticism Hertfordshire's elementary education rate had risen steeply in recent years, from eight pence in the pound in 1905–6 to eleven pence in 1909–10, and a salary increase in May 1914, adding a further 1½d to the rates, had not endeared teachers to county councillors.[73] They complained they had lost control of the schools because the Board encouraged initiatives which seemed to fit them less and less for the type of dutiful lives, modest careers and subservient attitudes they believed working-class pupils should be led to accept. As a result, little concern was shown towards the difficulties schools experienced as teachers volunteered for military service. It was this attitude, combined with the hysterical patriotism pervading all sections of society, which led the chairman of the county council, closely followed by local newspapers, to condemn the headmaster at Buckland, who had been a Territorial volunteer before the war, for apparently seeking to avoid the dangers of active service by still being in school in October 1914. The local vicar was accused of conniving at his desire to stay at home, and there were wild reports of outraged villagers resorting to 'rough music' – making loud noises all night outside his house – to show their contempt. After hasty votes of censure, and a great deal of publicity, it was all proved false. Everyone in the village knew the true story – that the headmaster was only working until ordered elsewhere by his regiment.[74]

The low view of teachers nevertheless persisted, and their requests for the LEA to make up the difference between their service pay and peacetime salaries, and to grant 'sick allowances' to wounded teachers, were received with undisguised hostility.[75] These allowances were made only with great reluctance, and later in the war county councillors had no hesitation in refusing to assure teachers in the Volunteer Reserve they would receive the same allowances as other enlisted teachers if they signed, as requested, for active service at home in case of invasion. Outraged councillors called the claim 'monstrous', and contemptuously added 'if the guarantee of their salaries ... was the only way to get the teachers to offer their services to defend the nation the sooner the Kaiser was here the better.'[76]

The boys' schools and the larger mixed schools containing mostly male teachers suffered particularly from frequent changes of staff. Unfettered enlistment, the delays in replacements, and the inadequacy, absences and sudden resignations of some of the supply teachers caused a swift decline in educational standards, and despair in headteachers. The experience of a school in Hoddesdon epitomised the problems. It had 140 boys and four teachers, including the headmaster. In September 1914 two of the teachers were new arrivals, and both enlisted in December. One supply teacher was appointed in January 1915 and a second a month later – just before the first resigned. The headmaster's wife acted as a supply teacher until July, and returned in September when her replacement also resigned after a few weeks in post. In June 1916 the headmaster enlisted, and as no replacement was appointed the school was reorganised into three classes. The sole Certificated mistress was made acting headteacher. Throughout 1917 the female supply staff proved inadequate as teachers of large classes of boys. Numerous 'indispositions' and absences were logged, and when the acting headmistress was taken seriously ill in the autumn a succession of masters transferred from other schools took charge for short periods. Twice – once for six weeks – the school had to be closed as no teachers were available. The same catalogue of absences and resignations blighted 1918, and despite Marvin's protests to the managers and LEA there was no improvement until, fortuitously, the masters returned safely from service.[77] Similar sequences of disruption to staffing and standards were recorded at Priory Park, St Albans and Sawbridgeworth Boys' School.[78]

The press followed the lead of county councillors and education committee members in castigating the cost-effectiveness of the schools, and dismissing any disruptions. In April 1915 one leader safely asserted 'there is less cause to grieve over the interruption of the business of elementary education which the war has brought about inasmuch as the results of forty four years of compulsion are so woefully small.'[79] Pank was delighted at the government directives urging economies. They were, he claimed, 'the very thing the committee had been want-ing for years and years – the power to stop expenditure.'[80] Henceforth their policy would be 'one not only of economy but of negation', and they would 'have the knowledge that they had done their best not only in the interests of the county but in the interests of the country in her hour of need.'[81]

The economies were implemented with vigour, even spite, and certainly to the great satisfaction of most members. There were immediate cries for reductions in stationery, coal allowances and the number of medical inspections. The exigen-cies of war, though, rendered all these areas of school life particularly difficult without the LEA's added intransigence. The chronic shortage of imported wood pulp eventually led many schools to reintroduce slates, the enlistment of nurses severely impeded the efficiency of the school medical service, and delays in coal and paraffin supplies led to freezing classrooms, curtailed sessions and tempo-rary closures. In 1985 a Stevenage resident, born in 1905, remembered the small and ineffective coal fire, the depressingly cold schoolroom and the prevalence of painful chilblains.[82]

Small items did not escape the education committee's attention. General approval greeted the suggestion that much less should be spent on brushes, paint and clay, and the discussion prompted one education committee member to recall with disgust that 'after they had the clay they were asked to provide wash-hand basins for the children to wash in after using it.'[83] Annual school repairs were reduced from £3,000 to £1,200, the lowest figure 'consistent with safety', and all new building work ceased.[84] 'The world would not stop', Pank exclaimed when a long-awaited project was suddenly axed, 'if this school in Bishop's Stortford was not enlarged.'[85]

In a far more controversial move, it was decided that staffing levels would be reduced to the absolute minimum required by law, largely by excluding all children under the age of five from schools. The scheme not only reversed the Board's moves to end the employment of Supplementary teachers but also included the dismissal of trained teachers. In December 1915 Hallidie, the chief education officer, dutifully calculated that 62 monitorial, 56 Supplementary, 41 Uncertificated and 6 Certificated teaching posts could be abolished. In addition, 21 Supplementary and Uncertificated teachers could be replaced by monitors, 32 Uncertificated and Certificated teachers by Supplementaries, and 6 Certificated teachers by Uncertificated ones.[86] Proponents of the cuts on the education committee drew harrowing pictures of children under five walking 'perhaps two or three miles to school in all winds and weathers', packed into overcrowded rooms, disrupting the education of older pupils, standing at lunchtime 'in the mud with no-one to look after them', and completely exhausted at the end of a long day away from home. However, this tactical error allowed their critics to appeal to an unlikely combination of modern educational practice and wartime needs. The teachers' representatives asserted that most under-fives had their own rooms in schools and that the 'system of teaching the very young had been revolutionised', with play dominating their activities. Using language as intemperate as their opponents, they warned that exclusion would lead to the resurrection of unsanitary and uncontrolled 'dame' schools. In one bitter exchange the accusation was hurled at those supporting the cuts that:

> there is no doubt that this kind of grandmotherly legislation is proposed by gentlemen whose wives are able to hand over their children to the care of a governess or a nurse, and thereby secure abundant leisure for themselves.[87]

Others were concerned that exclusion would render it impossible for many mothers to go out to work just at the time they were needed in factories and on farms. They repeated horrific tales of young children across London locked in rooms all day as a result of its county council barring them from school. The potential misery caused by Hertfordshire ratepayers saving 'a paltry' £1,800 was contemptuously compared with the nation spending that amount every thirty seconds on the war.

The education committee decided by a small majority to reject the proposal, but the full council, unimpressed by the sensitivities, immediately referred it back.[88] Hallidie ensured his second report was packed with statistics which emphasised the savings, disputed the rumoured evils in London, and claimed that under-fives were disturbingly susceptible to infection and absence from school. With Pank in full and forceful flow, enough members changed their minds for the proposal to be put into action.[89] The staff reductions began in earnest.

School logbooks record the exclusion of the under-fives and the departure of teachers without much further comment, but open criticism of official decisions would have carried the risk of severe reprimand. An open letter of protest by the Hitchin branch of the NUT highlighting the plight of dismissed teachers and the short-sightedness of the county council stimulated no response in the press.[90] In Barnet, managers successfully delayed the loss of a couple of teachers on the grounds that few suitable monitresses could be found as most eligible girls took advantage of the 'exceptional opportunities for employment' in shops and factories.[91] The grouped management body in Watford took more vigorous action, and twice contested the LEA's figures. In the initial 'round' affecting fourteen schools a compromise was reached, with nine married war supply teachers being dismissed and the permanent staff across the borough reorganised to avoid any further losses. A later proposal for reductions in eight schools met with challenges from six of them, four of which were successful. The arguments over the remaining two continued into 1917, effectively delaying further cuts until late in the war.[92] Managers and parents in the prosperous Chiltern village of Chipperfield also fought a determined but ultimately unsuccessful campaign throughout the summer and autumn of 1916 to avoid the destruction of their 'splendid school' and 'excellent staff' through the proposed replacement of their monitress and Uncertificated mistress by a Supplementary teacher.[93]

Despite the largely laconic logbook entries, there can be little doubt that many schools endured a relentless sequence of enlistment, staff shortages, lack of continuity, amalgamated classes and temporary school reorganisation in 1914 and 1915, followed by compulsory teacher losses and further disruption in 1916 and 1917, all interspersed with an increasing incidence of staff illnesses, absence and breakdown. When the headmaster at Buckland left on active service in October 1914, his wife, although Uncertificated, took charge for the remainder of the war. In February 1916 staff reductions left her with one Supplementary teacher for forty pupils aged five to fourteen. The strain made her seriously ill. For two months in 1917 she was without any assistant, and a senior girl had to be placed in charge of the infants.[94] At the boys' school in Sawbridgeworth there were delays a term long in replacing masters who enlisted early in the war, and in 1916 the enforced reductions left the headmaster and his wife permanently responsible for nearly 100 pupils. The couple became ill, but HMI Marvin's complaint that the staffing was entirely insufficient went unheeded by the LEA.[95] At Wareside, too, the numerous changes in staff, and the incompetence and inexperience of several of the replacements, contributed to the nervous breakdown of the headmistress in 1916.[96]

In these circumstances it is unsurprising that the Board of Education's report for 1916–17 reported a serious increase in juvenile delinquency. It was most marked in children aged between eleven and thirteen, and parents received much of the blame.[97] By then the issue had reached Hertfordshire, but there is little recorded evidence of an alarming tide of youthful crime, even though headteachers asserted that bad behaviour was far more widespread than hitherto. The constant rounds of billeting certainly affected some children adversely, and the well-substantiated rising tide of truancy probably had a multitude of causes – the opportunity to earn money, the lure of the army camps and the demand for domestic chores. No doubt in some cases the Watford headmaster was correct when he blamed the 'lack of control at home when the fathers are away wearing the King's uniform'.[98] In several schools there was an ominous rise in unruly behaviour when inadequate war supply teachers replaced permanent staff, and when the LEA's draconian staff reductions resulted in a combination of excessively large classes and a dilution in the number of trained teachers.[99]

In 1914 and 1915 local newspaper editors were far more interested in children's positive contributions to the war effort – the making of goods and raising of money for relief agencies – than in any of their nefarious activities.[100] During this early period of the war reports, editorials and articles concentrated upon heartening acts of patriotism, and local newspapers made light of sporadic incidents such as the closure of Lord Knutsford's park to the public after a gang broke a gate, damaged a boat and chased the ducks. The case was consigned to an inside page, under the title 'Mischievous Boys'.[101] It aroused no correspondence.

During 1916 the juvenile crime rate in Hertfordshire appears to have been no greater than in previous years. The *Hertfordshire Mercury* routinely reported the judicial proceedings held throughout the eastern half of the county, including courts sitting in Bishop's Stortford, Broxbourne, Buntingford, Cheshunt, Hatfield, Hertford, Hitchin, Hoddesdon, Knebworth, Much Hadham, Stevenage, Waltham Cross, Ware and Welwyn. In 1916 the *Mercury* recorded the conviction of twenty-two boys of elementary school age. Their offences included the perennial ones of damaging haystacks by using them as slides, breaking fences, and the theft of bicycle lamps, fruit from shops and small amounts of money from employers. One habitual thief was sent to a reformatory; the rest received small fines and probation orders. Editors and correspondents were too absorbed with condemning the 353 offenders against the blackout regulations to take any notice of the few petty misdemeanours of elementary schoolchildren.[102]

In December 1916 two incidents were reported in detail, and each reflected a wartime anxiety regarding the cause of juvenile crime. In the first, in Letchworth, the prosecution blamed wanton damage to a fence on the lack of parental control. In the second, in Hitchin, boys were convicted of stealing potatoes and onions, and the headline 'Cinema and Crime' followed the national trend in blaming such delinquency on the unhealthy influence of films on impressionable young minds. The culprits had admitted thieving to gain the entrance money to the cinema, and in court the probation officer received a round of applause for asking the magistrate to 'make the condition in the bond that these boys don't go to the picture palaces for a year'.[103] In the same month two passionate yet opposing letters were published. The first asserted that films, combined with the 'war fever', had 'inflamed' boys' imaginations, thereby fuelling criminal activity. The second, a reply to the first, reminded readers that films were carefully censored, and acidly argued that they were no more harmful to children than the moral 'cant and hypocrisy' practised upon them daily by many adults.[104]

A few months earlier the Earl of Lytton, who was not only a Hertfordshire landowner but also chair of the State Children's Association, had written an open letter to county newspapers about the rising tide of public opinion in favour of severer penalties for juvenile offenders. He made an eloquent plea for a greater understanding of the obvious problems facing children in wartime:

> In thousands of homes the father is absent; in many the mother is employed outside her home; school hours have been curtailed and there is a serious lack of men teachers in the boys' departments. The darkened streets, the lessened number of police and the absence of social workers from boys' clubs, church brigades and scout organisations all have their widespread effect. To these, though not a consequence of the war, must be added the exciting influences of sensational cinema shows, inciting imaginative youth to imitation.

Cautioning against a punitive approach to juvenile offenders, Lytton challenged the critics of the probation system, arguing that:

> report after report from magistrates and chief constables tells of the many cases of first offenders placed on probation who never come again before the court, as well as of many finally reclaimed after several appearances.[105]

Newspaper editors, and public opinion generally, were unimpressed by such arguments, and the *Hertfordshire Express* ridiculed a Home Office circular advocating the use of probation and the employment of female probation officers.[106] At the same time Stevenage magistrates were praised for having 'the courage and wisdom to discard that notoriously inoperative form of "correction" in favour of the older and in existing circumstances certainly preferable method of corporal chastisement'.[107] Later, in 1917, the *Express* devoted a complete column entitled *The Birch at Last* to publicising and praising the increased use of this humiliating punishment. The victims included two boys below thirteen years of age convicted of stealing chocolates, cigarettes and a toy gun from a shop.[108] Ironically, in that same issue evidence from Hitchin and Baldock suggested that probation was an effective method of both punishment and rehabilitation. During 1915 and 1916 twenty-seven schoolboys and older youths were put on probation for theft, wilful damage and fraud. The subsequent conduct of twenty-five of these individuals was described as generally satisfactory by the probation officer, although several had needed close supervision and considerable guidance. Only two had repeated their offences.[109]

A Board of Education circular and Home Office letter issued in December 1916 were ignored in Hertfordshire. They claimed a 34 per cent rise in urban juvenile delinquency between the winters of 1914–15 and 1915–16. They, too, pinpointed the blame on the lack of parental control, and urged LEAs to make schoolrooms available in the evenings for youth clubs.[110] There is no evidence that the circular or letter were debated by the county council or any of its committees, or that any Hertfordshire school was used for that purpose during the war.

Although some children might have welcomed and benefited from the youth clubs, they were probably not needed as agencies of social control. During the last two years of the war there were more juvenile crimes reported in the *Hertfordshire Mercury* than in previous years, but not many more, and, given the prevailing public mood, it can be assumed that newspaper editors would not have missed the opportunity to publicise any marked rise. In 1917 the *Mercury* reported the conviction of thirty-one boys across the eastern half of the county. As usual, the crimes were mainly petty theft and vandalism – one gang had broken windows, another group had overturned a beehive, and two boys had thrown 'missiles' at passers-by. Most were fined and put on probation, but birching was ordered for a boy aged ten who stole wood from a yard, two boys aged ten and twelve who stole two watches valued at 14s, two boys aged eleven and twelve who stole bicycle lamps, and a boy who stole an attaché case containing twelve white collars.[111]

Articles about the problem continued to appear, and local speakers claimed to have the answer. At a teachers' conference it was claimed 'Materialism was too powerful, and forces, physical and mechanical, too dominant.' The 'terrible facts' of the war had afflicted the minds of children who otherwise would never have acted illegally.[112] Clergymen blamed the decreasing value placed on religious instruction. One condemned the 'mere intellectual training with nothing added to it' which he believed prevailed in elementary schools. 'At present', he asserted, 'children might know the whole of the international lesson, but they would not come in at nights.'[113] In common with many others, he regretted the sudden passing of a comfortable era that existed more in his own mind than in the towns and villages of pre-war England:

> The wholesome, necessary and most essential government of the home by father and mother had largely gone, and the restoration of a true, beautiful, firm Christian discipline in British households was a most desirable and pressing British reform.[114]

In the war-weary years of 1917 and 1918 thoughts of long-term educational and social reform began to dominate public opinion. Greater emphasis began to be placed on the treatment rather than the repression of juvenile offenders and, not surprisingly, local newspaper editors dropped their support for punitive measures as more enlightened approaches gained popularity. Despite the fluctuations in adult opinion and the generally depressing news from the Western and Eastern Fronts, between January and November 1918 the *Hertfordshire Mercury* reported the conviction of only twenty-four children aged fourteen and under.[115] Besides the petty theft and vandalism, there was a case of rowdyism – 'hooting and yelling' – one of gambling with cards, and one of cruelty to farm animals. Birching was only ordered once, though, for the theft of a gold watch.[116]

Nevertheless, anxieties about juvenile indiscipline continued to surface. Among the many critics of the rising generation, the chairman of the county education committee complained loudly of the 'excess of energy diverted into wrong channels' by older children, and the vicar of Hitchin publicly condemned 'the undisciplined state of the scholars'.[117] The creation of School Cadet Corps in senior elementary schools was considered a sound remedy. This essentially public school way of introducing future officers to military life was recommended for the early taming and training of the other ranks. Local newspapers bestowed their blessing on the initiative, saying just what they thought the majority of their readers wanted to hear:

We have often admired the smart bearing of the older boys of the elementary schools of Hitchin as they have marched under their efficient instructor for their programme of physical exercises at the Gymnasium. This feature of their school life cannot but be productive of good results.[118]

The further step, the creation of cadet corps, would bring 'our boyhood into paths that lead to a sturdy British manhood'. It held little appeal for hard-pressed and under-staffed schools.

Troops as well as children were responsible for wanton damage. Drunkenness and disturbances of the peace were common and, invariably, requisitioned buildings suffered badly. The damage done to schools in Watford over the autumn and winter of 1915–16 had hardened managers' hearts against the army requisition order the following year, and their experience was not unique. After a month's occupation the headmaster of a Bishop's Stortford school found it in 'a very filthy condition'. 'The floors have been scrubbed with hot soda water', he wrote, 'but are still black in places.' Heating stoves had to be repaired and the whole building disinfected.[119] Damage was widespread in St Albans. Hearth curbstones, toilet roofs, cast-iron desk frames, wooden stools and music stands, and a piano were all broken, and a complete length of fencing was removed for firewood.[120] It seems compensation remained a vexed issue. In 1917 the county council had to bear the difference of £31 3s 4d between the actual cost of repairs to the schools in Watford and the £129 0s 3d received in compensation from the War Office.[121]

Hertfordshire towns, villages and schools also accommodated other wartime visitors. A number of soldiers' children accompanied their fathers to the camps around Much Hadham and were admitted to school.[122] They were from the families of instructors who were more permanently based in the county than the ordinary enlisted men. Some of the children orphaned or injured by the great explosion which destroyed the East London Munitions Works at Silvertown in 1917 were billeted at Much Hadham, and in due course also attended its schools.[123] The persistent air raids on London in 1917 and early 1918 led some parents to send their children to stay with friends or relatives in the country, and schools in rural Hertfordshire, including Hitchin, Great Wymondley and Ayot St Peter, began to admit these urban evacuees.[124]

At the outset of the war many thousands of Belgian refugees, fleeing from the initial German invasion of the Low Countries and France, had sought sanctuary in Great Britain. Most of them had been distributed among the larger towns in the north of England and south Wales, but by early 1915 549 had been received within Hertfordshire.[125] Local reception committees were enthusiastic in their

The windmill at Much Hadham, disused since 1895, converted
into accommodation for Belgian refugees (S. Ruff)

welcome, and the refugees duly appreciative. In Much Hadham, surrounded by
troops and already hard-pressed for billets, the welcome may have been warmer
than the accommodation. Admitting five boys 'driven from their homes by the
vilely cruel Huns', the headmaster noted that arrangements had been made 'to
make them comfortable in the disused mill near the Railway Station'.[126]

Understandably, after the trauma of invasion and flight from their homeland,
the refugees found it difficult to adjust to a new life. So many had settled in and
around Hitchin that the largest store started advertising its wares in French and
Flemish, and in 1917 the police interpreter was granted exemption from active
service because 'there are now so many Belgian cases heard in court that [the
Superintendent of Police] did not see what they were to do without him.'[127] The

early months of attendance at school must have placed great stress upon the refugee children, who spoke little or no English, and their teachers. The LEA merely stated that managers could refuse admission to schools on the grounds that the refugees could speak only French or Flemish, and there is no evidence that schools received extra staff. If any refugees were refused, it seems not to have been recorded in school logbooks, and certainly not in places such as Hitchin, Sawbridgeworth and Barkway, where refugee children were readily accepted in local schools. The first few months of the war were a time of heightened national patriotism, charitable activity and newspaper-incited horror at the barbarities of the Germans in Belgium, and rejection seems unlikely.

Across the country, in 1915 HMIs reported favourably upon 'the friendliness and sympathy with which the Belgian children have been received by their English school-fellows and … the progress they are making'.[128] Opinion in Hertfordshire, however, was divided on the question of the Belgian children's aptitude and abilities. At a NUT conference in 1917 one headteacher had noticed 'among the Belgian children at school an energy and alertness which made them outstrip the English boys and girls'. He added the perennial complaint that 'in the acquirement of foreign languages the English were singularly incapable compared with other nations.'[129] This was immediately contested by a colleague who

> at first … thought they were cleverer than the English, but he found that it was because they had been put back too far and that when they were put with children of their own age they had not evinced any superiority.[130]

In difficult and unprecedented circumstances, schools were simply learning by experience. Understandably, headteachers faced with children whose abilities and learning capacities were in doubt had resorted to placing them, at least initially, in classes largely made up of much younger children. It was common practice.

Hertfordshire did not escape from direct German aggression. The towns and villages near the eastern border with Essex were directly under the flight path of German airships and, later, the equally alarming Gotha bombers seeking out targets in London. The raiders crossed the North Sea, flew eastwards over East Anglia and turned south between Cambridge and Royston.[131] The airships first arrived in the autumn of 1915, presenting a novel source of excitement, as well as danger and stress, to children. In Hertfordshire the bombs caused several deaths, scattered damage to property, much inconvenience to family routine, and yet more disruption to schools.

Lombard House, Hertford: on 13 October 1915 bombs killed four people who had come outside to view a German airship held in the beam of a searchlight (HALS)

Cheshunt was attacked twice by airships. On the night of 7–8 September 1915 several dozen small bombs devastated rows of greenhouses which the Germans probably mistook for factory roofs, and a second raid on 1–2 October 1916 laid waste another six acres of greenhouses and also damaged 350 houses. No-one was killed.[132] Essendon was bombed in the early hours of 3 September 1916; a few houses and part of the church were destroyed, and two sisters killed. Two search-lights had been positioned in the village, and it had probably been mistaken for the outskirts of London.[133] Childhood memories identify the fear aroused by an airship as it flew over Hoddesdon on the night of 13–14 October 1915, 'for there was something ruthless and sinister about the slow relentless humming of its engines.'[134] It was an ominous 'drumdrumdrum', confirmed another witness.[135] Hoddesdon escaped bombing that night, as it had been blacked out since an ear-lier raid on London by several airships flying in over Suffolk, but nearby Hertford, 'blazing with lights', was struck by forty-eight bombs which destroyed several buildings in Bull Plain and North Street, killed nine people and maimed another fifteen. As so often happened, some of those killed had come out of their houses to watch the airship.[136] On their way south the airships had hovered over Sawbridgeworth, and the following day the pupils were 'very excited and tired'.[137]

The Hertfordshire village of Cuffley became famous as the spot where the first airship shot down over Great Britain crashed in flames on the night of 3 September 1916, earning the fighter pilot, Lieutenant Leefe Robinson, a Victoria Cross.[138] During the raids countless households were kept anxiously awake at night by the sound of engines passing overhead and explosions not too far away, and the blazing buildings and especially the lurid fire-ball created by a stricken airship could be seen for many miles around. Tourists flocked to Hertford to gaze at the gutted houses, and to Cuffley to stare with mixed horror and fascination at the scorched earth and heap of twisted metal. The reports of the flight and fiery destruction over Potters Bar of a fourth raider on the night of 1–2 October 1916 reveal the heady mixture of tense anticipation, anger, excitement, joy and danger which gripped people of all ages. As the *Hertfordshire Mercury* wrote:

> rumours of a probable raid on a large scale were floating about early in the evening, and everybody was on the *qui vive*, and despite the often expressed view that it is safer to remain indoors than to congregate in the streets, thousands of people in the various towns and villages in East and South Herts could not resist the temptation to sally forth, anxious not to miss any detail of the anticipated thrilling struggle.[139]

The descent of the airship in flames was witnessed as far away as Hertford, Ware, Hatfield and St Albans.[140] Yet again pupils in Sawbridgeworth were either absent the following day or arrived at school 'very tired, the result of being up all night'.[141] In Goffs Oak 'few children attended', in Hertford children fell asleep at their desks, and nearby in Bengeo the headmistress recorded that:

> The children who are present are unfit for work. Several children were taken to the tunnel for refuge for several hours during the night whilst Zeppelins were hovering around the district.[142]

Gradually more towns emulated those enforcing blackout regulations, and schools were measured up for blinds.[143] Cheshunt and Waltham Cross were especially vulnerable as they were directly beneath the most frequently used German flight path, sited on the outskirts of London and close to large industrial targets. In 1916 their local education committee was obliged to choose between providing blinds or closing the schools early during winter months. To avoid the expense of blinds the committee contributed to the disruptive effect of raids by curtailing the lunchtime break by three-quarters of an hour and shortening the schoolday, in full knowledge of the difficulties this would cause many working-class families providing meals at midday.[144]

Precautions were justified, as during the war bombs fell on Cheshunt, Clay-hill, Cockfosters, Essendon, Gordon Hill, Hadley Wood, Hertford, London Colney, Little Heath, North Mimms, Northaw and Ware – all in Hertfordshire at that time.[145] During 1917 and 1918 heavily armed aeroplanes replaced the increasingly vulnerable airships, and the later bomber attacks occurred in daylight as well as at night. Raids and warnings of raids over Hertford and Hoddesdon resulted in early dismissals and cancelled attendances.[146] Children were often collected by parents when raids seemed imminent, and they were usually kept at home for the rest of the day.[147] The noise of enemy aircraft, anti-aircraft gunfire and distant explosions unsettled children, and often shelter was taken under desks as the sounds grew louder.[148] Between June and November 1917 there was no respite, with raids occurring frequently. The results were predictable. In Hertford families stayed awake all night in fear of raids, and many huddled night after night in the railway tunnel. The children's health and standard of schoolwork declined through stress and the lack of sleep.[149]

In June 1917 the first official air raid warning siren sounded from a factory in St Albans. People were urged to stay indoors until they heard the all-clear signal.[150] The system proved controversial, and for some time only accentuated problems in schools. The *Hertfordshire Advertiser* soon realised that 'the area over which the signal is given is large and it may be that when the signal is given in St Albans the enemy aircraft are no nearer than Norfolk.'[151] The police, and especially special constables, were accused of creating unnecessary confusion and anxiety by false alarms and forgetting to sound the all-clear.[152] The sirens were only used during the day, but the *Hertfordshire Mercury* reported the farcical but annoying nocturnal activities of 'nervous' special constables trying to warn friends but 'clattering along the streets loudly knocking at the doors and shouting "they're about" in such a manner that everybody within hearing distance is disturbed.'[153]

During the bombing sorties of 1917, and with sirens now heralding imagined as well as real dangers, school managers sought a directive from the LEA regarding sending children home every time the warning sounded.[154] The problem of parents demanding to take their children away from school at such times had become acute. In addition to children's safety there was understandable anxiety about the disruption to timetables and attendance figures. The LEA was surprised to find that, two years earlier, Cheshunt schools had received a Board of Education circular issued to districts deemed vulnerable to raids which advised everyone to stay indoors and continue working during attacks. The LEA's belated circular could not improve upon this advice, or upon the recommendation to keep children away from windows and neither cramped together nor dispersed too widely to hamper escape from a fire. It added only the directive that the school had to remain in session, beyond normal time if necessary, until all danger had passed, but individual children could be collected by parents.[155] This advice, logical but demanding firm discipline and some courage, operated throughout the final phase of intense raids between January and March 1918. These resulted in the familiar pattern of false alarms, local destruction, cancelled attendances, unmarked registers, reduced classes, dislocated timetables and tired, nervous children.[156]

The strains and dangers imposed directly by the war were thus many and varied. The novelty of an army constantly on the move held children in fascination, and the novelty of billeting, bombing and life without fathers and older brothers was equally unsettling. The schools were in an unenviable predicament. Despite all that went on outside, including enemy bombing, the education regulations had to be obeyed until someone in higher authority decided otherwise. Teachers had very little freedom of action – indeed, that was the last thing desired by most managers, county councillors and officials. The LEA, though, was also enmeshed in a web of rules and directives, and the early problems of requisitioning were prolonged by the reluctance to contravene rules, incur expense or, indeed, to do anything except 'by the book'. Parents moved to complain about wartime shortages and billeting orders ran the serious risk of counter-charges of a lack of patriotism. In the prevailing emotional as well as military mobilisation of public opinion elementary education was the lowest of priorities. Only H.F. Hebert, the vituperative Hemel Hempstead councillor, argued logically, publicly – and vainly – that troops undergoing training could put up with improvised conditions far better than children under instruction. Basically nothing was too good for the troops and anything was good enough for the children.

CHAPTER FOUR

Schools at war

A SCHOOL'S CURRICULUM, broadly defined as not just the subjects taught but all the activities undertaken by the children under the auspices of the school, reflects the priorities of the society it serves. During the First World War those priorities crystallised into the defeat of Germany and its allies, the preservation of the British Empire and, later in the conflict, the nurture of the next generation into citizens sufficiently healthy in body and mind to maintain Britain as a major commercial and imperial power.

Schools were expected to take and, indeed, they often wanted to take, a positive approach to the promotion of the war effort. After all, they were in daily contact with the families who were fighting it. As a result the syllabuses and activities undertaken by the children changed dramatically. Most of the changes arose from the widespread view that it was right and proper for the elementary schoolchildren to contribute as much as they could to their country in its hour of need. Mass war work, and the inculcation of patriotism in the masses, went hand in hand, and the actions of government ministers, county councillors and newspaper editors revealed that both elements applied as much to children as to adults.

These new national priorities did not mean greater freedom for the elementary schools – far from it. A few of the wartime innovations, especially in the early weeks, were initiatives on the part of the schools, but usually changes were thrust upon headteachers, irrespective of their own views or timetables, by local assumptions regarding the schools' role. Often the schools' goodwill was taken for granted by local dignitaries – the squire, the parson and often their wives – who were keen to recruit the children as knitters and needleworkers, gardeners and gatherers, morale-boosters and fund-raisers. The local dignitaries, usually school managers with considerable influence over the teachers, were quick to judge the patriotism of teachers and pupils through their war-related activities, and more than willing to criticise schools whose efforts failed to match their expectations. As the war dragged on, national charities, such as the Red Cross, and several government ministries, such as the Board of Trade, Board of Agriculture and Ministry of Munitions, worked through the Board of Education and the LEA to reinforce and extend the demands on schools. Despite all the additional anxieties and pressures, which sometimes brought teachers to the point of collapse, schools were usually willing to play the fullest possible part in the war effort.

At a time when elementary education occupied a lowly place in national affairs, the schools' involvement in local patriotic and morale-boosting events became a source of pride to both children and teachers. Participation gave importance and relevance to the school community during a period of local sacrifice and anxiety. Eventually such service led to welcome praise for the schools, which had been so maligned as expensive luxuries by county councillors and newspaper editors prior to and immediately following the outbreak of war. Nevertheless, the war gradually turned the elementary schools into mass producers of food and goods, with syllabuses devoted to training skills in handicraft and gardening for boys and domestic subjects for girls. At other times history, geography and reading were dedicated to the glories of British history and the nation's greatest heroes and heroines. The war finally raised the status of the schools, and engendered a national willingness to invest further in them. As later chapters will argue, though, the war also reinforced the lingering conviction that the primary purpose of these schools was the production of God-fearing citizens armed with the appropriate attitudes and training for them to become skilled workers in local factories, farms, offices and shops.

The war pervaded the classroom in very personal ways from the outset. Many of the men volunteering were fathers and brothers of pupils, many were ex-pupils, and some were the teachers themselves. Contact was maintained with them during their training and while serving at home or abroad, and the close links held a great emotional appeal for the children – and sometimes for the men as well. In the village of Sacombe, for example, the pupils sang the National Anthem when the new school year opened in September 1914, and soon began cultivating an extended school garden in their own time to raise funds to buy blankets for local soldiers. They made socks and belts to send to the troops via an early national collection patronised by the Royal Family, and received a printed note from Queen Mary thanking them for their work.[1] In Bishop's Stortford, a month after returning to school a headmaster reflected with pride on the way his pupils were already actively engaged in the war. Special reference had been made to the causes and course of the war in History and Geography lessons, and:

> The girls have made the flags of the Allies which now float on the flag staff. The girls are knitting socks for the soldiers, and the children have brought £1 4s 6d this week to pay for the wool that is being used. This money represents the pence which would otherwise have been spent on sweets etc. The boys have coloured the 'Times' War Maps, and made small flags to show the progress of the war on the maps. 48 old boys are in His Majesty's Forces, ie. 25 permanently in the Army and 23 in Lord Kitchener's Army.[2]

The Board of Education noted and even eulogised examples like these, but admitted it could not quantify such instances across the country that 'may serve to suggest (better, perhaps, than any systematic summary) the way in which a great stir of national feeling manifests itself in our elementary schools.' It praised the 'largely spontaneous' efforts of teachers, saying 'they are characteristic of what is best in our elementary education of to-day.'[3]

The Board's conclusions were certainly borne out in Hertfordshire in 1914 and 1915. The personal links allowed the adventures, the triumphs and the tragedies to be shared by everyone. Ex-pupils visited schoolrooms to say goodbye before their embarkation. The welcome given to youths in uniform was enthusiastic, and their final departure often poignant. The visits were pervaded by the volunteer's pride, and the teachers' awareness of his possible mutilation and death. Headteachers not only recorded farewells but were moved to record the mood of the occasion. During the autumn of 1914 the headmaster at Much Hadham noted the visit by two 'old boys' going shortly 'to the front to help our country in this most awful war', and the boys of Ashwell gave another ex-pupil 'a hearty "Send off" and many were the expressions that God would protect him and bring him back safe and sound.'[4] Many male teachers volunteered for military service. At Buntingford a master received 'a hearty send off from all present ... the boys cheering lustily again and again.'[5] The teachers corresponded with their schools and the children followed their fortunes keenly. In Sawbridgeworth two teachers on active service sent postcards to the school, visited it on leave, and presented it with the nose cap of a German 'Aerial Torpedo'. When one was incapacitated by a bullet in the thigh the pupils immediately subscribed money to send him chocolates and cigarettes. The headmaster recorded with pride the other master's promotion to sergeant, his head wound during an air raid, his commission as an officer, his award of the Military Cross and his safe return to teaching as a captain.[6]

On occasion the headteacher's patriotism was overshadowed by concern for the well-being of the school once the teacher had volunteered and departed. One by one the assistants at Cowper Testimonial Boys' School in Hertford enlisted, and in May 1916 the headmaster recorded with anxiety rather than enthusiasm that 'my last remaining masters have gone to Bedford to be medically examined before joining the Army'.[7] A year before this date schools had generally ceased to record the farewell visit of local volunteers. No school recorded such visits, if they were made, by the conscripted men later in the war. The excitement could not be sustained, the novelty had long since palled and the casualties were now too heavy for the mood of the early outbursts to be recaptured and repeated.

As local families began to endure casualties some elementary schools honoured their names, following the practice of the far more prestigious public schools. On 12 October 1915, for example, the children of Sandridge brought to school flowers for crosses and wreaths for the memorial service that evening in the parish church for Charles King, the fourth ex-pupil to die in combat.[8] Unusually eager to foster a warlike spirit in his pupils, in December 1914 the headmaster at Ashwell hung up in the school a 'handsomely framed' engrossed Roll of Honour of ex-pupils serving in the armed forces. This, he wrote:

> excited among the scholars much interest and a patriotic spirit and many were the glances at the list of names, some of whom were the Fathers and Brothers of the boys. They numbered 64 boys in all who had volunteered for active service. Two on the list … had died the deaths of Heroes in trying to save England from the ravages of the 'Cultured Hun', being killed in the retreat from Mons.[9]

The elaborate ceremony accompanying the event was widely reported and praised, and from time to time imitated.[10] By the end of July 1915 ten of those on the Roll of Honour had been killed.[11]

Few elementary schools had such consistently jingoistic headteachers as at Ashwell, where the headmaster's deep admiration for the British armed forces, past and present, led to an enthusiastic procession of special lessons, commemorative anniversaries, patriotic concerts, military-style parades, charitable collections and talks by serving soldiers. The school embraced all local war-related activities, and was foremost in many of them.[12] Elsewhere, the mounting casualties generally led to more restrained actions. In October 1916 in one small village a sombre

> little ceremony that witnessed the stern realities of War took place in the School-room … An enlarged photograph of Herbert Dash, a former pupil who went down

in the battle of Jutland Bank in the 'Black Prince' on May 31st, was hung on one of the walls by the head boy ... and a chaplet of laurel leaves placed above it by one of the girls ... After the fixing of the photograph in its place, the children, headed by the Rector, who gave a short address, marched past it in a single file, saluting as they went.[13]

During the first year or two of the war the visits of ex-pupils on leave or during convalescence were recorded with obvious warmth which reflected the welcome they received from staff and pupils. One soldier gave his school a picture of King George VI, but the major attractions were the souvenirs illustrating personal experiences.[14] Many visits involved the soldiers taking over the lesson. This could be a lighthearted occasion, as when children passed round Queen Mary's 1914 Christmas present to the troops – an embossed tin box containing a pipe, tobacco, cigarettes and a greeting card.[15] Sometimes, as at Ashwell, the visitors talked about their experiences in training camps. On occasion, however, the sights and stories must have stunned the pupils. Ashwell was also visited by an ex-pupil 'recovering from a bullet wound in the face', and another soldier gave 'a graphic account of his experiences in the trenches'. This included showing the boys 'the bullet (an explosive one from a Maxim gun) that had penetrated through his right shoulder permanently incapacitating him from serving again at the front'.[16]

Such tales must have thrilled and horrified the impressionable young audience. Details of battles and the winning of medals were freely given. One wounded soldier, with a map behind him, traced in detail his journey on the ill-fated expeditionary force to Gallipoli and back.[17] In a second school a soldier told of his participation in eight engagements with the Germans on the Western Front.[18] Other servicemen enthralled classes with stories of bravery culminating in awards for gallantry, including the Military Medal, Distinguished Conduct Medal and Military Cross.[19]

The efforts of schools to keep in contact were appreciated by the local volunteers, and gratitude as well as pride contributed to the men's readiness to visit them on leave. No doubt, too, it enhanced the popularity and standing of the school with their pupils' families and the local community generally. For Christmas 1914, letters were written in Royston:

by upper boys and girls to all the old boys of the school serving in His Majesty's Forces. Each envelope contained a Xmas card painted in school, and a Khaki handkerchief having the old boy's initials worked on it by a school girl.[20]

During this early period of the war newspapers were very interested in such stories. The public imagination was caught and stirred by the strong yet simple vein of gratitude and mutual sacrifice in a letter pinned to a soldier's blanket by a St Albans schoolgirl on behalf of her class:

> Dear Soldier,
>
> We are sorry you are cold at night, so we are sending you a blanket. We mean to send one every week if we can, because we love you so, for being so brave, and taking care of us and our dear country. We all send our love, and pray God to end the war soon and bring you back safe.
>
> Your loving little friends
>
> Garden Fields School Girls
>
> P.S. We are not going to buy sweets till the war is over, but save our money for blankets and tobacco.[21]

All over the county the handknitted gifts of socks, mittens and balaclava helmets were the products of much time, care and sacrifice of money by children.[22] They were fully involved in the war effort. The county education committee refused schools' requests to allow money it had allocated for attendance prizes to be diverted to the purchase of raw materials to make useful gifts for the troops. The schools, with the pupils' families' agreement, therefore used contributions from pocket money, collections from special concerts, gifts from managers and other well-wishers, and in one case 'prize money from independent sources' to further their efforts.[23]

In only a small minority of schools does this intensive personal contact with soldiers seem to last throughout the war. Certainly the press and, therefore, perhaps, the general public, gradually lost interest in such stories. Most, although not all, school logbook entries on this theme fade away during 1916, but again this does not prove that individual schools did not perpetuate the gifts and letters to local soldiers. However, the major relief agencies, and in particular the Red Cross, much preferred all donations of goods and money to be channelled through county centres without specific people or even units or destinations in mind. In a few schools feelings remained strong enough to resist this pressure and, more pertinently, the wishes of influential local charity organisers. In Anstey and Gilston knitted garments continued to go to local men throughout 1915 and 1916, and in Harpenden until 1918.[24] In Harpenden, too, fruit collected by the children was reserved for one particular ship whose captain lived locally.[25] In

1916, however, few schools were acting independently on the scale of the one in Bishop's Stortford which packed 124 parcels containing wallets, cigarettes and letters as Christmas presents to old boys – after first raising £16 to pay for the materials.[26]

The schools became increasingly involved in the collection of money for a number of charities. This represented a new attitude towards community affairs as hitherto direct giving had not been requested of elementary schoolchildren, and it was likely that some of the children themselves had been the recipients of charitable donations. As the war ground relentlessly on, and relief activities intensified, charities began to recognise that children were particularly effective publicity agents and fund-raisers.

The Royal Family's prestige and patriotic appeal was used to boost several relief funds. Schools rallied to Queen Mary's fund to provide warm clothing for the troops, and to the Prince of Wales' fund to support injured soldiers and their families.[27] Schools in the north and east of Hertfordshire contributed to the Belgian relief fund, with a local newspaper noting that 'the admirable object of helping a fund to feed starving children in Belgium, whom the Germans brutally refuse to feed, has appealed to all English children.'[28] The French flag day in July 1915 held far less appeal in the county. In Bishop's Stortford one headmaster initiated a collection for the French Red Cross and Relief Fund, but in Eastwick, the only other school to mention a collection, it was undertaken at the request of the vicar's wife.[29] By this time public interest in the children's patriotic activities was becoming a double-edged sword. Schools had been praised for their efforts. It had been acknowledged they were setting an example to some communities, but they had also set precedents for future calls upon them and standards by which their future efforts would be judged.[30] The schools started to bask in newspaper approval, but the demands for fund-raising never ceased.

School concerts were invariably linked to wartime themes, and especially the valour of British soldiers and sailors. There were also sentimental eulogies of English pastoral life, ignoring the hardships many in the audience must have experienced working in that same countryside.[31] Drills, mimes, paper-cutting, country dances, recitations, patriotic sketches and costume tableaux were interspersed with traditional and wartime songs. In one concert there was a sketch on 'Our Food Supply', and in another a display of paper-cutting entitled 'His Majesty's Fleet' and a character piece called 'The Farmer'.[32] The recitations and songs included old and new favourites such as 'We love our country', 'I want my daddy', 'The soldier's pardon', 'Merry soldiers', 'The burial of Sir John Moore', 'The

Charge of the Light Brigade', 'Keep the home fires burning', 'Tipperary' and the national anthems of the Allies.[33] The *Hertfordshire and Cambridgeshire Reporter* comforted its readers that the purely educational value of the time-consuming concerts for the young performers 'cannot be over-emphasised'.[34] Certainly the singing, dancing, and art and craft aspects of the curriculum received a boost, and the children must have felt their work in schools possessed a genuine relevance to the momentous events taking place outside.

As casualties soared the concerts and collections became primarily concerned with alleviating the discomfort and injuries of troops from Great Britain and its Empire rather than our continental allies. In 1915 and 1916 schools held functions to help the YMCA install recreational huts in rest areas behind the front lines.[35] The care of blinded and limbless men became a priority, with collections targeting the Star and Garter Homes and St Dunstan's Homes for the Blind.[36] The opportunity was not missed to use the memory of Field Marshall Earl Roberts VC, who died in the autumn of 1914, to fire a patriotic spirit and elicit relief funds.[37] Two years later, the stirring story of Jack 'Boy' Cornwall, who stayed at his post although mortally wounded during the battle of Jutland, swept the country. Gaining a posthumous Victoria Cross, the young sailor became the special hero of many children, and they responded with enthusiasm to collections in his name.[38]

By 1916 the fund-raising capacity of schoolchildren was well known. The days when local charity committees had ignored schools, and refused to allow children supplies of wool, had long passed. Now the wives of rectors and other managers besieged schools with badges to sell and wool to knit.[39] The children were proving themselves an unsurpassed source of disciplined labour and local publicity. Early in 1916 the children of Buntingford were congratulated for raising money for the RSPCA's fund for the army's sick and wounded horses. In a well-publicised campaign they had sold badges in school, undertaken a house-to-house collection and, the local newspapers reported, 'few were able to resist the touching appeal "Buy a badge and help a horse".'[40]

'Our Day' was celebrated amidst widespread publicity from 1915 onwards. Despite the title, it occupied several days of fund-raising on behalf of the Red Cross each side of Trafalgar Day in October. Many children were involved in rattling collecting boxes around the streets and at special sales. In addition, they sold 'Our Day' flowers, and gave out and later collected charity envelopes inviting donations.[41] In St Albans, out of a total of £203 14s 9d raised in the city in 1918, the children collected £95. 'This latter sum – a splendid one', stated the *Hertfordshire Advertiser*, 'was the result of the ingratiating industry of mainly children from the local schools; and – as one little philosopher remarked: "it is wonderful where all the money comes from".'[42] As part of the vigorous publicity attending 'Our Day', Ernest Catlin, a ten-year-old crippled child, merited the rare distinction of two photographs in a county newspaper – one in 1915, when he handed in 720 farthings, and the second in 1918, when he had collected a further 1,153.[43] One local collection was described in detail, and reveals the major part children were playing in fund-raising by 1916:

> The children, who had each a red cross conspicuously attached to their clothing ... first marched in procession down the principal street of the village, singing national airs and drawing the attention of onlookers at the doors and windows of the houses. At the ... end of the street they turned about and parted in pairs, one armed with a pincushion decked with flowers for sale, and the other with a money box, to visit every house and make raids on the pockets of their elders. Their raids were expeditiously and merrily made and met with willing and even eager welcome; for satisfactory results were secured, it may be said, everywhere they went, with scarcely a single exception.[44]

The newspaper made a point of adding that 'a word of praise is deservedly due to the schoolteachers for the preparatory drills that did much to make the operation successful.'[45] Schools and teachers were climbing back into public favour.

Nevertheless, the experiences of schools in Hemel Hempstead reveal the pressures that built up regarding fund-raising, and the shifts in public attitudes. In April 1915 the borough education committee heard the news that one school had dispatched parcels of 'comforts' to local volunteers. The outspoken H.F. Hebert immediately – and successfully – advocated the extension of the idea to all the schools under their control. He stated that:

> there should be some little organisation and that occasional collections be made and small parcels sent to soldiers at the front. There was an average of about 1,650 attendances, and if only one fourth of the children contributed ½d a week an appreciable sum would be got together.[46]

He added, 'the scheme would be the means of bringing home the nature of the struggle in which we are engaged to the children.' He spoke as though mobilisation, enlistment, billeting, the requisition of schools and news from the front had completely bypassed local families.

The imposition of Hebert's proposal through an official education committee letter to schools had limited appeal and very limited success. Some schools raised money for the Overseas Club Fund later in 1915 but, pointedly, others did not, and in November 1916 the education committee bemoaned that collections 'appeared to be dropping out now'.[47] Undaunted, Hebert proposed that all the borough's elementary schools should participate in charity work approved by the committee. He condemned the schools' reaction to the Jack Cornwall appeal as half-hearted and 'very unsatisfactory for a great occasion'. They had 'some small amounts collected and two sums of £1, which looked suspiciously as though they had been made up to that amount.' He argued that no collections should be made without the committee's sanction, and when that was given 'they should be taken up in a proper spirit'. His outburst included criticisms of the children's behaviour and, by implication, their training by their teachers. He believed 'some of these collections had been rather abused. Children had been going round to people's houses and bothering them for subscriptions.' Despite some members' doubts about the propriety of compulsory collections, Hebert carried the day.[48] All initiative passed to the borough council and, one suspects, much goodwill and enthusiasm were lost in the process.

The county education committee adopted a completely different approach. In 1915 the Overseas Club sought to extend its fund-raising activities from the Dominions to Great Britain. At least one Hertfordshire school, Much Hadham, had encouraged pupils to give 1d to provide 'gifts and comforts to the brave soldiers of the British Empire' and in return each child had received an illustrated certificate from the Club.[49] Education committee members expressed sympathy with the Overseas Club's charitable aims, but, when asked, refused to give official sanction to the certificate scheme as it seemed 'rather difficult to hold an official collection in the schools for any particular fund out of the many funds which have claims upon the public'.[50]

The numerous war-related activities were tangible signs of local patriotism, a virtue which became deeply embedded in all aspects of school life. Patriotism incorporated both a belief in the rightness, even righteousness, of Britain's cause, and a desire to contribute the utmost to that cause. Increasingly, the elementary schools became instruments through which children would not only serve the nation in its current emergency but also be trained to serve it well in the inevitable economic and military conflicts of the future. The inculcation of patriotism had a powerful future as well as present imperative.

Practices varied, but schools seized the opportunity to celebrate British achievements past and present, and to mark the lives of significant historic and contemporary figures. In Hoddesdon, Field Marshal Sir John French was given three cheers at the time of the battle of Loos in 1915.[51] In Gilston, the drowning of Field Marshal Earl Kitchener, the publicly revered Secretary of State for War, on his way to Russia in 1916 prompted a study of his military exploits in the Sudan, South Africa and India.[52] In Pirton, the commemoration of the execution of the British nurse Edith Cavell for assisting Allied soldiers to escape from Belgium led to subscriptions for the purchase of her portrait.[53] In Ayot St Peter, St George's Day was marked by the distribution of roses.[54] In Sawbridgeworth, perhaps forgetful of both the Prussian contribution to final victory and the current status of the French as allies, the centenary of the battle of Waterloo was highlighted as a signal feat of British arms.[55]

The National Anthem was sung more frequently than before the war, and sometimes was accompanied by renditions of those of Russia, France, Belgium and Serbia on the piano or harmonium.[56] Two songs, both well publicised in Hertfordshire, blatantly exploited children, encouraging enlistment and defending a romanticised view of English life. One acquired national fame, and was aimed at shaming men into volunteering. Part of it asked accusingly:

> Where will you look, sonny, where will you look
> When your children yet to be
> Clamour to learn of the part you took
> In the War that kept men free?[57]

The other, printed originally in the *Daily Chronicle*, was a wartime variation of 'Jesu, Lover of my Soul', sung, it was claimed, by men of the Hertfordshire Territorials on marches and in the trenches. It incorporated the names of several Gade valley villages, evoking memories of the songs and hymns taught in the day and Sunday schools. Hemel Hempstead had a strong and continuing Nonconformist tradition, and groups of local volunteers may well have used these words alongside the other sentimental – and more risqué – songs popularised by the war. The song – it is hardly a hymn – tells of:

> Weary British soldiers
> Sodden through the rain,
> Singing 'Tipperary',
> Leave the trench again;
> And the men of Hertshire
> Take their place to-night,
> Where the shells are screaming
> 'Mid the winter's blight
>
> But amid the rattle
> Of the cannonade
> From the flooded trenches

> Where the Hertshires wade;
> Hear the voice of music
> Falling on the ear:
> 'Tis the men of Hertshire
> Singing strong and clear:

It ends:

> At the front in Flanders
> Sing the Hertshire men
> Songs they learnt on Sundays,
> In the Hertshire glen:
> Songs they sang at Apsley,
> Hempstead, and Boxmoor,
> Or within the Langleys,
> On the schoolroom floor.
>
> Still the schools are standing,
> And the songs are sung
> By the little children
> Where no shells are flung:
> And a prayer is offered
> For the boys of old,
> Fighting now in Flanders
> In the trenches cold.[58]

Special lessons, songs and salutes, and concerts and collections also marked Trafalgar Day on 21 October and Empire Day on 24 May, but these two occasions were used primarily not to raise money but to instil patriotism. Trafalgar Day celebrated the genius of Horatio Nelson and Britain's century of naval supremacy, and now it looked forward to equally crushing victories over the Germans. The anniversary had been commemorated before the war, but usually in a low-key way. In some schools in 1914 special lessons noted the historic importance of the day, but there were no elaborate ceremonies.[59] At Callow Land in Watford the pupils also sang the Marseillaise, neatly combining past English victories over the French with modern rapprochement.[60] In 1915 the anniversary soared in popularity. The county council issued a circular expecting all schools to do their duty and make a special effort to mark the anniversary.[61] It joined the growing number of wartime occasions when schools hoisted and saluted the Union Jack and sang the National Anthem. The commemoration became much broader in outlook and more emotional in character, and usually embraced the local community. The growth and power of the Royal Navy since Nelson's day was the heart of the new message to the children.[62] Admiral Jellicoe, the commander-in-chief of the

Grand Fleet, was held to have inherited 'the Nelson touch', 'Hearts of Oak' was sung to celebrate the spirit of the ordinary sailor, and the children were made to understand that they owed a great debt to the navy, especially in 'the present crisis'.[63] The intention of all schools, especially after receiving the county circular, can be summarised by one headteacher's formal logbook entry:

> Special reference has been made today in all the classes, to the 21st October 1805, and to the present work of the Fleet in protecting our trade, and our own shores from invasion.[64]

Timetables were altered for the special lessons, and sometimes patriotic entertainments were staged to honour past and present admirals, followed by the rare treat of a half-day holiday.[65]

From 1915 onwards the local rector or vicar, where he was also a school manager, was increasingly likely to take charge of a topical lesson on Trafalgar Day. There were hymns and sermons as well as parades and salutes, implicitly or explicitly ensuring the children were aware that not only Nelson's successors but also God were on their side.[66] Christianity and nationalism quickly combined in this tidal wave of patriotic fervour.

Trafalgar Day ceremonies reached a peak in 1916. In June the British and German fleets had clashed heavily but indecisively off Jutland, and the nation needed reassurance that Admiral Jellicoe's failure to annihilate the enemy did not mean the dissipation of the much-vaunted 'Nelson touch' in British admirals. That summer the county council commended to school managers the Navy League's resolution that British naval history and 'the use of British Sea Power' be recognised as 'an essential branch' of education.[67] New editions of class readers contained sections on the subject, and Trafalgar Day ceremonies became far more formal, intense and prolonged. In Buntingford the flagstaff was decorated, Guides and Scouts formed a guard of honour, the war hymn composed by the Dean of St Albans was sung, the vicar offered dedicatory prayers, the chairman of the managers – a lieutenant colonel in full uniform – unfurled a brand new flag, and parents, guests and children sang 'Rule Britannia'. This was followed first by silence in memory of Nelson and old boys of the school, and then by three cheers for the navy.[68] Elsewhere in the county, too, the religious element was significant, and sometimes the link with Trafalgar seemed tenuous, with sermons reported on themes of 'The Freewill Gifts of Our Day', 'Hospitals and the Red Cross' and 'Cups of Cold Water'.[69] The 'Cups of Cold Water' sermon centred on the dying Elizabethan courtier and soldier, Sir Philip Sidney, passing a cup of water meant for him to a mortally wounded ordinary foot soldier lying nearby on the battle-field of Zutphen. The famous story encapsulated the virtues of courage and self-lessness which British warriors, and especially their officers, were held to possess in abundance.

The role of the modern navy loomed larger and larger in later celebrations as the German U-boat campaign against merchant ships grew in intensity. Navy League lecturers toured Hertfordshire, and by 1918 the children were thoroughly imbued with tales of the enormity of Germany's maritime crimes, and 'of the unceasing vigilance of the "King's Navy".'[70] Six hundred boys from elementary schools in St Albans, accompanied by their teachers, attended a 'lantern lecture' on 'Mines, Torpedoes and Submarines' given by a League speaker. Popular war songs preceded the show. Hatred of Germany and its people was raised to fever pitch by the lecturer's choice of phrases and arguments. The boys were reminded that only the Royal Navy stood between them and the destruction of St Albans, starvation and defeat. Conversely, the German fleet was ridiculed for skulking in Kiel, the speaker mocking that:

> in the British naval ships ... most of the guns faced forward and there were only two at the stern, but in the German ships they had as many guns as possible facing backwards; and they needed them, for they were good at running away.[71]

The children were told the story of the sinking of the unarmed liner *Lusitania* by a U-boat, and warned that 'that brutal act ... should never be forgotten by British boys, who should when they grow up, refuse to work or be associated with Germans.' In the theatrical finale the audience 'vehemently' shouted a series of 'Noes' when asked, 'Are we downhearted? Do you love the German emperor? Shall we forgive him?'[72]

Girls never attended such lectures, and not one all-girls' school records commemorating Trafalgar Day. All the children in mixed schools seem to have participated in the celebrations and ceremonies connected with special occasions during the war, but the instillation of an aggressive patriotic spirit was reserved primarily for the boys. They were the ones likely to be conscripted; the days of relying on volunteers had passed.

The development of Empire Day took a different course. By far the most widely honoured day in schools, it was subject to close scrutiny regarding its relationship to the war, the future of the country and its influence upon children. In 1914 the day was noted but not commented upon further in Hertfordshire school logbooks. It was a time for treats – buns, or a trip to the cinema.[73] In 1915 a wide variety of activities were reported, revealing the different interpretations managers and teachers were now placing upon Empire Day. Special lessons were given, and flags hoisted and saluted nearly everywhere, with the ceremony usually accompanied by songs and dances. In one St Albans school strict formality dominated the day. The morning lessons were devoted to lectures on 'The Duties and Responsibilities of British Citizenship'. These were followed by a parade, the National Anthem and 'God bless the Prince of Wales', after which a county alderman gave an address on the Empire and the duties of its subjects.[74] At a nearby school over 300 parents and the chairman of the district education committee enjoyed a programme of folk songs and dancing. The whole affair was light-hearted and 'caused much merriment'.[75] At a third school in the city the newspaper report noted that 'there was quite an undertone of seriousness and sadness, especially among the older girls, throughout the celebration.' One of the plays, 'Britannia and Her Friends', aroused deep emotions, 'especially among the Territorials present, one of whom seized by a sudden impulse, borrowed a bag and made a collection among the spectators'.[76] As one headmaster wrote, Empire Day had a fuller significance after the gratifying response 'of the Colonials to the military needs of the Motherland'.[77] Convalescing troops from the Dominions, as well as refugees, attended school Empire Day ceremonies and, one local newspaper observed, 'greatly increased the interest and gave pathos to the occasion'.[78]

In 1915 children were beginning to be taught the watchwords of the League of Empire movement – 'Responsibility, duty, sympathy and self-sacrifice, and the rally cry "For God, duty and Empire".'[79] In Harpenden the national flag was endowed with a moral significance when pupils received a lesson on 'Duty, Sacrifice, Freedom and Safety, as taught by the Union Jack'.[80] In 1916 the government formally recognised Empire Day, and the Union Jack had to be flown from all public buildings. The *Times Educational Supplement* duly reported that 'in more than 70,000 schools addresses were delivered on the privileges and duties which attach to Imperial citizenship.'[81] The Earl of Meath had fervently advocated a day like Empire Day since 1901 but, the report went on, 'before the war it seemed remote, unreal, too high for ordinary men and women' but now 'it is gradually being recognised as merely a statement of the common heritage.' The goals of Empire Day were clearcut:

> It aims at preserving the proud memories of the past; it designs instruction in the facts of the present; it dreams of the realisation of great ideals in the future.[82]

The task of inculcating what was vaguely termed a 'tradition of kinship' with the peoples of the Empire was thrust upon the schools, as 'in no place but the school can these traditions be adequately preserved and vitalised.' To achieve this it seems that a selective view of History was acceptable, in the hope that children 'will know nothing of times when it was still a matter of speculation whether the Empire would hold together or not'.[83]

For the remainder of the war the children of Hertfordshire learnt much about the growth of the Empire, drew flags, marched, saluted and sang, but above all were exhorted to love and preserve the Empire, defend the new-found values it stood for, and reciprocate the undoubted filial attachment of the Dominions and colonies.[84] The verse about the Dominions was added to the National Anthem, which children duly learned along with the songs 'What can I do for England?', 'Who'll fight for England?' and 'The Red, White and Blue'.[85]

Personal qualities of character and willing service became all-important, as the League's watchwords and rally cry proclaimed. In 1917, a year of intense U-boat attacks, bloody stalemate on the Western Front and Russian collapse in the east, one St Albans headmaster spoke 'on the deadly peril of the British Empire in the present war and pointed out to the boys how each might do his share towards victory'.[86] Clergy addressed schools, as in Barkway, on each child's 'duty as a citizen of our wonderful Empire'.[87] By 1917, Empire Day in Hitchin had become an important religious festival. The minor celebration of 1915 had been replaced by a formal service conducted by the Dean of St Albans.[88] Nothing less than devotion to the Empire was required of the next generation.

To a large extent, however, the schools celebrated Empire Day in a social vacuum. In 1916 the *Hertfordshire and Essex Observer* noted that the observation of Empire Day in Bishop's Stortford 'with the exception of flags flown from private residences, was confined to the schools'.[89] Rarely does any county newspaper mention any institution other than a school marking the occasion but, nevertheless, few people doubted that the schools should mark it. In 1917 the *Times Educational Supplement* strongly implied that the real importance of Empire Day was its impact on children.[90] Locally, only H.F. Hebert in Hemel Hempstead spoke out against the dangers of inculcating a bellicose nationalism. He sided with the Liberal MPs who wrote in the *Daily Mail* that 'inherent in the word Empire is the idea of force rather than freedom, and of constraint rather than goodwill.'[91] He condemned 'the aggressive arrogance it carries with it to the minds of the great peoples of other nations', and he argued that rampant imperialism created armed conflicts the League of Empire was claiming to prevent. With striking provocation, he asked:

Can anyone now to whose lips rises the word so glibly tell us what is the share in the calamity under which the whole world is groaning, of our proud and arrogant adoption of the word Empire?[92]

Finally he attacked the hymns popularised by the war and frequently sung in schools, particularly 'O God our help in ages past', and ridiculed the assumption that the British had a monopoly of either truth or appeals to God. He considered 'We are but little children weak' and 'God moves in a mysterious way' to be far more educational and appropriate for children's use.[93]

The press, well aware of public opinion, had long thought differently. It regretted the pre-war neglect of Empire Day and its lessons for children, arguing that:

we should have heard a great deal less about conscientious objectors had the spirit which Empire Day seeks to inculcate in our children been more generally fostered.[94]

As early as February 1915 the *Times Educational Supplement* offered teachers more reasoned guidelines. It did not criticise the Empire, but it did recognise that teachers were 'troubled' about how best to impart not so much the facts but the principles associated with the war. The teacher's duty was not to communicate to children his or her 'own natural moods – the anger against the Germans which we must all feel at times, the instinctive hatred of enemy for enemy', nor to assert 'that England stands in the war for all that is holy and good and Germany for all that is wicked. To say that is to make a religion of patriotism and a partisan of God.' Children sorely needed a patriotism that was 'sane and modest but none the less passionate for that', and their maturing attitude towards their country should be much the same as their maturing love of their parents – both were to be defended stoutly, but accepted with affection as fallible.[95]

The *Times Educational Supplement* was asking much of the elementary school teachers and, probably, too much, bearing in mind the relentless propaganda and tight censorship of the government, the daily news of casualties reaching local communities, the horrors of civilian bombing, and their own level of education and training. All the evidence suggests that teachers eschewed the most lurid features of British anti-German propaganda but simply ensured their pupils celebrated famous British figures and anniversaries, supported the country in its hour of adversity as much as they could, and understood current events as far as their ages and the available news allowed them to. Understandably in such perilous times, the British could do nothing wrong and the Germans nothing right militarily or morally, but local newspaper editors, the ever-vigilant guardians of public opinion, were sometimes far from satisfied with the lessons the children were receiving. In 1916, during the prolonged slaughter on the Somme and the mounting air raids over southern England, the *West Hertfordshire Observer* dramatically announced that schools were failing to foster patriotism with sufficient vigour. With a sweeping disregard for the evidence, teachers were castigated for being 'too much pre-occupied with a stereotyped curriculum to pay much regard to national ideals.' Too many showed too little inclination 'to fire the souls of their scholars with the passion of patriotism'.[96]

The same newspaper urged drastic alterations to syllabuses. It exhorted the county education committee and schools to:

> pay more attention to the geography of the British Empire, and leave no page of its thrilling story untold ... the sublime patriotic pages of Shakespeare, which stir the blood today as does nothing else in English letters, should be learnt by heart, as should a number of moving poems. [97]

One of the chief aims of elementary education, the newspaper went on to argue, was to ensure pupils understood 'that they belonged, not to themselves, but to their country.' In the light of these criticisms, it is ironic that the constant publicity given to stirring tales of British valour in the current war served to raise the standing of the elementary schools which had educated the overwhelming majority of combatants. The *Hertfordshire and Cambridgeshire Reporter* frequently mentioned Ashwell school, whose headmaster was so proud of the regular enlistment of ex-pupils and the 'plucky spirit and determination of a true British lad.'[98] Likewise, the *West Hertfordshire Observer* ensured that a wide audience read about the public statement of the chairman of managers of Watford Higher Elementary School that 'it was unthinkable that children brought up in the traditions of a British school would ever be guilty of such an atrocity as the shelling of Scarborough', and the spontaneous round of applause that followed.[99] The killing of forty civilians by the German warships bombarding Scarborough, Whitby and Hartlepool had provided a major propaganda coup for Britain.

Many classes spent much time talking about the causes and progress of the war. This was particularly true in the autumn of 1914. As the headmaster of Hoddesdon wrote, 'the boys bring so many questions regarding the War that the Geography and History lessons turn on the topic more than any other.'[100] Lessons had to be altered to explain the latest news. History and Geography soared in popularity, having an immediate appeal and possessing a relevance never experienced before. Many of the dates, places, rivers, bays and capes the children had learnt parrot-fashion now meant something to them. In September 1914 several lessons for older pupils at Barkway were revised to discuss the countries engaged in the war, the causes of the war and the prominent leaders. By November the war dominated Barkway's History and Geography lessons, and the original syllabuses were relegated to the wings. By 1917 the children's vast accumulated background knowledge enabled them to follow each new campaign closely and clearly.[101] In Braughing the novelty of lantern slides added to the drama.[102]

Extensive changes to a school's syllabuses had to be sanctioned by HMI Marvin. One detailed record of such a revision survives for St Mary's Boys' School in Hitchin, and it reveals a comprehensive coverage of the history and geography of all the combatants, alongside a significant increase in pro-British literary texts. For 1915–16 Geography was revised to include Egypt, the Persian Gulf, German West Africa and the Balkan States as well as other European protagonists. In October 1915, for example, the older boys studied the Balkans, and 'amongst the salient points dealt with were the history of Turkey from 1453, the Balkan War 1913, and the present crisis now existing in Eastern Europe.' The additions to English Literature were calculated to enhance pride in British arms and overseas achievements, and included 'St Crispin's Day', 'Men of England', 'Trafalgar Day', 'Queen Elizabeth at Tilbury', 'Hubert and Arthur', 'Ring Out Wild Bells', 'To India and the Colonies' and 'There is no Land Like England'. A study of airships was added to the list of Science Observation lessons. The school received consistently high praise from Marvin, and it seems safe to assume that the 'sane and modest but none the less passionate' patriotism sought by the *Times Educational Supplement* prevailed here.[103] The school epitomised the Board of Education's own publicly expressed view that the most successful teachers consistently taught present-day events in the context of the past histories, established positive links with 'old boys', and incorporated a range of war-oriented songs, poems and prose into the curriculum.[104]

Occasionally a school overstepped the bounds of patriotic outrage at German aggression. Early in 1915 the *Hertfordshire Express* published a school's essays entitled 'What I would do with the Kaiser'.[105] They satisfied the most rabid anti-German feelings:

> If I had the Kaiser I would banish him to the Isle of St Helena, and there he could think he was king of the world.

If I got hold of the Kaiser I think I would take him up Queen Street and let the people up there give him it. It would be better if it were their washing day, for then they would hit him with their copper-sticks. If I did not do that I should put him in an iron cage and take him round to the market and then let the people do as they liked with him.

If I caught the Kaiser I should make him give me all his money and I should give it to the poor. I should put him in prison and feed him on bread and water, and then I should make him suffer like he has made some of the Belgians. Then I should put him on an island and make him stay there and starve to death.

If I caught the Kaiser I would cut him and put some salt in his cuts and punish him well; if he did not die with that, I would hang him straight away so he would not make any more wars.

If I caught the Kaiser I would take him to Belgium and show him everything he had done, and I should make him build everything up again that he had destroyed ... I would make him bring all his own beautiful things and put them in the houses of the Belgians and in the cathedrals and churches.

If I caught the Kaiser I should first of all take all his money and put it towards building up what he has damaged. Then I should put him in prison and torment him, and to kill him I should make up a big furnace and throw him on.

If I caught the Kaiser I should put him in prison, feed him on dry bread, with dirty water to drink, and if he would not have it he could starve to death.

One girl suggested pulling out the Kaiser's moustache, and another, imbued with the contemporary working-class aversion to a pauper's funeral, advocated burying him as cheaply as possible. Bearing in mind the more rabid propaganda accusations of German atrocities, it is not surprising that such sentiments received publicity. They did, though, attract great criticism. Correspondents condemned the essays as 'blood thirsty and vindictive' and 'repugnant to the teaching of the New Testament'.[106] The newspaper should have condemned them with shame, critics asserted, not published them with pride. They were held to be proof of the war's 'debasing effect upon children's minds'. The school was castigated as thoroughly irresponsible for instilling hatred and a love of cruelty that boded ill for future parents and peaceful co-existence with other nations.[107]

Early in 1917 every child in Hertfordshire was made to feel personally involved in the war when the War Office, at the height of the spy mania, requested that lessons were given on its pamphlet *Inadvertent Disclosure of Military Information*.[108] The county was a sensitive military area, and the request was obeyed, especially as German agents had long been suspected, although never actually caught, around the numerous camps.[109] The 1914 Aliens Restriction Act was enforced strictly. In February 1915 Hertfordshire County Council was informed that 483 'enemy aliens' had been registered, of whom 134 had been interned and 162 obliged to move to less sensitive areas. Those allowed to stay were watched closely.[110] Anxiety persisted about the possibility of spies masquerading as Belgian refugees.[111] A professional journal, *The Teacher's World*, issued a specimen lesson, complete with illustrative stories, which unlike any logbook entry reveals the melodramatic, alarming and urgent tone which characterised many wartime exhortations. It claimed:

> British boys and girls have all unknowingly given Germany help of a kind that she could have got in no other way. We may have sacrificed ourselves in every possible way; we may have been brave and strong when news has come that our dear ones will never return to us again; we may have worked and worked until we have become but shadows of our former selves; and yet patriotic as we are, we may have helped Germany more than once. Without knowing it, we have been traitors to our country.[112]

The aim was to ensure that children were too shocked, scared and suspicious to speak or write to anyone about local military activities.

The war led to a resurgence of military drill in Hertfordshire schools, reversing the tentative moves towards organised games and gymnastic exercises.[113] Drill exercises were popular as entertainment in patriotic concerts and at Empire Day parades, but it was the discipline as much as the pageantry that led to their restoration. The potential value of drill as an early preparation for military life, coupled with the growing fear of juvenile delinquency, led to it being the only aspect of the curriculum to be formally debated by the county education committee during the war, in July 1916. Members upheld that, with a predominantly female influence both at school and at home, 'something a little sterner and stronger would be an excellent thing'. Military instructors were advocated, with drill written into the curriculum. The example of the public schools, where this was common practice, was used to strengthen the argument that 'it would give a feeling of self reliance and altogether a good tone to boys in elementary schools.' Once again the neglect of war-oriented lessons was lamented as:

> had all the children in the schools for years past been in the habit of receiving military training they would now have been in a better position to take up the sterner work.[114]

The committee took no further action as it became abundantly clear that military drill, occasionally led by army personnel, although usually by civilian teachers, was already the rule rather than the exception.[115] It had crept back on the initiative of local schools and their managers, and against the wishes of HMI.

If Physical Education was degraded educationally in wartime, Science fared no better. It, too, became an adjunct of the war effort. Initially the Board of Education encouraged a diversity of approaches. Its pamphlet *Elementary Science, including Nature Study*, published in 1915, confirmed the place of Object Lessons during which, week by week, children learnt by heart the given characteristics of a multitude of common objects.[116] Sometimes the objects were placed in front of each child, but usually they were held up by the teacher or portrayed in a picture. During the year 1915–16, for example, the infants at Bengeo studied 'shells, a lighthouse, cup and saucer, teapot, kettle, watering can, wheelbarrow, scissors, a flag, a sponge, a bell, an umbrella, water, milk, cocoa, sugar, an egg, a loaf, salt, coal and cork'.[117] However, the Board recognised that Object Lessons merely supplied 'useful and interesting information' rather than encouraging 'first-hand observation and inquiry.' Rural schools were urged to study plants and animals first-hand and in different seasons, and urban schools encouraged to make full use of zoos and museums.[118]

Practice in Hertfordshire continued to fall short of the Board's expectations outside the traditional Object Lessons. A microscope was so rare that possession of one called for special comment in a Hitchin school logbook, when pupils studied flies.[119] Nature walks were uncommon. In just two small schools children were given the opportunity to observe, comment upon and draw the living fauna and flora of the locality. Rare treats even in these schools, they were joyous occasions. In May 1915 Barkway infants 'plucked flowers in the meadow, noticed the various trees, buds, leaves', and asked many questions. That autumn they:

> walked through the stubble of the cornfields, and by the farm chatted about stacks. They also talked about a binder, plough, and dragging machine which stood near by. Teachers and children picked hazel nuts, hips and haws, blackberries, acorns and sloes. The little ones were delighted and their observation was very keen. This afternoon they are learning the words of a song 'To the woods'.[120]

Nature Study was given a new purpose in 1917. By then the children's success as fund-raisers and publicity agents, and their availability as a source of cheap labour, were well known. As Allied merchant ships succumbed in large numbers to German U-boat attacks the supplies of imported foodstuffs and industrial raw materials dwindled. At the beginning of the year Germany had adopted a policy of unrestricted warfare against all ships that U-boat commanders suspected of aiding the Allied war effort. As national timber stocks fell, nut shells and fruit stones were found to produce a satisfactory charcoal for use in gas masks. Schoolchildren were asked to collect them, and to publicise the need for this unusual salvage operation.[121] In some Hertfordshire villages dandelion and white bryony roots were collected in large quantities for their medicinal qualities. A ready market existed in London for bulk consignments, and in King's Walden the children collected 800 pounds in one week.[122] The dearth of imported animal feed led to official requests being directed to headteachers to organise acorn-collecting walks. Occasionally local squires stimulated the children's efforts with promises of treats. Thus motivated, the pupils in King's Langley collected 90 bushels, and those in Much Hadham a ton.[123]

The demands became more intense as the shortages grew more acute. Only a few Hertfordshire schools collected nuts or acorns, but the next requests, although couched in permissive terms, had the force of directives. In August 1917 all schools received an urgent plea via the Board of Education from the Food Controller and Minister of Munitions to collect horse chestnuts.[124] After the schools had delivered their collections to local depots they were transported to a destination and used for a purpose that remained closely guarded secrets. In fact horse chestnuts were an alternative to imported wood and maize for the distillation of acetone, a solvent used in the manufacture of cordite. The experiments and manufacture were carried out in a secret factory near King's Lynn, Norfolk.[125] The air of mystery coupled with the salutary announcement that every ton of horse chestnuts released half a ton of grain for food appealed to the public imagination. Nature walks proliferated with horse chestnuts solely in mind. As Wareside School recorded, Marvin's permission was readily given as the Board was keen for schools to make a 'definite contribution to national efficiency'.[126] Efforts varied widely, from the occasional walk undertaken at the managers' insistence in Eastwick to frenzies of intensive collecting spread over several weeks in Hitchin.[127] The children in Barkway collected 2 tons 2½ cwts and the Buntingford schools 3 tons 15 cwts – 'a gratifying response', conceded the press.[128]

Not everyone was enthusiastic. Some collectors in the county raised the question of payment, and received indignant refusals as well as accusations of unpatriotic conduct.[129] Property owners complained of acts of trespass and wanton damage to trees. The county press, sure of readers' sympathies, loudly bemoaned 'the wet blanket ... thrown over the kiddies' efforts to help with a little bit of win-the-war work', especially as the collections had been an emergency measure requested by the government.[130]

The shortage of labour and the heightened demand for jam by the armed forces led to more nature walks in 1918, this time for blackberries.[131] An average of three half-days harvesting per week was required by the compliant Board of Education at the request of the desperate Ministry of Food. The Board expected the 'hearty co-operation of both teachers and children', but the strain on patriotism was offset by the promise of 'substantial remuneration to the actual pickers'.[132]

Blackberrying became a universal pastime across Hertfordshire in the late summer and early autumn of 1918. The press had whipped up enthusiasm by forecasting a prodigious crop, but bad weather blighted early ripening, the influenza epidemic depleted school numbers and a railway strike hindered the speedy dispatch of the fruit.[133] Some schools, too, were keener than others. One headteacher, under instructions to cooperate, grumbled that rain ruined one walk and the garden had to be neglected because of another.[134] The *Hertfordshire Express* complained that many children picked unripe fruit, and provoked a short-lived but bitter exchange of correspondence with those outraged by its assertion that this practice should be made a 'heinous offence' by parents, teachers and clergy, and be backed up by threats of visits by the police.[135]

Despite all the impediments several schools picked over 30 pounds, and one 200 pounds, in a single afternoon.[136] Many devoted three half-days a week for a fortnight or more, with the small village schools at Ayot St Peter collecting 500 pounds and Sandon 1,533 pounds.[137] The eleven schools in and around Buntingford picked 1½ tons.[138] A particularly determined Hertford school sacrificed sixteen afternoons to gather 18½ cwts and win the silver cup awarded by Lady Pearson to the Hertfordshire school collecting most blackberries.[139] Overall, ninety-eight Hertfordshire schools sent in 14.7 tons of fruit.[140]

The collections were part of a national obsession with economy and efficiency. The children were a source of cheap and obedient labour, and it was widely believed that their war work, undertaken alongside the new patriotic syllabuses, would infuse them with a greater understanding of their country's needs and a lasting readiness to serve them. Many of the virtues deemed necessary during the war were those that had been promoted by teachers, clergy and employers during the previous century. The nation in 1914 required of children the same qualities that the popular writer and social reformer Samuel Smiles had demanded of their parents and grandparents – they should be 'honest, truthful, polite, temperate, courageous, self-respecting, and self-helping'.[141] For generations employers, school managers and teachers had taken it as axiomatic that habits of respect, obedience, temperance, industry, perseverance and thrift should be engrained for life in the schoolroom.[142]

In the summer of 1915 the Board of Education re-emphasised the importance of thrift.[143] No new syllabus was required, only an emphasis upon the nation's dire wartime needs in addition to the traditional benefits of saving money for periods of ill-health and old age. In reality the savings of adults were the main target, but once again the government recognised the propaganda and publicity value of children – as 'what is said and done in the schools has effect in many homes'. In 1916 all pupils took home a leaflet entitled *War Savings – How Everybody Can Help to Win the War*. Allying personal thrift with national victory, it promoted the War Savings Certificate with the twin catchphrases *Save for the sake of the country. Save for your own sake*. Publicity coupling the promise of good times to share with the men on their return home with the threat of bad times striking without notice was avidly propagated in schools nationwide.[144] Hertfordshire County Council issued supporting circulars, and local newspapers urged everyone to 'spend less, save more and lend all you can to the government.'[145]

The schools did what was expected of them. The importance of thrift was reaffirmed and war savings clubs launched.[146] Waterford School recorded its procedures in detail, and probably other communities followed a similar course. A public meeting was held at the school, agreement reached to form a War Savings Association, and War Savings Certificates were purchased for members once the necessary 15s 6d had accrued in their account in the school's Post Office Savings Bank.[147] In Braughing the children introduced the inaugural meeting with a play, *Patriotic Pence*.[148] At Norton, 'Tank Bank Week', complete with a mock-up tank, firmly linked family savings to the war effort.[149]

The children's efforts became a source of pride to the teachers, who sometimes ran schemes that incorporated the whole village. In remote Pirton, with ninety children on roll, thirty families joined the new Association.[150] By October 1918 the neighbouring villages of Sacombe and Tonwell had purchased 391 certificates between them.[151] At Sawbridgeworth Boys' School 159 certificates were sold in a month – a rare achievement.[152] Headteachers in poor areas were sometimes surprised at local efforts. It took two and a half years for one Hitchin school to save £100, but all of it was 'saved in comparatively small sums, no certificate having been brought as the result of a single payment.'[153] On 9 May 1918 forty-one boys and a teacher from Callow Land in Watford marched triumphantly into the town to buy forty-six certificates.[154] By the end of the war the schools in Hemel

Hempstead had raised £1,217 17s od and for once received the approbation of their education committee.[155] Nevertheless, the praise had been hard earned, and possibly by then any comments from the persistently interventionist education committee were not particularly welcome. In 1917 committee members had publicly criticised a non-participating school, and then used the variations in each school's total as crude evidence that not all the teachers 'were doing their best'.[156]

Thrift was extended in other ways. Domestic Subjects had appeared in an increasing number of Hertfordshire schools before 1914, and during the first year of the war most cookery syllabuses and centres continued in use as before. From the autumn of 1915 the emphasis changed. In the interests of national economy cookery was revised 'so that children may have practical instruction on how to live cheaply.'[157] Cookery instructors were asked to give evening demonstrations to mothers' meetings and parish guilds, using school premises and equipment.[158] The press was sceptical, asking:

> whether the young ladies engaged in this kind of work will be able to teach much to a working class mother who has brought up a family of, say six or seven children on a small weekly wage.[159]

It anticipated ribald comments from housewives, and resentment from their husbands, at the insulting suggestion of family poverty and domestic inadequacy. Nevertheless, as part of this initiative cookery classes for girls became compulsory if local Domestic Subjects Centres were accessible. In Hertford all girls attended their centre in rota, and in November 1915 they were preparing a two-course dinner for a family of six for a shilling.[160] Menus included meat and vegetable pudding with rice pudding, potato soup and fruit pudding, and Irish stew with currant dumplings. Later on, a penny a head became the target. The children popularised the county's policy, and the newspapers' fears proved unfounded. The *Hertfordshire Mercury* acknowledged that the children became 'so proficient that their mothers are glad of their aid in the preparation of meals at home'.[161] Families followed the schools' examples of careful budgeting, including groups of householders in some streets agreeing bulk purchases among themselves in order to negotiate cheaper prices from stores. In January 1916 the LEA's intensive efforts to foster domestic economies merited a detailed report in the *Times Educational Supplement*.[162]

As food shortages became acute, a Board of Education circular urged schools to promote jam-making, bottling and pickle-making using the cheapest possible fruits.[163] Lessons were given on the evils of sweets and on ways of using less sugar and bread.[164] In conjunction with the lessons for children and demonstrations for adults, in some communities the schools helped arrange local exhibitions and competitions to stimulate families' interest in, and imitation of, the cheapest possible dishes.[165] Marvin was impressed.[166]

Thrift and economy pervaded some other subjects to such an extent that they became adjuncts of the war effort rather than aspects of education. Gardening was one. Until 1916 it continued to be encouraged by Marvin much as in pre-war days. He advocated its full integration with other subjects, such as Nature Study, Mathematics, Drawing and English, although in this he was usually disappointed. Nevertheless, by December 1914 boys from fifty-six Hertfordshire schools were cultivating plots.[167] The enlistment of many male teachers and skilled instructors made it difficult for some headteachers to maintain regular gardening lessons, but throughout 1915 schools continued to acquire plots and secure county grants. Gardening appealed to the education committee, and a garden in each school was its avowed aim. Members welcomed the host of benefits – physical exercise, disciplined training and horticultural knowledge – it gave future farm and estate workers.[168]

With justification, schools felt their gardens made a significant contribution to the war effort. They sold some of their produce locally, not least because the LEA still demanded that schools covered all their gardening costs, but many gave away surplus vegetables, fruit and eggs to soldiers on leave, to navy personnel to take back to their ships and, especially, to the military hospitals at Royston and Cambridge. These hospitals sought over 15,000 eggs a week from local sources, and several schools arranged intermittent collections from chicken coops at school and at home.[169]

In 1917, however, the food shortages, the obsession with economy and the value of schools as propaganda agents combined to turn gardening classes into a primary industry contributing to national survival. Gone were thoughts of an integrated curriculum, simple scientific experiments, neat plots decorated with flowers as well as vegetables, and the need for skilled instruction in horticulture. Instead, the Board of Education, in association with the Ministry of Food, urged LEAs to concentrate solely upon potatoes and cheap green vegetables.[170] Acreage and tonnage became the criteria of success. Educational advice was now limited to warnings about potato diseases, and the usefulness of soap suds and animal droppings swept up from the roads as fertilisers.[171] Marvin changed tack, too, and urged school managers to order their schools to dig not so much for victory as to avoid starvation.[172] Local Church of England clergy, many of them managers, took up their bishop's cue in ensuring that their schools cultivated every scrap of land, including the gardens of absent servicemen.[173]

Hertfordshire school plots increased by twenty-seven acres in 1916–17, a total exceeded only by Durham's forty acres.[174] The *Times Educational Supplement* approved wholeheartedly of patriotic gardening, 'even if the time devoted to this occupation had to be increased at the expense of other subjects'. It welcomed the vocational training it gave to 'the country boy', and it welcomed, too, Hertfordshire's new scheme under which the school managers secured land and tools, the pupils provided the labour, and the county council gave the seed – for which it would be reimbursed once the produce had been sold.[175] The remaining proceeds would be used to buy stock for the following year, with any final profit being divided among the pupils.

Some months later, in October 1917, Marvin told Hallidie, the chief education officer, that Hertfordshire had 'done better ... than any other English county'.[176] The *Times Educational Supplement* was in error, however, in saying that nearly all its schools now had 'war gardens'.[177] By March 1918 141 Hertfordshire schools were concentrating upon vegetable production. In total, forty-five acres were being worked by 3,600 boys and 800 girls. Ninety schools with older pupils were still not participating, but the combined efforts of Hallidie, Marvin and school managers ensured that twenty-six of these were actively clearing and planting plots by the end of the war.[178] In September 1918 Hallidie singled out a Hitchin school which represented the epitome of wartime achievement. Here, 200 boys in ten groups cultivated three acres of previously derelict land, largely without the aid of manure. The chief education officer was now concerned solely with production in bulk, and conceded that experimental work and subject integration had been ousted. He comforted education committee members with the confident claim that the boys were 'more observant, more eager to know the reason of things, more self-reliant and self-respecting'.[179]

An increasing number of girls worked on the war gardens, breaching the generally accepted division of practical subjects between the sexes. Some headmasters approved, others did not, but headmistresses had no doubts. They reported that girls worked plots without harm to themselves, and in 1918 the county instructor conceded they did the job 'nearly as well as the boys'.[180] Newspapers recorded the crops with interest, and also a little surprise at the girls' achievements.[181]

Just once was a detailed record kept of what was taught in a wartime gardening class. Written in the summer of 1917, it comes from the Stevenage school hailed as possessing the best garden in Hertfordshire, and belies the LEA's total commitment to mass production. This school managed to combine an impressive output with a well-thought-out integrated curriculum. The one-acre garden had twenty-eight plots, plus experimental beds, and cultivated a complete range of kitchen garden plants, including fruit trees. The children were taught about soils, fertilisers and the weather. Accounts, records and drawings were important, as was the aesthetic side of gardening. The garden served, but also transcended, utilitarian aims, and was hailed by the *Hertfordshire Express* as a supreme example of 'Practical Defiance of the U-boat'.[182] The garden would have gladdened Marvin's heart, but in the straitened circumstances of 1917 and 1918 it was almost out of place.

The pressure on many schools to embark upon the cultivation of large and sometimes difficult plots with diminished staff, inadequate expertise and little financial assistance was relentless, and hard to resist when managers were enthusiastic, susceptible to national fears and subject to the arguments of the Board, the LEA and HMI. Certainly, dilatory managers were pestered by Marvin – war gardens were 'a necessity', he told those at Pirton.[183] Hallidie and his assistant visited schools to praise successful efforts, with a clear brief from the education committee to overcome local indifference and difficulties.[184] Ignorance was no excuse, as teachers' courses were started in every district.[185]

The LEA was parsimonious and Marvin, and some managers, were over-enthusiastic in their selection of new plots, but schools had little choice but to cooperate, whatever the headteachers' views of their circumstances. At Sandon, Marvin and the managers presented the school with a *fait accompli* – a plot of land to begin cultivating immediately.[186] At High Wych nothing happened for two and a half years after Marvin's first request for gardening to appear on the curriculum until a patriotic landowner surprised – and perhaps alarmed – the headmaster by donating a plot specifically for potatoes.[187] In Hoddesdon the boys cultivated the spaces around the VAD hospital, and at Harpenden Marvin advocated converting the gravel playground into a vegetable plot.[188] One school in Hemel Hempstead dug up a strip of concrete to plant beans, and the managers of a second viewed favourably a piece of derelict ground that required 'ploughing two or three times'.[189] Only the headmaster in Much Hadham recorded his opposition to the pressures. First he told the LEA by letter, and then Marvin to his face, that no suitable and 'easily get-at-able' land was available, and 'besides, the boys have a good deal of practical experience from and with their parents.' After that, his logbook intimates, he was ignored. The LEA persuaded the school managers to acquire land and to set a date for cultivation to begin. Marvin dispatched the teachers to observe gardening lessons in other schools, and the rector gained the boys' agreement to bring tools from home. The managers and Marvin then altered the timetable to include gardening, and in due course the Much Hadham boys trudged across the village to their new plots.[190]

Perhaps the greatest effort and enthusiasm were displayed by the new headmistress at Waterford. With thirty pupils on roll, and just a monitress for help, during 1917 the school cleared, dug and planted a completely derelict plot. The children collected waste paper to sell so they could buy tools. At any one time half the pupils worked on the garden while the other half worked in the schoolroom, often on projects linked with the garden. After all their efforts most of the emerging crop was eaten by rabbits and the garden had to be hastily replanted with potatoes. Despite this, the children won prizes for their 'war' soup and puddings, and were praised for producing the best potatoes in the county.[191]

The changes in cookery and gardening were mirrored in handwork, and overall they contributed to a utilitarian and vocational bias that long outlasted the war. Boys' and girls' handwork was beginning to flourish before the war. Marvin was urging its development, and the county organiser, R.R. Bunn, was preaching the gospel of manual training around the county.[192] As we have seen, the outbreak of war led to a spontaneous upsurge in handwork, partly at school and partly at home, as numerous scarves, mittens, balaclavas and belts were produced for friends and relatives in the forces. It was mainly, although not exclusively, the preserve of girls.[193]

These activities did not cease, but inexorably the schools were drawn into handwork more associated with production lines in workshops as both the number of wounded and the demand for munitions soared. District Red Cross organisers, who were usually notable local figures in their own right, descended upon school managers to incorporate teachers and children into the nationwide efforts to maintain a constant supply of warm clothing and bandages created out of recycled wool and linen.[194] Such work became increasingly onerous, repetitive and time-consuming. In December 1914, for example, the schools in Hertford were already being coordinated for the conversion of 1,000 pairs of disused woollen stockings into mittens.[195]

A year later the pace intensified, and the divergence between educational aims and current practice became complete. Addressing Buntingford's Educational Handwork Association in April 1915, Marvin upheld that handwork was 'not a subject but a method' embracing practical activities across the curriculum. It allowed pupils to be creative, to continually refine ideas and to demonstrate growing skills. It also minimised, he suggested to the teachers, 'the monotony of daily routine'.[196] Bunn, though, had different ideas. A rota of classes visiting his Technical Centre in St Albans was giving the lead in the production of arm splints, crutches and stretchers for the Red Cross and hand grenade boxes for the Ministry of Munitions.[197] Already totals were important, and in the autumn of 1915 the county council dispatched a circular urging all schools to offer their services to the Red Cross if they had not already done so.[198] By the end of that year the girls in 175 schools had been organised into sewing parties for the Red Cross, using wool and linen found at home, donated by well-wishers, supplied by the Red Cross, or purchased out of funds raised by the school.[199] The manufacture of finger splints replaced painting and modelling for both boys and girls in Hitchin.[200] In Braughing 'every odd moment' was spent making 150 splints a month and then covering them with linen.[201] In Sacombe the girls spent the autumn producing swabs for hospitals, knitting mittens for soldiers and sewing heavy hessian into sandbags for the trenches.[202]

In the autumn of 1915 the education committee approved the establishment of vocational training links between Bunn's Technical Centres and munitions factories.[203] Under Bunn's direction older boys from elementary schools received technical instruction qualifying them to take up semi-skilled posts in the munitions factories scattered across the south of Hertfordshire and north London.[204] It was a partnership unique in the country, and much admired.[205] Under Bunn's direction, too, the Technical Centres became the major points for distributing materials to schools, and for collecting and finishing off products. The mass production of splints and crutches was significantly enhanced by several schools working cooperatively with their local Centre so that each undertook just one particular stage in the construction.[206] Boys tended to make the wooden parts of splints and crutches, and pass them on to girls to pad and cover. Schools began to specialise in other ways, too. Sometimes each class concentrated upon one item from a list sent to the school, such as cane baskets, raffia mats, writing pads, cigarette boxes, darning socks or filling 'hussifs' – satchets containing needles, thread, thimble and buttons.[207]

Local newspapers and the *Times Educational Supplement* praised the heightened utilitarian and vocational aspects of Hertfordshire's policy.[208] The *Hertfordshire Advertiser* stated that the aim was not only to help the war effort, but also 'to bring the children into closer touch with the conditions that are prevailing in the country now', forgetting that most families were experiencing those conditions only too well.[209] Bunn's reputation with county councillors, HMI, employers, the Red Cross and newspaper editors soared, along with his production figures.[210] In 1915–16 he visited 362 schools and departments, and held teachers' courses in Berkhamsted, Bishop's Stortford, Buntingford, Hertford, Hitchin and Ware.[211] In St Albans alone, 4,500 splints, 100 pairs of crutches, 1,000 hand grenade boxes and 2,500 other articles were made that year. A number of elementary school leavers in the city were securing well-paid permanent jobs in manufacturing companies, and Bunn lost no opportunity to promote his vocational training programme. In June 1916 Hallidie celebrated that handwork in wood and metal, not just card and clay, had come to stay, and would lead to a reassessment of the curriculum, as:

> it is quite certain that whatever changes may be made in elementary education in the future, the chief improvement will be that it will come to rely much more on practical work and less on books.[212]

He was right.

Headteachers imposed the repetitive tasks upon their children, but some doubted the educational value of what they were doing. Logbooks, though, rarely criticised the wisdom of policymakers. Only the exasperated headmaster at Much Hadham, who vainly argued against a school garden, recorded his more general objection to the incessant demands: 'with so many subjects in the already overcrowded curriculum the necessary and essential foundation work is being ruined.'[213] The three elementary school headmasters elected to the county education committee had greater freedom of speech, however, and in 1916 they united in persistent and forceful opposition to Bunn. Bunn consistently lauded the articles children made 'to alleviate pain and suffering and to afford comfort and enjoyment to our brave soldiers and sailors', and in obvious irritation at his self-congratulatory and emotional style the teacher-members did not mince their words. They argued that far too much praise was being heaped on Bunn's activities, and far too little consideration given to the adverse effect it was having on pupils. They criticised his annual salary of £300 as excessive, especially as it exceeded the top of the scale for a Certificated class teacher. They denigrated the employment of three handwork instructors 'in order to tickle the ears of the Government inspectors' just when the general teaching force was being reduced. They condemned the much-vaunted industrial training courses as merely 'done for the benefit of the employers who wanted cheap labour', and they revealed that in many cases they led to wages of just 6s a week.[214]

The argument of educational priorities made no impression on other education committee members, and the accusation of providing cheap semi-skilled labour was hotly denied. Pank resolutely asserted that 'it was the most successful work carried on by any one', and Bunn continued to bask in the approval of everyone but the teachers.[215] In the autumn the ill-tempered exchanges re-occurred when a Red Cross circular issued with Hallidie's approval suggested that each girl in the county should produce, on average, one knitted article a week. The teacher-members protested strongly, reminding the education committee that wool cost 5s a pound and schools were already pouring out garments. Pank had little sympathy, coolly observing that he saw 'no harm in asking the children to do all they could'.[216]

The schools' output continued to be prodigious. In the year ending April 1917 Bunn visited 350 schools and departments, and supplied raw material to 250 of them. In his St Albans woodwork and metalwork classes the children turned out 10,587 wooden and metal splints, 50 iron beds, 543 new crutches, 1,995 repaired crutches and 4,000 other articles, including stretchers.[217] Production continued unabated throughout 1918.[218]

It was generally accepted that wartime expediencies had given handwork and gardening permanent places in the curriculum. In August 1917 the *Times Educational Supplement* discussed Hertfordshire's practical and vocational training initiatives, and argued that the wartime pressures had 'led to much increased appreciation of the value of technical and specialised training, and to a consequent demand for the supply of such instruction.'[219] The leader writer, like Hallidie, fully supported Bunn's proposal to continue and extend these programmes after the war. By then, Bunn's senior school classes were already manufacturing furniture for schools, toys for private companies and war shrines for churches.[220]

The war had a significant impact upon the schooling of both girls and boys. For all the traumas, it probably enlivened many days as far as the children were concerned. The revised syllabuses and patriotic activities bound the schools more closely to the attitudes and emotions of the local community, and schools and homes became linked in a common enterprise. Current affairs and national needs had never loomed so large in schools and children's lives. Both girls and boys studied the geography and history of nations involved in the war, collected for diverse charities, marched, acted, danced and sang in patriotic concerts, promoted thrift, grew vegetables in bulk, and produced thousands of useful products inextricably associated with modern warfare and its heart-rending casualties. The boys, though, were the prime targets in the drive for enhanced patriotic fervour and vocational training. Drill, handwork, gardening, war history, war geography, and lessons by men on leave were most prominent in the all-boys' departments and schools. They were the ones who would fight the inevitable imperial and commercial wars of the future, and for them the necessary physical and mental training could not start too early. Contrary to the famous catchphrase, few believed, although many hoped, that the present conflict was the war to end all wars.

There remained, though, plenty of dull moments. By 1917 and 1918 the mass production of potatoes, knitwear and Red Cross artefacts must have become monotonous work as well as being severely limited in educational value, and it has to be said that many of the children's ordinary class lessons during the war were as lacklustre and depressing as they had been before 1914. Although infants' schools were becoming increasingly happy places, as the cramped staged galleries and fixed desks were at last being removed and more liberal approaches to teaching and learning were catching on, they served to highlight the sullen faces HMI found in a number of unenlightened junior and senior schools. Even when Marvin took into account the dislocation caused by the enlistment of teachers, the reductions in staffing levels, and the headteachers' criticisms of the quality of some wartime replacement teachers, he had to condemn the stultifying effect of uninspired instruction, the unproductive reliance on rote learning, and the excessive degree of silent work in many schools. Such phrases as reading 'not well understood', arithmetic 'very defective', written work 'hardly fair', and general knowledge 'lacking even on simple matters' were alarmingly common.[221]

The war, though, had brought physical training, handicraft, gardening and domestic subjects to the fore and, as we shall see, they remained to the fore during the 1920s and 1930s. New and more stimulating teaching approaches to these utilitarian subjects were to make their appearance after the war, with the LEA making a massive investment in facilities, equipment and staffing. The war had reinforced the primary purpose of these subjects in the hearts and minds of government ministers, county councillors and urban and rural employers – and this was nothing less than the intensive training of the next generation in the mental qualities and physical skills it would need to serve the needs of industry, commerce and agriculture, and defend the Empire.

CHAPTER FIVE

Children at work

D URING THE WAR it was easy to hide self-interest behind pious sentiments of patriotism, and nowhere was it easier than in the realm of child labour. With very varying degrees of enthusiasm, however, most people accepted that older elementary schoolchildren were needed as workers in factories, workshops, offices, shops and farms at a time of unprecedented national emergency. Local authorities in Hertfordshire transcended nearly all other counties in creating favourable circumstances for children to be employed with little or no fear of action against them, their families or their employers. Schools became a reserve of labour to be tapped at will.

In 1914 many county councillors and education committee members remained unconvinced of the merits of the elementary schools for the working-class and lower-middle-class families who attended them, especially as the local rates to pay for them continued to soar.[1] In common with many other employers and ratepayers, they saw the war as the moment to call a halt to what they considered to be the unrestrained and ill-considered expansion of public education. They much preferred a return to past practices when, within living memory, a modest schooling in the basic skills of literacy and numeracy, and the tenets of Christianity, led to early employment and the life-long application of that useful everyday knowledge. In their eyes, too, the daily lessons could easily be complemented by some useful work in the locality before and after school when children would supplement the family income, acquire discipline and skills, and learn respect for their employers.

Parents placing little value on education but much on their children's earnings were also quick to take advantage of the changed wartime attitudes of county councillors, employers and magistrates. Under consistent pressure from rural and urban employers, with no leadership or direction from the county council and often scant sympathy from magistrates and local education sub-committees,

schools could do little but watch the rapid erosion of the long and hard-won campaign to secure free and compulsory education for all the nation's children. In
examining these interwoven trends, this chapter looks first at the abuses and controversies surrounding the part-time labour of children out of school hours, and
then at the virtually unfettered resurgence of full-time child employment. The
attitudes which resurfaced during the war were to play a significant part in shaping policies towards children and schooling in the 1920s and 1930s.

The part-time employment of children before and after school attracted little
attention before the war. County byelaws barred employment on schooldays
except between 6.15am and 8.15am and after 4.30pm, and under the 1903 Employment of Children Act it was illegal to employ children under the age of fourteen
on any day before 6.00am and after 9pm.[2] No survey had been made of the extent
of schoolchildren's paid employment early in the morning or late at night, and it
must be supposed that ignorance had engendered a general belief that no problems existed in Hertfordshire because the numbers were probably low and the
work probably light and fairly rewarded. Many, no doubt, assumed that throughout the centuries children had always worked and there was no sound reason to
interfere with a useful tradition.

In 1913 Dr Francis Fremantle, the county and school medical officer,
unearthed the true extent of child labour on schooldays.[3] He revealed that numerous errand boys were employed each day in the northern and central towns, such
as Royston and Harpenden, and he discerned ominous signs of exploitation in the
southern conurbations of Barnet and Watford. Many 'tired and listless' children
were arriving at school after two hours' work. In one Watford school, 84 of the 225
boys regularly worked out of school hours as paper boys, house boys and errand
boys. The paper boys started work before 6am. They were often late for school
'and then have no energy left for schoolwork'. If the papers were late, or the
weather bad, they missed the whole of the morning session. In another school, 37
boys started work before 8am, 24 before 7am and 17 before 6am; 41 were
employed during the lunch hour, and 29 until after 8pm. Fremantle isolated the
extreme case of a child working six and three-quarter hours a day, in addition to
attending school. His findings, though, were buried in his long and detailed
annual report exploring all aspects of child health, and there is no evidence that
the county council, education committee, newspapers or the public took the
slightest interest in them.

The outbreak of war created the conditions to exacerbate the situation while
denying Fremantle the opportunity to quantify it. However, the reports from

local school medical officers enabled him to state that 'in nearly every district ... children appear to be engaged in some capacity or other for a few hours before or after school.' He cited a forthright Watford headmaster who asserted that the situation required 'serious attention, especially the street hawking of newspapers, which lowers the children morally, physically, and mentally'.[4] Once again, there was no response from the county council or education committee.

HMI Marvin, though, seized the initiative, and confronted the LEA with his own corroborative evidence of widespread, lengthy and sometimes illegal part-time employment of school-aged children. In June 1915 he identified a school in Cheshunt:

> where 104 out of 184 were employed out of school hours, the effect of this employment was most pronounced, the children present at the inspection ... being physically incapable of benefiting from the instruction.[5]

Hallidie was obliged to bring the matter to the attention of the county's school attendance sub-committee, and identify some course of remedial action. An inefficient district attendance officer took much of the blame, but the LEA asserted that its own local survey revealed a far less worrying situation. It found that, throughout Cheshunt, 306 children were employed outside school hours. Although 202 of these infringed the byelaw, Hallidie argued that 192 did so only technically by signing on at 6am – in practice, apparently, they waited until 6.15am before starting work. Hallidie pushed the LEA's case even further by not only denying any ill effects of such labour but claiming it had significant benefits, upholding:

> that with some three or four exceptions, the children employed appeared to be well nourished and healthy. They were probably better fed than if they had not been employed. Their morning work did not make them late for school, but many of them were sleepy and apathetic during the after-noons. This was doubtless due in part to a heavy midday meal.[6]

Having blunted the edge of Marvin's attack, Hallidie acknowledged that stricter byelaws might prove necessary, but 'the present is hardly a propitious time for recommending to the County Council any action restrictive of the labour supply.'[7]

Hallidie's comforting report actually hid an array of alarming statistics. It revealed that 92 children in Cheshunt were working for five hours or more each schoolday, and 182 worked for 10 hours or more each Saturday. Table 5.1 summarises the survey.

Table 5.1 Hertfordshire County Council Education Department: Cheshunt Survey, summer 1915[8]

	Employment of children on school days Hours employed							
	Under 4	4	5	6	7	Total		
Ages between								
7–8	1	2	0	0	0	3		
8–9	7	2	1	0	0	11		
9–10	10	12	5	0	0	27		
10–11	18	14	17	0	0	49		
11–12	26	18	14	0	1	59		
12–13	38	20	27	3	0	88		
13–14	28	17	23	1	0	69		
Total	128	86	87	4	1	306		

Employment of children on Saturdays

Hours	Under 8	8	9	10	11	12	13	14	15	Total
Numbers	98	7	10	60	83	10	14	13	2	297

Employment of children on Sundays

Hours	Under 4	4	5	6	7	8	9	10	11	12	13	Total
Numbers	38	20	7	12	7	4	0	3	1	0	3	95

The county council did nothing, and Hertfordshire could continue to boast, along with London and the cities of the Midlands and north of England, extreme examples of child exploitation, with one eight-year-old boy regularly working three and a half hours each schoolday, ten and a half hours each Saturday and another ten and a half hours each Sunday.[9] At least one Hertfordshire head-teacher was well aware of children working up to five hours before school during the soft fruit harvest.[10]

In June 1916 Hallidie was pressurised into initiating the lengthy procedure necessary to revise the byelaws. He adjudged four hours' employment on school-days and Sundays, and eight hours' worth on Saturdays and during holidays, to be the maximum acceptable amount.[11] The county council agreed with these modest revisions, and the Home Office helpfully pointed out that the byelaws need not apply to agriculture and suggested that domestic service could also be excluded.[12] At the end of October 1916 the education committee formally resolved that:

> No child may be employed while under the age of 10 years. No child may be employed after 7pm between the 1st October and 31st March or after 8pm between the 1st April and 30th September in any year. No child who is liable to attend school full-time, shall, on days when school is open, be employed except

between the hours of 6.15 and 8.15 in the morning and after 4.30 in the after-noon.[13]

This still left children over ten with four and a half hours in winter and five and a half hours in summer during which to work on schooldays. Only the very worst abuses had been officially eradicated, and this no doubt accounts for the ease with which the revisions passed through the committees. As usual, Pank neatly sum-marised the prevailing mood by commenting that the education committee 'recognised that in these troublous times they must do nothing to interfere with labour', but they had 'thought it necessary to do something'.[14]

In November 1916 the county council approved the revisions but, as local objections had to be formally invited and considered, their implementation was delayed by another six months. Objections were received from an Anglican rector, six grocers, two drapers, three booksellers and newsagents, five trades-men's associations, an invalid who needed 'a lad for errands and light domestic work', and also from Royston District Council and the East Barnet Education Sub-Committee. The newsagents feared for the regular delivery of papers, the trades-men's associations lamented the hardship falling on poor families relying on children's wages, and the education sub-committee revealed its contempt for ele-mentary schooling by condemning the byelaws as 'objectionable in normal times and oppressive under existing conditions.'[15]

At this late stage Dr Fremantle re-entered the public debate. His 1916 annual report condemned part-time employment without reservation, and was reported in the local press.[16] Part-time work made children 'tired and disinclined to work', and he painted a grim picture of children going to work without breakfast and fainting in the humid Lea valley greenhouses. He castigated the 'poor and careless parents' who allowed these practices to flourish, and he reminded his readers that many children not only worked long hours but often had to travel considerable distances to work and then to school. Many were 'unfit' for lessons. By the middle of 1917 the significantly heightened interest in children as a national asset obliged the county council to reject the objections and confirm the new byelaws. They came into force on 1 August 1917.[17]

The wartime opportunities for the full-time employment of school-aged chil-dren proved particularly attractive to many vested interests in Hertfordshire, including the great majority of rural employers, county councillors and county and local education committee members, numerous urban employers and a sig-nificant number of magistrates and clergy. Many parents, and no doubt many children, had similar sympathies.

It was, however, the much-admired Boy Scouts who hit the headlines first. The moment war was declared, patriotism rose to the fore in the effort to bring order into local chaos. Early in August 1914 the Scout Commissioner for Hertfordshire placed the services of 1,000 boy scouts at the disposal of the Chief Constable.[18] With towns such as Ware 'in a state of ferment', Hitchin 'full of much excitement ... due to alarming rumours', and St Albans 'in a state of disorganisation' owing to the sudden influx of troops, the threats to sanitation, the dislocation to transport and the fears of food shortages, the Chief Constable accepted the offer with alacrity.[19] In St Albans up to 180 scouts were on duty at any one time. Their duties were many and sometimes onerous, and continued well into the autumn. They included whitewashing huts and fences, reporting the arrival of troops, directing troops to their quarters, assisting billeting officers, searching for lost children, delivering troops' washing, collecting parcels, distributing letters, posting recruiting notices, making sandbags, conveying patients to RAMC ambulances, moving furniture for the Red Cross and making bandages. The army appreciated the scouts' 'keenness and discipline'.[20] It employed many of them in permanent posts as messengers, and they were also entrusted with conveying pay money to troops.

The scouts' undoubted usefulness in freeing many soldiers from routine tasks led the army to request the arrangements stay in place after the reopening of the schools. The county education committee acquiesced immediately, exempting from school all scouts attached to military posts. In practice the scouts voluntarily attended school on a half-time basis, as occurred in some of the requisitioned schools.[21] Towards the end of September the LEA wrote to the Board of Education, arguing that as the scouts:

> are receiving considerable training in discipline and duty the attendance of such boys at military headquarters should be allowed to claim for grant as though such attendances had been made at a public elementary school.[22]

Alerted by the letter, Board officials grew concerned at the worryingly large numbers of boys that could be involved. Bishop's Stortford, Hemel Hempstead and St Albans were each surrounded by three army brigades, with further brigades in and around Berkhamsted, Harpenden, Hatfield, Hertford, Hitchin and Tring. The Board expressed sympathy and understanding to the LEA, and it did not bar exemptions, but it refused to allow absentees, whatever the reason, to be marked in the register as attending school.[23] The Board's willingness to recognise some justification in the requests for child labour, while refusing to relax the regulations governing the grant formula, remained unchanged throughout the war. In effect it left decisions to the LEA, and this was to have a profound effect upon the county's children.

Several weeks later it was the War Office itself which terminated the scouts' term-time assistance, to the consternation of both the Scout Commissioner and the county education committee. Both protested that the half-time schooling arrangements which provided squads of scouts throughout the day for the army worked well for the army and the boys.[24] The appeals were in vain; the army was becoming better organised, and on 5 November 1914 the scouts returned to school 'with great regret' that their war work had come to an end.[25] However, their work outside school hours as reliable messengers and clerks for army personnel, and also for charities working with local troops, continued unabated throughout the war.

The enthusiasm and trustworthiness of the scouts led to their well-publicised identification as the epitome of British youth, the ideal to be emulated by all schoolboys. They received no payment, and few, if any, seem to have evaded the duty to attend school half-time. In December 1915 one local newspaper pinpointed the sense of duty, efficiency and modesty it held to be the hallmark of the good scout, adding that:

> when it has been a question of delivering recruiting notices or Red Cross parcels it has always been, 'Oh, the Boy Scouts will do that', and the Boy Scouts have always done it promptly and well.[26]

They were involved in parades, in uniform, with army detachments and on most ceremonial occasions in schools.[27] In December 1917, as the new Education Bill with its clauses providing compulsory part-time education for school leavers was under intense debate, Marvin went so far as to tell a public meeting that a boy enlisting as a scout 'would have more real practical education than at a Continuation School'.[28]

The LEA's ready support for the scouts' wartime work may have encouraged civilian employers to believe that wartime labour shortages could be alleviated easily by the relaxation of the school attendance byelaws. The Hertfordshire byelaws were made in 1910 and incorporated the agricultural byelaw of 1899. Parents had to ensure their children attended school between the ages of five and fourteen, but total exemption could be granted to children over twelve if they had passed the Fifth Standard prescribed by the Elementary Code. In the urban districts of Barnet, Bushey, East Barnet and Watford, the higher Sixth Standard had to be attained before exemption. The agricultural byelaw allowed children over eleven who had passed the Fourth Standard to be employed full-time for part of the year on farms. Such children, while between the ages of eleven and thirteen, had to attend 250 sessions (mornings or afternoons) in school in the year between 15 October and 15 June, and were not entitled to total exemption until the age of thirteen.[29]

As early as October 1914, a debate was forced upon the county education committee by the actions of two Rural District education sub-committees. Berkhamsted sought a ruling that legal proceedings need not be taken against boys required 'for agricultural purposes', and Ware submitted a resolution that:

> in cases where farmers have lost members of their staff who have been called to the Colours, school boys over the age of twelve should be allowed to take their places where necessary. The substitution to be at the rate of not exceeding two boys for each man and such an arrangement to remain in force during the period of the war. [30]

Pank tried to avoid a debate by saying that no action was necessary as the harvest was over, but his vice-chairman, Sir Thomas Halsey, who exercised great influence as chairman of the full council, argued more bullishly that 'the children would be receiving in the opinion of some [members] just as useful an education as learning to read and write', and 'they could turn a blind eye to these cases'.[31]

The assumptions of Pank and Halsey caused a furore, but not much of it on behalf of the children. Many councillors pleaded the special case of farmers, but there was strong opposition from those who felt that tradesmen and factory owners had as strong a case as farmers for the employment of children. Nevertheless, loud cries of 'No' greeted a member from Watford who formally asked whether the same exemption privileges would be extended to occupations outside agriculture. A few used this dissent to urge the strict enforcement of the byelaws. One member claimed that widespread urban and rural exemption would mean 'they would never get the children back to school.' A teacher-member passionately condemned the Ware proposal and the farmers he believed were behind it:

> We know very well that this is a dodge to get cheap labour and comes from a class of people who for forty-four years have opposed the Education Act. The farmers can get plenty of adult labour if they will pay for it, but they won't. There are plenty of middle aged and elderly men in the towns who would gladly do the work if they were adequately paid, but they won't do it for about 10s a week. [32]

He believed, too, that 'it will be most fatal to the interests of our children if we allow this to go through.' Eventually Pank disingenuously proposed a compromise, whereby they

> leave things as they were and trust to the good sense of the managers and the school attendance officers not to take proceedings where it was shown that the boys were engaged in agriculture, and that it was a real necessity to the neighbourhood that this should be so.

This was carried in effect, though not officially, when by a large majority the committee moved to the next item of business.[33] Henceforth, most people thought the regulations had been relaxed, and the proponents of child labour gave little thought to any restrictions.

Throughout the first autumn and winter of war headteachers watched attendances plummet. As usual, all the reasons for absenteeism that had been given by the children's parents and grandparents were recorded once again in the logbooks. In Much Hadham, for example, currant-picking kept attendances low in late summer.[34] At Anstey, children stayed away 'to carry meals into the harvest fields'.[35] Families in Hoddesdon tried to use the measles epidemic to cover the children's annual casual employment digging and picking up potatoes.[36] The attendance officer at Ashwell continued his endless pursuit of farmers illegally employing local pupils.[37] By Christmas the situation was changing. Headteachers were finding absences getting longer and becoming more frequent, without explanation or retribution. In Hitchin 19 out of 167 girls were absent from one school for 'no particular reason.'[38] The headmaster at High Wych found the attendance officer 'very slow to act' against an incorrigible defaulter. The boy was absent every Monday and Friday, his father was in the workhouse and his mother 'simply defies the law'.[39]

By early 1915 successful action to stop a child working illegally was becoming a rarity. In January falling attendances at Stanstead Abbots were blamed on children who were approaching their fourteenth birthday 'acting as if they were entitled to leave', and, shortly afterwards, the headteacher in nearby Hoddesdon complained that 'magistrates refused to convict [the] parent of a boy who is 14 years of age in April and who has been absent since Xmas.'[40] That March, the senior school headmaster at Barkway lamented the 'idea prevailing among the parents and children that the law has been altered for the children to work at 12 during the war'.[41] In September 1914 the attendance officer had diligently investigated cases of illegal employment in Sandon, but by the following spring absences were frequent, prolonged and unchecked.[42] As a Sawbridgeworth head-master complained, 'it is useless to report them'.[43] At Ashwell three farmers curtly told the headmaster that they had need of the boys they were already keep-ing off school, and that they would inform the LEA of that fact. There was no thought of gaining permission.[44]

In February 1915 another confused county council meeting exacerbated the situation. An alderman from Baldock urged the release of twelve-year-old boys to work on farms. Once again, Pank opposed any ruling by the council as setting a 'difficult and dangerous precedent' and sought agreement that decisions should be left 'to the good sense of employers of labour and the school attendance com-mittees'. He believed that if a genuine shortage of labour existed anywhere in the county, and if schoolboys were suitable replacements, 'the school attendance committees would not prosecute for non-attendance'.[45] There was no proposal and no vote, but Pank's words were put into an LEA circular to local sub-com-mittees, and were widely reported in the press. One member equated the 'discre-tion' allowed to the sub-committees with a licence 'to do as they liked'.[46] The comment was uncontested, and prophetic. The 'good sense' of rural employers quickly drained many schools of their older pupils.

Officially the LEA had taken no lead, and neither did the government. Both, though, sent clear messages to all interested parties. Although ministers, like most county councillors, sympathised with employers, they ensured that any odium for condoning child labour would fall elsewhere. There were several ques-tions asked in the House of Commons, and the Board took the unusual step of sending a circular to LEAs with the answers given by ministers.[47] In March 1915 J.A. Pease, President of the Board of Education, said that if a farmer resorted to schoolboy labour after offering 'good wages' and failing to find any adults to replace his men who had enlisted in the armed forces, 'I do not think there is a bench of magistrates who would convict the parent for having kept that boy away from school.' A week later H.H. Asquith, the Prime Minister, studiously avoided being charged with the restoration of child labour by refusing to countenance the suspension of any clause of the Education Acts. As Pease had done, Asquith placed all responsibility for exemption from prosecution, tacit or official, on local authorities. He acknowledged that the nation under arms should not be bound by 'any pedantic regard for rules and conventions', and he made a virtue out of local autonomy. Only the LEAs knew 'the local conditions, they are responsible to the ratepayers, and they are in touch with the parents of the children'.[48] Walter Long, the President of the Board of Agriculture, also made the government's position crystal clear. No-one, he replied to a Commons question, wanted a return to the bad old days of child labour, but local authorities should ensure that boys are allowed to work on farms where they are needed and take measures – 'we do not very much care what they are' – to avoid the situation being abused.[49] The ensuing advice from the Board of Education was that each application for a schoolboy labourer should be considered on its merits, that any exemption from prosecution should be for a limited period, that the work should be light in character, and that frequent checks were made to ensure the conditions were kept.[50] The delegation of responsibility was complete.

The *Hertfordshire Mercury* had already noted with disapproval the moves by both the government and the county council to pass 'the onus of breaking or observing the law to the humble local committees much in the same way as ... the dirty work of an office is relegated by easy stages from the chief to the office boy.'[51] The *West Hertfordshire Observer* added its condemnation of the opportunities being given to the managers of rural schools, as 'they were the farmers, and could do as they liked.'[52] The newspapers were not, of course, opposed to schoolchildren working on farms if they were really needed. Even the teacher-members of the county education committee acknowledged in April 1915 that 'genuine shortages' of labour existed.[53] However, when they accused some local education sub-committees of going 'recklessly to work', especially by asking schools to draw up public lists of boys 'who and whose parents consent to their being employed in agriculture', Pank terminated the discussion with the sarcastic comment that 'he did not think any difficulty would arise that would terrorize those who held the education of the children to be foremost and paramount.'[54]

The LEA issued its own circular based upon the Board's recommendations regarding any exemption from prosecution for non-attendance at school. Its major difference was the omission of limiting exemptions to work on farms. When the omission was challenged during a county education meeting Pank blandly stated that if any urban industry was short of labour the same rule would apply as to farmers.[55] It is impossible to say whether the original omission was accidental or deliberate, but it seems reasonable to suppose that intensive lobbying from urban county councillors and employers had occurred. The circular was not rescinded or amended.

War exemptions soared in number, but the complacent LEA remained in ignorance of the accelerating trend for several months. In May 1915 the *Hertfordshire Mercury* reported that up to 31 January just twenty schoolchildren in the county had received official exemption, and of these fourteen worked on farms.

This was out of a national total of 2,352. The *Mercury* sneered at 'the fear existing in many quarters that education would experience a setback by the proposal to employ school-children in agricultural pursuits.'[56] It noted that the worst offenders were mainly agricultural counties such as West Sussex, Gloucestershire, Hampshire, Somerset and neighbouring Bedfordshire, and, reflecting the dominant view of rural children, it added smugly:

> In view of their destined vocation it is highly probable that in the great majority of instances the lads who have gone on the farms have actually benefited educationally by being allowed to step into the breach and do what they can for the country.[57]

In fact, in May 1915 Hertfordshire had the third-highest war exemption figures in England and Wales, but the figures were not published until many weeks later. For the period from 1 February to 30 April its total of 177 was exceeded only by Bedfordshire's 203 and Kent's 507, and these referred only to children employed on farms.[58] When education committee members were faced with the true figures, their immediate concern was the damage done to the Treasury grant. The Board was castigated for its failure to take a lead or to allow exempted pupils to be counted as attending school, and the lack of evidence did not stop rural county councillors accusing urban employers of abusing the emergency as much as the farmers.[59]

The war was nearly a year old before the LEA knew what was happening to attendances. Table 5.2 reveals the inexorable downward trend. Several factors besides the exemptions caused the decline. The winter of 1914–15 was unusually wet, and on many days children had to be sent home as their clothing was soaked.

Table 5.2 Attendances: autumn 1914 to spring 1916[60]

	% for this term last year	% for this term	% difference
Urban Districts			
1914 Autumn Term	91.6	90.8	−0.3
1915 Spring Term	89.3	85.9	−3.4
1915 Summer Term	90.7	88.8	−1.9
1915 Autumn Term	90.8	89.0	−1.8
1916 Spring Term	85.9	85.7	−0.7
Rural Districts			
1914 Autumn Term	93.0	91.5	−1.5
1915 Spring Term	90.3	85.8	−4.5
1915 Summer Term	92.1	88.1	−4.0
1915 Autumn Term	91.5	87.3	−4.2
1916 Spring Term	85.8	85.4	−0.4

There was an abnormal amount of sickness, especially measles, which Hallidie believed had been exacerbated by the influx of army camps and intensive billeting, and the inevitable problems of inadequate hygiene and overloaded sewers. Schools were closed for an aggregate of 192 weeks in the spring term 1915, compared with 44 weeks a year earlier. The appalling weather continued into the summer of 1916, and so did the sickness. As we have seen, too, the constant presence of army camps, manoeuvres and parades was a contributory factor to absenteeism and, headteachers asserted, a significant minority of children took casual jobs in defiance of any regulations. Hallidie ensured the county education committee appreciated that neighbouring LEAs were faring as badly or worse. In the spring term 1915 attendances in Essex fell by 5.3 per cent, and those in Bedfordshire by 8.4 per cent, compared with a year earlier.[61]

In the spring of 1915 attendances in the rural districts fell below those in the urban districts for the first time, and they remained lower, and increasingly so, for the rest of the war. The number of persistent truants reported to attendance officers rose in urban districts from 623 in autumn 1913 to 731 in spring 1915. Over the same period the numbers reported in rural districts fell from 355 to 308, but only because headteachers realised that no action was likely to be taken against persistent defaulters by local education sub-committees or magistrates.[62] The number of fines for absenteeism across the county began to fall, from 107 in autumn 1913 to 89 a year later and 93 in spring 1915, and the average fine fell dramatically from a heavy 8s to a far more bearable 3s 6d. There were twenty-two fines for the illegal employment of children in autumn 1914 and twenty-three in spring 1915, with the great majority in and around Ashwell and Hitchin, where the farmers' flagrant attempts to secure schoolboy labour had had to be challenged.[63]

For the next two years these trends intensified with few checks. The new leniency was taken for granted, and even elevated to a virtue. In June 1915 the rural dean of Buntingford made a stirring speech on the wartime duties of Church of England clergy. As school managers, he stated, 'where there was a dearth of labour in agricultural parishes it was their duty to see that boys should be spared from school.'[64] At a county education committee meeting in July, Pank silenced a critic of children being exempted in direct contravention of the county circular with the glib comment that 'it used to be much earlier when I was young'. No-one knew what jobs were undertaken by the girls who were exempted from school attendance, though Pank hoped it was milking, and no-one knew the hours the children worked.[65] In December 1915 a drama staged in court in Hitchin revealed the confusion and leniency of magistrates, the difficulties under which attendance officers worked, and the pragmatism of rural employers. A farmer near the border with Bedfordshire, a county even freer with its exemptions than Hertford-shire, had been prosecuted for employing an eleven-year-old boy. He claimed other farmers were doing the same:

> ... and he did not think he was doing wrong.
>
> Mr King (school attendance officer): The boys working for the other farmers are not under 12.
>
> A magistrate: Why 12? Is that a new order?
>
> Mr King: Yes, sir. It has been issued about three months. A farmer may get permission to employ a boy if he is over 12.
>
> The chairman: You ought to have applied for permission.
>
> Defendant: I have applied for permission, but they will never grant it. Other farmers can get it; why can't I?
>
> Mr King: That is in Bedfordshire.
>
> Defendant: Yes, in Bedfordshire. I can shift them into another cottage and then they will be in Bedfordshire; he can leave school there.
>
> The chairman: Well, these are very hard times; they are difficult times, but we have got to administer the law, and until we can get it altered you must obey. In this case we will only impose a nominal fine of one shilling. The law will probably be altered.[66]

The number of regularly defaulting pupils reported to attendance officers stayed well over 1,000 a term, reaching 1,305 in autumn 1915. Just a quarter of these were prosecuted, and fines stayed modest, averaging 4s for summer 1915, 2s 10d for the autumn and 4s for spring 1916. The overwhelming majority of prosecutions in urban districts were for non-attendance, and in the rural districts for illegal employment. In a few districts, and notably Watford, great efforts were made to stem the tide of absenteeism but, overall, the figures reveal a rising number of tru-ants, a decline in prosecutions and fewer successful cases, and hide all those absent children headteachers thought it a waste of time to report.[67]

During the summer term 1915 540 boys and 12 girls were formally exempted from school attendance in Hertfordshire, 149 of them – 27 per cent – for jobs other than on farms. Nine were under the age of twelve.[68] New-style returns were required from this time onwards and they show the general upsurge in exemp-tions and the high proportion working in shops, offices and factories – 44 per cent in autumn 1915 and 39 per cent in spring 1916. Many exemptions significantly exceeded the limit of three months originally recommended. In autumn 1915 a total of 961 children – 886 boys and 75 girls – were working with official exemption – 536 on farms, 193 'for errands' and 232 'for other work'.[69] In spring 1916 the total was virtually the same but the information was more detailed. Of 963 children exempted that term, or carried over from previous terms, 700 had been exempted for three months, 120 for up to six months and 143 for up to a year. A total of 587 were working on farms, 189 in retail trades and 187 in offices and works.[70]

The official returns told only part of the story. The widespread absenteeism adversely affected the atmosphere and achievement of many schools. The spectres of parental apathy, grossly irregular attendances, contempt for byelaws and despair in headteachers which had characterised the late Victorian struggle to transform fee-paying voluntary schooling into a free universal and compulsory system all appeared again, and extensively so, just as the high pre-war attendance figures suggested that the battle might have been won. For example, in September 1915 in the small school at High Wych there were twenty-one persistent absentees, only ten of whom were war exemptions. Many were minding younger children. The headmaster complained that 'very little value indeed is placed on Education by the majority of the parents.' A month later, the attendance officers had done nothing, the byelaws were considered 'a farce' and children were absent so much that they 'lose all interest in their work, and become lazy and careless'. Following up a case of a parent falsifying a child's age to gain exemption, the headmaster found that this was common practice. Children also frequently started work long before their parents received the results of their application for exemption.[71] The situation was similar in nearby Sawbridgeworth, where parents now did 'as they liked'.[72]

Frequent absences of a week or a fortnight for a whole variety of once-traditional reasons were recorded again and again across the county. They included beating for country house shooting parties, threshing, gleaning, gathering wood, minding sheep, clearing stones from fields, potato planting, gathering flowers for market, haymaking, strawberry- and pea-picking, cutting raspberry canes, kitchen gardening and baby minding.[73] In Hemel Hempstead the education committee suspected that it had become customary for some families to keep their children at home or in casual employment for one day each week. Parents believed, with some justification, that this would not result in prosecution as the child's average attendance would remain an acceptable 80 per cent.[74] In small village schools, such as Sandon and Great Wymondley, where thorough investigations were unlikely to be carried out by local sub-committees sympathising with local farmers, some children under eleven, and even under ten, were absent at work as often as they attended school.[75]

It proved difficult to gauge the true extent of the plight of rural employers. The evidence suggests there was a shortage of men, but it suggests more strongly that the attraction of cheap and malleable labour and the attack upon what was widely perceived as an unnecessarily expensive and prolonged schooling went hand in hand. The Agricultural Labourers' Union believed that adequate wages would resolve the situation instantly, and the Board of Education was unconvinced that farmers had made 'any systematic effort' to deal with their labour problems.[76] However, a survey by Watford Labour Exchange in March 1915 estimated that Hertfordshire farmers had a 13 per cent deficiency, and needed 893 more full-time labourers – an average of just under one per farm – although it went on to claim that 2,779 more pairs of hands were required during the harvest.[77] In January 1916 the county war agricultural committee confirmed the general shortage but said the incidence was very patchy. It found there was sufficient adult labour in some eastern parishes, mainly those surrounding Much Hadham, Buntingford and Hertford, but a shortfall as high as 30 per cent existed elsewhere, with the figure rising to 50 per cent on farms near Watford and Hemel Hempstead. The committee admitted that enlistment was not the only problem. The increasingly high wages offered in the major towns were tempting the remaining men away from the land and also many of the women who might have replaced them cheaply during the war. Many local agricultural sub-committees called for even more leniency in the recruitment of children. The urban districts of Barnet, East Barnet and Stevenage, the rural districts of Hatfield, Hemel Hempstead, St Albans and Ware and the borough of Hemel Hempstead all urged the complete suspension of the school attendance byelaws to free all children over the age of twelve for work.[78]

The fast-deteriorating situation in Hertfordshire caused the Board of Education to seek ways of not only curbing exemptions there but also limiting them to agriculture. The flow of internal Board minutes and exchanges of correspondence achieved very little but they reveal a great deal about attitudes. A 'snapshot' Board survey of agricultural exemptions on 31 January 1916 revealed Hertfordshire's 441 was exceeded only by Norfolk's 525.[79] In a pointed circular soon afterwards the Board noted that out of the sixty-two English and Welsh counties nine allowed no exemptions, nineteen had granted under fifty, and most of the others had carried out 'the spirit and letter' of the Board's 1915 circular. Hertfordshire was among the small minority strongly suspected of 'defects of organisation', thereby allowing local sub-committees 'unfettered control'.[80] HMI Marvin confirmed that the sub-committees 'on the whole tend to slackness', and cited Ware and Hoddesdon as notable examples. Their sympathies lay entirely with employers, not the children, he asserted, going on to state: 'I certainly don't think that any effective means are taken to level up the bad areas. With this A[uthority] and at this time it w'd [*sic*] be impossible to get this done.'[81] An internal Board minute also reveals that Hertfordshire was the first LEA to allow extensive exemptions for employment in shops, offices and factories.[82]

In May 1916 the Board demanded an explanation from the LEA about the apparently unchecked decline in attendance at particularly badly affected schools identified by Marvin. It expressed concern at the 'unduly large' number of exemptions overall, especially for occupations outside agriculture, and intimated that motives less than patriotic were guiding local sub-committees.[83] The LEA was unmoved. Its bland reply denied laxity anywhere, affirmed the efficacy of its own circular, and assured the Board that no child under twelve had been or would be granted exemption.[84]

Marvin, meanwhile, was unearthing the extent of the abuse of procedures across the county. In East Barnet, for example, an area of abysmal attendance, exemptions were 'freely granted' without regard to the nature of the work. Out of forty-seven boys exempted from one school only '2 or 3' went to farms, and out of twenty-five girls exempted the majority were 'acting variably as general servants.'[85] After this, the Board's second letter in July 1916 was chiding in tone. It cited some of Marvin's findings, deeply regretted that, overall, 7 per cent of boys in the county between the ages of twelve and fourteen, and 18 per cent of those between thirteen and fourteen, were exempted for farmwork alone, and asked how the LEA planned to regain control of its affairs.[86] The LEA's reply, a month later, merely explained away all the individual cases of irregular attendance raised by Marvin, and made no attempt to outline any controls over local sub-committees.[87] Officials at the Board could not decide 'whether this is wilful defiance or mere negligence', and Marvin was dispatched to discuss their concerns with Sir Charles Longmore, the Clerk to the County Council, but to no avail. The breakdown of the attendance regulations, Marvin reported, is 'now tacitly accepted by everyone'.[88]

Marvin continued his surveys. In October 1916 he provided evidence of St Albans children 'being exempted wholesale for non-agricultural employment'. Boys from one school were found working in a boot factory, silk mill, brush works, shops and as odd-job hands at Mill Hill public school. In the small market town of Sandon, the elementary school regularly supplied house boys, errand boys and poultry-keepers to the neighbourhood.[89]

The Board of Education was in a quandary. It took a second 'snapshot' on 31 May 1916 of schoolchildren across England and Wales working on farms. As a result it identified ten counties whose exemption figures were high and policies suspect. Gloucestershire, Kent, Peterborough and Rutland were able to satisfy the Board that they had had merely temporary labour difficulties, and they acceded at once to the Board's request for remedial action. In contrast, Bedfordshire, Huntingdonshire, Somerset, Warwickshire and Worcestershire, along with Hertfordshire, gave unsatisfactory explanations and refused to discuss tighter controls.[90] Board officials, including the Permanent Secretary, L.A. Selby-Bigge, considered a number of approaches to the recalcitrant LEAs. These included asking HMI to intensify their fact-finding surveys, securing a mandamus – a judicial writ ordering the LEAs to perform their statutory duties satisfactorily – and seeking legislation, but all were ruled out on the grounds of time, cost and the likelihood of widespread protest. As one senior official lamented:

> It would be contended that what the Board of Education were doing was not endeavouring to stop illegality but to prevent Authorities from committing any other illegality than the precise illegality which the Board were prepared to sanction.[91]

Selby-Bigge finally confessed that one must stop barking 'unless one has power to bite', and Lord Crewe, the President of the Board of Education, agreed it was 'undesirable to try a fall with the LEAs on this question'.[92]

A final 'snapshot' survey was ordered for 16 October 1916 in the hope that the situation had improved after the harvest. Its results are itemised in Table 5.3, along with the 'snapshots' earlier in the year for the ten LEAs falling under greatest suspicion. It shows an improvement in most counties by the autumn, with the notable exceptions of Huntingdonshire, Worcestershire and the greatest offender, Hertfordshire.

Marvin and Board officials were correct in thinking that little would be done in Hertfordshire to stem the flow of child labour. The local arguments, though, centred as much on hostility towards modern elementary education as on the wartime need for youthful employees. H.R.G. Crauford was a county councillor and education committee member, and also chairman of the War Agricultural Sub-Committee in Berkhamsted. As chairman he upheld publicly that 'it would be a good thing if the children at the present time could be taught farm work',

Table 5.3 Summary of returns supplied by county LEAs of the number of children normally liable to attend school but excused from attendance for the purpose of agricultural employment[93]

LEAs in correspondence with the Board of Education regarding excessive exemptions

	31 January 1916	31 May 1916	16 October 1916
Bedfordshire	403	549	452
Gloucestershire	301	451	328
Hertfordshire	441	564	770
Huntingdonshire	377	588	645
Kent	321	1668	331
Peterborough	51	104	53
Rutland	13	54	47
Somerset	424	715	488
Warwickshire	301	499	316
Worcestershire	189	649	654

thereby provoking like-minded colleagues to voice their deep-seated fears of elementary education, with children, one asserted:

> brought up unfortunately to think of nothing else but a black suit and clean boots, and to work in an office, then when they got on they would not look at farm work. They would not adapt to it, and that was mainly through their being kept at school so long.[94]

Farmers brought great pressure to bear upon schools of which they were managers. In January 1917 a farmer-manager at Digswell persuaded the rector to close the school while his potatoes were harvested. When school reconvened he continued to illegally employ five children aged eleven or less to complete the task.[95] Rural families and employers took full advantage of the county's agricultural byelaw, passed in 1899, which allowed children over the age of eleven who had passed the Fourth Standard to work on farms full-time during the busy period between June and October, and then gain total exemption at the age of thirteen. The last published figure for Hertfordshire was in spring 1915, and this reveals that another 860 children each year below the age of fourteen were added to the rural labour force.[96]

The parental attitudes encouraged by the leniency of so many sub-committees are epitomised by the unrepentant mother who informed a Hitchin magistrate in February 1917 that 'I think when they get to that age (13) they ought to be doing *us* a bit of good.'[97] Later that year, the headmaster at High Wych could do little but give a boy a 'good talking to' after his family had conspired to deceive a local farmer with a forged note of absence from the school.[98] Occasionally there are

hints that local education sub-committees realised the implications of their decisions, but still the exemptions rose. In Waltham Abbey a deeply divided sub-committee excused children aged thirteen to work in a government munitions factory
with public expressions of concern for their safety as well as their education.[99]
Hoddesdon sub-committee equally publicly bemoaned parental defiance of the
attendance regulations, but it granted numerous exemptions because of the
needs of the labour-intensive local market gardens.[100] In Hemel Hempstead the
borough's plan to impose a weekly wage of 6s as the minimum payment for a
pupil's loss of education backfired when it was widely interpreted as the sole criterion for an exemption certificate. In an equally ineffective compromise girls
were automatically excused from school for household chores if their mothers
had secured work on farms.[101]

The press, sensing mainstream opinion, remained set on encouraging child
labour and condemning the inappropriateness of much elementary education. In
October 1916 a local newspaper claimed that:

> whether on harvest work or other occupations there is a consensus of opinion
> that these children have acquitted themselves well, and doubtless they will return
> to their respective schools physically invigorated and better able to cope with the
> multiplicity of subjects that somewhat confuse the issues of education in primary
> schools.[102]

Although the county education committee was faced with an average attendance
falling below 83 per cent in rural areas, Pank stubbornly defended the devolution
of decision-making to local sub-committees. Each sub-committee, he insisted in
April 1917, 'must be the judge of the requirements of its own district, and during
the war they must expect to be confronted with variations in the attendance.'
Members agreed, and staunchly defended the exemption practices in their own
localities. They laughed at the jocular comment that some district had to be
bottom of the county attendance list, and did nothing. They were content to
blame the attendance officers for slackness in dealing with truants and the magistrates for undue leniency towards the minority of miscreants eventually
brought to court.[103] Only in the autumn of 1917 was there the first sign of an
improvement, as the figures in Table 5.4 show.

The total official exemption figures in Hertfordshire peaked at 1,314 children
between 1 July and 30 September 1916, and they remained above 1,000 until the
autumn of 1917. Exemptions were granted less freely from the summer of 1917,
and much less freely in 1918, but the total number of schoolchildren at work

Table 5.4 Attendances: summer 1916 to spring 1918[104]

*No explanation was given why the figure was adjusted, but 89.1% seems correct. This means that there was a slight rise in urban district attendances in the summer of 1916.

	% for this term last year	% for this term	% difference
Urban Districts			
1916 Summer Term	88.8	88.6*	–0.2
1916 Autumn Term	89.0	87.8	–1.2
1917 Spring Term	85.7	84.2	–1.5
1917 Summer Term	89.1*	87.2	–1.9
1917 Autumn Term	87.8	88.6	+0.8
1918 Spring Term	84.2	85.2	+1.0
Rural Districts			
1916 Summer Term	88.1	86.9	–1.2
1916 Autumn Term	87.3	85.7	–1.6
1917 Spring Term	85.4	82.5	–2.9
1917 Summer Term	86.9	86.4	–0.5
1917 Autumn Term	85.7	87.5	+1.8
1918 Spring Term	82.5	84.4	+1.9

Table 5.5 War exemptions: summer 1916 to spring 1918[105]

	Districts	Total	County total	% of roll excused	Type of employment: Agriculture	Retail shops	Office & works
April–June 1916	Urban	473		N/A	187	201	85
	Rural	762	1235	N/A	626	98	38
July–Sept 1916	Urban	583		2.0	225	243	115
	Rural	731	1314	4.8	593	91	47
Oct–Dec 1916	Urban	464		1.6	145	217	102
	Rural	634	1098	4.2	495	87	52
Jan–Mar 1917	Urban	512		1.8	135	238	139
	Rural	610	1112	4.7	467	87	56
April–June 1917	Urban	535		1.9	179	225	131
	Rural	655	1190	4.3	530	75	50
July–Sept 1917	Urban	447		1.6	157	160	130
	Rural	592	1039	3.9	489	70	33
Oct–Dec 1917	Urban	365		1.2	98	162	105
	Rural	499	864	3.3	402	71	26
Jan–Mar 1918	Urban	297		1.0	81	136	80
	Rural	379	676	2.5	274	67	28

declined only slowly. This was because a far greater proportion of exemptions, especially in rural districts, were for longer periods than previously, and often up to a year. This blatant reversal of earlier practice was the local sub-committees' response to the belated pressure from the LEA to tighten up their procedures.

The pressure did not extend to other occupations. While the agricultural figures declined from over 800 in the middle of 1916 to 600 in the winter of 1916–17 and 350 a year later, the non-agricultural exemptions hovered around 400 all through 1916 and 1917 and fell only slightly in early 1918. The figures in Table 5.5 (above) chart the trends from April 1916 until March 1918. The column entitled '% of roll excused' highlights the rural bias, but the figures mask the fact that the vast majority of exemptions were for pupils in the last two years of compulsory schooling – those aged from twelve to fourteen – and the exact, and no doubt alarmingly poor, attendance returns for these two vital years were not routinely recorded.

The number of girls exempted varied between approximately a quarter of the number of boys earlier in the war and half the number of the boys later in the war. For example, between April and June 1916 the number of new exemptions totalled 107 girls and 483 boys, and a year later 149 girls and 278 boys. Between October and December 1918 the new exemptions comprised 75 girls and 161 boys. Although the returns do not say, it is likely that the great majority of girls still gaining exemption went to work in local shops and offices. Either deliberately or carelessly, some local sub-committees also granted exemption to schoolchildren under the age of twelve – at least 14 are recorded in 1916 and 15 in 1917.[106]

In addition to the official exemptions during this two-year period, the number of persistent absentees reported to attendance officers exceeded 1,000 each term until early 1918. Approximately a third of these resulted in prosecutions, and of these between 40 per cent and 60 per cent resulted in fines, most of which were a little higher than in previous years. The figures are presented here in Table 5.6.

In 1917 Hallidie, the chief education officer, made some attempt to stem the

Table 5.6 Attendance defaulters: prosecutions and fines summer 1916 to spring 1918[107]

	Pupils reported	Prosecutions	Fines	Average fine
1916 Summer Term	1074	325	182	4s 3d
1916 Autumn Term	1334	314	184	5s
1917 Spring Term	1011	241	154	4s 3d
1917 Summer Term	1008	347	120	9s 10d
1917 Autumn Term	1157	348	194	5s 6d
1918 Spring Term	739	214	123	5s

tide of absenteeism and exemptions. No doubt Marvin had subjected him to pressure, but by then county education committee members were balancing their deep-seated desire to assist employers, as well as parents who 'in these hard times wished to have their children earning money', with mounting anxiety that the falling annual grant would necessitate higher local rates.[108] In addition, social reform was very much in the air, with the clauses of the Education Bill proposed by H.A.L. Fisher, the new President of the Board of Education, reaching the local press in the summer of 1917.[109] In December 1916 Hallidie had gained the education committee's sanction to ask those local sub-committees particularly free with their exemptions to take 'a less liberal view in future of the local requirements for child labour', and six months later he secured agreement that the Board of Education's recommendation of 1s a day should be the minimum wage linked to any exemptions.[110]

Hallidie and his assistant visited local sub-committees to enlighten them. He found committees who were obliging attendance officers to consult with them before issuing warnings to parents or taking proceedings against them, thereby delaying action in each case by a month or more. He found, too, magistrates who persisted in merely issuing attendance orders to notoriously negligent parents. When these parents were eventually brought before the bench they much preferred to pay a small fine than lose their children's wages.[111] Even on those rare occasions when a local sub-committee, such as Rickmansworth, genuinely desired stricter controls on attendance, it claimed magistrates made 'no secret of their objection to the Education Acts'.[112]

Pank was unsympathetic with greater controls. In October 1917 he defused a potentially explosive education committee debate on the wide variations in local exemption rates by asserting that no district was either lax or strict, it was merely a matter of 'different authorities, different policies'. A deep Conservative himself, he deflected any serious attempt at revision by joking that Barnet, with few exemptions, 'adhered to the more conservative policy' of his critics, while East Barnet, with more exemptions than any other urban district, 'supported the more liberal policy as perhaps represented by himself'.[113] The ensuing laughter at the heavy irony ended the discussion. Nevertheless, Pank realised that he was fighting a last-ditch defence against child-centred reforms. The now inevitable Education Act would almost certainly mean the end of all exemptions. He did not hide his regret, publicly confessing that 'it seemed absurd to him that a child could not combine education with industry.'[114]

Pank was speaking at the height of the national debate on educational reform.

During 1917 the pre-war pressures for social reforms were intensified by the wave of feeling that the unprecedented and never-ending sacrifices families were making on behalf of their country should not be in vain. Countless families of all social classes had lost husbands, fathers and brothers, many more men had endured injuries and traumas, thousands of women had returned to work while still maintaining responsibility for homes, and Fisher estimated that 600,000 children across the nation had been put 'prematurely to work', not counting those employed in total violation of the law, during the first three years of the war.[115]

There was a groundswell of opinion fuelled by the meetings and publications of numerous reform groups that victory, even if it seemed remote in 1917, should bring well-deserved rewards that would touch all citizens.[116] Lloyd George, the Prime Minister, recognised the need for a clear sign to a war-weary nation that this would be so. He had asked Fisher to compile a radical Education Bill and promised him full personal and cabinet support. The ensuing Bill sought to end the loopholes in compulsory schooling, stimulate the provision of a broader curriculum, and extend the final leaving age. Introducing the Bill in the House of Commons in August 1917, Fisher believed that it would 'put a prompt end to an evil which has grown to alarming proportions during the past three years – I allude to the industrial pressure upon the child life of this country – and it will greatly facilitate the solution of many problems of juvenile employment.' He added that 'the same logic which leads us to desire an extension of the franchise points also to an extension of education.'[117] The government was now prepared to allow all men the vote, and also extend it to all women over the age of thirty, but generations of tradition and class divisions survived unscathed to ensure that it never contemplated any erosion of the rights of wealthier parents to purchase places for their children at public, private and grammar schools. Fisher did, though, surmount the vigorous opposition from urban and rural employers to the clauses completely prohibiting any exemption from school attendance until the age of fourteen. The proposal to introduce compulsory part-time continuation classes for pupils between the ages of fourteen and eighteen met with equal outcry from many employers, and from many others convinced that the socialist and collectivist inclinations of the Lloyd George government had gone too far.[118] Nevertheless, these proposals, too, reached the statute book.

The mounting casualties of war had meant that a greater value was placed upon life, and especially the life of the next generation. The care of babies and young children fell under the spotlight of reformers, and Fisher included the provision of medical treatment, playing fields, school camps and health education in his Bill. The healthy upbringing and education of future citizens began to replace the immediate needs of employers, and newspapers dutifully followed the trend in highlighting the exhibitions, speeches and publications devoted to better child-rearing techniques, wide-ranging educational reform and the country's long-term need for plentiful skilled workers.[119]

In 1918 the incidence of exemption started to fall. However, wartime habits and pre-war inclinations died hard. Fewer children were exempted during 1918 but the seasonal increase in the summer and the longer periods of exemption which had become customary combined to ensure that the overall decline in the number of schoolchildren in full-time employment was slowed down. During the last quarter of 1918, 691 children were at work with exemption certificates: 22 of them were under the age of twelve, 310 had been exempted for up to three months, 212 for up to six months and 169 for up to a year. In the first quarter of 1919, 295 were still working: 18 for up to three months, 104 for up to six months, and 173 for up to a year. A total of 158 schoolchildren were still working all day in shops, factories and farms seven months and more after the Armistice. This was in direct contravention of the Board of Education's directive in March 1919 that all exemptions were to be withdrawn.

Attendance figures were even slower to improve, for a variety of reasons. Education committee members remained quick to uphold the right of managers to close schools if local farmers needed harvest hands.[120] More schools than in

Table 5.7 War exemptions: spring 1918 to summer 1919[121]

	Districts	Total	County total	% of roll excused	Type of employment		
					Agriculture	Retail shops	Office & works
April–June 1918	Urban	296		1.0	93	112	91
	Rural	416	712	2.6	306	61	49
July–Sept 1918	Urban	337		1.1	124	123	90
	Rural	410	747	2.7	295	58	57
Oct–Dec 1918	Urban	301		1.0	129	94	78
	Rural	390	691	2.5	304	42	44
Jan–Mar 1919	Urban	131		0.4	34	52	45
	Rural	164	295	1.2	117	18	29
April–June 1919	Urban	71		0.2	16	24	31
	Rural	87	158	0.6	54	15	18

Table 5.8 Attendances: summer 1916 to spring 1918.[122] The period for the returns changed in 1919 from termly to quarterly, but although the comparison with the previous year is not exact the trend is clear

	% for this term last year	% for this term	% difference
Urban districts			
1918 Summer term	87.2	86.7	−0.5
1918 Autumn term	88.6	84.2	−4.4
1919 Jan–March	85.2	79.6	−5.6
1919 April–June	86.7	89.4	+3.7
Rural Districts			
1918 Summer term	86.4	86.5	+0.1
1918 Autumn term	87.5	83.5	−4.0
1919 Jan–March	84.4	81.8	−2.6
1919 April–June	86.5	89.8	+3.3

previous years closed for the hay, grain and potato harvests, and the definition of harvest was stretched in Hertfordshire to include fruit, much against the Board of Education's wishes. Sometimes schools closed for a week, only to find that the wet summer of 1918 obliged farmers to spread the work over a longer period than envisaged, thereby wrecking school timetables and attendance figures for a further week. Parents continued to defy headteachers and attendance officers and keep children away from school for household chores and casual labour. Children whose applications for exemption were refused still stayed away with impunity.[123] Absenteeism was greatest among the older children; as the headmaster at High Wych commented, parents were eager 'to get rid of the younger ones' to school.[124]

Reasons beyond the control of the LEA exacerbated the situation. Numerous schools recorded the heavy falls of snow early in 1918, and then the gales and persistent rain which did not fade away until the summer.[125] The shortages of meat, margarine and bread at the height of the German U-boat campaign led to long queues outside shops, with parents using their children to hold places in them.[126] On 22 January 1918 fifty boys were absent from St Mary's School in Hitchin when news of a margarine delivery was heard, and ten days later forty-one boys from Callow Land School in Watford were also queuing outside shops.[127]

Following hard upon an outbreak of measles, the virulent worldwide influenza pandemic struck north-west Hertfordshire in June 1918. It had covered the county by October and only died away in early 1919. There were 373 school closures and reclosures in 1918, many for a fortnight, some for a month at a time.[128]

As usual in these circumstances, headteachers noted that 'healthy children appear to be taking advantage of the situation generally'.[129] Teachers and pupils fell ill, routine was wrecked, and many families found it a frightening and desperate time, with food shortages, the full range of chores to do and less income as a result of the adults' and children's absence from work. Families also had to endure the news from the battlefields. The final year of the war witnessed another savage phase with Germany's massive onslaught on the Western Front during March and April 1918 and the Allied counter-attack during the summer. Few expected Germany to collapse so suddenly in the autumn. As always, the county education committee was concerned primarily for employers. In October 1918 one clerical member noted the 'very serious epidemic of influenza and a very serious epidemic of potato picking', and urged colleagues to close the schools so that the remaining children could gather in the crops.[130]

The revival of child labour had rekindled the dormant, but far from dead, coals of the Victorian controversy regarding the value of elementary education to working-class children, and the threat it posed to society by inculcating in future labourers a deep dissatisfaction with the *status quo* and their likely humble lot. Patriotism, prejudice, tradition and confusion – as well as the desire to meet the needs of the moment – all combined to produce new priorities in 1914. The unprecedented upheavals caused in national life by the war cast the children back a generation or more in their place on that list of priorities. County councillors, education committee members, magistrates, managers and local sub-committees possessed far more sympathy with the needs of employers than the needs of children, who were expected to make their own direct contribution to the war effort. The ambivalence of the government, including the Board of Education, contributed much to the confusion and rendered any attempts at remedial action little more than bluff. Hertfordshire LEA called the bluff, proving that no mechanism existed that would stand a chance of success in wartime to alter the policies and practices – and predilections – of those local groups once they had combined, tacitly but powerfully, to erode the progress of elementary education that had been made over the previous fifty years.

Only in the last year of the war, with Fisher's reforms on the statute book, was this erosion offset by the changes in national attitudes towards the health and welfare of children. Even then, it was with reluctance that Hertfordshire LEA moved towards protecting children's full-time education up to the age of fourteen. As we shall see, the needs of local rural and urban employers and a strong desire to preserve the distinctions between the social classes would continue to shape education across the county throughout the 1920s and 1930s. The war did not significantly break down the barriers of social class, and neither did the 1918 Education Act. They did, though, create the mood and the means for a considerable strengthening of the vocational features of elementary education and, thereby, ensure that children continued to serve the needs of the local economy in line with the wishes of their social superiors.

CHAPTER SIX

The war and health

I N 1914 A HOTCHPOTCH OF LEGISLATION governed the policies of local authorities towards child health. Much of the legislation was new, and its provision was severely hedged about with conditions which reflected the struggle between those who argued that the state should take greater responsibility for the welfare of the poor and those who believed in the sufficiency of charities and the Poor Law to alleviate distress. Although the promoters of collectivism and extended state provision were growing in number, seeing the sound health of the working classes as an invaluable national asset, they were sharply challenged by the enduring body of nineteenth-century opinion which asserted the primacy of self-help, individual responsibility and personal liberty over any further growth of state obligation, expenditure and control. The detailed Victorian and Edwardian surveys might have revealed the numerous poverty-stricken urban ghettoes, but their publication never overcame the deep-seated fears that too much public support pandered to, and enfeebled, the numerous parents who, given the choice, would be only too happy for others to bear the burden and cost of bringing up their children.[1] Among middle-class commentators there was a well-publicised maxim that every free meal for a child meant another pint of beer for the parents. It was a prolonged and bitter controversy, and continued several decades into the twentieth century.

A number of inquiries in the late nineteenth and early twentieth centuries had revealed the inadequate diet and poor constitution of many working-class children. In 1899 the London School Board caused controversy by recommending the use of public money for school dinners in poor areas, and soon afterwards the humiliating British defeats at the hands of the Boers in South Africa generated widely publicised fears of racial degeneration. It was revealed that over a third of the 700,000 recruits medically examined between 1893 and 1902 were unfit for service, and probably many more did not even qualify for inspection.[2]

An Inter-Departmental Committee on Physical Deterioration went to work, and its 1904 report contained extensive evidence of child malnutrition and urged the provision of state-subsidised school meals to supplement the efforts of charities. In 1905 another Inter-Departmental Committee concentrated specifically upon medical inspection and school meals, and the Trades Union Congress gave the campaign its wholehearted support. In the face of vigorous opposition, in 1906 an Education Act finally empowered LEAs, but fell short of compelling them, to spend money out of the rates on feeding necessitous children. The Act also obliged LEAs to recover wherever possible the cost of the meals from the parents. By 1910–11, 100 LEAs were providing meals; Hertfordshire was not one of them. All attempts up to 1914 to press for an amending Bill to make provision compulsory ended in failure.

In 1907 the Education (Administrative Provisions) Act gave LEAs the duty to provide for the medical inspection of children in elementary schools. Prior to this a few progressive School Boards had strained the clauses in the 1870 Education Act which allowed them to employ 'other necessary officers' by appointing school medical officers, most of them part-time. Their work was primarily concerned with the inspection of school buildings, but some were engaged in the identification of pupils manifestly unfit to attend lessons.[3] Very few school medical officers treated any ailments they found in pupils. Dr James Kerr headed London County Council's team of school medical officers, and maintained a firm commitment to the extension of public health, the improvement of sanitation and the prevention of contagious diseases. Nevertheless, along with many other public officials and doctors, he believed that free medical treatment turned parents into paupers.[4] People of all social classes, and especially the poor themselves, believed that the very act of accepting publicly financed aid, even outside the strict operation of the Poor Law, created a new pauper who was immediately burdened with all the social, economic, legal and psychological stigmas attached to that unwelcome status. Across London and the few other towns and cities where pupils were examined, the school doctors and nurses limited their work to telling the children, or their parents, what was wrong and informing them of the remedy. In general, where inspections took place, great attention was paid to dirty heads and poor eyesight but far less to diseases of the ear and teeth. In a few towns charities contributed towards the cost of treatment, but otherwise poorer parents resorted to loans or, in many cases, were unable to take any action at all.

Other legislation also reflected the contemporary tensions between relieving the appalling conditions in which many children grew up – or failed to grow up –

and avoiding the serious erosion of a proper sense of parental duty among the poorer classes in society. In 1908 the Children's Act gave local authorities the power to prosecute parents for failing to provide their children with adequate clothing, food or medical treatment. Poverty *per se* did not enable parents to escape their legal responsibilities, as they could be prosecuted for not applying to the Poor Law Guardians for relief. In 1909 another Act obliged LEAs to charge parents for medical treatment unless it was certain that they could not pay. The tortuous struggle for improved public health stemmed as much from a deep-seated suspicion of the moral character of the working classes as it did from the humanitarian instincts and social conscience of campaigners and collectivist politicians.[5]

Under the 1907 Education Act children were inspected twice during their elementary school lives – on entering school, and on leaving it. In 1907, too, a Medical Branch was formed at the Board of Education, and Dr (later Sir) George Newman became its chief officer and driving force. The Act left the detailed method of its implementation, and the use of permitted powers above the minimum demands of inspection, to be clarified by local initiative and experience. Rate-subsidised treatment was not permitted until 1912, and only then as a result of Newman's persistent agitation and the increasing evidence of need provided by school medical officers in the field.

By 1911, 900 medical officers were engaged in the school health service nationwide, some full-time but most part-time. They were far from universally welcomed, and the undoubted success of the school medical officers in raising the standards of children's health, school sanitation and health education has to be measured against the opposition they encountered from education committees, LEA officers, and teachers and parents who often resented the rising public expense, the arrival of new 'experts' in educational affairs, and the official interference in family life. As historian Jose Harris has shown, medicine as a science had advanced in status during late Victorian and Edwardian Britain, and doctors were moving 'from the margin to the mainstream of social life'.[6] She has highlighted, too, how doctors were 'widely resented', not least by those unqualified practitioners whose skills and influence they had downgraded, by those compelled to undergo physical and mental examination, and 'by individuals in all classes who resisted the creeping "medicalization" of what had previously been viewed as "common sense" areas of human life, such as child care, sexuality, physical fitness, diet and crime.'[7] In contrast, Newman himself saw public health reform in messianic terms, describing his book *The Health of the State* as 'a missionary handbook, sent forth as a reminder that the physical health and fitness of the people is the primary asset of the British Empire and the necessary basis of that social and moral reform which has for its end "the creation of a higher type of man".[8] He strove to ensure that all school medical officers shared and promoted his vision. It is not surprising that the deference usually given to the well-paid medical experts was accompanied by a lingering hostility from all levels of society towards their ever-expanding roles and responsibilities.

In 1913 Newman was urging school medical officers to expand the frontiers of their work by analysing the incidence of childhood ailments in their locality, identifying the conditions contributing to particular diseases, and recommending the most effective measures of treatment and longer-term prevention.[9] However, he was not thinking primarily of environmental factors. Throughout his professional life, which lasted until 1935, Newman remained convinced that parental ignorance and inadequacies were the main causes of debilitating diseases and child mortality. He asserted that 'the most injurious influences affecting the physical conditions of young children arise from the habits, customs and practices of the people themselves rather than from external surroundings or conditions.'[10] In an early circular giving LEAs operational guidance, he stated unequivocally that 'one of the objects of the new legislation is to stimulate a sense of duty in matters affecting health in the homes of the people, [and] to enlist the best services and interests of parents.'[11] This perception of parents and the need to educate, persuade and coerce them was never doubted by Hertfordshire's first school medical officer, Dr (later Lieutenant Colonel Sir) Francis Fremantle, and his deputy and successor, Dr H. Hyslop Thomson.

Fremantle was in the forefront of the pioneering movement to collect and evaluate all the data being produced by the nascent health service. He showed no hesitation in interfering in school or home affairs. Writing in 1914, he revealed a determination locally as great as Newman's nationally to ensure that county councillors, education committee members, teachers, parents and the public at large appreciated that the:

> system of public elementary education includes the development of the body as well as of the mind and character. Medical inspection provides for occasional advice and the discovery of defects, with a view to remedy, but the proper care and training of the body and the cultivation of cleanly and sanitary habits must be part of everyday life in the school.[12]

In Hertfordshire children were examined soon after entry to school, again between seven and eight years of age, and finally at twelve. No treatment was

Dr (later Lieutenant Colonel Sir) Francis Fremantle (HALS)

given, and Fremantle was not an advocate of publicly subsidised treatment centres, but school nurses followed up cases with home visits to explain what should be done. They also endeavoured to visit each school once a month to examine children brought to their attention by teachers. The 1908 Children's Act was invoked to enforce the inspection and reinspection of lice-infested children who were excluded from school until cleansed. If parents proved dilatory in achieving this, they could be prosecuted under the attendance byelaws.[13]

In common with Newman, Fremantle sought greater cooperation and coordination between the numerous professional groups, voluntary organisations and charities concerned with children and public health. The aims, Fremantle asserted, were nothing less than:

> to discover and use the services of every agent and agency concerned with child-life both at home and in school to the same end – nurses, attendance officers and caretakers, managers, clergy and other benevolent persons, medical practitioners and institutions, the National Society for the Prevention of Cruelty to Children, the Guardians and other Authorities – and to inspire the whole educational

system and the community at large with the determination to bring up a race of children healthy in body as well as in character and mind.[14]

He remained totally opposed to the expenditure of public money as anything but a last resort, to be used when local voluntary efforts and parental ability to pay were clearly exhausted.

In 1914 Hertfordshire had more school medical staff than any other county – four full-time and twelve part-time district medical officers, and 59 nurses, mainly part-time, hired from the County Nursing Association – but its scheme was restricted in scope and limited in effect.[15] Fremantle recognised this more than anyone else, and he used his annual reports and the newspaper publicity they generated to ensure that county councillors, education committee members and the public were aware of it too.[16] He believed that the professional attitudes and personal skills of doctors and nurses were as important as their technical expertise. They must possess the broader view and the longer aim. They should, he argued, 'be in close and constant touch with the schools and homes of the pupils and teachers' and they must be 'permanent, tactful and experienced; not temporary, dictatorial and unknown'.[17] Currently, he stated, district medical officers were not 'sufficiently concerned ... in the more important part of school health, the daily life and daily curriculum of the schools'. Always the interventionist, Fremantle wanted teachers, nurses, caretakers, attendance officers and school managers to be in constant receipt of 'advice and encouragement' on physical drill, hygiene, school cleansing and the ways parents could access treatment as easily and cheaply as possible. He went so far as to argue that the 'school doctor should be able to count on the teachers as his agents'.[18]

Fremantle appreciated the crucial role teachers played in the promotion of child health. An uninterested teacher was a serious impediment. By 1913 on average just 1 per cent of Hertfordshire parents refused to allow their children to be inspected, but in one village, where 'the headteacher is very apathetic, shows no sign of interest in children, and appears bored at inspections', refusals totalled 75 per cent. In another, the efforts of a zealous nurse to help parents secure treatment were frustrated because of the lack of back-up by the teachers.[19] Sometimes, though, inadequate school buildings and strict school timetables disrupted visits. In Hertford and Bishop's Stortford district medical officers complained it was impossible to carry out inspections in the same room as 100 children were being taught. In Watford a medical officer pleaded that 'teachers should be allowed full liberty to alter their programme so that noisy classes, such as singing and marching should not be held during the hours of inspection.'[20]

As Fremantle recognised, the opposite qualities of self-respect and carelessness were the common causes of refusals and absences on the day of inspection. In Cheshunt 'a good many stop away (mainly dirty) when inspection is expected', and at St Andrew's, in Hitchin, 'the dirtiest school in the district', where there was much evidence of malnutrition and poverty, the district medical officer claimed it was 'difficult to interest parents in their children and get anything done to remedy defects'. At Kimpton, one parent refused as she 'did not want to know if anything was wrong with her child as the cost of correcting it was the distasteful part'. Conversely, medical officers noted that 'the better class parents' often said they preferred their own doctor to examine their children.[21]

Although Fremantle believed in a sympathetic and persuasive approach to parents he remained convinced that the full force of the law was essential in a small minority of obdurate cases. He criticised the LEA for being more lax than neighbouring Buckinghamshire and Essex in prosecuting parents under the attendance byelaws for refusing to cleanse excluded pupils and under the Children's Act for failing to provide adequate food, clothing and medical aid or seek relief through the Poor Law. He argued that the derisory fines imposed by most Hertfordshire magistrates only encouraged parents to act irresponsibly. He advocated setting up 'cleansing stations' so that the LEA could invoke its right to treat dirty children consistently neglected by their parents. He found attendance officers were usually far more concerned with getting sick children back to school as soon as possible, to maximise the attendance percentages, rather than ensuring they were completely cured and free from infection. 'Ill-health', Fremantle reported acerbically, 'is simply an inevitable obstacle to their aim.'[22] Attendance officers were not responsible for the closure of schools due to epidemics, and many had little interest in keeping children at home in the early stages of infection to encourage a quicker recovery and avoid diseases spreading across the school. Fremantle sought a drastic revision of their role, including frequent meetings between them and school medical officers to exchange information on epidemics, exclusion, absenteeism, home visits, advice to parents and the need for legal action.

In 1914 Fremantle possessed a clear view of the aims and objectives of the school health service, and their fulfilment involved the subservience of other professional groups to its decisions and strategies. He could draw upon a host of local statistics as well as national legislation to support his arguments, and he did not hesitate to do so. A significant minority of Hertfordshire children were found to be inadequately clothed and shod (Table 6.1). A comparison of the urban and

Table 6.1 Children inadequately clothed and shod

	Aged 5		Aged 7		Aged 12	
	Boys %	Girls %	Boys %	Girls %	Boys %	Girls %
Urban districts	7.6	4.2	9.0	5.1	11.7	3.2
Rural districts	3.9	2.3	4.9	3.5	5.3	3.3

rural figures revealed a hard core of poverty in the towns as, Fremantle believed, 'clothes can hardly receive rougher wear than they do in the country.'[23]

Urban children, in particular, suffered from malnourishment (Table 6.2),[24] and dirty and verminous children were common. Thanks mainly to their longer hair, girls were far more prone to infestation by lice than boys (Table 6.3).[25]

Table 6.2 Children malnourished

	Aged 5		Aged 7		Aged 12	
	Boys %	Girls %	Boys %	Girls %	Boys %	Girls %
Urban districts	5.6	5.3	10.8	13.0	10.4	5.8
Rural districts	2.5	2.6	5.1	5.4	7.0	8.1

Table 6.3 Children with infested heads and/or bodies

	Aged 5		Aged 7		Aged 12	
	Boys %	Girls %	Boys %	Girls %	Boys %	Girls %
Infested heads						
Urban districts	5.5	14.3	5.5	22.3	4.8	13.0
Rural districts	4.6	17.0	4.4	23.7	13.8	30.8
Infested bodies						
Urban districts	4.6	4.6	6.4	6.1	9.4	3.2
Rural districts	1.3	2.7	2.3	3.8	2.5	2.7

The incidence of infestation was in slow decline, due, Fremantle believed, 'to the general spread of the desire for cleanliness, owing to medical inspection, resulting in some unpleasantness towards the offenders and a slow hardening of public opinion in that direction.'[26] However, no such change in popular expectations attended the very high percentage of dental defects (Table 6.4).[27]

Table 6.4 Children with defective teeth

	Aged 5		Aged 7		Aged 12	
	Boys %	Girls %	Boys %	Girls %	Boys %	Girls %
Urban districts	25.5	28.8	45.1	39.6	26.6	25.6
Rural districts	31.6	36.9	46.2	53.4	30.1	34.1

Table 6.5 Children with defective eyesight

| | Aged 7 | | Aged 12 | |
	Boys %	Girls %	Boys %	Girls %
One eye defective				
Urban districts	5.8	7.5	5.8	4.8
Rural districts	2.6	4.2	5.1	5.3
Both eyes defective				
Urban districts	13.4	16.5	11.1	6.8
Rural districts	6.1	7.4	9.1	14.3

District medical officers also found a significant minority of children had defective eyesight (Table 6.5). Fremantle believed the fine focusing required for needlework contributed to the problem for girls, and many children were wearing totally inappropriate glasses originally provided for other people, or prescribed and made by untrained opticians.[28]

School medical officers found many school buildings lacked basic sanitation, and by 1914 Fremantle's persistent lobbying, and a Board of Education grant, had persuaded the county education committee to take action in the worst cases. Very gradually schools were being provided with cloakroom space, better lighting, improved ventilation, piped water and water closets instead of earth closets and middens. A few of the dangerous gravel yards were being tarred, and more school floors were being scrubbed from time to time with disinfectant.[29]

Fremantle was a reformer, but a moderate one. He had no thoughts of radically changing, let alone abolishing, the current system of medical provision and legal obligations based upon the 'liberty of the subject, compulsion of parent or guardian to take necessary care of a child, encouragement of self-support and voluntary effort, and the provision by the Guardians of help to all who need.'[30] For example, he saw no need for the LEA to provide meals. In Watford, he noted, voluntary groups easily satisfied the demand, and in St Albans the soup kitchen had closed for want of clients. In just two villages, North Mimms and Weston, cocoa was provided for long-distance pupils, and penny dinners were popular in two others, Braughing and neighbouring Standon. Fremantle was convinced that 'similar philanthropy' would cater for such needs anywhere else, and he made it clear that 'voluntary action has this advantage over official action, that it is less likely to err on the side either of disregard for or of too rigid insistence on economic principle in the execution of parental duties.'[31]

However, he condemned the inadequacies of the Poor Law. He cited the fever hospitals, tuberculosis dispensaries and school clinics as proof that it could not cope with severe and persistent outbreaks of contagious and debilitating diseases 'on a broad scientific basis, without reference to social and financial status'.[32] Nevertheless, he believed that greater parental knowledge and cooperation brought about by sympathetic doctors, nurses and teachers, the greater coordination of facilities and expertise possessed by professional bodies and voluntary agencies, and the greater use of legal sanctions by LEAs, attendance officers and magistrates, would alleviate most problems.

In every respect but one he believed the Hertfordshire system had been 'successful to an unexpected degree, sufficient to justify a continued development along the same lines'.[33] The exception, he went on to say, was the chronic need for dental clinics, 'for the simple reason that no treatment is available except in a few towns and at private fees.' In the summer of 1914 he sought to employ and equip two school dentists, and he was at pains to point out that no precedent would be set, as sufficient professional and voluntary medical agencies existed to treat other ailments and impediments.

His modest request met a mixed reception. A vociferous minority of education committee members, ignoring his reassurances and clear statement of policy, publicly evoked deep fears of state collectivism and runaway charges on the rates. Pank was particularly hostile, suspecting that Fremantle had underestimated the cost in order to get his scheme accepted. He reminded members of the strong opinions held by many members of the public 'on the question of relieving the parent at the expense of the ratepayers'. Cries of approbation greeted the assertion that the LEA's duty ended with the £2,700 spent each year informing parents of their responsibilities. 'If they started to do as suggested with the teeth', one horrified member interjected, 'why not the noses, the flat feet, the ruptures, the eyes and the rickety bones?'[34]

The panic-mongers overplayed their hand, and Fremantle had enough support for the proposal to be deferred rather than defeated. The press, though, gloated and continued where Pank and his associates had left off. Many children, asserted one editor with particular venom, were 'already clothed, fed, educated, and medically inspected at the expense of the ratepayers and it would almost seem that the State recognises no responsibility on the part of the parents beyond that of adding to the population.' As in all areas of elementary education at this time, the expansionist tendency of bureaucracy met with considerable press hostility. The same editorial which denigrated working-class parents went on to lament the burdens imposed upon the middle classes, as 'the outstanding feature of all these schemes is the multiplication of officials which they involve and the vast increase in their salaries.'[35]

The reliance upon voluntary efforts alongside the meagre relief offered through the Poor Law prevailed in Hertfordshire well into the war. It was significant that the Honourable A.H. Holland-Hibbert was a leading opponent of Fremantle's proposals on the county council while at the same time being a prominent figure in the county branch of the NSPCC. Addressing members of the society in the week war broke out, and confident of their support, he highlighted the need for even greater fund-raising and the massive extension of the charity's welfare aid, including the expansion of its residential homes. He took it for granted that the NSPCC and other voluntary agencies, rather than the state and local authorities, would bear the brunt of succouring those who were in distress.[36]

Holland-Hibbert also became a member of the County Relief Committee set up in August 1914 to alleviate any working-class distress arising out of the war.[37] The fear of unemployment due to the dislocation of trade had led to the hurried passage of the Elementary Education (Provision of Meals) Act through both Houses of Parliament. The Act combined some awareness of the possible need for rapid action on an unprecedented scale with the narrowly restrictive tenets of Victorian public aid. On their own initiative LEAs could provide meals for elementary schoolchildren, but only to those whose education would obviously suffer and where no voluntary provision was available.[38]

The County Relief Committee saw no reason to implement the Act in Hertfordshire.[39] Others, though, anticipated widespread hunger and unrest. Watford's Local War Assistance Committee and Trades and Labour Council, Letchworth Parish Council, and Bishop's Stortford's clergy and Urban District Council all urged the county council to activate the scheme without delay.[40] When inquiries were made, however, Bishop's Stortford could produce no evidence of distress or Watford that the local soup kitchens were inadequate, and Letchworth had to admit that its school managers had established their own relief agency.[41]

County newspapers saw the Committee's actions as commendable steadfastness in the face of unwarranted panic. With the recent rejection of Fremantle's scheme in mind, they took pride in the county's resolve to resist the war 'being used as a lever for the carrying out of costly experiments in social reform'. The past was seen as the pointer to the future. It was deemed a virtue to be 'old-fashioned enough to believe ... the less the State trespasses upon the sanctity of the home, with its family life, its duties, and its responsibilities, the better will it be for the future of our country.'[42] Editors did, however, present readers with a bias in their columns that was greater than on the ground. The speeches of Pank and other opponents of state-subsidised feeding and social reform were reported and supported in all local newspapers, but only one carried quotations from an education committee member who had a different perspective. He argued that the reliance on voluntary efforts placed an unfair burden on 'the good nature of the people who were continually financing objects of this kind, whereas it was a duty which ought to be cast upon the whole community'.[43] It remained, however, a minority view.

The school attendance prizes were early casualties of the war. The most coveted were the watches awarded for five years without a single absence. After an outbreak of scarlet fever had been traced back to an infectious child who had attended school rather than forfeit a prize, thirteen urban and rural districts combined to petition the LEA for the abolition of the watches.[44] Fremantle had consistently opposed the awards as liable to encourage epidemics, but education committee members persisted in the unsubstantiated belief that their watches – despite, or because of, the fact that they cost £320 a year – did more good than harm in securing high attendance percentages.[45] For once, local editors were in the vanguard of public opinion. They asserted that the scheme was 'utterly worthless' and contributed mainly to perpetuating 'one of the fetishes of State managed education' – the strict formula tying Treasury grants to attendance.[46] After lengthy debate, and with some reluctance, all the prizes were finally phased out during a series of economy measures imposed in the autumn of 1915.[47]

In 1914 Fremantle received a commission in the army. Dr Thomson, his senior assistant, became acting school medical officer and continued Fremantle's campaign to coordinate the efforts of all statutory and voluntary parties.[48] He had a high regard for the work of the nurses and, unlike many at the time, for teachers. By 1915 the school nurse system at last covered the whole county, and the numbers of undernourished and unclean children continued to decline, despite the disruptions of war.[49] Several schools started selling hot drinks for a penny a week, not because of domestic difficulties brought on by the war but, on the advice of district medical officers, to offset the hardship of long walks from home.[50] Thomson believed that teachers should be empowered to exclude all pupils suspected of suffering from infectious diseases, and then report their action to the medical officer for further investigation. This radical, although common-sense, approach was aimed at replacing the current crude and inflexible procedure whereby schools closed when attendances fell below 50 per cent. At the Board of Education Newman was impressed and quoted Thomson at length in his annual report. He agreed that each teacher's 'daily contact with the children gives him special opportunities for effective appeal, and there is abundant evidence of the success of his efforts.'[51]

The war abruptly curtailed the programme of building improvements begun in 1911, and postponed indefinitely all thoughts of dental treatment.[52] However, Thomson was a formidable advocate of good sanitation and ventilation, and the traumas of war gradually changed public attitudes towards welfare issues and especially the health of the rising generation. Fremantle, who rose to the rank of Lieutenant Colonel in the Royal Army Medical Corps, contributed a powerful public plea for reform born out of his first few months on the Western Front. In an open letter to the county council he argued that 30 per cent of recruits were still rejected as unfit, and 'most of these defects could have been prevented or cut short by proper treatment or by proper habits in childhood.'[53] Hertfordshire was one of only twelve counties barring any form of treatment out of the rates, and Fremantle now cast aside the way it had 'hitherto approached the subject timidly in the hope that private enterprise might meet the need.' He urged the county council to undertake 'the systematic treatment of defects on a complete scale' or, better still, to petition the government to adopt a national insurance scheme to cover the treatment of children's illnesses and conditions reported by the school medical officers.[54] It was a dramatic change of mind.

Fremantle and Thomson were far from being isolated voices in the wilderness. Public opinion was changing, and the press was quick to note the trend. As a result, Fremantle's letter and Thomson's annual report received extensive publicity. In Spring 1915 the *Hertfordshire Mercury* acknowledged that the 'terrible wastage of the war' would direct attention towards the greater health of the next generation and 'any steps taken by our education authorities in that direction are of the utmost importance to the welfare of the nation.'[55]

The school health service remained immune to the economy measures keenly imposed upon local public expenditure by county councillors during 1915 and 1916. In May 1915 there was no opposition to the appointment of six more health visitors.[56] In Autumn 1915 the county accountant suggested a reduction in medical inspections from three to two during each child's school career, thereby saving £600. Hallidie refused to support this measure, and so did the Finance and General Purposes Sub-Committee, the Education Committee and the full county council.[57] Half a dozen older schools even had sanitary improvements carried out in 1916–17.[58] In 1917 Thomson felt confident enough to draw attention to the contrast between the council and church schools, the latter falling steadily behind the standards laid down by the Board of Education since 1902.[59] He gave notice that remedial action would be required in due course if the worst buildings were to escape the withdrawal of the Treasury grant. The greater attraction of war-related appeals meant that some Church of England parishes had difficulty in maintaining their school funds.[60] Belatedly, the diocese of St Albans realised the daunting task ahead in matching the council schools' improvements in sanitation, heating and ventilation, and early in 1918 it began the painful task of raising funds for a major maintenance programme.[61]

The war did not delay the implementation of either the 1913 Mental Deficiency Act or the 1914 Elementary Education (Defective and Epileptic Children) Act. The first defined, and required LEAs to identify, mentally deficient children up to the age of sixteen.[62] The second came into force, without postponement, on 1 January 1915 and obliged LEAs to make suitable provision for those incapable of receiving instruction in ordinary elementary schools.[63] Ever since an 1899 Act had permitted it, the LEA had dispatched a few mentally and physically handicapped children to distant special schools. The vast majority, however, had had to survive without additional help in ordinary schools or, with tacit approval, had stayed away from school altogether. Now, in the midst of the war, the LEA had to intensify its efforts.

An initial list submitted by Hertfordshire headteachers contained the names of 300 pupils for specialist investigation. The LEA was entitled to build, equip and maintain its own special schools, or pay other authorities or voluntary agencies to board and educate designated pupils. In peacetime it had had no thoughts of financing its own residential schools, and during the war the Treasury banned capital expenditure on buildings. This led to the hurried reservation of beds at Stoke Park Colony near Bristol.[64] Forty places were reserved at 10s 6d a week for 'educable, clean and healthy' children and 14s for 'low grade, dirty and hospital cases', but these were obviously insufficient in the longer term. To the estimated annual charges of £1,150 for the beds, there had to be added travelling expenses and clothing allowances. Many of the families with mentally deficient children were very poor and the LEA was unlikely to recoup the costs of care from parents.[65] Throughout the war a steady trickle of children boarded trains to Bristol, and in due course others entered homes, hospitals and asylums in Kent, Norfolk, Somerset, Staffordshire, Buckinghamshire, Derbyshire and Yorkshire.[66]

By 1917 Thomson, Hallidie and the education committee were becoming alarmed at the numbers continually being identified as requiring special education. Thomson calculated the number to be 1 in 200 of the elementary school population, making a total of 194.[67] There was, though, the dawning realisation that malnutrition and defective sight and hearing could contribute to a preventable backwardness which could be easily mistaken for congenital stupidity.[68] For the first time children's special educational needs were being considered seriously on a county-wide scale.

Although wartime attitudes protected and stimulated health care provision, the war severely impeded the efficiency of the service. The shortage of nurses was a major problem. Early in 1915 Hemel Hempstead's nurse volunteered for duty overseas, and with difficulty and after long delays four replacements were appointed over the next eighteen months, each one staying only briefly until securing a permanent post elsewhere.[69] Constant changes of staff also occurred in Watford, St Albans and Barnet, and in 1916 the County Superintendent of Nurses, Miss Margaret Burnside, had to report that 'the work in consequence was so behind that it has been impossible to bring it up to the usual standard.' The lack of continuity, and perhaps the lack of diligence, had predictable results. Miss Burnside complained that the replacement nurses 'do not know the children or the districts, and in consequence their work bears little fruit'. Some schools were not visited at all during the year, and routine inspections and reinspections for infestation and minor ailments were often ignored. In 1916 only 27 per cent of defects were remedied, largely because medical inspections were not followed up, and, Miss Burnside concluded, 'a great deal of time and trouble and public money is wasted.'[70]

During the latter part of the war more nurses were employed, although Miss Burnside remained critical of their genuine interest in children and capacity to win over parents to the need for effective treatment. 'Much of the work', she complained, 'is done in far too mechanical a manner to convince either parents or children of the truth of the facts being urged upon them.'[71] Nevertheless, the remedial rate crept up to 37 per cent in 1917, and rather reluctantly she recorded that, considering the shortage of doctors and problems of public transport, 'it really means more interest is being shown in the health and well-being of the children.' By then Miss Burnside, too, believed that voluntary efforts to provide advice, care and treatment were insufficient for the future, and she argued alongside Thomson and Fremantle that 'the State should take up the matter seriously if the nation is to improve in health.'[72]

Food shortages caused great anxiety, and sometimes panic, in 1917 and 1918. Imports had been vital before 1914, and although the wartime demand for labour ended unemployment, and wages rose accordingly, working-class families were constantly uneasy about the remorselessly rising food prices and the possibility of shortages. The government remained anxious about profiteering as well as scarcity, and the ominous tendency of both to incite widespread civil unrest. Price controls and rationing were discussed in 1916, but it was the ravages of the unrestricted U-boat campaign in 1917 that finally obliged their introduction.[73]

In 1915 Thomson reported very few cases of malnutrition, and even a distinct improvement in the health of children from poorer homes because of the higher urban wages, the forces' separation allowances and the army billeting money.[74] That autumn Hallidie saw no need to distribute the Board of Education's pamphlet on food economy, as 'special teaching on the subject will not be of much use while so many families ... have more money to spend than usual.'[75] The main call in the schools and evening classes at that time was the patriotic avoidance of waste rather than the imaginative use of cheap ingredients.[76]

In 1916 Thomson found that only 2.2 per cent of Hertfordshire's elementary schoolchildren were malnourished, far fewer than in 1913. Nearly half of these were due to tuberculosis, and most of the others lived in the slum areas of Watford, St Albans, Baldock and Hitchin.[77] In 1917 just 209 children – 1.6 per cent – suffered some degree of malnutrition, but the district medical officers remained confident that once the tuberculosis cases were taken into account only a few families had not benefited from the high employment and rising wages of the war.[78]

Food shortages became apparent locally in the middle of 1917, and they grew acute in 1918. Lord Robert Cecil, MP for Hitchin and son of the Marquis of Salisbury, was one of many wealthy commentators hurrying to give advice to both rich and poor. In an open letter to the *Hertfordshire & Cambridgeshire Reporter* he urged the well-to-do 'to leave the cheaper foods for the poor, such as potatoes, bread, cheese, dried flesh, rabbits and so forth', and he exhorted the poor to be:

> careful that there is not a scrap of any food wasted in their homes, bread should be cut as required, puddings should be made of stale bread that is left over, potatoes should not be peeled before cooking, oatmeal porridge and barley porridge, especially where there is a large family of children, should be eaten for breakfast.[79]

The dearth of wheat and flour led to renewed attention being given to the provision of cheap meals in schools. The 'practically breadless and flourless' but adequately nutritious menu introduced and subsidised by Viscount Knutsford, the brother of Holland-Hibbert, in his local school just across the border in Cambridgeshire was widely praised and publicised. It comprised:

Monday –   Roast beef or mutton, 1 potato, greens (in season), boiled rice or
                beans. Flaked maize or sago pudding.

Tuesday –   Stew, potatoes, cabbage or beans. Porridge (in the form of
                pudding).

Wednesday – Pea Soup or Bean Soup, ¾ oz bread. Cornflour or ground rice
                mould, or steamed rice and treacle.

Thursday –   Cottage pie or mince or fried liver, potatoes, beans or any
                vegetable in season.

Friday –   Soup of beans or peas, ¾ oz bread. Rice pudding or steamed rice,
                or cornflour shape.

The charge to parents was 8d a week, to which Lord Knutsford added 2d.[80] The
Daily Mail agreed that 'no diet could be better chosen for growing children ... If
generally adopted throughout the country the saving of wheat would be
immense, about 25,000 tons a month.'[81]

    Throughout 1918 long queues formed outside shops for the dwindling sup-
plies of some basic commodities and, as headteachers complained, parents often
used their children to hold places in them. Tea, sugar, butter, margarine and
potatoes were in particularly short supply, and the news or just the rumour of a
local delivery would cause a sudden rush to the shop. However, although shortages were commonplace, deliveries erratic, prices high and the fear of hunger
widespread, the nation had enough to eat.[82] Despite the obvious anxiety, in 1918
Thomson noted the 'general prosperity of the working classes' and recorded just
167 children who were malnourished. In just a few very poor districts the medical
officers believed rationing took its toll, with children becoming thinner and
'slightly anaemic' due to the 'shortage of meats, fats and possibly wheaten
flour'.[83] Compared with the pre-war situation, however, a far greater percentage
of families were better nourished.

    They were not, though, much cleaner. In 1915 several district medical officers
urged the full force of the law to be invoked against parents who used the domestic disruptions of wartime as an excuse for failing to keep their children free from
vermin. Others were more cautious, realising that 'in places where soldiers are billeted the children are more dirty and untidy owing to the fact that the mother's
time is more occupied and there is less bestowed on the children.'[84] In 1916 many
more children attended school in 'a neglected condition', largely, the medical
officers believed, because their mothers were engaged in war work.[85] Sometimes
all the good housekeeping was in vain, as nurses became convinced that many

children were infected by men returning home on leave.[86] In 1917 the shortages of nurses meant that inspections failed to cover every school, but still 827 children – 6.3 per cent – were referred for treatment for verminous heads.[87] Magistrates tended towards leniency when the worst cases came to court during the war, but Thomson thought they were totally misguided. Their lack of appropriate action, he asserted, 'amounts to cruelty' to children who were enduring the loss of health, care and schooling.[88]

The never-ending bloodshed of the war and frequent revelations of the poor physical health of recruits contributed to the dissatisfaction felt in Hertfordshire, as everywhere else, with the care and attention being given to the rising generation. In particular, the widespread problems associated with eyes and teeth among the troops effectively completed the case for the immediate treatment of children as the corollary of their inspection. In 1915 and 1916 Thomson re-emphasised the difficulties Hertfordshire's scheme imposed on the working classes in seeking out opticians and dental clinics, and finding the costs of travel as well as treatment.[89] He was not alone. In June 1915, the director of the NSPCC had addressed a meeting in Watford, and adopted a far more progressive stance than Holland-Hibbert. He had taken it for granted that 'life was never of such value to the nation as now', and placed responsibility for its nurture jointly on the state as well as the individual.[90]

Despite all the evidence, and the groundswell of support, the education committee refused to sanction subsidised treatment of any sort. The pressure on members was relentless. Thomson and Miss Burnside were able to prove beyond doubt that the combined efforts of voluntary agencies, legal compulsion and private practice were grossly inadequate to cope with the disparate needs of thousands of working-class families. Switching from arguments of social care to national efficiency, they asserted the local situation was rendered intolerable by the growing realisation that the children's good health was essential to the nation's continuing survival, let alone prosperity. As they made clear, medical inspection had provided valuable data for local authorities as well as advice for parents, and the accumulation of statistics served to reinforce the futility of providing diagnosis and prognosis without ensuring treatment. Accompanying Thomson's analytical reports were well-publicised conferences, speeches and rallies which turned the screw on an already tightly wound war-weary populace.

The national and local campaign for increased welfare provision reached its height in the summer of 1917. It was a time when the trench warfare seemed to have no end, U-boats were ravaging commercial shipping, and German fighter aircraft had established their supremacy over the Western Front. Campaigners were fired by the declining birth rate and the mortality rate of 15 per cent during the first year of life, and by the widely held suspicion that child neglect was significantly accentuated by the increased employment of women. They argued that as female patriotism, rather than irresponsibility, was now the primary cause of placing so many children at risk the state had a duty to provide some measure of support.[91]

The health of succeeding generations was the central theme of numerous well-coordinated local garden parties, fetes and baby shows. Conspicuously supported by socially elevated local figures, they received extensive publicity. They tended to be emotional as well as fashionable occasions, with speeches combining statistics of infant and war casualties with confessions of the culpable neglect of children before the war and exhortations to provide, as one dignitary proclaimed, 'a heritage of health for every child born in this country.'[92] An unusually large number of eye-catching photographs of well-known local supporters, and contented babies, accompanied the lengthy press reports.[93]

A speech by the Duchess of Marlborough in June 1917 in Watford epitomised the shift in attitude from contempt for the working mother's apparent ignorance of child care to remembering 'that she had to be constantly waging a war against inadequate housing and poverty' and deserved credit for doing so. Speaking at the same garden party, the Earl of Clarendon was just one of many across the county and country who linked the million rejected recruits with the half-million children leaving school each year with untreated defects. 'The war', he reiterated, 'had thrown a new light on the value of healthy children.'[94] Here, and elsewhere, speakers successfully rallied support by describing the welfare campaign in terms of military conflict – it was a struggle, they asserted, that would both supersede and complement the one in the trenches, in the air and at sea.[95] By the summer of 1917 Watford's borough council already supported the local voluntary dental clinic, and it readily agreed with the Countess of Clarendon's Welfare Committee that the most appropriate form of war memorial would be a health centre funded by public subscription but largely maintained out of the rates.[96] A precedent had been set for the county council.

Medical officers also spoke on the same platforms as distinguished guests, with the same fervour and forthrightness, and to the same enthusiastic response. Their high status in local affairs was reflected not only in their salaries but also in their acceptance as equal and committed partners in the welfare campaign, rather than merely hired experts. Fremantle himself possessed an assured position in society. The son of the Dean of Ripon and the grandson of Lord Cottesloe, he had attended Eton and Balliol College, Oxford, before training at Guy's Hospital. After serving on the Western Front and in Mesopotamia, where his experiences converted him to state-initiated reform on a national scale, he was elected Coalition-Unionist MP for St Albans in December 1919, a seat he held until his death in 1943. He remained an advocate of public health and welfare services, chaired the Parliamentary Medical Committee (1925–1943) and was knighted in 1932.[97] He continued to take a personal interest in county affairs. Although less patrician in background, Thomson still far exceeded the chief education officer in status and salary: £1,250 in 1919 compared with Hallidie's £700.[98]

No elementary school teacher, education officer or HMI had such freedom of speech and prestige. Speaking in Hitchin in July 1917, the district medical officer called the nation 'semi-civilised' for failing to have child health as its first priority, and rejoiced that the need for state action was overcoming the lingering prejudices against public interference in family life.[99] Another doctor wrote with more than a hint of guilt to the *Hertfordshire Express* urging readers – he assumed they were equally middle-class – to:

> think of the constant expert care and tendance that surrounded our own childish lives – the games, the songs, the stories, the pictures that filled and influenced our early days, and compare with those joyous days the life of the child brought up in the one room in which its mother (doubtless as loving and devoted as our own) has to cook, wash, iron and take her meals with husband and family.

He believed the stark domestic comparison, combined with the rewards due to working-class families after the war, more than justified the extension of national welfare care to the provision of state-supported nurseries.[100]

In that summer of 1917 Thomson had no hesitation in publicly highlighting the dire effect of the lost army of youthful recruits upon the nation's military and economic efficiency. It was a telling argument for cost-conscious voters and ratepayers. Losing no opportunity, he asserted that the ill-health of the rising generation, coupled with the slaughter of their elders, placed the very survival of the British Empire in jeopardy. 'Fit and hardy men' were essential to develop and protect the colonies. He did not believe the current war would be the war to end all wars, as many hoped. Playing on the fears of his audience, he foresaw 'a strenuous time of commercial rivalry, and the progress of it depended upon the health of the individual'.[101]

By July 1917 Thomson was proposing nothing less than sweeping preventative measures on a national scale. During the war the government had assumed control over a host of industries and civilian affairs, including price controls and rationing, and Thomson looked towards the provision of cheap medical advice and treatment through a Ministry of Public Health.[102] These views, so radical a few years earlier, met with the fervent approval of his audiences of teachers, doctors, nurses, local councillors and others engaged in social work. Indeed, in Hitchin and Stevenage, as well as Watford, local councils were enthusiastically supporting health and welfare clinics, and the press was right to describe them as 'semi-official in character'.[103]

Many clergy supported reform, and some added a further dimension. One based the need for state intervention upon the moral depravity supposedly rife in 'the overcrowded state of cottages, where decency is almost impossible'.[104] In Stevenage the rector noted how popular the council-subsidised maternity centre had become, but he feared the secularisation of welfare services, as 'the danger always was when the State took over a work that it did not venture to bring God in – it was a system which worked and lost sight of souls and characters.'[105] A third clergyman, however, reinforced the argument of collective guilt and shame which characterised the speeches at garden parties and fetes. 'It needed the war', he confessed, 'to force us to realise the shameful conditions of our social life, of which the waste of child-life is the most glaring symptom.'[106]

Table 6.6 Number of authorities which had made arrangements for medical treatment[107]

Year	Made some arrangements for medical treatment	Provided school clinics	Contributed to hospitals	Made provision for spectacles
1908	55	7	8	21
1912	167	97	37	101
1913	241	139	53	125
1914	266	179	75	165
1915	279	212	78	210
1916	276	219	87	216
1917	279	231	95	223
1918	287	252	110	235

By 1918 Hertfordshire was one of a tiny and shrinking minority of local authorities without any treatment arrangements. Elsewhere, as Table 6.6 above reveals, the greatest strides had been taken in the years immediately preceding the war but, such was the interest and concern, the strict wartime economies had not halted progress towards the universal provision of at least some subsidised treatment.

The national and local pressures were proving irresistible, but the education committee was in no hurry. In June 1917 Thomson had been authorised by the education committee to submit proposals for treatment, and the likely expense, 'for consideration after the termination of the war'.[108] Pank was obliged to acknowledge that parental poverty had caused the county's existing scheme to be far from cost-effective, but he cautioned against any hasty decisions about its extension. Indeed, it had been only the prospect of government aid in the wake of Fisher's Education Bill that had prompted the committee to commission Thomson's costing exercise.[109] Ignoring the example of nearly every other LEA, sympathetic local newspapers lavished praise on the education committee, first for its foresight in agreeing to consider the treatment of children's ailments, and then for its prudence in deferring any action until military victory was assured and the government's grant formula had been clarified. 'A few years ago', waxed the *West Hertfordshire Observer*, 'there would have been bitter opposition to what is being proposed. We should have been told that it was socialistic and that to relieve parents of their responsibility at other people's expense was to establish a dangerous precedent.'[110] The newspaper could well have added, as Sir Charles Longmore, the Clerk to the County Council, readily acknowledged early in 1920, that most members had not changed their attitudes at all as a result of the war.[111] They bowed, briefly they hoped, before the highly charged current of public opinion, but in reality they sought the restoration of their world as it had been in 1914.

Thomson's proposals were not published until April 1918, although the education committee had considered the details, and the likely cost, several months earlier. Thomson envisaged a comprehensive health service, including the establishment of permanent and travelling dental clinics; the establishment of permanent school clinics for the treatment of minor ailments, and incorporating the maternity and welfare clinics, in Barnet, Berkhamsted, Bishop's Stortford, Buntingford or Royston, Cheshunt, Hatfield, Hemel Hempstead, Hertford, Hitchin, St Albans, Tring and Watford, with travelling clinics serving outlying villages; arrangements with specialists in refraction work and opticians to supply spectacles, with parents paying half the cost, and with local hospitals for the operative treatment of enlarged tonsils and adenoids; and arrangements with London hospitals for the X-ray treatment of ringworm.[112]

This scheme was adopted by the education committee in October 1918 with a slim majority just sufficient to overcome the fierce last-ditch opposition of those seeking to impose a means test on families benefiting from the new clinics.[113] Pank made the best of it, reassuring colleagues that half the cost would come from the Treasury. At the end of the debate he attempted to cast the begrudging committee in a more favourable light by asserting that 'they would more than get their money back in the better health of the children, and in preparing them for better citizenship.'[114] Local newspapers were equally platitudinous. The costs were heavy, they said, but, now occupying the moral high ground, they concluded that 'public opinion is sufficiently educated to appreciate the point of view that what is best is cheapest in the long run.'[115]

Thomson had also stated that further measures were vital for raising and maintaining children's health. The LEA should ensure children were adequately fed, and provide meals if necessary. Schools should be well lit, heated and ventilated. They should have sufficient grass and asphalt for open-air lessons and games. Regular lessons should be devoted to inculcating habits of personal hygiene.[116] These recommendations did not form part of Thomson's formal proposals, but the pressure exerted by the school medical service, nationally and locally, for their adoption never went away.

Progress in implementing Thomson's core treatment proposals was slow. By the summer of 1919 houses had been purchased in Hatfield, Hertford, Hitchin, St Albans and Stevenage, but none yet converted into school clinics. Negotiations were still proceeding with hospitals over the fees to be charged under the county scheme.[117] The newspapers had lost interest, but at least the 1918 Education Act now guaranteed elementary schoolchildren would have easier access to the range of treatment recommended at their medical inspections.

Despite the enduring reluctance of Hertfordshire's education committee and county council to spending ratepayers' money on children in general and welfare schemes in particular, the war had provided an immense stimulus to developments in medical care which were already struggling into national existence. As life became cheap in the trenches it grew more precious at home, and the good health of future recruits was more readily appreciated than good schooling as essential to the nation in its time of crisis. Although the reduction of staff due to enlistment caused the school medical service to falter during the war, there was no opposition to the expansion of its work – except when this involved subsidising treatment. Over the question of treatment the advocates of reform, increasingly riding on the crest of a wave of public support, met head-on the entrenched opponents of spending money on the working classes before the resources of voluntary agencies and the remit of the Poor Law Guardians had been exhausted.

Both extremes saw the question in terms of national efficiency. The reformers believed easily accessible and publicly subsidised health services would lead to fitter workers and soldiers, while their opponents remained convinced of the efficacy of moral sanctions, legal compulsion, charity and the Poor Law. Both extremes also saw the question in moral terms. The reformers believed the wealthier sections of society, and the state itself, were guilty of culpable neglect in failing to alleviate the suffering of many poor children, and saw the sacrifices of war as a clear justification for rewards in terms of social reform. They saw poorer working-class families as the victims of hopeless circumstances rather than the feckless perpetrators of their own misery. Their opponents retained a far less elevated view of the working classes, and feared the capacity of enhanced public aid to erode even further their fragile sense of personal morality and responsibility. The war gave the reformers a brief moment of hope, and in 1919 Thomson was determined not to lose the initiative provided by the heightened, if fragile and short-lived, mood of national unity and state obligation.

CHAPTER SEVEN

Continuity and change: Hertfordshire 1914–1939

A T THE END OF 1918 many people sought a return to the world as they thought it had been at the beginning of 1914. However, the dreams of an unchanging ordered society buttressed by British world supremacy were just that – dreams. The disillusion festering in many major industries in the early 1920s reflected the discontent and strikes of the decade before the war, while the constant battle for world markets and the uncertain European peace were problems faced before as well as after 1918. Probably the fervent desire to turn the clock back to halcyon days of the imagination stemmed from the unnerving thought that British society, and perhaps the world, was disintegrating. Across Europe the war had been catastrophic, shattering families, destroying cities, wrecking landscapes, and replacing monolithic kingdoms and empires with unstable republics. For many, a belief in the essentially beneficent qualities of modern culture and civilisation had been dashed for ever.[1]

In Britain the social, political, religious and educational institutions of the pre-war world remained in place, no doubt comforting many people, but these institutions were not quite the same as they used to be. Thanks to Lloyd George's pre-war budgets major landowners faced 40 per cent death duties and taxes on land and leases, as well as the continuing poor returns from agricultural rents. Many decided to sell off at least part of their estates during the 1920s, sometimes to speculative builders, sometimes to wealthy industrialists. Thousands of Nonconformist chapels and Anglican parish churches were witness to the nation's deep but divided religious past, but their congregations were being eroded by the accumulative effect of the scholarly 'higher criticism' of the Bible which discredited its literalism, the rationalisation of science, the nation's increasing if unevenly spread material prosperity, and a reaction against the clergy's general blessing of the war effort. Nevertheless, the chapels and churches remained the social centres in many communities, and most people still desired a church or chapel wedding and funeral.

Class divisions were not eroded by the shared experiences of combat. Although many ordinary servicemen received commissions later in the war, the vast majority of officers continued to come from families well above those of private soldiers in social status. The paternal concern they showed towards the men they commanded did not mean that the differences in social status had been forgotten, or even set aside for the duration. Officers, as always, dressed differently, lived separately and were expected to behave as leaders.

Many women, some middle class but many working class, had taken up posts vacated by men enlisting in the forces. Numerous photographs were published of women bus conductors, railway porters and munitions workers which revealed the novelty of the wartime circumstances as much as the patriotism. The images did, though, belie the fact that many thousands of working-class women had been employed in textile factories and clothing workshops throughout the last century. As the men were demobbed in 1919 many women found they had become unwelcome members of the factory or transport workforce. Depending on their circumstances, the vast majority went back to comfortable unemployment, became full-time housewives or returned to posts in domestic service. Nevertheless, their overall contribution to the war effort had impressed Members of Parliament. After the vigorous, sometimes bitter, and unsuccessful campaigns of the Suffragettes before 1914, the vote was extended to women with little opposition in June 1918 – although until 1928 they had to wait until their thirtieth birthday. Generally speaking, though, the war was remembered more by the erection of thousands of granite crosses on village greens and brass plaques in parish churches than by broadening employment opportunities for women, increasing harmony between the classes, or the creation of sound labour relations by employers and trades unions.

Prices had risen significantly after 1914, especially for food in short supply, and as a result agitation for higher wages was common. Some strikes had taken place among miners, textile workers and munitions workers during the war, although these were as much about union recognition and the rights of skilled workers as about pay. For all the undoubted patriotism pervading the working classes, there was a gradual souring of relations between the government and the trades unions which persisted into the 1920s. Prior to the war the government had stood aloof from disputes between employers and employees, seeing itself as

The war memorial at Harpenden, unveiled by Lieutenant General the Earl of Cavan (HALS)

a conciliator if needed, but mass mobilisation and industrial reorganisation for a conflict fought across the globe had brought it constantly face to face with the nation's workforce. After the war there lurked deep suspicions within the middle classes of the inherent malevolence of the working classes in seeking higher wages when the nation was under threat. On demobilisation the courageous soldier seemed to change out of all recognition when he discarded his rifle for a miner's helmet, riveter's hammer or railwayman's oil can.

Despite the military victory, issues overseas continued to disturb the peace. The legacy of the peace conference at Versailles was the seething discontent in Germany at the humiliating loss of its colonies and territory to Poland, France and Czechoslovakia. The seeds of the crises of the later 1930s and the Second World War had been sown. In addition, the spectre of Bolshevism loomed increasingly large as Lenin established himself in the Soviet Union and preached the gospel of global revolution against the capitalist nations of the West. The fear of revolution never entirely disappeared in Britain after 1918, with repeated utterances from the extreme left and right wings of the political spectrum feeding the unsettling thought that the ambitions of the Labour Party were perilously close to those of the Bolsheviks.[2]

In fact, most Labour supporters disliked what they heard about the Bolshevik terror in former Imperial Russia, but at the same time they had sympathy with anti-capitalist views and the notion of a 'workers' state' or at least a government strongly biased towards the aspirations of the working classes. In the period between the wars socialism, broadly defined as the growth of the collectivist state providing a multitude of welfare benefits through the control of the nation's economic life, was viewed with only marginally less hostility than Bolshevism by Conservatives. Many Conservative parliamentary candidates were only too happy to coat their Labour opponents with the tar of high taxation, the prospect of national bankruptcy, excessive government intervention in ordinary lives and the loss of individual freedoms.

General elections between the wars witnessed the rapid decline of the Liberal Party and the steady consolidation of the Labour Party in the face of the largely dominant Conservative Party. The overall picture, though, belies the periodic swings in party fortunes as particular issues, and the downturns and upturns in the economy, influenced voters. It was the early 1920s that witnessed the most significant realignment in voting patterns, with the Labour Party rapidly establishing itself as the main opposition to the Conservatives and even forming a minority administration between January and November 1924. The Liberals, elected overwhelmingly into government in 1906, had split themselves asunder ten years later when H.H. Asquith, the Prime Minister, was ousted from power in the middle of the war by his vibrant Minister of Munitions, Lloyd George. The mantle of opposition to the Conservatives was taken over by the Labour Party, with its more obviously populist tenets, and the Liberals never recovered.

The 1920s were hardly a time of domestic harmony, although towards their end many families, but far from all, were enjoying a greater degree of comfort than ever before. When the miners lost a bitter strike in 1921 there was widespread rejoicing among the middle classes. By then the post-war overproduction of raw materials had led to prices tumbling, and unemployment soared to two million in 1920–1. During the war Lloyd George had extended insurance against unemployment, which had existed for building, engineering and shipyard workers since 1911, to virtually the entire working class. However, during the 1920s and 1930s the recipients often held the payments to be grossly inadequate and grudgingly given, while many middle-class commentators and politicians believed them to be overly costly to the nation and far too freely available.

The old industries – iron and steel, mining and shipbuilding – failed to recover fully from the 1920–1 depression. Polish and German coal was far cheaper than British coal, and in 1925 the mine owners called for wage cuts. The miners refused and called for improved working conditions. In May 1926 mutual intransigence led to a general strike, with many workers in transport, printing, engineering and power stations joining the miners. After eight days the strike collapsed, the miners were forced to accept the owners' offers, and Stanley Baldwin, the Conservative Prime Minister, ensured tougher anti-strike laws were passed. Government ministers were among the most violently outspoken opponents of the strikers, and national newspapers and meetings abounded with mutually antagonistic cries of capitalist conspiracies and Bolshevik plots. In prosperous Hertfordshire the newspapers hardly noticed the event.

The 1929 general election returned Ramsey Macdonald and the Labour Party to power, although without an overall majority over the Conservatives and the Liberal rump. The government had time to secure Dominion status for India, improve relations with Soviet Russia, pass a Housing Act to attack slums, and fail in several attempts to raise the school leaving age before the effects of the spectacular economic depression in the United States hit Great Britain. British export markets collapsed, and unemployment soared again to 2.5 million by the end of 1930. Conversely, however, the prices of imports fell, and the purchasing power of wages grew. People in work were little affected, and the depression stayed as remote as the general strike to most families in Hertfordshire and other Home Counties.

Nevertheless, the political repercussions were severe. Early in 1931 an economies committee, chaired by Sir George May, recommended reductions in the salaries of all public service workers, and a massive 20 per cent cut in unemployment benefits. The hostility towards the unemployed and the fervent desire to reduce wages ran deep in most industrialists, including those on the May Committee. However, the Cabinet split irreconcilably on the unemployment benefits issue and, to most people's astonishment, in August 1931 Macdonald and Baldwin, with Conservative and some Liberal and Labour support, formed a National Government. As a result Macdonald was expelled from the official Labour Party, which aggressively opposed the coalition. Nevertheless, the cuts came, the unemployed and most public workers, including teachers, losing 10 per cent. Another election in October 1931 confirmed the National Government in power, and although the Labour opposition improved its position in 1935 it was not nearly enough to prevent the National Government serving a further term.

1931 was followed by several years of government parsimony in public spending. The salary and benefits cuts persisted, import tariffs were imposed, and unemployment stayed at around two million.[3] In the end the nation spent itself out of the slump. For many families outside the depressed heavy industrial areas the 1930s were a time of prosperity. Domestic comfort and convenience descended the social scale. By 1930 one house in three had electricity, and by 1939 two houses in three. Householders were soon striving to buy vacuum cleaners, electric cookers, hot water heaters, wireless sets and refrigerators, and a host of products moulded from the new plastics such as Bakelite. They also purchased the ever-widening range of pre-packed processed foods which were entering the shops. Brands such as Kelloggs, Quaker, Heinz, Crosse & Blackwell, Nestle, Bisto and Ovaltine were heavily marketed and quickly popular. The factories that made these and many other consumer products were not dependent upon coalfields and steam power, and they preferred cheap sites nearer key markets, main roads and railways, often on the outskirts of London – including southern Hertford-shire. As the 1930s Hunger Marches of unemployed men from depressed north-ern towns and villages approached London, the housewives of the Home Counties who plied them with refreshments almost certainly made full use of the new convenience tins and packets. Many were probably dressed in the new nylon and rayon dresses and skirts, and used a range of cosmetics that few marchers' wives and daughters could afford.

Between the wars Hertfordshire was a prosperous place. New industries were arriving, and the population explosion made house-building, road improve-ments, town planning, school-building and educational reorganisation subjects of constant debate within and outside the county council and its committees. In 1911 the county's population was 311,284, 20.5 per cent more than in 1901. In 1921 the figure was 333,195, a rise limited by the war to 7 per cent. Thereafter, expan-sion accelerated again to 20.4 per cent, the 1931 census recording 401,206, an increase of 68,011.[4] This rate was consistently in excess of the national average for England and Wales. Between 1911 and 1921 it was 40 per cent greater, but between 1921 and 1931 it was nearly four and a half times as great, exceeded only by nearby Middlesex and Surrey, both more immediately subject to London's pressures.[5] A mid-1939 estimate suggested a county population of 499,200, an increase of 24.4 per cent in eight years, the highest rate in the country.[6]

The uneven distribution of the population was as striking as its overall growth. Those districts easily accessible from London grew fastest, a process accelerated in the south-west from the late 1920s, and around East Barnet from the mid-1930s, by the extension of the Underground railway lines. The 1939 esti-mate showed three distinct zones within Hertfordshire, illustrated here on the

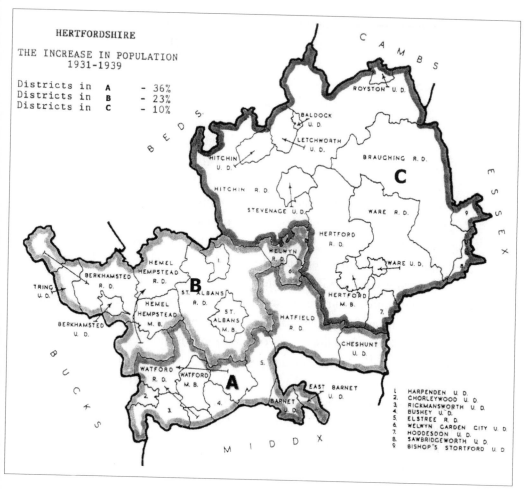

Map of population growth in Hertfordshire

map of population growth.

An area (labelled A on the map) bordering on or extending into Greater
London and comprising the urban districts of Barnet, Bushey, Cheshunt, Chorleywood, East Barnet and Rickmansworth, the rural districts of Elstree, Hatfield
and Watford, and the borough of Watford, increased its population by 36 per
cent in the years since 1931. The population of an adjacent area (labelled B) to the
west and north, comprising the urban districts of Berkhamsted, Harpenden,
Tring and Welwyn Garden City, the rural districts of Berkhamsted, Hemel
Hempstead, St Albans and Welwyn, and the borough of Hemel Hempstead and
city of St Albans, increased by 23 per cent, which was the average for the 'Outer

Ring' of Home Counties. A more distant area (labelled C) further east and north, comprising the urban districts of Baldock, Bishop's Stortford, Hitchin, Hoddesdon, Letchworth, Royston, Sawbridgeworth, Stevenage and Ware, the borough of Hertford, and the rural districts of Braughing, Hertford, Hitchin and Ware, increased its population by only 10 per cent.[7]

The urban–rural divide was stark. In 1931 the twenty-three urban districts and boroughs of Hertfordshire contained 70 per cent of the population in 17 per cent of the available land area. In contrast, the rural districts contained the remaining 30 per cent of the population, thinly scattered over 83 per cent of the land.[8] Of deep concern to the county council was the obvious unattractiveness of country life, with the massive urban influx being accompanied by steady rural depopulation. All areas were affected, but the east and north, and far west, strikingly so. Between 1921 and 1931 three rural and three urban districts, all dominated by agriculture despite their official appellations, suffered a net *loss* of population through migration – the urban districts of Royston, Ware and Tring lost 0.2 per cent, 2 per cent and 2.6 per cent respectively, and the rural districts of Hadham, Ashwell and Buntingford lost 2.5 per cent, 3.2 per cent and 7.2 per cent. A seventh, Ware rural district, barely made the positive list with a rise of 0.8 per cent. These negative trends had existed in 1911, and they had as dramatic an effect upon county policies as the remorseless urban growth.[9]

The censuses reveal the accompanying changes in people's employment. Although the alterations in job descriptions and occupational categories in the 1911, 1921 and 1931 censuses make exact comparisons difficult, the trends are clear. There was a slight but consistent decline in agricultural employment, a category that also included those engaged in commercial market gardening and outdoor work on landed estates, from 22,181 in 1911 to 21,111 in 1921 and 20,320 in 1931.[10] Agriculture's importance was undoubted, but the National Farmers' Union and county agriculture committee were perpetually pessimistic about its ability to survive. All agricultural prices began to spiral downwards in 1921 after the Ministry of Food relinquished control over prices and markets. There were several years of widespread losses when output prices were lower than production costs, until prices eventually stabilised at a level a little higher than pre-war days. The numerous arable farms in the county, as elsewhere, suffered from the rising world production of grain and the consequent price squeeze.[11] A 1929–30 survey of Hertfordshire showed that only the most intensive and scientifically run arable or mixed farms were worthwhile.[12]

Although the national agricultural lobby failed to secure more than minimal tariffs, subsidies gradually grew during the 1930s to £40,000,000 a year. The 1930s also saw the agricultural marketing boards given greater powers to encourage particular aspects of agriculture, notably milk, pork, and potato production.[13] No government, however, halted the emigration of workers. Farmers strove to maintain a working week of sixty hours while many industries were moving towards forty-eight hours. Wages were reduced to an average of 28s a week in the early 1920s, and the lure of urban living was entirely understandable when 28s represented merely a 55 per cent increase on the pre-war average wage of 18s, whereas the cost of living index was at least 75 per cent higher.[14]

The largely depressed Hertfordshire countryside contrasted sharply with the largely prosperous towns. Unemployment was present, but even in 1931, one of the worst years of depression, male unemployment was 6.2 per cent, around half the national average of 12.7 per cent.[15] The preponderance of modern commercial occupations inured the towns against the recessions blighting the traditional textile, mining and iron and steel industries of South Wales and the North. In 1933 the popular writer J.B. Priestley made an extensive tour of England and the following year his *English Journey* was published. He had found three different Englands. The first was the England of scattered villages, farms, churches, squires, craftsmen and workers, complete with a traditional cycle of festivals and customs. The second was the England of grimy industrial towns, with towering factories, the sounds of trains, trams and hooters, endless mean streets, and men on the dole. The third was the new England of modern houses surrounded by small but neat gardens, with mains water, electricity and gas supplies, easy access to shopping arcades, cinemas and other recreational facilities, and a variety of employment opportunities in clean new factories and offices. Hertfordshire incorporated much of the first, very little of the second and a great deal of the third.[16]

In all the occupations associated with a modern urbanised society, numbers grew significantly – sometimes steadily, sometimes soaring. Indoor servants remained numerous, increasing from 17,535 in 1911 to 20,033 in 1931 after a small fall to 16,095 in 1921, but the roles were becoming far more diversified than the large and strictly regulated staff maintaining a major country estate or the lonely 'skivvy' in a far more modest household.[17] The post-war rise was almost certainly a response to the influx of hotels, restaurants, works canteens and affluent middle-class families as much as to the continuing residence of many wealthy titled and non-titled families.

Those categorised as clerks, including typists and the lower grade of local and central government officers, almost quadrupled in number, from 4,876 in 1911 to 13,068 in 1921 and 18,367 in 1931. Those engaged in commerce other than as clerks, such as bank staff, retail proprietors and sales assistants, nearly doubled: in 1911 they numbered 10,612, in 1921, 13,643, and in 1931, 20,992. Those employed in heavy and light metalwork more than doubled, from 4,477 in 1911 to 7,464 in 1921 and 9,095 in 1931. Included in these totals were just 13 motor mechanics in 1911, but 656 in 1921 and 1,102 in 1931. Similarly, the growing demand for electrical goods, accessories and services caused numbers to multiply five-fold, from 473 in 1911 to 1,319 in 1921 and then to 2,453 in 1931. The renowned paper-making and printing industries, largely concentrated around Watford and Hemel Hempstead, continued to grow: in 1911 5,326 people were employed, in 1921 the total was 5,982, and in 1931 it was 7,520. Equally steady growth occurred in the numbers employed in road, rail, and to a now miniscule extent, canal transport, from 10,551 in 1911 to 10,299 in 1921 and 13,937 in 1931.

The furriers, skinners, tanners and leather-dressers, well-known in several northern and eastern towns, continued to employ about 400 people throughout the period, but other labour-intensive traditional industries proved uncompetitive, and faded away. The making of willow baskets occupied only 84 in 1911 and just 35 in 1931, and straw hat making and plaiting employed 1,496 in 1911 but by 1921 had disappeared as separate census categories. These casualties, and also the slow decline in local malting, were offset by the arrival of large hosiery factories and food processing plants, notably in the Garden Cities and St Albans, which kept the overall numbers engaged in the clothing and food industries in 1931 at 6,716 and 2,346 respectively. These were somewhat lower than the 1911 figures of 9,266 and 2,763, but many employees, for better or for worse, were working in very different industrial environments from the cottage and small-scale family businesses that had hitherto prevailed.

Not surprisingly the building trade thrived, employing 11,514 in 1911 and, after the wartime standstill, 16,132 in 1931. The proliferation of new housing estates reflected the gradations of wealth and class. Between 1921 and 1931 Hertfordshire witnessed a 34 per cent rise in housing, from 76,159 to 102,853, and the 1951 census intimates that the pace accelerated during the 1930s.[18] A few estates were luxurious, such as Moor Park and others at Tewin, Chorleywood and Park Street, but most houses in the speculative developments were aimed at a mass market of modest mortgage payers. The advertisements for the large Marshalswick estate in St Albans in 1925 were aimed directly at lower-middle-class aspirations for status, health, happiness, comfort and security, and many other advertisements followed suit.[19] They made greater play with the easy access to the adjacent countryside than the undoubted conveniences of town life. Paradoxically, as the towns spread across the fields, they tended to be represented as dirty, depressing and decadent while the countryside they eroded was presented as clean, revitalising and pure. The new residential estates were very much urban cuckoos in rural nests.

The largely semi-detached houses, with their variety of hipped roofs, ornamental gables, pebble-dashed walls, brick entrance arches, leaded windows, flower beds and privet hedges, spread thickly over southern and western Hertfordshire, and appeared in clusters around the market towns of the north and east. Although all the new properties pandered to suburban dreams, some were more obviously middle-class than others. A few had two bedrooms, most had three; some had garages, most left space for one; all had bathrooms, two reception rooms, kitchen fittings and deep narrow gardens. Nearly all new houses had electricity by 1930.[20]

Not everyone welcomed their arrival in such numbers. Lieutenant Colonel Fremantle, MP for St Albans, railed against the unfettered 'ribbon development' straddling the roads on the outskirts of most Hertfordshire towns, and he viewed the 'little houses of stucco and yellow brick' and 'the new blocks and streets' created by speculators and district councils alike as the slums of the next generation 'being created under our very eyes'. He condemned, too, the prolonged failure to halt London 'oozing out, like a blotch of tar' to engulf Middlesex and threaten the continuing independent existence of Hertfordshire.[21] Despite many agreeing with Fremantle, effective action was frustrated by a combination of the county council's fears of expense and controversy, the farmers' and country house owners' willingness to sell their fields, and the government's failure to protect stretches of land, compensate owners and bestow mandatory powers upon local authorities.[22] The Restriction of Ribbon Development Act of 1935, despite the precision of its title, was a case of far too little far too late.

With varying degrees of interest and enthusiasm some district councils made efforts to reduce the number of existing slums. 'Homes for Heroes' had been a 1918 election cry, and housing was the major post-war domestic issue. In 1919 Christopher Addison, the Minister of Health, implemented a generous subsidy scheme to encourage local authority construction. In Hitchin, for long derided by Letchworth as 'Sleepy Hollow', the paralysing grip of the reactionary Quaker-dominated council was loosened sufficiently by a coterie of progressive councillors to allow plans to be prepared for the eradication of a notorious warren of slums. Seventy-eight council houses were built in 1920, and five years later 190 decrepit properties in the town's centre were demolished and the families rehoused on new municipal estates.[23]

In Watford the task was greater, but so was the commitment to reform. After the war a united council proposed 2,000 new homes, 500 of them to replace 'insanitary areas'. The first 50 were completed in 1920, and although progress was erratic, largely due to administrative delays, shortage of materials and trades union action, by 1935 few slums survived and 1,352 council houses occupied three large estates.[24] At the other end of the spectrum, St Albans City Council steadfastly delayed all action until 1924, when it was faced with incontrovertible evidence of the evil conditions in its midst in a well-publicised housing report initiated by the Bishop of St Albans. The inquiry had surveyed 718 houses – a 20 per cent sample across the range of working-class homes – and found:

> 296 houses with no sink; 38 houses with no copper; many coppers shared by several families; many defective; only 50 out of 718 houses with any ventilated store for food; 94 houses sharing sanitary arrangements with others; 156 houses sharing their tap with one to eight other houses; houses with leaking roofs, tins in bedrooms to catch rain; houses infested with vermin, although occupied by tenants who do their best to cleanse them.[25]

By the end of 1928 8,892 council houses for rent had been or were being erected in Hertfordshire. The waiting list still totalled 4,912, but subsidies had been secured for another 3,269 houses under the Small Dwellings Acquisition Act. Sir Edmund Barnard, chairman of the county council, felt justified in expressing cautious satisfaction with the general progress.[26]

Highways were another persistent bone of contention, with the rising costs of new roads and improvements to old ones causing as many protests from economically minded county councillors as the rising costs of elementary education. In 1927, for example, the *Hertfordshire Mercury* reported the acerbic Holland-Hibbert's satisfaction 'that the Highways Committee was gradually coming round to his view that it was not necessary to round off all narrow and so-called dangerous corners.'[27] Accusations that much of the wear and tear was caused by 'foreign traffic' passing between London and the Midlands and North were often used to pare down the Highways Committee budget, amid strident criticisms of grossly inadequate government grants.[28] In 1935 Sir Joseph Priestley, the county council chairman, bemoaned the lack of coordination and investment. 'No-one who lives out of the town', he observed, 'can fail to be impressed by the failure of our Hertfordshire roads, as a whole, to accommodate the modern needs of traffic.' He thought the A-roads were 'fairly satisfactory', but the older roads winding through the countryside were 'so dangerous, with their turns and twists and narrow sunken levels, that in many places two vehicles cannot pass each other.' 'They are positive death traps', he concluded, completely unsuited to the vans and lorries now using them.[29]

HMI E.F.D. Bloom, who had suceeded Marvin as District Inspector in 1919, shared Priestley's concern. He accepted that unimproved country lanes had as much impact as fast arterial roads upon the success of educational reorganisation schemes, especially in the eyes of anxious parents whose children might have to traverse them each day. Most districts contained both dangerous extremes, and Bloom took them into account in his recommendations.[30] It was only in 1935 that the county council announced a five-year road improvement programme, largely on routes into or around East Barnet, Hatfield, Hertford, Rickmansworth, St Albans and Watford, taking advantage of the increased grants offered by the Ministry of Transport.[31] Mounting traffic congestion, an alarming rise in accidents and an intensive road-safety campaign in newspapers and schools led to an acceptance by the county council of the need for traffic lights, warning signs and roundabouts, but not until 1938. By then local censuses showed that traffic had increased by 128 per cent between 1928 and 1938, and the numbers killed and injured each year had kept on rising – from 30 and 584 in 1924, to 74 and 1,737 in 1934, and 78 and 2,053 in 1938.[32]

Motor buses made regular daily runs within and between major towns, and they were reaching most villages at least once or twice a week. Car ownership soared. The first car and travel supplement appeared in the *Hertfordshire Express* in April 1923 and the first Olympia Motor Show Supplement appeared that November.[33] Local newspapers also encouraged the penchant for domestic tourism with articles celebrating the beauty of the hills, valleys and villages of Hertfordshire.[34] The county also figured prominently in more widely available books popularising the Home Counties. In 1927, for example, the author of *London's Countryside*, a title neatly reflecting the perspective of the capital, bemoaned the 'indiscriminate buildings' and 'succession of motorways' radiating into the Home Counties, but delighted in the antiquities of St Albans, the Cecil influence upon unindustrialised Hatfield, and the undulating park scenery still to be viewed around Elstree and North Mimms.[35] Ten years later such explorations had become commonplace. Modern public and private transport, claimed one London author in 1937, 'have made the Home Counties seem like one vast playground laid out almost at our doors'. Once there, 'one need only leave the main roads to enjoy complete solitude.'[36] The depressed countryside and its communities, that were causing so much anxiety among all those with a vested interest in rural affairs, were being hailed as gems of the national heritage at one of the most worrying times in their history.

The railways reached their greatest extent in Hertfordshire between the wars. Many of them maintained important commuter links with London, but not all the lines prospered commercially. In the east the LNER line through Bishop's Stortford to Liverpool Street was too slow to attract many long-distance commuters but it did cater well for the factories and market gardens of the Lea valley. Its branch to Ware and Hertford, serving the local foundries, maltings and breweries, prospered, but the winding rural line to Buntingford encouraged only intermittent house-building in Much Hadham, Standon, Puckeridge and Buntingford itself.[37] Other lines also failed to fulfil expectations. The east–west branch lines from Hatfield to Welwyn and Hertford proved failures due to sparse services and under-investment, and the lengthy 'Hertford and Cuffley Loop', which opened in 1924 to supplement the main LNER line north of Hatfield, was damned the following year by Fremantle in a Commons debate as 'the most ineffective and the most useless service that was ever put on any main line in the United Kingdom.'[38]

In contrast, the original, faster, Hatfield route did contribute significantly to the development of towns along its route. Hitchin expanded, with electrical and aero-engineering factories, Hatfield was transformed by the vast de Haviland aeroplane works and associated industries, and Welwyn Garden City hosted the arrival of numerous manufacturing concerns after its own creation in 1924. Flanked by Letchworth's industrial estates, the Royston and Baldock line provided a fast and popular service via Hitchin to London, including the 'Garden City Express' inaugurated in 1932.[39]

By 1914 both Watford and St Albans were terminating points for regular if limited suburban services to London, but between the wars daily trains increased to sixty each way and, as HMI Bloom carefully noted, a branch line took many St Albans residents to work in Watford.[40] In the 1920s electrification reinvigorated the struggling branch lines to the mills and market gardens of Croxley Green and Rickmansworth, and soon stimulated extensive residential developments.[41] These lines also benefited from the nearby Metropolitan Railway's vigorous promotion of suburban traffic through Middlesex, south-west Hertfordshire and into mid-Buckinghamshire by a policy of electrification, frequent services, cheap fares, lavish advertising and speculative building. In 1925 the Metropolitan line was electrified to Rickmansworth and an extension opened to Watford. Between then and

1939 the flood tide of 'Metroland' commuter housing swept across this corner of the county.[42] Once again, the *rus in urbe* dream was successfully invoked.

The difficulties caused to the users and improvers of roads by the ridges and valleys along the south Hertfordshire plateau, which Bloom had noted in his reports, also delayed the extension of rapid and frequent railway links to the Barnets. The LNER's lack of investment prolonged the unpopular slow suburban steam services on the Totteridge and High Barnet branch lines until the 1940s but, in final proof of the dramatic impact of electrification, the extension of the Piccadilly line to Cockfosters in 1933 transformed East Barnet from a patchwork of farms, villages and small estates to continuous suburbia in six years.[43] As a result, the county council was almost overwhelmed with the demands for schools and other public services.

The proximity to a main railway line and the availability of the necessary acres had been primary factors in the creation of Ebenezer Howard's first Garden City at Letchworth, and the same reasons of convenience led to his second being sited between Welwyn and Hatfield in 1920.[44] Both Garden Cities became primarily manufacturing towns, employing most of the working population resident within their boundaries. Major manufacturers turned out motor vehicles, heavy machinery, piping and sheeting, and office equipment. Numerous electrical companies made wireless sets, heating systems and lighting equipment. There were mass producers of furniture, clothes, cosmetics, medicine, books and processed foods, including the famous Welgar Shredded Wheat.[45]

The aims of Letchworth and Welwyn Garden Cities were nothing less than the overt avoidance of the evils of overcrowded towns and the wasting depopulation of the countryside through the democratically agreed planned development of a society fully integrating the resources of the land, industry, technology and human skills. Wide and easily accessible employment opportunities were an integral part of Garden City planning, and so was the philosophy that those involved in commerce and industry should contribute to the common good as much as those involved with schools, civic amenities, public health and social welfare agencies.[46]

Contemporary attitudes towards children and education perturbed the pioneers greatly. They believed, and they were not alone in believing, that the current mix of educational provision perpetuated class divisions, encouraged religious divides, inculcated an unhealthy competitive spirit, and preserved the assumption that the vast majority of occupations in industry and commerce where workers' hands got dirty were markedly inferior to those in offices and administration

Birds Hill, Letchworth, c.1927 (HALS)

where hands stayed clean. To a significant extent, the Garden Cities saw social reconstruction in terms of radical educational reform.[47]

Although the Garden City pioneers challenged many contemporary educational practices, ideologically they did not wish to stand outside the public system, and financially they could not afford to do so. They exerted influence through elected membership of local, district and county councils, well-orchestrated local campaigns and impeccable educational and financial arguments. During the economic crises and political anxieties of the inter-war decades, the two Hertfordshire Garden Cities stood for partnership and peaceful change, and certainly not revolution in the Bolshevik sense so feared by many at this time.

After the war Letchworth's growing prosperity, and diminishing self-glorification, earned the grudging respect of more ancient towns, and none more so than neighbouring Hitchin. In 1932 Reginald Hine, the Hitchin historian, recalled that the overthrow of the Quaker dominance of his town owed much to Letchworth's example. Hitchin initially condemned as 'dithering' Letchworth's predilection for discussing every issue at length in public but, as Hine recorded in imaginative but not unbelievable prose, attitudes changed in the early 1920s as:

> first one and then another of our people took their lives in their hands and spoke,
> even from the house-tops, of grievances to be redressed, of old things to be made
> new, of town planning, of road building, of slum clearing, of many other things,
> and with us, as with the pioneers of Letchworth, the modern world with its chal-
> lenge, and its calls to social service, lay open to our view.[48]

It was the Letchworth architects who eventually organised the slum clearance
schemes in Hitchin, and assisted with the provision of civic improvements. Hine
recalled how the new town helped out in other ways when declining rural market
fortunes obliged:

> the strait-laced people of Hitchin ... [to] send their sons and daughters to Letch-
> worth to make corsets, which Letchworth women obviously never wear, but
> which their husbands sell at great profit to the less enlightened women in other
> towns.[49]

Letchworth also promoted the educational use of museums and historic sites
across north Hertfordshire, and in 1924 it was feeding electricity from its own
supplies to Baldock and adjacent villages.[50]

For deeply held reasons of social justice and educational opportunity the idea
of sequential and universal primary and secondary education was supremely
important to Letchworth, and in due course to Welwyn Garden City. Writers and
speakers argued that this reform would not only enhance the educational and
vocational choices available to children but also would remove the pernicious
association of types of education with particular social classes. The integration of
subjects was important, too. As W.R. Hughes explained, a fundamental principle
was:

> to arrange and relate our courses, practical and theoretical, that from the begin-
> ning knowledge will appear to the child as a unity and synthesis and not as a hap-
> hazard collection of facts, only accidentally related.[51]

As many studies as possible would be related to real life – to farming, to industry,
to civics, and to household management – and to personal expression and fulfilment through oral lessons, poetry, music, dance and a range of arts and crafts.
Cooperation, not competition, was the teaching watchword, with an emphasis
upon individual projects, group activities and mutual support. Strong
home–school partnerships were essential, with parents fully consulted about
their children's abilities, interests and progress.[52]

In a striking passage Hughes pinpointed the irreparable damage he believed

Aerial view of Welwyn Garden City under development in the 1920s (HALS)

was done to children by teachers who themselves had been deeply damaged by their environment and upbringing. They could only be compared, he wrote, to 'the much-talked-of mother who feeds her baby on the pressed beef and pickles and tea which satisfy her own distorted appetite.'[53] With more than a hint of Garden City glorification reappearing, Hughes equated the school buildings and teaching methods generally to be found outside Letchworth with the unjust imprisonment of children and crippling mental and physical malnourishment. Letchworth certainly did not possess the monopoly of sound school buildings and good teaching in the county, but it did put its principles into practice in its first schools. They were relatively spacious, with Garden City Company funds and donations contributing to their facilities. They were genuinely co-educational, they adopted a liberal curriculum, and they paid close attention to children with physical handicaps and learning difficulties. The town's Parents' Educational Association became a vocal discussion and pressure group.[54]

The same was true of Welwyn Garden City, which grew from green fields to prosperous industrial town at breakneck speed during the inter-war years. The construction of its first all-age school was threatened by the 1921 economic depression, but the Garden City presented the LEA with a financially attractive offer of Garden City architects and builders it could not refuse.[55] In May 1923 the new-style part-timber, part-concrete slab and wholly flat-roofed building, designed by Louis de Soissons, was opened amid great publicity by Edward Wood, President of the Board, and heralded as a masterpiece of light, airy and spacious design. It was surrounded by woodland, allotments, tarred playgrounds and games fields – all reserved exclusively for the children's use. As the deeply Conservative Wood and other dignitaries were confidently informed at the opening ceremony, secondary education for all would follow on naturally from primary education, and not be separate from it. Wood duly, and maybe wryly, wished the town good luck in its aspirations.[56] His conception of a socially elevated secondary grammar school education catering largely for fee-payers and a miniscule percentage of scholarship entrants was far removed from the Garden Cities' ideas of a wide-ranging and well-resourced programme available to all.

The avowed aim of the new school's managers was to 'make the school so efficient and attractive that parents will have no occasion to look elsewhere.'[57] Part of this attraction was the appointment of an experienced headmaster holding the degrees of Bachelor of Science and Master of Arts. Up to the age of eight play methods would dominate the school's work; between eight and eleven a careful balance would be struck between academic, aesthetic and practical education; and between eleven and fifteen or sixteen academic, agricultural and technical courses would be developed, each possessing equal staffing, facilities and status. The elementary–secondary divide would be ignored.[58] Certainly, the new all-age school buildings, grounds and equipment were proof of this intention, and the term 'elementary' was never used in local newspaper reports or speeches. Letchworth's Parents' Educational Association warmly endorsed Welwyn's actions, including the 'linking up of voluntary with public resources', stating they would 'give a chance to all children in the school to benefit by secondary education without seeking a fresh school.'[59]

The political face and public policies of the county council were far removed from those of the Garden Cities, but nevertheless some aspirations were held in common, and the LEA had far fewer disputes with these new communities during the inter-war years than it did with many other towns. Partly this was due to the financial incentives the Garden City Companies brought to negotiations, but the importance they attached to practical, technical and vocational education was mirrored by the LEA's own clear-sighted policies during this period, even though they stemmed from very different social assumptions, economic arguments, and perceptions of education. In addition, the reports, correspondence and editorials in county newspapers, and education committee minutes, all reveal that although many perceived the Garden Cities as rather odd, they also came to recognise and admire, if sometimes grudgingly, the ideals they practised and promoted. Town planning, slum clearance, civic services and educational reorganisation were all pressing questions between the wars, and the Garden Cities seemed to have constructive answers to them all.

After the war, as before it, the county council and education committee made a virtue out of listening to, and whenever possible acceding to, local wishes regarding capital expenditure on school buildings. Not surprisingly, the disparate villages and towns across Hertfordshire varied widely in their opinions on the subject, and the district education sub-committees were important links in the decision-making process. The sub-committees were composed of representatives, usually nominated rather than elected, from among the ranks of county, district and parish councillors, school managers and churchmen, and co-opted members with educational interests and local prestige. Local deliberations were sharpened by the fact that civil parishes had to bear up to 75 per cent of the county council's share of the cost of capital improvements to schools. No doubt the stricture helped to wreck or minimise many proposals, although the Garden Cities were adept at using it to their advantage. In 1926, for example, a spate of paralysing disagreements within some towns over improvement schemes led Captain Morris, the chairman of the education committee, to state complacently that:

> the aim and object of the Education Committee was in every way possible to meet the wishes of the locality concerned, recognising that upon it fell the great proportion of the expenditure which must be incurred.[60]

Hertfordshire was the last county to relinquish this practice, which persisted until 1937, when extensive parish boundary revisions and the creation of large senior schools and broader catchment areas rendered it impossible to implement.[61]

In 1918 the county council was still run on essentially patrician lines with minimal public expenditure and change remaining the major guidelines. Sir Charles Longmore, the Clerk of the County Council, continued in the office he had held since 1894, with his influence probably reaching a peak during the chairmanship of his friend, Sir Edmund Barnard, between 1920 and 1930. Longmore died, reportedly of shock, shortly after Barnard suffered a fatal seizure during a council meeting, and he was succeeded in all his offices for another eighteen years by his son and deputy, Major Elton Longmore.[62] It is an indication of the Longmore influence that the succession was immediate and unchallenged, and an indication of the father's pre-eminence that the county council reduced the son's emoluments.

As late as 1938, when Sir Joseph Priestley, Barnard's successor, was praising the loyalty and diligence of long-serving officers, including the accountant, land-agent, surveyor and education officer, he noted with approval that all of them were 'legacies from Sir Charles Longmore, brought up by him in his tradition.'[63] If the role of the chief education officer was an example of that long-lasting tradition, fundamentally it meant the efficient execution of education committee and county council policies without making any significant contribution, outside technical advice, to those policies. Archibald Hallidie and his successor Samuel Howe made no public speeches, were only rarely quoted in newspapers and remained completely subordinate to Sir Charles and his son. Indeed, both remained little more than senior clerks in the Clerk's Department throughout their periods in office. They were far removed from dynamic directors of education such as James Graham of Leeds, Percival Sharp of Sheffield, Spurley Hey of Manchester and William Brockington of Leicestershire, who took responsibility for policymaking, relished innovation and often dominated their education committees.

It is not difficult to imagine Sir Charles' control of Howe's appointment when Hallidie retired in 1926. The education committee accepted without demur that:

> the real essentials for the post of Education Officer are experience, tact and common sense to cope with the various contingencies which daily present themselves. [64]

They accepted, too, that these worthy, if less than illustrious, qualities, together with a mastery of technical detail and intimate local knowledge, were conveniently identified in S.W. Howe who for the past twenty years had been an assistant solicitor specialising in educational and agricultural affairs in the Longmore family firm. Howe fully justified his superior's confidence until his own retirement in 1940. He was one of few remaining English and Welsh chief education officers during the period without any teaching experience.[65]

The county council and its major sub-committees, such as education, highways and agriculture, kept firm hold of policymaking, and their chairmen remained influential figures. They were sensitive to ratepayers' opinions, but when education issues were under consideration it was the needs of urban and rural employers that were uppermost in mind. Attitudes had barely changed since before the war. Indeed, old attitudes were stronger than ever as the volatile post-war economy rocked the confidence of councillors, employers and parents.

Sir Edmund Barnard (HALS)

Most people accepted that the grammar schools were the preserve of fee-payers and a few fortunate scholarship winners, who were destined for 'white-collar' occupations largely beyond the reach of the vast majority of the county's children attending the elementary schools. Certainly, most county councillors believed that the role of the elementary schools was to do what they had done in the previous century – namely, to prepare the vast majority of children for semi-skilled and unskilled posts in agriculture, industry, commerce and domestic service, and inculcate in them the virtues of diligence, honesty, humility, perseverance, cleanliness, self-respect and grateful acceptance of one's lot.

When Edmund Barnard succeeded Sir Thomas Halsey as chairman of the county council in 1920 the tradition of Liberals and Conservatives alternating office continued, although until the 1930s all members assumed Independent status and eschewed party politics in local affairs. The Barnard family had owned extensive farmland in and around Sawbridgeworth for several generations, and they had founded and endowed local elementary schools in the previous century. Knighted in 1928, Edmund Barnard had been Liberal MP for Kidderminster between 1906 and 1910, and was chairman of the Metropolitan Water Board and

The Rev. Canon G.H.P. Glossop (HALS) Captain Edward Morris (HALS)

Lea Conservancy Board.[66]

He was succeeded by two chairmen whose wealth and influence stemmed from professional and business interests rather than land, although both possessed modest country estates. Sir Joseph Priestley was a successful lawyer, created KC in 1903 and knighted in 1927. He had purchased Tatmore Place, Hitchin, and chaired Hertfordshire Quarter Sessions for over twenty-five years, and the county council for nine, from 1930 to 1939.[67] Sir David Rutherford, the owner of Powis Court, Bushey Heath, and director of two national assurance companies, succeeded Priestley in time to welcome members to the wartime opening of the new council chamber.[68]

Liberals and Conservatives also alternated as chairmen of the education committee, but again party politics never overtly invaded debates until the 1930s. John Lovell Pank was elected chairman in 1902, and dominated the committee until his death in 1923. He was perfectly in tune with most members' opinions regarding the 1918 Education Act when he gloomily forecast that it 'will be a most expensive one to work'.[69] In an unusual but clearly popular appointment, the Reverend Canon G.H.P Glossop was elected Pank's successor. Liberal in politics, Glossop was admired for his acumen in guiding the financial affairs of the diocese of St Albans, and universally recognised for his work on behalf of the foster care of orphans, the education of blind and deaf children and promotion of the

William Graveson (left), S.W. Howe (far right) and R.R. Bunn (next to Howe) (British Library)

County Museum. 'For education', the press acclaimed, 'he had an unusually keen enthusiasm.' His ecumenical qualities were recognised by the gift of a car from fellow councillors and diocesan friends on his election, and he had the rare distinction of holding governorships of Nonconformist foundations such as Bishop's Stortford College.[70]

Glossop died suddenly in 1925, to be succeeded by a prominent east Hertfordshire farmer, Captain Edward Morris. During five years in office, Morris successfully marshalled local support for policies aimed directly at the promotion of rural education and regeneration. Closely involved with the National Farmers' Union, Morris was elected the national chairman in 1930 and resigned his post on the education committee.[71] William Graveson succeeded Morris, holding office until a few months before his death in August 1939. Liberal, and a staunch

Quaker, Graveson had relinquished active involvement in the family draper's business in Hertford to concentrate upon public affairs. A noted naturalist and lover of literature, Graveson promoted local libraries, published popular books on Hertfordshire wildlife and was devoted to the preservation of the county's countryside.[72] He shared the concern of Captain Morris, an Anglican and Conservative, to quench the fires of sectarian controversy which seemed likely to be rekindled over religious education and school reorganisation in the late 1920s.

In 1931 George (later Lord) Lindgren, a railway clerk from Welwyn Garden City, became the first Labour county councillor in Hertfordshire.[73] He had already contributed significantly to the Labour dominance of his district council. In 1932 he was joined by H.J. Bridger, a self-made businessman, and T.R. Clark from Watford, and after the 1937 county council elections the Labour caucus numbered seven. To the mixed amusement and disgust of most other members, they announced a new era in county affairs by declaring themselves the 'official opposition'.[74] Self-confident, energetic and articulate, Lindgren made adroit use of the club-like style of debating and decision-making which had long characterised county affairs. His partisan challenges to majority assumptions and opinions were made all the more discomforting by his meticulous respect for the rules of the chamber and mastery of detail.[75] Both Holland-Hibbert and Lord Salisbury were avid promoters of absolute economy in public spending and, typically, in 1932 Holland-Hibbert proclaimed with pride that 'of the 48 counties in England … 42 exceeded Hertfordshire in the cost of education.'[76] Such repeated assertions led Lindgren to give a speech the following year utterly condemning the parsimony and paternalism which had governed the provision of the county's services for so long. He stated with contempt what others claimed with pride, 'that in almost every department of the County Council the minimum required by the legislation of the Central Authority had been the maximum of Hertfordshire.' The best that could be said, he lamented, was that 'a particularly high level of charitable benevolence, especially in the rural areas, has made the meagre nature of some of the County's services less grievous than it otherwise would have been.' He gave warning of mounting dissatisfaction with such superannuated class-ridden practices.[77]

The warnings did not count for much before 1939. Outside Watford and Welwyn Garden City, Labour maintained only a minority and patchy presence on local councils, and was in decline during the late 1930s. By 1936 Labour had lost all its seats on Barnet, East Barnet and Friern Barnet urban district councils, and despite determined campaigns it failed to advance in Baldock, Hitchin and

Letchworth in 1937, and Stevenage and Ware in 1938.[78] The Labour 'opposition' on the county council faced fifty-nine Independent members with marked Conservative or Liberal leanings. When it came to educational debates, Lindgren argued for more practical, more technical, more vocational and more secondary education. Ironically, with regard to the first three he was preaching to the already converted, and he stood no chance of success with the last.

A national study by historians Brian Keith-Lucas and Peter Richards, and a local study of Cheshire by J.M. Lee, have revealed how unusual Hertfordshire was in retaining the active interest and involvement of so many major landowners, especially titled ones, in county council affairs after 1918.[79] The Marquis of Salisbury, the Earl of Clarendon, the Earl of Strafford, the Earl of Verulam, Viscount Hampden, Lord Brocket, the Honourable Arthur Holland-Hibbert, Sir Frederick Halsey Bt, Sir Lionel Faudel-Phillips Bt, Sir Charles Hadden, Sir Edmund Barnard and Colonel Abel Smith all possessed county estates, were all local benefactors, were all actively involved in county agricultural circles, and all attended county council meetings as Independent aldermen or elected members for all or part of the inter-war period.

Throughout the period it continued to be made easy for such families to take part in county council business. It remained customary for the heads of major county families to be invited to fill the next aldermanic vacancy after inheriting the estates, and even to become a county councillor involved no loss of dignity as no well-known members had their election contested. In 1920 Sir Charles Hadden was unusual only in emphasising publicly that he accepted his nomination in the agricultural interest on condition he was not opposed.[80] Indeed, as late as 1937, when Labour mounted its greatest challenge for seats, thirty-five out of the forty-seven sitting members were returned unopposed.[81]

As the Liberal party faded nationally amidst bitter arguments between its warring factions, and as the Labour party grew in strength largely, but not exclusively, across the industrial conurbations of the Midlands, the North, Scotland and South Wales, the Conservative party attracted an increasing percentage of voters in parliamentary elections in prosperous constituencies such as those in Hertfordshire. In Hertfordshire the days of close-fought elections between Liberals and Conservatives faded away, and the last Liberal MP in the county briefly held the seat of Hemel Hempstead by just seventeen votes from December 1923 until ousted by a large Conservative majority the following October. Here, and also in Hertford, a strong Nonconformist presence usually kept the Liberals in second place, but in St Albans, Hitchin and Watford the Labour party was increasingly the one to beat. All five county constituencies saw comfortable victories for Conservative candidates in 1918 and 1922, except in Hertford where Noel Pemberton Billing, a colourful right-wing Independent and popular proponent of British air power, triumphed in 1918 because no official Conservative candidate stood against him. The Labour and Liberal votes rose in the 1923 election when the Conservatives nationally were in brief disarray, but not enough to dislodge any Conservative candidate outside Hemel Hempstead. Afterwards, comfortable majorities in 1924 and 1929, and soaring ones in 1931 and 1935, rendered all the constituencies very safe Conservative seats. Stanley Baldwin's confidant J.C.C. Davidson at Hemel Hempstead, Lieutenant Colonel Fremantle at St Albans, Rear Admiral Murray Sueter at Hertford, and Dennis Herbert at Watford all served their constituencies for all, or nearly all, of the inter-war years. All four were knighted for their political services, and when Davidson was made a viscount in 1937 his wife was immediately nominated and elected Conservative MP in his place. Only Hitchin experienced frequent changes of MP, but all of them were Conservative – Lord Robert Cecil, son of the third Marquis of Salisbury (1911–23); Major Guy, later Lord, Kindersley (1923–31); Viscount Knebworth, a popular sportsman, aviator and son of the Earl of Lytton (1931–33); and the soldier, explorer, colonial administrator and author, Lieutenant Colonel Sir Arnold Wilson (1933–40).[82]

In addition, many other county families maintained the tradition of local patronage: Lady Desborough regularly donated prizes to local schools near Panshanger; Lady Reynolds and Sir Arthur and Lady Acland supported schools in Sandridge, Digswell and the Ayots; the Beit family patronised village sporting activities near their Tewin estate; the McMullen brewery family provided Hertford with a health centre; and Tresham Gilbey gave Bishop's Stortford land and grants towards an elementary school, hospital, playing field and swimming pool.[83] As late as 1931 the coming of age of Lord Verulam's son was a noted St Albans event, involving a banquet and ball for distinguished guests one day, and tea and lantern slides for estate workers the next.[84] Old traditions died hard, and so did old interests in controlling public opinion and public affairs.

Hertfordshire was in rapid transition as industrial and residential estates spread across the county, but the traditional vested interests with the most powerful say in local government policies remained much the same right up to 1939. The irony is that those vested interests took radical decisions that dramatically affected a generation of families growing up during and after the First World War.

CHAPTER EIGHT

Education, social class and employment

S OON AFTER LLOYD GEORGE took office as Prime Minister in December 1916 he sought to maintain the nation's flagging morale with a significant measure of social reform which would tangibly improve the lives of ordinary families. The ensuing Education Act was passed in August 1918 on a rising wartime tide of concern for child welfare and support for state intervention, but beneath the general approbation many viewed its sections on school attendance and continuing education with open hostility. Many tradesmen and textile manufacturers feared for their profits, and the numerous opponents of extended schooling for the working classes despaired at the expense, and prophesied massive social unrest.[1]

The Act abolished all exemptions from attending school between the ages of five and fourteen. Practical instruction was encouraged for all senior elementary school pupils, and 'advanced' courses were to be provided for those wishing to stay in full-time education after the statutory leaving age. In addition, free and compulsory continuation schools, aimed at bridging the transition from elementary schooling to adult employment, were to be introduced over a period of time. Children leaving elementary schools would attend continuation classes for 320 hours a year, or the equivalent of eight hours a week for forty weeks. There were a number of sanctions in the Act to stop children working excessive hours on the days they attended continuation classes, and classes could not be held on Sundays or on any other traditional local holidays.[2]

In Hertfordshire these reforms met a mixed reception. As elsewhere, for many months few understood what 'advanced', 'practical' and 'continuation' schooling meant within the new legal framework. The *Barnet Press* welcomed the prospect of greater curriculum diversity at eleven being provided through a rich variety of readily accessible schools, and correspondents in the *Letchworth Citizen* felt the same.[3] The Watford Teachers' Guild and Barnet Labour Party petitioned the LEA to extend generous provision 'downwards' to nursery schools and 'upwards' to continuation schools and also to 'central' schools catering for pupils willing to stay in full-time education after the age of fourteen.[4] Nevertheless, many county councillors and education committee members considered the Act to be totally misguided. They agreed with one of their number who condemned it as yet a further collectivist blow 'weakening the moral sense of duty among a large section of parents.'[5] Another feared that improved secular education and the likely demise of church schools would fulfil the Duke of Wellington's pessimistic prophecy a century earlier that publicly funded schooling would turn working-class children into 'clever little devils' fermenting widespread discontent, even revolution.[6] The Honourable A.T. Holland-Hibbert stated that henceforth his 'principal interest' on the county council would be monitoring the cost of new schools.[7]

The press, whipped up by the restrictions on child labour, made great play with the dire threats extended compulsory schooling posed to individual self-determination and free will. The right-wing *Hertfordshire Record* castigated the whole concept of continuation schools as 'typical Prussianism', crude, cranky and costly, and later luridly portrayed the 'education maniac' forcing 'his peculiarities on other people, regardless of the taste or predilections of his prospective victims, and with a majestic indifference to expense.'[8] Other articles in the same vein condemned the Board of Education as the 'archwaster', and damned as pernicious folly the attempts 'to force youths and maidens to continue as learners against their will'.[9]

After a year's desultory deliberation, in June 1920 the LEA published its report on the possible provision of advanced, practical and continuation education across the county. Based largely on the views of local education sub-committees, it is not surprising that the ramshackle document contained a mix of vacillation, local biases and genuine difficulties. To house the continuation classes, private rooms and halls had been found for hire in Harpenden, Hitchin, Letchworth, Royston and Sawbridgeworth, and spare space identified in Bishop's Stortford's small Technical Institute. Elsewhere, solutions still eluded the sub-committees. There was a little more optimism when it came to practical and advanced instruction facilities. Barnet, Cheshunt, St Albans, Ware and Watford opted to establish central schools, all by reorganising existing schools. Other districts, including Bishop's Stortford, Berkhamsted, Harpenden, Royston, Sawbridgeworth, Stevenage and Tring, found themselves able to free a few rooms and workshops by rearranging existing schools and these, along with hired halls and houses, were considered adequate for a start. However, a third group, comprising Baldock, Bushey, Hitchin, Hoddesdon, Letchworth and Rickmansworth, stated that nothing could be accomplished until new building works were agreed and completed.[10] The borough of Hertford uniquely attempted to resolve the issue by asserting the new elementary school classes would have to wait until the grammar school erected its new buildings and vacated the old one.[11]

During the recession of 1920–1 most education committee members openly welcomed the demise of universal compulsory continuation schooling. Shrill cries for economy were in the ascendant nationally and locally. Late in 1920 several editorials urged utmost frugality on the county council, with the message that public profligacy in elementary education was elevating the working classes, 'killing the middle classes' and destabilising society.[12] Pank, the chairman of the education committee, could not have put it better, and in February 1921 the county scheme for continuation education was formally placed in abeyance, never to be considered again.[13]

Nevertheless, the 1918 Act was far from dead, even in apparently unsympathetic Hertfordshire. The key sections on attendance, advanced courses and practical instruction remained operative despite the continuing and sometimes panic-stricken cries for savage economies. The rabid *Hertfordshire Record* railed that the ruinous cost of elementary education was 'the inevitable result of Socialism in practice', while Rear Admiral Murray Sueter openly condemned as 'impatient and unreasonable' those constituents who lobbied against educational savings, and Lord Robert Cecil bemoaned the national failure to implement all the savings recommended by Sir Eric Geddes' public spending committee.[14] A more measured view was given by Lieutenant Colonel Fremantle, who believed that the temporary halt on developments would provide time 'to devise schemes more adaptable to the varied needs and capacities of different children'.[15] Fremantle was attempting to calm local anxieties, but his comments proved surprisingly accurate. Once the economy began to recover in the mid-1920s the county became increasingly committed to enhancing the practical and vocational opportunities within elementary education. It was a policy popular with teachers, employers and parents – and also with all those who sought to preserve the exclusivity of the county's secondary schools.

No group sought to preserve that exclusivity more than the county council and education committee and, of course, their expansion of the vocational aspect of elementary education was but one half of their overall policy. Captain Morris summed this up in 1929 when he reiterated, to the immediate applause of the education committee and ensuing praise of the press, that 'bookish learning' was for the few and most children 'should be taught that doing was as fine a thing as thinking'.[16] Farmers continued their cries for a pool of willing youthful workers, factory owners consistently prioritised the need for skilled machine operators and mechanics, and the growing number of offices, hospitals, hotels and cafes as well as middle- and upper-class homes created a never-ending demand for girls with domestic skills. As historian Harry Hendrick has stated, the desirable outcomes of education between the wars were new skills relevant to changing economic times firmly tied to old values of patience, perseverance, honesty, humility, obedience and self-respect.[17] Far from losing their wartime emphasis, gardening and rural studies, handwork and practical instruction, and a range of domestic subjects retained their dominance in the adjustment to peacetime priorities.

It was all very different in the secondary schools. They were small, and few and far between. They possessed largely graduate staff, and enjoyed more extensive facilities, far smaller classes and greater freedom from LEA control than elementary schools. They followed a curriculum that placed a high value on literary skills, they prepared their more able pupils for external leaving examinations and admission to higher education institutions, and they were highly regarded for opening up avenues of professional employment not usually available to elementary school leavers. They possessed more imposing buildings, some ancient, some modern, and they enjoyed far greater prestige, which stemmed from their socially superior intake, academic records, sporting achievements, fee levels, uniforms and ceremonies, and their passing resemblance in these respects to the even more prestigious public schools. Although secondary schools did accept a small percentage of elementary schoolchildren who had passed a stringent scholarship examination at the age of eleven, the vast majority of pupils had been admitted several years younger from families who were able to pay the annual fees and bear the cost of uniforms, books, sports kit and, if necessary, transport to and from school.

In Hertfordshire in 1919 there were up to forty annual county scholarships to local grammar schools, twenty each for boys and girls. They covered the cost of tuition, uniforms, books and stationery, but not 'extras' such as games kit, club subscriptions and examination fees.[18] Other free places, the entrance scholarships, were awarded by the governors of the secondary schools. The county was divided into seven districts centred on the available secondary schools. All the scholarships were limited to children in that district and, as Table 8.1 reveals, the numbers of scholarships varied widely. Additionally, following a patrician English tradition, half a dozen 'tied' scholarships had

Table 8.1 County and entrance scholarships in Hertfordshire: 1919–20

Districts and schools	County Scholarships Boys	Girls	Entrance Scholarships Boys	Girls
Barnet	2	3	16	26
Berkhamsted	2	2	10	4
Bishop's Stortford	1	2	1	7
Hertford & Ware	3	3	10	18
Hitchin & Stevenage	3	2	13	12
St Albans	4	3	17	3
Watford	5	5	39	39

been endowed by benefactors of specific elementary schools.[19]

It was the unevenness of the provision that became the major bone of contention. The comparative lack of scholarships for girls in St Albans and boys in Barnet and Bishop's Stortford caused endless dissatisfaction. The disparity in population among the seven districts meant that Berkhamsted, for example, had proportionately twice as many scholarship places as Watford. Soon after the war the First Garden City Company offered the county council a contribution of one-third of the building costs of a secondary school in Letchworth partly because of the steadily worsening odds against pupils in that rapidly expanding district gaining the scarce scholarships to nearby Hitchin Grammar School.[20]

The LEA made great play with the fact that the ratio of free places to the total secondary school accommodation matched the national average of about 30 per cent, but the all-important figure – the overall percentage of elementary school pupils winning admission to these rare establishments – was never published. However, a comparison of secondary and elementary school statistical returns for 1920–1 reveals that 4.21 per cent of the total number of Hertfordshire elementary pupils over the age of ten had gained and accepted scholarships. This was well under half the average of 9.2 per cent for England as a whole. There were just 493 scholarship places for boys in Hertfordshire, and far fewer –403 – for girls. These figures represented 4.76 per cent and 4.0 per cent respectively of the total number of elementary school boys and girls over ten in the county.[21] As the school population expanded during the 1920s the LEA proudly publicised its additional secondary school accommodation. By 1924–5 the number of scholarship places for boys had risen to 580, and those for girls to 451, but these increases masked the decline in boys' places to 4.3 per cent of elementary schoolboys over ten and the girls' places to a particularly lowly 3.3 per cent.[22]

Local support for secondary school expansion fluctuated with the state of the economy. Cheshunt probably epitomised the aspirations and frustrations across the county. In 1919 the idea of a secondary school in the immediate locality was popular, but within a year support had died away. The high post-war building costs, the large share falling on the borough and the uncertainties about the 1918 Education Act, especially over the provision of continuation classes, were largely to blame, and the recession delivered the *coup de grace*. By early 1920 a local editor was castigating the dwindling advocates of the secondary school as extravagant and unrealistic idealists.[23] Among the economies agreed by the LEA in 1922 was the redefinition of the 'free place' to mean only the place was free, and the maintenance and book allowances became subject to means testing.[24] Despite the charges of blatant unfairness, these rules became applicable to scholarship pupils already in secondary schools as well as to new entrants.[25] Only towards the end of 1925 did the agitation for a secondary school begin to surface again in Cheshunt.[26] The continuation schools had not materialised, the economy was recovering, new residential estates were being built, and the nearest secondary school was in Hertford, but for another ten years the LEA showed little sympathy towards Cheshunt's cause.

To the LEA's chagrin, in 1924 the Labour government encouraged an increase in the numbers of elementary pupils transferring to secondary schools. Board of Education Circular 1340 offered additional grants for free places in excess of 25 per cent of the total number of pupils in a secondary school, up to a maximum of 40 per cent.[27] In response, the LEA conducted a time-consuming survey which eventually confirmed the all too obvious disparities between the districts and the inaccessibility of secondary schools to families living in many rural areas.[28] The well-publicised debates on the survey show that county councillors, education committee members and LEA officers were convinced that only about 4 per cent of elementary schoolchildren were suitable academically or socially for secondary education. They viewed with abhorrence any thoughts of elementary school headteachers coaching candidates for the scholarship examinations.[29] In the end modest increases in free places were agreed, strictly according to the new definition, in a few districts significantly below 4 per cent, such as Berkhamsted, Hertford, Hitchin and St Albans. An attempt was made, although ultimately frustrated by local outcries, to reduce the 7.2 per cent of elementary schoolgirls accepted by Barnet Grammar School – where, the survey claimed, a significant proportion were 'not up to the usual standard'.[30] This limited response was hailed by the LEA as bringing secondary schooling fully into line with modern needs across the county.

The County Teachers' Association (CTA), which represented the elementary schools, made great efforts to ensure parity and accuracy across the county in the scholarship examination processes. Ironically, in doing so it created greater tensions within the elementary schools themselves as they strove to foster their time-consuming practical subjects, such as gardening, handicraft and domestic subjects, while not neglecting potential scholarship pupils. The elementary sector of education was accelerating in a different direction to the humanities and literary pathways prevailing in secondary schools. The 1924 revision of the scholarship examination for places in the grammar schools and Central School in Watford reveals the trend. It involved a preliminary test to eliminate obviously unsuitable candidates, a second stage comprising written arithmetic and English tests, and then oral examinations and critical consideration of the pupils' elementary school record.[31] Its demands for academic abilities of a high order bore heavily upon those elementary schools with a tradition of scholarship success to maintain.

In 1928 the Watford branch of the NUT condemned the evils of examination cramming at a meeting devoted to modern teaching methods. Letters appeared in newspapers arguing over the classroom tensions that contributed to over-wrought pupils. The increasing expansion of the curriculum and the academic pressures, including the scholarship tests, were blamed in about equal measure. In 1928, and again in 1932, the CTA condemned, and the LEA banned, all scholarship coaching in schools – sure signs that the practice was believed to be persistent. Neither the LEA nor the CTA wished to encourage the passage of crammed pupils from elementary to secondary schools, and the CTA remained very sensitive to any accusations that senior elementary schools were the depositories of their own failures at eleven-plus.[32] No doubt some headteachers concealed their coaching efforts, but searches through numerous newspapers and logbooks suggest that it was actually a small minority of headteachers who consistently and publicly fostered a highly competitive spirit within their schools, and usually this embraced both scholarship and sporting success. Out of sixty elementary school logbooks examined, just five reveal a consistent interest in scholarship success, with St Mary's School in Hitchin being the prime example. Its academic and sporting successes occupied much space in the logbook as well as regular columns in the press.[33]

The county council and education committee had different futures in mind for most brighter elementary school pupils. In 1920, as a direct result of the 1918

Education Act, the LEA compiled a scheme incorporating a two-year higher elementary course specifically 'in advance of what is usually provided at an elementary school' for the estimated 33 per cent of pupils 'sufficiently intelligent to finish the ordinary elementary school course by the age of 12' – that is, up to two years earlier than usual.[34] The initiatives included not only a heavy investment in numerous Practical Instruction and Domestic Subjects centres and their structured programmes for older pupils, but also the establishment of two selective central schools and a handful of selective 'advanced tops' in ordinary schools. They were all funded and managed, however, under the Board of Education's Elementary, not Secondary, Code.

The LEA became an enthusiastic promoter of practically biased elementary schooling. Handwork and modelling were fostered in younger pupils, then gardening and woodwork for older boys and cookery, laundrywork and housecraft for older girls, with technical, commercial and secretarial courses becoming available for those aged about fourteen who showed interest and ability. Clear pathways were established, completely outside the secondary sector, from the junior schools to specialist colleges. The county council and education committee saw technical institutes, with syllabuses informed by local employers leading to a variety of vocational qualifications and skilled posts in commerce and industry, as the most appropriate targets for diligent elementary schoolchildren. They found it entirely appropriate that this bias led elementary schools further and further away from the ethos and courses dominating secondary schools.

The LEA acted decisively. Early in 1919 most education committee members were relieved to learn that R.R. Bunn, the county's supervisor of handwork, was to be released by the Admiralty after a brief period of war service. His wartime transformation of school handwork into the mass production of military and Red Cross equipment had gained their unbounded admiration. The objections of the elementary school representatives on the education committee to Bunn's excessive mimicry of industrial and commercial practices resurfaced on the news of his return, only to be brusquely quashed. As Sir Charles Longmore himself stated, Bunn's ideas were perfectly in tune with the aims of the 1918 Education Act, and, he could have added, the aspirations of the LEA.[35] By May 1924 Bunn supervised eighteen new or refurbished urban Handicraft Centres attended by 3,005 older boys, many for a whole day a week.[36] Later that year HMI praised the 'steady progress' since the war.[37] At the end of 1926 3,550 boys aged twelve and over – 66 per cent of the total – were receiving weekly Handicraft tuition, and just two years later there were twenty-five instructors teaching 4,600 boys – 74 per cent of the total – in eighteen schools and seventy full-time and part-time centres.[38] Bunn saw handicraft in vocational terms, and in 1929 his annual report strongly supported the move for all older boys to spend a complete day each week at the centres 'doing advanced work with a view to apprenticeship later on to some trade where craft skill is essential to their advancement.'[39] In 1930 metalwork appeared alongside woodwork in the more specialised centres.[40]

Despite the new facilities and syllabuses, Bunn consistently blended traditional utilitarian arguments with modern educational ones. Not surprisingly, he believed that 'the arts and industries are among the greatest factors in social progress, and the schools should provide experience and training in those manual process which make for social efficiency.'[41] To Bunn, social efficiency for most individuals meant productiveness in manual occupations, for which Handicraft developed many appropriate attitudes, such as patience, persistence and self-discipline, as well as life-long skills. The training could not start too soon. Making a book of paintings epitomised the highly disciplined activity he valued most in junior schools. To accomplish this, he explained, a young child needed to measure and divide, appreciate the qualities of paper, card, cloth and glue, master various tools, collect and select the contents, and understand something of the painters and their work.[42] A range of early activities using paper, card, crayons, chalk, paint and clay, accompanied by the increasing mastery of various tools, laid firm and particular foundations for the syllabuses at his numerous centres.

Although some new centres were postponed during the depression in 1931, Handicraft escaped any cutbacks. Indeed, the 1930s as a whole witnessed the greatest expansion, with thirty-one full-time instructors employed in 1932 and thirty-eight in 1935–6. By then most instructors were qualified teachers with additional Handicraft certificates. In 1932 HMI deemed the provision and the children's work 'very satisfactory'.[43] Many of the centres built in the later 1930s were on the same sites as the large new senior schools they served. In addition, many pupils now started three- or four-year specialised courses at the age of eleven rather than twelve, a reduction in age long desired by the LEA but frustrated by the depression. Utility was the watchword. Pupils made items of furniture for their homes, such as kitchen drainers, bread boards, trays, book ends, stools and small tables, while rural classes constructed gardening tools, seed trays, coops and hutches, and urban groups fashioned Science and Mathematics equipment.[44]

In response to the Board of Education's revised *Suggestions*, issued in 1937, the scope of Handicraft was extended to include weaving, basketry, printing, beaten metalwork, pottery and technical drawing. Bunn's senior woodwork and metal-work groups produced much of the necessary equipment in bulk, ensuring the utilitarian value of the skills they had acquired was not forgotten.[45] By then, Hertfordshire's infant and junior classes were spending up to 20 per cent of each week on aspects of Handicraft, and seniors up to 30 per cent.[46]

The selective central schools envisaged by the LEA soon after the war were achieved quickly and cheaply. One was created instantly by renaming Watford's Higher Elementary School in 1919, and another a year later by putting the spare daytime capacity in St Albans Technical Institute to productive use.[47] Watford Mixed Central School had an intake of at least 120, and sometimes 150, pupils a year and quickly became popular and overcrowded. As early as 1921 it had the choice of 338 candidates for 120 places. In 1922 HMI confirmed that the school had got the balance in its curriculum about right, noting that 'though regard is paid in the later years to the respective needs of commercial and industrial occupations and of the teaching profession, there is, on the whole, no attempt at specialism in a narrow sense.'[48] In the final analysis the school was judged by HMI on two pragmatic criteria – the number of pupils staying for four or more years and the quality of jobs secured by leavers. Three years later HMI recognised the excessive workload of the teachers, who not only provided Industrial and Commercial pathways for older pupils but also entered some for the Cambridge Local Examinations, normally the preserve of the secondary schools. He did, though, caution the headmaster against any 'check' on the 'special characteristics of a Central School' – that is, its thorough preparation of pupils for careers in industry and commerce.[49]

The temptation to diversify the programmes of study to include the prestigious Local Examinations reveals the tension between the Board's definition of a central school and local perceptions of its place in the community. Many parents, like the LEA itself, saw the school as an opportunity for the children to secure the practical skills for a better job than they originally envisaged, but to others it was the consolation prize for children just failing the scholarship examination, and they favoured a curriculum far closer to that of the grammar school. The local selection procedures and some of the Central School's working practices accentuated the problem. Children between the ages of ten and twelve sat the Watford scholarship examination only if their parents had applied for the opportunity and their elementary school headteachers had approved. Watford Boys' and Girls' Grammar Schools had the first pick of the candidates, and rather than oblige children to take further tests the Central School customarily took the best of the rest.

Early in its existence the Central School had clouded its status further by comple-menting its essentially elementary curriculum with the secondary school practice of appointing prefects and creating rival Houses to stimulate academic and sport-ing competition.[50]

Nevertheless, the school heeded HMI's warning. It pitched its work firmly between Watford's ordinary elementary and grammar schools, and managed to serve several purposes well. After a general education, it gave most children well-targeted courses for local employment, some a preparatory training for advanced courses in technical institutes, and a few the opportunity to sit the Local Exami-nations, while steadfastly resisting the temptation and pressure to become a pale imitation or rival of the grammar schools. It bridged the gap, while also conceal-ing the gulf, between the elementary and secondary sectors. The balancing act lasted well into the 1930s, and HMI was particularly impressed with the employ-ment record. A detailed survey of the years 1931–4 revealed that 11 per cent of boys and 12 per cent of girls had entered teaching, and 72 per cent of boys and 65 per cent of girls had embarked upon sound clerical careers with the Civil Service, rail-way companies, insurance companies, banks and local councils. This left just 17 per cent of boys and 23 per cent of girls who had accepted low-grade posts in fac-tories, hospitals and shops. The school was fulfilling its selective vocational func-tion well. By then, handicraft, needlework and housecraft were specialist subjects from the age of entry at eleven, with a wide range of commercial subjects, includ-ing shorthand, typing and book-keeping being introduced at fourteen.[51]

St Albans Central School developed differently, largely because it was expected to offset the comparative lack of secondary education for girls in the city. Throughout the 1920s HMI consistently praised the dedication of the staff in transcending the severe limitations of the cramped, stuffy and noisy building. There was no playground or field, and the building was also used during the day for School of Art classes and as a cookery and handicraft centre.[52] For all this, HMI reports reveal an institution quickly reaching beyond the range of ordinary elementary subjects and standards of attainment, but deliberately paying far less attention than its counterpart in Watford to practical training. Like Watford, it introduced uniforms, prefects, houses and colours, and these trappings of gram-mar schools met with HMI approval as contributing to an *esprit de corps*. The cur-riculum was altogether another matter. The 'A' stream prospered impressively well, with French, botany and mathematics taught particularly thoroughly, but practical needlework, housewifery, laundrywork, handwork and drawing remained stubbornly undeveloped despite HMI's repeated criticism.[53] The

Workers' Educational Association was another vociferous critic, not only challenging the school's neglect of practical instruction, especially for the 'B' stream girls, but also considering its secondary school pretensions entirely inappropriate and a grave impediment to the provision of a county girls' secondary school to complement the direct grant High School.[54]

The school's lowly origins denied it secondary status, despite its obvious aspirations. During the reorganisation discussions in 1927, the city's education subcommittee agreed that the school filled the gap between the elementary and grammar schools perfectly. Significantly, the headmistress of the High School agreed, arguing that the early leaving of 58 per cent of her free-place pupils proved the LEA's generosity in this respect was already excessive.[55] The school, though, continued to deny its original purpose, and in 1936 HMI, the LEA and the city council finally condemned it as an anachronism. It had consistently rejected Commerce, given only passing attention to housecraft, and HMI asserted its 'B' stream – half the intake – was still particularly ill-served. As a result plans were made to close the central school when the proposed new senior elementary school was finished. The central school's buildings would be used to expand the girls' grammar school and its pupils would be divided equally between the grammar and elementary schools according to their ability.[56] The reorganisation took place in 1938.

Another selective central school opened in Hemel Hempstead, the independent LEA within the county. With strong Nonconformist and Liberal traditions, and with most families employed in the local paper and stationery mills, the borough felt it was different politically, socially and economically from the rest of Hertfordshire. Its education committee was convinced that expensive educational reforms were unnecessary for the borough's children, whose secure and respectable futures were largely mapped out. The arrangements whereby a few able children could secure scholarship places at the grammar schools in Berkhamsted and Watford affirmed rather than contradicted this conviction. They allowed the dominant pattern of elementary education within the borough to proceed unaltered while not denying other opportunities to the tiny minority for whom it was obviously unsuitable and whose families were prepared to accept the extra costs and inconvenience.

For a century the owners of the mills, the Longman, Evans and Dickinson families, had endowed hospitals, churches, parish halls, libraries and sports fields in and around Hemel Hempstead, and the mills had a lengthy tradition of free further education and training. At Apsley Mills the original trades school had been restructured from time to time in the light of government legislation, changing technology and working practices, and in 1920 it received Board of Education recognition as a continuation school. Its day programmes included English language and literature, arithmetic, civics, commercial geography, physical training, nature study, book-keeping, typing, and geometrical and mechanical drawing. All factory and office workers between the ages of fourteen and sixteen had to attend for six hours a week, studying a combination of general and vocational subjects. The school also ran evening classes on commercial art, printing, workshop mathematics, salesmanship, trade developments and manufacturing processes. The school awarded certificates and prizes, and overtly aimed to identify talents beneficial to the company.[57] In 1921, eighty-nine workers attended the day school and, in addition to adults, the various evening classes attracted 130 employees under the age of eighteen.

HMI had nothing but praise for the quality of the facilities, organisation and instruction, confirming that 'the scheme in effect provides a voluntary continuation school for the district without any charge on the rates, since nearly all the young people of the neighbourhood find employment in the Apsley Mills.'[58] Throughout the inter-war years it remained a popular facility with employees, the borough council and county council. Its name changed again in the mid-1920s to the Efficiency Training Centre, which was a reminder of its underlying vocational purpose. Nevertheless, the numbers attending the day classes grew to 200 in the 1930s, and to all intents and purposes it transformed itself into a voluntary part-time technical institute with a strong commerce bias.[59]

In 1921, after immense arguments, Hemel Hempstead borough council decided to start a selective 'higher top' school in a few spare rooms in an unwanted building. It represented the cheapest possible solution to the anticipated overcrowding of the local schools over the next few years, and even then many resented the expense.[60] Nonetheless, under a vigorous headmaster the school quickly became immensely popular for its breadth of courses and quality of tuition.[61] Pupils were admitted at eleven on the basis of a competitive examination and interview, parents had to confirm their children would complete a minimum three-year course, and there were no maintenance grants. After two years' general education, pupils studied physics, chemistry, algebra, geometry, advanced arithmetic, art, French and English. They had a longer day than an ordinary elementary school, and substantial homework assignments.[62]

The school's success, and indeed its very existence, caused a local furore. For some, it was sufficiently secondary in character and curriculum to cater for all the largely working-class borough's needs in this direction; for others, it offered cheap and easily accessible advanced instruction to prepare able children for sound and secure posts in local industries. For a third group – as in St Albans – the Central School was an impediment to the provision of a 'proper' secondary school.[63] In 1929 the headmaster made his position crystal clear, proudly proclaiming his fulfilment of 'the demand ... for instruction of a practical nature, it being recognised that better results were produced by actually doing a thing than by bookish instruction'.[64] As the economy recovered, so the controversy intensified. Eventually, in 1929, plans for a secondary school were agreed between the borough and county councils, and a school serving not only Hemel Hempstead but also the industrialised valley beyond its borders opened in 1931.[65]

Yet, the Central School remained open, popular and full. It retained its vocational bias, rendering it easier for the new secondary school to create its own distinctive ethos. HMI Bloom thoroughly approved of the range of local interests and abilities being met through a coherent hierarchy of grammar, central and senior elementary schools, the first two selective.[66] Many in the borough, however, were grievously disturbed by thoughts of the heightened mobility and social dislocation the secondary school's curriculum and atmosphere would encourage. They believed the district could not provide employment for all the academically educated pupils, and the mills would suffer a chronic shortage of labour. In the event, the secondary school, the Central School and the Efficiency Training Centre co-existed successfully until 1939, when the Central School was absorbed as an 'advanced stream' into a new purpose-built senior elementary school. 'It died happy', said the press report, preserving to the last its popular specialisms.[67]

In addition to the central schools, other selective 'higher tops' were created in a few schools across the county. They had a practical and, increasingly, a technical bias. In 1924 an anxious audience of parents in Barnet was told that those children just failing the secondary school scholarship, and others 'who had shown special aptitude in the general test by his Majesty's inspector', would be eligible to join the new 'top' class about to be opened. Admission was a privilege, but a minor rather than a major one, with the 'top' itself designed as a cheap alternative to secondary education but definitely not imitating it in its syllabuses, surroundings or ethos. Nevertheless, the initiative was popular with Barnet parents, as well as employers, with both groups seeing it as contributing to the range of options available to children whose abilities were above the average. The 'top' offered French, science and mathematics, and:

for those who desired it, there would be classes with a commercial bias, for instruction in shorthand, book-keeping, and probably, typewriting. Others, who were likely to go in for handiwork, would be able to spend extra time in the handicraft centre.[68]

In 1925 a Board of Education inquiry identified three other Hertfordshire 'higher tops' – in Kimpton, Letchworth and Royston.[69] A marked practical bias was evident in them all. At least one more 'top' appeared later, in Knebworth in 1927. Significantly, the school managers stated it was for 'those brighter pupils' in and around Knebworth, Stevenage and Welwyn with a genuine desire and aptitude for advanced practical courses, and for those 'precluded by various reasons from attending secondary school'. The latter group included children whose parents had no interest in the secondary schooling their children had won, or who could not afford the extra costs of travel and equipment, and a few who had narrowly failed to gain a scholarship.[70] The 'top' would offer these families a readily accessible, more vocational and considerably cheaper alternative. In 1985 a Stevenage resident recalled with some pride her admission to Knebworth's 'top' – an 'experiment' she called it, foreshadowing secondary education for everyone – where she studied more English, History and Geography and began French, shorthand and book-keeping.[71]

Not surprisingly, Letchworth Garden City had educational and egalitarian aspirations which far exceeded those of the proponents of central schools and 'higher tops', and, indeed, all those who saw elementary and secondary schools as two distinct systems. In April 1924 it announced its vision of a Civic College, a single system incorporating a wide range of equally valued educational options for all children, based on the precepts published by W.R. Hughes and his colleagues a few years earlier.[72] The College was to be part of the state-maintained system of education, although grants from the Garden City Company and local employers would significantly enhance the facilities. The concept received wide local and national support. The College Committee included representatives from local councils, employers' associations, trades unions and schools, while the Garden City Company's solicitors, medical officers and architects provided expert advice. The principals of the University of Birmingham, Woolwich Polytechnic, Brighton Technical College, Manchester College of Technology and the City of London School were among those on the Consultative Committee.[73] Sir Douglas Hogg, the Attorney General, well known for his advocacy of Polytechnics, agreed to be the College's president.[74]

although the definitions shaded into one another technical education did possess distinctive features. During the inter-war years it was primarily the preserve of older pupils, mainly over the age of fourteen, and programmes of study usually contained a general education element as well as the theoretical and practical preparation for skilled, and often highly skilled, posts in specific industries. Technical education was offered in a range of institutions which ran 'junior' and sometimes 'senior' courses applicable to local employment opportunities, and these courses, often carrying certification, could be full-time, part-time, in the day or during the evening. Its growth was initially *ad hoc* and hesitant, but increasingly subject to pressures from local employers, district councils and government ministries for greater coherence, relevance and accessibility.

The practical skills and theoretical knowledge embraced by the term 'technical education' lay largely outside the curriculum expected in the secondary schools. In fact, they largely lay outside the curriculum found in most elementary schools, too, but their associations with essentially working-class spheres of employment inevitably led most people to assume that moderately able elementary school pupils would be those most likely to be interested in technical education courses. Secondary schools did not entirely eschew programmes of study in technical colleges and institutes for their less distinguished leavers, especially those leaving early, but their headteachers ensured that such sops to modern business life were not their schools' primary concerns. Inevitably, the cultures surrounding the two sectors meant that technical education courses and certificates became valued accolades for many elementary school pupils but poorly regarded consolation prizes for those in secondary schools.

Although Hertfordshire LEA promoted a practical bias in elementary education, technical education in the early 1920s largely comprised a handful of evening classes and part-time courses at the small schools of art, commerce and science in Watford, St Albans and Hertford, which had evolved since the last quarter of the nineteenth century. However, after a hesitant post-war start the pace of development dramatically quickened, with technical education becoming highly valued by parents and employers. Indeed, a few months after the Armistice a small technical institute had been founded in Berkhamsted as a war memorial by the family of Sir Richard Cooper, and a technical institute as well as a cross was supported by war memorial subscriptions in Hemel Hempstead.[86]

Far from denigrating either technical or vocational education, local speakers sought to elevate both. However, their reasons varied, usually according to their perceptions of the places of such provision in the educational hierarchy.

The elementary school teachers and newspaper leader writers urged greater efforts to identify children's aptitudes, and to 'broaden avenues of opportunity'. The progressively inclined Letchworth and Welwyn Garden Cities were more specific and sought easily accessible, even universal, secondary schools with both grammar and technical sides. Conversely, others welcomed the trend towards vocationalism because their aspirations for elementary schoolchildren remained limited, and they believed national efficiency demanded a rigorously cost-effective and socially biased system of national education.[87] An enthusiastic example was Rear Admiral Murray Sueter. He had been a pioneering director of the Admiralty's air service during the war, and he openly advocated the early identification of practical abilities in pupils, not only to ensure the nation had a ready supply of skilled artisans but also to prove the utter inappropriateness of secondary education for most working-class children. His confident arguments extolling an education system driven by the characteristics he believed to be inherent in each social class were very well received, and he was largely confirming rather than challenging the dominant view in his constituency.[88]

Fuelled by these economic anxieties and educational aspirations technical education started to flourish in the county. Watford was in the vanguard, and squeezed every advantage out of the special relationship it had established with the county council when, unlike Hemel Hempstead, it had chosen to relinquish its status as an independent elementary education authority some years after the 1902 Education Act. It had been absorbed into the county LEA, but its price had been four extra seats on the education committee and an additional annual 'special agreement' grant. It had also retained its own education sub-committee and, just like the Garden Cities, Watford was never short of positive, if rather more pragmatic, ideas on education and social welfare provision.[89]

In 1922 the borough embarked upon a programme of expansion in technical education, and did its utmost to raise its status in the community. An early move was the restructuring and revitalisation of the School of Art, Science and Commerce, and the securing of the Countess of Clarendon's agreement to present a newly created range of annual prizes in a well-publicised ceremony. An illustrated prospectus publicised a range of courses closely related to local businesses, and a sympathetic local press highlighted the good posts and business commissions gained by the students. In 1926 HMI noted with approval that the School's work was tightly coordinated with the borough's four evening continuation classes, all of which took students at the age of fourteen, mainly direct from elementary schools. Since 1922 the School's intake had nearly doubled to 393, of whom 256 were ex-elementary school pupils and 120 were from secondary schools, many of them early leavers.[90] Soon afterwards the LEA reduced the age of admission to evening classes to thirteen, and embarked upon a vigorous publicity campaign to foster elementary schoolchildren's interest in commercially and industrially biased evening courses.[91] It worked, and the number of fully recruited evening courses across the county rose from 255 in 1921–2 to 335 in 1927–8 and 402 in 1928–9.[92]

Watford marched on. In 1929, with full LEA support, a Junior Technical School opened in the old public library premises. Its annual intake was 120 pupils rising fourteen years of age who undertook two- or three-year full-time courses specialising in industrial art or commerce interspersed with general studies. It was instantly oversubscribed. The following year all Watford's technical education sites were made components of a newly designated Technical School. In 1931 Lord Eustace Percy opened a new annex during a week of demonstrations by students, displays by local firms and guided tours for elementary school pupils.[93]

Percy was an interesting choice of visiting dignitary. A scion of the ducal house of Northumberland, he had been Conservative President of the Board of Education between 1924 and 1929. During his lengthy tenure of office he had actively encouraged the expansion of technical education while at the same time striving very successfully to limit the growth of secondary schools. Developments in Watford were exactly those he had envisaged nationwide as President. In 1927 the Ministry of Labour's Departmental Committee on Industry and Trade had urged firms to survey local technical education facilities and work with LEAs, schools and colleges to fill the gaps. In 1928 the Malcolm Committee's report saw the elementary schools as the main preparatory training ground for skilled workers, and it encouraged vocational training for older pupils in central schools. It urged a firm lead from government, and so did Lord Emmot's committee, which investigated the overall role of technical education in relation to industry and commerce.[94] They were addressing the converted, and knew it. Percy had long ago decided that national interests, the existing initiatives in the field, and the overall cost of public education all contributed to policies which encouraged technical rather than secondary education pathways.[95] Hertfordshire LEA had come to much the same conclusion.

In 1934 HMI praised the high proportion of Watford Technical School leavers who entered skilled trades, and in the light of local employment priorities urged the LEA to lower the age of entry from fourteen to thirteen. The move was popular, and the Technical School soared in prestige as a selective school, although

staying firmly second to the grammar schools in repute.[96] In a small but significant move at this time Watford Boys' Grammar School appointed a Commerce
teacher, largely under parental pressure. The headteacher, governors, HMI and
education committee members agreed that its pupils would be those unlikely to
reach the School Certificate Examination standard of attainment. It was a second-
rate subject for second-rate students, and everyone associated with the school
knew it.[97]

Barnet followed suit, with County Councillor, later County Alderman, Harold
Fern taking a leading role in seeking a range of educational facilities closely linked
to local employment needs in his 'home' borough. With Howe's support, during
the 1930s Fern guided the transformation of Barnet Handicraft Centre into a
multi-faceted Technical School. He involved local industrialists, borough councillors, headteachers, school managers and governors in planning meetings and
publicity initiatives, and ensured local pressure was consistently brought to bear
upon the LEA for improved facilities. The Handicraft Centre expanded its courses
for senior elementary pupils, developed new evening classes, and then took over
the rambling buildings vacated by the grammar school when it moved to its new
site. The aspiring Technical School knew its place in the educational hierarchy,
which was to fill the gap between the secondary schools and ordinary elementary
schools, and to respond to the needs of local employers. Not surprisingly,
Barnet's grammar schools encouraged the Technical School's expansion, and
made no secret of the fact that it freed them from undue contact with commerce
and industry. In 1935, for example, they urged the Technical School to introduce
applied biochemistry and civil engineering. In an unusual public outburst, the
persistent air of superiority displayed by Barnet's grammar schools led enraged
borough councillors to condemn them as financially pampered and vocationally
useless.[98]

A few years earlier Lord Eustace Percy, the distinguished visitor to Watford,
had taken a momentous decision as President of the Board of Education which
affected the future of elementary and secondary as well as technical education. In
May 1928, with full Cabinet approval, he had published *The New Prospect in Education*. This was the government's politically and educationally biased response
to the 1926 report of the Board of Education's Consultative Committee, chaired
by Sir William Hadow, which had envisaged two main stages of education – 'primary' and 'post-primary' – with eleven-plus being the dividing age and with the
leaving age extended to fifteen. The Hadow Report justified the definite break at
eleven with the memorable phrase – 'There is a tide which begins to rise in the

veins of youth at the age of eleven or twelve' – and asserted, equally memorably, that 'If that tide can be taken at the flood, and a new voyage begun in the strength and flow of its current, we think that it will "move on to fortune".'[99] It delved no deeper into the phenomenon of adolescence, but asserted the need for a variety of 'post-primary' schools to provide for the needs of all children, and for all these schools to be 'secondary' in status and funding. Pragmatically, however, the report rationalised the numerous types of schools that currently existed to fit its recommendations, and as historian Ross McKibbon has said, in doing so it 'formalised a rather messy status quo'. For a small minority of children, 'post-primary' schooling should continue until eighteen in the traditional secondary 'grammar' schools. For others it could go on to sixteen-plus in secondary 'modern' schools, a term including the various selective and non-selective central schools. For the vast majority, it would end at fourteen-plus, or perhaps fifteen, in the senior classes of ordinary elementary schools, or preferably, completely separate senior schools.[100]

The New Prospect celebrated the Hadow Report while side-stepping its major recommendations. The government remained firmly wedded to the social class foundations of English education, and steadfastly eschewed any ideas of equating elementary education with secondary education. It did, though, accept the need for more investment in the practical education and training of older elementary school pupils and in the convenient, if far from thoroughly researched, notion of a change of schools at eleven.[101] The junior–senior divide became an educational shibboleth, and a long-term Board of Education campaign got under way to encourage LEAs and voluntary schools to agree local schemes in which some all-age elementary schools became 'junior' schools by 'decapitation' at the age of eleven, thereby allowing older pupils to be grouped in educationally more effective and financially more efficient numbers in 'senior' schools. Where this was not possible, schools could divide internally into clear junior and senior departments. Henceforth the emphasis was to be on varied elementary school courses to suit the varied abilities of elementary schoolchildren. Percy saw no need to raise the leaving age, expand secondary schooling or increase scholarship places.[102]

In October 1928 Hertfordshire established a Schools Reorganisation Committee (SRC) to consider each district's needs in the light of *The New Prospect*, and to confer with managers, local councils and other interested groups.[103] The LEA recognised the need for leadership as urban pressures soared, and it prepared for a heavy investment in elementary education. The difference between the LEA's triennial programmes of work for 1927–30 and 1930–3 reveals the impact of both the population growth and government policy. The first, agreed early in 1926, resulted in six new elementary schools and various extensions, while the second, compiled early in 1929, planned for twenty-three new schools and seven major enlargements. Five were in Watford, four in St Albans, three in Letchworth, two in Welwyn Garden City, and one each in Baldock, Barnet, Cheshunt, East Barnet, Elstree, Harpenden, Hatfield, Hitchin, King's Langley, Knebworth, London Colney, Rickmansworth, Royston, Stevenage, Waltham Cross and Ware.[104]

The depression in the early 1930s delayed much of the building work, and so did the local disagreements which arose over many reorganisation proposals. In St Albans the plans for two new senior schools failed to mask the fact that several old, cramped and awkwardly shaped buildings were converted into senior schools at negligible cost without adequate workshops, gymnasia and playing fields.[105] In a bitter episode in Watford, the irate parents of 110 children under the age of eleven went on strike for three months from September 1929 when their all-age school reopened as a senior school and they were allocated places at an allegedly inferior school which could only be reached after a lengthy and danger-ous walk.[106] The SRC also caused widespread disruption and discontent in Barnet between 1928 and 1932, when several church and council schools were decapitated and others refurbished and extended as senior schools. As a result, 550 of the 1,350 elementary pupils had to transfer schools, ninety parents made written protests, numerous teachers suffered compulsory relocation, and two headteachers lost their posts.[107] To many families in these large urban communi-ties the purpose of the changes remained unclear, and the benefits far from imme-diately recognisable, especially as many of the 'new' senior schools were no more than the old all-age schools with minimal refurbishment.

Hertford's experience probably cast the difference between elementary and secondary schools in the harshest light. Here, the long-awaited purchase of the old boys' grammar school in 1930 paved the way for a cheap and speedy reorgan-isation of elementary education. In September 1931 the borough council, LEA and voluntary school managers considered reorganisation complete. The Roman Catholic school was allowed to stay all-age provided that it reorganised internally, the impoverished Anglican schools agreed to survival through decapitation, most of the council schools were decapitated as well, and a senior school was opened in the redundant grammar school buildings, which William Graveson, the chair-man of the county education committee, thought 'were extremely good for the purpose'. In marked contrast, a few months earlier an outburst of speech-day laughter had greeted the grammar school headmaster's joke that 'they would have a fit' if they were required to return to the old school.[108]

Despite this inauspicious start, as the 1930s wore on a series of new, light and spacious senior elementary schools were built on green-field sites to serve the large new estates surrounding most of the old towns. The schools impressed all observers, including parents. They were a stark contrast to the patched-up and extended Victorian buildings to be found nearer the town centres. The new schools possessed purpose-built laboratories, domestic science and handicraft centres, gymnasia and playing fields, and the LEA proudly announced that building standards were far above the minimum laid down by the Board of Education. Articles, photographs and letters in newspapers, and speeches by school managers and distinguished guests, emphasised how superior the new schools were to those built a generation, even a decade, earlier.[109] They give the feeling that the speakers and writers believed elementary education, with its high-quality modern buildings, host of practical and sporting facilities, and links with local employers and colleges, had 'come of age' and could improve little more. There were numerous references to satisfying the educational demands of local districts, frequent emphasis on the range of courses now available, and many pious hopes that pupils would prove worthy of the huge investment. Even HMI Bloom agreed there was 'a fresh conception of the standards of accommodation which such schools should possess'.[110]

Such praise camouflaged the separateness of the elementary and secondary sectors, and no doubt that was often the intention. Few, though, complained, and most fully approved of how the range of post-primary schools was meeting the needs of pupils and employers. In an address to the CTA in 1937 William Graveson was roundly applauded when he 'welcomed the fact that the great division which existed between elementary and secondary schools was being bridged', and cited the improved buildings as his evidence.[111] CTA conferences during the 1930s said nothing about the extension of secondary education, but much about utilising the findings of Cyril Burt and other psychologists to refine selection procedures, develop streaming criteria, and map programmes of study for A, B and C 'type' pupils.[112] In this context it is significant that the large elementary school in Hatfield was highly regarded by HMI, employers and parents because most leavers had no difficulty in securing office or manual posts in firms associated with the local aeronautical industry. In 1931, and again in 1936, HMI acclaimed the instruction given in typing and shorthand outside school hours to the 'A' stream, the strong practical bias in 'B' stream work, and the untiring efforts of the headmaster to match pupils' abilities to outside occupations and training programmes.[113]

With more well-equipped senior elementary and technical schools urged by HMI, local councils, chambers of trade, trades unions and employers' associations, the controversy about the worth and relevance of secondary schooling to most elementary school pupils became sharply focused. In 1930 the LEA had a disagreement with HMI Bloom, who advocated compulsory universal scholarship testing in urban elementary schools in preference to the county's customary reliance on parental initiative to enter children.[114] The education committee was convinced, by experiences with compulsory testing in Watford, that persuading the unwilling or indifferent family of a bright child to accept a secondary school place was utterly futile. The child usually left early, and might well have deprived a slightly less able child from a more supportive home of a place in a school in which he or she would have flourished. To revise the system, Howe argued, would be a waste of money.[115]

In 1932, when the county council was considering every avenue of economy, Howe recommended that the pressure for secondary school places should be relieved by raising the standard of all entrance examinations rather than providing more accommodation.[116] At a time when secondary school leavers could not 'be absorbed into suitable professions and occupations', he assumed any reductions should be first at the expense of the elementary schools. At a county conference the secondary headteachers agreed. They claimed that ex-elementary school pupils, narrowly versed in English and arithmetic at the age of eleven, were likely to be overtaken in academic achievements by fee-payers who had appeared inferior in tests initially but only because their early private schooling had included a far broader and richer curriculum, including Latin and French.[117] Howe and the headteachers saw the elementary school, and its pupils' homes, as no adequate cultural substitutes for the preparation given by middle-class families and fee-charging schools.

Throughout the inter-war years local secondary schools continued to accept children under ten years of age, and many at eight. Until 1928 their parents were charged the usual fees, which amounted to 60 per cent of the full costs, with the Board's grant making up the deficit. In 1928 the Board withdrew the grant for pupils under ten, but in a significant decision the education committee agreed to subsidise these places out of the rates. Parental willingness to pay secondary school fees from the earliest possible age was deemed as accurate a criterion for a child's suitability for its curriculum as any scholarship examination.[118]

Bloom strongly disagreed. In a full survey of Watford in 1934 he argued that the borough's socio-demographic make-up merited far more secondary school places than the present twelve places per thousand of the population, and contrary to the opinion of secondary headteachers, education committee members, and Howe, he asserted that 60 per cent of Watford's Central School pupils were self-evidently 'of secondary school calibre' despite failing the highly competitive local scholarship examination.[119] He failed, however, to make any impression.

In 1932 the Board itself had made it more difficult for families of limited means to accept scholarship places when it replaced 'free' places with 'special' places. Special places carried no maintenance grants, and there was a sliding scale of fees if parental income was above a certain level. Hertfordshire education committee welcomed the decision, as it confirmed the financial and educational appropriateness of means testing that it had operated for the last eight years.[120] After analysing the 1933 'special' place examinations, Hertfordshire's secondary headteachers confidently reported that very few, if any, of the unsuccessful candidates would have been able to profit from a secondary grammar school education.[121] With little controversy, therefore, the percentage of Hertfordshire elementary school pupils gaining and accepting special places at eleven-plus remained under half the national average, rising from 4.66 per cent in 1931 to 6.42 per cent in 1937, and only creeping above half to 7.68 per cent in 1938.[122]

In 1933 the county's problems in keeping pace with residential expansion, promoting technical education, limiting the rate of secondary grammar school expansion, and keeping costs down, seemed to be eased in one stroke by the introduction of the 'modern' secondary school. It was an idea imported from neighbouring Middlesex, but had been recommended in the 1926 Hadow Report. After a conventional secondary course between eleven-plus and thirteen-plus, pupils opted either to continue that conventional course or to pursue a commercial or industrial course up to an approved first examination at sixteen-plus. The new schools would be cheaper to build and run than grammar schools, as at sixteen-plus pupils either entered employment, stayed on for a one-year course in business studies, or transferred to a grammar school for the higher certificate.[123]

The 'modern' secondary schools sounded progressive. They increased children's options, and they were staffed and equipped under the relatively generous Secondary Code. They carried much of the prestige of secondary status, while possessing strong vocational overtones and serving national economic interests. They also broadened the definition of secondary education, while doing nothing to improve the overall ratio of secondary school places to the child population. As Howe made clear, that was not the intention.

In August 1933 the new stratagem got under way. First Howe reiterated publicly that too many children were attending grammar schools, both as fee-payers and subsidised scholarship entrants, and then went on to argue that 50 per cent of their pupils would benefit far more from 'parallel' secondary schools 'arranged in co-operation with the requirements of industry and commerce in the areas served by the scholar.'[124] Probably it was no coincidence that a year earlier the county's secondary headteachers had called for tighter controls upon elementary pupils' access to their schools, with one headteacher bluntly asserting that 40 per cent of the free-placers 'were not worth spending money upon'.[125] Their unsurprising analysis of the 1933 'special' place results gave added weight to the campaign to preserve their exclusivity.

In due course, the LEA was to bask in wide-ranging praise for both its prudence and its initiative. The 'modern' school was introduced into the county at a time when the population explosion made a significant increase in secondary school places inevitable. In 1932, new secondary grammar schools opened in Letchworth and Hemel Hempstead, and several others had modest extensions.[126] A year earlier, requests for secondary schools from Royston and Cheshunt had been turned down, but by 1933 pressure on the LEA from these and other towns was becoming intense. Henceforth, the LEA decided, the new 'modern' secondary schools, rather than grammar schools, would be provided in the more commercial and industrial towns.[127] In 1934 the Board agreed with the LEA that they would be eminently suitable for Cheshunt and East Barnet. Indeed, they hinted to the local councils that it was a 'modern' secondary school they would get or, probably, nothing.[128] East Barnet Mixed Modern School opened in 1937, Cheshunt Mixed and St Albans Boys' Modern Schools in 1938, and building work started on Welwyn Garden City Mixed Modern School in 1939.[129]

The new concept quickly gained local support. The press praised the schools for helping match pupils more accurately to careers, and for breaking down the snobbery (which it now acknowledged had existed) between particular types of education and occupations.[130] St Albans, now as much an industrial and dormitory town as ancient cathedral city, exemplified the trends. Here, a 'modern' boys' secondary school was planned to complement the existing boys' grammar school and the new boys' senior elementary school. The grammar school headmaster welcomed the variety and perceived no rival, and the city council praised the wide opportunities soon to be available to diligent elementary schoolchildren.[131] In

East Barnet, too, the 'modern' school was welcomed by Harold Fern and many others as completing the range of educational provision.[132] Its prestige was just a shade below the grammar schools, as reflected in the fees. During its first speech day, the headmaster pinpointed its difference. A 'modern' school, he said, 'relates secondary education to real life' and is designed 'for the requirements of the large percentage of secondary school pupils who enter industry and commerce and the Civil Service'.[133]

The development of the 'modern' schools was accompanied by an upsurge in investment in technical education. Several intensive HMI surveys of Hertfordshire's provision convinced the Board that the growing industrialisation of the southern half of the county merited greater investment in technical institutions, greater links between them and senior elementary schools, and greater coordination between all schools and local employers.[134] The heightened attention given to technical education nationally was thought worthy of emphasis in the Conservative Party's election manifesto in 1935, and soon after the Conservative victory a Board of Education circular gave notice of positive government support and, indeed, control of future developments.[135]

As a result HMI recommended a massive programme of five new multi-faceted regional Technical Schools across Hertfordshire. For the first time the LEA was to plan and build far ahead of demand. The schools, for day and evening students aged fourteen and over, would have close contact with elementary and secondary schools, and their courses would be fully informed by local industry and commerce.[136] Clear and increasingly accessible pathways from general education to advanced vocational courses were opening up for a growing number of children. To ensure local employers were satisfied, representatives from local industries as well as county and local councillors and 'people experienced in education' were to serve on the schools' management bodies.

Over the next three years the LEA proved very willing to tackle the huge task. In 1938 HMI noted 'no apathy' in Hertfordshire, unlike the penny-pinching and neglect witnessed in Surrey, Oxford and Buckinghamshire.[137] As early as October 1936 the county council agreed to spend £80,000 on a new Technical School in Watford, £26,500 on a smaller school in Welwyn Garden City, £36,000 on a new Evening Institute in Hertford, £25,000 on extensions in Barnet and £9,000 on improvements in Letchworth.[138] Two years later even these sums seemed inadequate. Technical education was fast broadening its scope, with more evening classes acting as preparatory courses for advanced part-time and full-time programmes of study, and a host of new courses linked to the building, transport, chemical, electrical, printing and engineering industries. In addition, at HMI's behest far more courses were created for girls in office administration, secretarial skills, domestic science, catering, dressmaking, hairdressing and skin care.[139] During 1938 and early 1939 the LEA dramatically expanded its building proposals. Conferences throughout the five regions ensured that specialist facilities were appropriate to local industrial, commercial and agricultural needs, and the results were indeed comprehensive. In mid and north Hertfordshire, for example, the new Technical Schools in Welwyn Garden City and Letchworth would have day and evening senior and advanced courses in science, technology, engineering, building, commerce, domestic science, arts and crafts, and English language and literature, with preparatory and junior classes held in the evening institutes throughout the districts.[140] By the time the final plans were drafted the costs for the new schools had soared to £61,995 for Welwyn Garden City, £63,310 for Letchworth, £64,485 for Barnet, £137,954 for Watford and £50,000 for the institute in Hertford.[141] The war, of course, halted the implementation of this well-funded and widely supported development plan.

In 1918 the county council and education committee had been content to see elementary education continue at its 1914 standard of provision, with additional practical instruction dominating the later stages of schooling. Scholarships to secondary schools identified the tiny minority who could be elevated out of this utilitarian system, and practical instruction was considered highly appropriate for the majority who stayed in it. Their likely jobs and domestic circumstances would demand the various skills practised in school. The late 1920s were a major turning point, when the government and LEA decided that elementary education would be linked strongly with technical education. Well-targeted practical instruction followed by intensive vocational training was popular with parents and employers, and the growth of population, industry and commerce created the will in many expanding towns to acquire a full range of educational facilities. They did not spurn grammar schools for their fee-paying families and scholarship holders, but 'higher tops', central schools, technical schools of various hues and 'modern' secondary schools were equally in demand educationally if not equally regarded socially. The late 1930s witnessed the promotion of technical education at its height, for which the elementary schools were clearly providing a broad and firm foundation. All of this was very popular, but for many it had the added advantage of preserving the social and academic exclusivity of the grammar school – still the brightest star in the educational firmament.

CHAPTER NINE

The countryside

THE ACUTE WARTIME CONCERN for increased agricultural production gave a new lease of life to the old argument that elementary education should prepare children for an externally imposed station in life rather than give them ideas above it. In Hertfordshire the strength of the agricultural interest in county affairs had been amply demonstrated by the extent to which the school attendance regulations had been subverted to employers' advantage. Although the Armistice and the Education Act ended the blatant indulgence of sectional interests, the county education committee continued to seize the many opportunities that came its way to pursue policies conducive to rural employment. Major landowners and farmers remained well represented on the county council and its major committees, and their attitude towards rural children did not change – they merely perfected the art of using modern educational arguments to perpetuate and refine well-established practices. In many respects government policies and national educational trends worked to their advantage, and they embraced them wholeheartedly.

After the war there was continuing concern over the future of the English countryside, and also over the role of rural schools in shaping that future. Agricultural prices and wages were falling, and labouring families were attracted by the better-paid jobs and modern lifestyles of the towns. In Hertfordshire those towns were usually not far away. As we have seen, they were rapidly enveloping the southern and south-western landscape, and throughout the 1920s great publicity was given to the possibility that the county would be swallowed up by London and cease to exist. Ironically, the increasingly urban outlook across the nation was creating a new attitude towards the countryside as an asset that should not be allowed to decay beyond redemption. The 1920s witnessed the arrival of mass tourism into the hills and forests, vales and villages of rural England – by train and foot, by bus and coach, by bicycle and tandem, by motorbike

and sidecar and, for a few, by car. Indeed, there was more than a hint that the factories, offices, shops and cinemas of the burgeoning towns did not fully compensate for the healthy air and beauty of the countryside, however dire the cottages,
scarce the employment and sparse the facilities. Fewer and fewer people wanted
to live in the country but more and more wanted to preserve it.

Rural schools were particularly vulnerable to criticism. In 1919 rural teachers
everywhere were felt to be so out of touch with curriculum developments that
HMI organised annual summer courses to encourage more stimulating and practical teaching approaches.[1] In 1922 one Hertfordshire newspaper made much of
the NUT's confession that rural education was 'too bookish and towny' and, proceeding on the assumption that the interests of farmers were the same as those of
pupils, it asserted that the village schoolboy 'is wasting time which might be prof-
itably spent in becoming acquainted with the things that will matter in his after-
life'.[2] With politically charged rhetoric Hertford's MP, Rear Admiral Murray
Sueter, promulgated similarly simplistic ideas, publicly arguing that

> Surely [children] would do better if trained properly in practical work such as pig
> and cow-keeping and general agricultural work, than pumping into their heads
> 'Shakespeare'.[3]

By 1926 the Board of Education felt the situation had improved very little. It justified the continuing investment in rural teachers' courses on the grounds that
they offset the enervating surroundings increasingly faced by rural teachers. The
Board bleakly asserted that,

> The exodus from the country side – too often of the brighter element – has tended
> to make the human environment of the pupils unreasonably dull. There is often
> too little variety, movement and energy in country life.[4]

By 1926, however, many village schools in Hertfordshire were beginning to enjoy
a surprising and popular educational renaissance.

The 1918 Education Act required LEAs to provide facilities and teachers for
'advanced' instruction and for part-time continuation classes. This presented
LEAs with the dilemma of whether they should provide central schools for older
pupils from groups of rural schools or send peripatetic teachers to undertake specialist work in individual villages.[5] This question also involved the key issue of the
degree of vocational bias to be incorporated into the new courses. H.A.L. Fisher
had recognised the problem, but his important speech on the educational estimates in 1917 had contributed to the confusion. Undoubtedly he saw schools as
major bulwarks against rural depopulation, but not as the conditioners of human

fodder for use by farmers. In detailed public argument, however, the clarity of this division became obscured. Fisher cited the fact that three-quarters of village children eventually migrated to towns to commend the compilation of new syllabuses which would counter the consistent criticisms of country schools' excessive devotion to textbooks and neglect of outdoor education without pandering to the farming lobby's demands for a strong rural and vocational bias. Nevertheless, he sought to perpetuate the Board of Education's links with – if not its subservience to – the Ministry of Agriculture in promoting in rural schools 'a taste for country life, an interest in all the sights and sounds of the countryside, and an intelligent use of all its various opportunities.'[6]

In Hertfordshire the balance promulgated by Fisher was never perceived as axiomatic, and there was no shortage of conflicting advice for education committee members to consider in their response to the Education Act. At meetings across the county some argued for the establishment of a series of identical urban-based continuation schools drawing pupils from both the towns and the surrounding countryside, while their opponents sought the provision of a decentralised system of infinite variety sensitive 'to the special needs of the locality' which included limiting continuation classes to the winter months when farm workers were less in demand.[7] Overall, though, there was widespread agreement that elementary education should be in far closer touch with the children's surroundings. Probably most teachers agreed with Spencer Holland's aphorism at a Hertfordshire conference that in country areas an environmentally based schooling 'might well be rural without being agricultural'.[8]

Sensing the appropriateness of the moment, in October 1920 the Hertfordshire branch of the National Farmers' Union (NFU) sent a resolution to the county education committee urging that education in all country schools, not just continuation classes, 'shall have a distinctly rural bias'. For good measure it re-emphasised the agricultural lobby's long-standing complaint that elementary schools educated children to scorn all farming pursuits.[9] The LEA responded sympathetically, and there can be little doubt that the resolution was far from a surprise. Indeed, a new and close partnership was being forged between the county agricultural and education committees which reflected the common interests of many members. Sir Charles Longmore agreed wholeheartedly with the NFU's resolution, and a minute records his deceptively modern assertion to education committee members that 'all teaching must be based upon what is already in the minds of the children and must draw its illustrations from their daily experiences.'[10] The committee gave immediate notice that Hallidie and HMI Bloom would be issuing advice on appropriate textbooks, that all rural schools should have properly equipped gardens, and that all syllabuses should have 'special reference to the surroundings of the scholars, the natural and historical features, and plant life of the locality, and the industries of the inhabitants'.[11] Henceforth, the LEA decided, local studies, farm visits, nature study, gardening, animal husbandry, rural crafts, rural poetry and literature, country traditions and practical Mathematics were to become key features of school life. To a large extent, they did.

This policy was in tune with the times. HMI and many teachers were sympathetic towards more lively and practical educational approaches. In July 1919, at the behest of the Earl of Lytton, the county council voted £300 to allow twenty-five schools selected by Hallidie and Bloom to undertake Regional Surveys under the guidance of the County Museum.[12] These detailed and comprehensive studies of the local environment aimed at exciting the children's interest in rural churches, manor houses, markets, farms, crafts and traditions, and they represented the interwoven historic, patriotic and aesthetic threads within the resurgent concern for English country life. As the passionate idealist Lytton stated, the objectives of the Regional Surveys were nothing less than the restoration of national pride and the stemming of rural depopulation through 'a more subtle and sensitive appreciation of the lure of the countryside'.[13]

The popularity of the Regional Surveys with headteachers and the education committee led to a combined outcry in 1921 which rendered short-lived the county finance committee's decision to discontinue the grant during the national economic crisis.[14] Although the grant was lost for a year, its subsequent restoration and renewal represented the recognition among those fearful for the future of agriculture, those concerned at the decay of village life and crafts, and those convinced of the educational value of practical outdoor studies, that all these interests were more complementary than conflicting.[15] A few records survive. The autobiography of Vicars Bell, headmaster at Great Gaddesden, mentions a major parish project, and at Hexton a full-scale local survey was published as a book subsidised by the local squire in 1936.[16] The chapters, in order, cover the local geology, climate, watercourses, plants, animals and birds, agriculture, rural industries, roads, village and families, manor and squires, church and vicars, the earthworks of Ravensburgh Castle, field names, ancient customs, court rolls, local organisations and Hexton Park. The older pupils engaged in the study, and in writing the book they must have benefited from a significant amount of expert support.

The early 1920s witnessed the belated recognition of the worth of another initiative – the county's nascent agricultural institute recently established at Oaklands, near St Albans, to provide courses for intended farmers and skilled farm workers. In 1921 its future seemed bleak under a storm of criticisms from county councillors stemming partly from the ominous implications for county ratepayers, despite the Treasury grants, and partly from hazy perceptions of its contribution to Hertfordshire's agricultural and educational affairs. In the end not only was closure avoided but expansion was encouraged into horticulture, dairying and poultry-keeping – all prominent local occupations – and strong links were anticipated between Oaklands and the elementary schools. The institute was now seen as providing substantial vocational opportunities for older elementary schoolchildren and school leavers, and this, education committee members comforted themselves, would offset to some extent 'the huge sums being given to grammar schools and secondary education'.[17] Such arguments effectively countered the objections of those suspicious of the agricultural lobby's sudden enthusiasm for particular educational developments. County Councillor Captain Morris, for example, had extensive farm holdings and was customarily unsympathetic to expenditure on elementary schools, but despite the recession he became a vociferous advocate of subsidised agricultural education. This was, he said, because of its benefits to 'people who were in no better position than the large majority of those for whom they provided secondary education on a generous scale.'[18]

Survival became Oaklands' primary concern, and through vigorous self-promotion it rapidly became part of the accelerating movement to give a significant vocational bias to rural schools. In 1923 it launched weekend and summer courses for elementary school teachers, and hosted visits by classes.[19] In 1924 the principal shrewdly promoted a far more comprehensive programme to educate both teachers and older pupils in the joys of rural living and the satisfaction of rural occupations.[20] The teachers' courses were widened to include Nature Study, Rural Science and Agricultural History. Oaklands staff gave lantern slide lectures in schools, and the institute created preparatory courses for older pupils to whet their appetites for more specialised agricultural education programmes at the age of sixteen. The initiatives proved popular, and by April 1926 the county agricultural and education committees, with the active encouragement of the County Teachers' Association, had agreed a scheme of maintenance grants and subsidised residential courses at Oaklands for children aged fourteen and over who had committed themselves to farming careers and whose parents were in agricultural employment. The scheme sought to secure young skilled farm workers by providing a further year's education with a marked rural bias, followed by a year combining work on an approved farm with evening classes, and culminating in an advanced residential course at Oaklands at the age of sixteen.[21]

Other developments were equally calculated to revitalise interest in the countryside and restore prestige to rural occupations. In 1922 the Board of Education commissioned specialists to undertake lecture tours on various aspects of local studies. HMI Bloom verified their popularity in Hertfordshire, and this contributed to the education committee's decision in 1923 to underwrite the costs of compiling and publishing a school manual on the Natural History of Hertfordshire.[22] This appeared in 1925, sold 2,418 copies over the next five years, and was firmly established in school syllabuses by 1927.[23] Two education committee chairmen, Canon Glossop and William Graveson, were key figures in the burgeoning movement to stimulate interest in the country through the Regional Surveys and the textbook. Glossop personally subsidised several Regional Surveys during the year the grant was withheld, and Graveson, a keen naturalist, wrote part of the new manual. Graveson, too, lost no opportunity in committee debates, newspaper articles, at prizegivings and at the opening of new schools to promote 'county patriotism' in children – a concept synonymous with an appreciation of, and respect for, all aspects of Hertfordshire's countryside, history and traditions.[24] In the interests of rural regeneration and the preservation of England's cultural heritage both Glossop and Graveson were enthusiastic advocates of the circulating libraries which operated in rural Hertfordshire from March 1925 with the support of grants from the county council and Carnegie Trust. Often the village school and teacher acted as library and librarian.[25]

The Regional Surveys, the Oaklands programmes, the Hertfordshire book, the libraries and the HMI courses all prospered throughout the inter-war years. They were manifestations of a new and widespread desire to promote a specifically rural type of education. To some – teachers and HMI Bloom – they offered stimulating methods of instruction combining practical activities with subject integration. And to some – such as Lytton, Glossop and Graveson – they represented a means of preserving the local heritage and crafts. To others – such as Captain Morris and most Hertfordshire farmers – they were essentially an opportunity to produce school leavers with interests and skills readily applicable to rural occupations, and to create a pool of teachers conditioned by the same rural bias. Under the guise of modernity it was the last set of objectives which Hertfordshire's education committee set out to achieve with most determination.

Village schools, so long and so recently derided, were soon to be hailed as the means of social, cultural and, above all, economic regeneration.

The idea of an approved Hertfordshire Rural Syllabus originated with Captain Morris, who became chairman of the county education committee on the sudden death of Canon Glossop in 1925. He readily acknowledged that the NFU, in which he was a key county and national figure, was closely involved in the compilation of the Syllabus and that it had been approved by the National Council of Agriculture.[26] The local content and teaching approaches were worked out by a county sub-committee including teachers, farmers, HMI, education officers and the principal of Oaklands.[27] The end product was published in February 1927. Fundamentally the Rural Syllabus invoked modern teaching approaches in the service of an intense programme of agricultural and vocational education. With characteristic bluntness Morris stated that its advantages were that if children:

> settled on the farms they became better workers. If they went to the towns they would take with them a knowledge of the countryside, and a love for the country. If they settled in the Colonies it would fit them better for the Colonies, and make them better citizens.[28]

The Board of Education published *Rural Education* a year before Hertfordshire's Rural Syllabus, and although it was not mentioned in any county minutes or newspaper reports it must have prepared the ground for Morris's initiative. The Board envisaged a rural bias permeating and enriching most subjects of the curriculum, but *Rural Education* effectively blurred the distinction between vocational training and education. It asserted that many practical crafts and skills:

> are equally valuable in urban and in rural schools, but in rural schools they have perhaps a more direct bearing upon everyday life, their practical utility is more evident, and there is therefore, in this sense, a certain natural connection between education and vocation.[29]

In *Rural Education* Science embraced plant and animal studies, elementary mechanics and the properties of air, water and soil. The gardening syllabus identified the articles produced in Handicraft lessons and provided many of the subjects for Drawing. Mathematics included school garden accounts, scale plans, map work and an analysis of local markets. Domestic Science concentrated upon dairy products, the use of herbs and the preservation of local fruits. Geography was studied partly through the local climate, physical features and land use, and History involved a shift in emphasis from political to social and economic developments.

Hertfordshire's Rural Syllabus complemented all this, but directed it differently. The intensity of the experience was its telling feature. All subjects were to possess a definite rural bias within the classroom, and beyond it. Indeed, total immersion in rural life was the aim. Every local farm, field, fruit, house, hill, hedge, stream, skill, song, crop and craft was studied in depth through a host of walks, talks, practical activities and integrated projects. The Syllabus had many exciting features, with tasks and approaches clearly laid out for teachers and attractive to children. Nevertheless, despite the impressive range of themes to explore, the Syllabus ensured the distance the children travelled literally and conceptually was limited. Epitomising this point was the positive discrimination that operated in the selection of textbooks and readers, those 'bearing on country life and subjects' being paramount. Another significant feature was the central place held by the story of British agriculture in History.[30]

Hertfordshire's greatest departure from the Board's recommendations was in the emphasis on farming. The Board advocated wide-ranging parish surveys and expected them to have a strong historical bias. In Hertfordshire the dominant feature was detailed agricultural studies made on site, reinforced by work back in school. Farm surveys were to be in depth, with each class making a minimum of two and a maximum of six visits each term. The farmer, the teacher, and sometimes an Oaklands member of staff would guide the visits. So important were these visits that ten of the fifteen pages of the Syllabus were devoted to detailed questions children should ask about crops, animals, buildings, equipment and the host of daily and seasonal tasks.[31] Other intensive studies were to be made of rural industries such as mills, malthouses, wheelwrights and blacksmiths.

Hertfordshire's Rural Syllabus included numerous opportunities to corner and channel children's interest in local agriculture. As early as January 1927 the local press saw the vocational motive as obvious, but no less welcome for being so clear. It commended the LEA for boldly providing 'specialised educational facilities' for rural children 'fitting them to undertake, on leaving school, agricultural occupations'.[32] With Edmund Barnard as chairman of the county council, Sir Charles Longmore as Clerk, Captain Morris as chairman of the education committee and William Graveson as his vice-chairman, the rural lobby was at the height of its influence.

The year 1927 saw the Rural Syllabus launched in twelve schools, chosen because their existing rural bias impressed Captain Morris and HMI Bloom. Six more schools were added during the first year and another fifteen during 1928.[33] A Hertfordshire curriculum initiative was so rare that a measure of prestige was attached to selection for the Rural Syllabus. This was enhanced by the special courses for their teachers at Oaklands, a £7 equipment grant and a temporary initial increase in staffing. Such willing expenditure confirmed the high standing of the Syllabus in the minds of county councillors and education committee members.[34]

Undoubtedly all parties wanted the Rural Syllabus to work. The years 1927 to 1930 saw a flurry of specialist projects by enthusiastic schools, with the regular farm visits as central features.[35] The LEA pursued publicity avidly, and in 1928 an education sub-committee was created, with a budget of £50, to display a selection of the children's practical projects at the prestigious County Agricultural Show.[36] In the light of press eulogies, the budget was doubled for succeeding years.[37] Approbation reached its climax with the visit in July 1928 of the Duchess of Atholl, Parliamentary Secretary at the Board of Education, to a selection of the schools using the Syllabus. Captain Morris told the education committee, and the press told the rest of the county, that the Duchess not only believed the schools were recapturing children's interest in country life but the example of the first pupils who had taken up the Oaklands agricultural scholarships indicated 'that this work is full of possibilities and hope for the future'.[38] No-one in Hertfordshire had any reason to doubt that this meant the Board approved all aspects of the Syllabus. In the summer of 1929 an emboldened LEA revised the Syllabus, extending the farming topics and adding new sections on woods, villages and different types of country houses.[39]

The fame of the Rural Syllabus became national, and then international. By 1930 Howe could report that copies of the Syllabus had been requested from Canada, the United States of America, India, Australia and Jamaica, and that it 'has been adopted in its entirety by three or four English counties'.[40] The school at Hertingfordbury, a few miles from the county town, achieved an exceptional rural bias and attracted an exceptional range of visitors. The headmaster had turned the campus into a miniature rural estate and based much of the curriculum on its detailed running. From 1927 until 1930 his logbook records a host of distinguished visitors – the Duchess of Atholl, Sir Charles Trevelyan, Sir Michael Sadler, the BBC to record programmes for its series 'Elementary Agriculture for Rural Schools', the directors of education for Cyprus and Jamaica, officials and councillors from other LEAs, training college principals, and a steady stream of inspectors from the Board of Education and Ministry of Agriculture. In due course the headmaster received an MBE, membership of the BBC's Natural History and Science Committee, and invitations to broadcast and lecture.[41]

Wilstone School, c.1910 (HALS)

Wilstone School: pupils spinning, 1939 (HALS)

Wilstone School: pupil dyeing wool, 1939 (HALS)

Wilstone School: pupil weaving, 1939 (HALS)

The Syllabus flourished throughout the 1930s. The wave of interest by distinguished figures subsided, but from 1932 onwards the visitors to Hertingfordbury were no less important, comprising mainly classes of children and their teachers and a stream of training college lecturers seeking advice.[42] HMIs continued to use the children's projects in major displays, and the headmaster was prominent in organising the Rural Science Exhibition at the Royal Agricultural Society's Centenary Show held in Windsor Great Park in the summer of 1939.[43] At this event Wilstone, another much-publicised Hertfordshire village school, contributed an exhibit called 'Sheep to Scarf' which celebrated a curriculum based largely upon countryside studies and handicraft. A farmer had donated fleeces and the pupils also collected tufts of wool caught on briars, hedges and fences. The wool had been washed and then coloured in saucepans over the classroom fire using dyes made from tree bark, rhubarb, walnut leaves, onion skins, tea leaves, elderberries and ink. Using an array of looms loaned by parents, given by the LEA and made by older pupils, the children had woven material, including a tartan, to make scarves, caps, cushions and ties, and they had also used the wool to knit cardigans, gloves and tea cosies. Many of the finished articles had been sold.[44]

HMI Bloom was keen to promote the Syllabus. He was astute enough to recognise the LEA's utilitarian motives, but in 1929 he believed the occasional accusations of social conditioning to be an acceptable price to pay for the 'definite invitation to schools to experiment freely' within the Syllabus's relatively broad framework.[45] In 1932 a major conference at Oaklands revealed the way the Syllabus was satisfying all parties. Farmers were proving cooperative with schools, the Ministry of Agriculture was keeping the LEA up to date with agricultural developments, and a wide range of rural crafts and well-designed projects were flourishing in village schools.[46] HMI and the schools defined success more in terms of teaching approaches than vocational training – the new freedom for children to talk in class, work independently, plan in groups, integrate subjects, engage in genuine investigations, deal with people and things in context, and draft their findings without excessive concern for spelling and handwriting.[47] The Wilstone pupils were engaged in particularly active learning processes, but a file of in-depth essays compiled by older pupils at Watton-atte-Stone during 1936 confirms the continuing attention given to written work. The essays, each several pages long, are probably carefully composed final copies of corrected drafts, perhaps for public display. They combined detailed factual information, lengthy eulogies of the countryside and its seasons, and a familiarity with well-known poems celebrating the natural world, all of which helped fulfil the cross-curriculum criteria of the Rural Syllabus and imbue a particular view of the local environment.[48] An essay on a ploughing competition gave close descriptions of the horses, tractors, ploughs, furrows and competition rules, interspersed with a celebration of autumn colours and fruits. Another essay centred on hedging and ditching, and led on from the plants and wildlife observed by the writer to accounts of the farm workers' traditional skills. A third was devoted to a walk through the village and, with A.H. Clough's poem 'Green Fields of England' as a backcloth, it described the old Roman road, the overhanging Tudor houses, and the continuing age-old use of the village pump, laundry, animal pound, allotments and chalk pit providing garden lime. The arrival of the railway and hopes of mains water supplies were the only concessions to the outside world. The attraction of the visits and multi-discipline projects might well have been conducive to a renewed interest in rural life and work, although equally well they could have emphasised to young people the isolation and relative backwardness of village life. However, county education committee members never doubted the Syllabus's capacity to stem rural depopulation, and to lead more school leavers to register on the county's agricultural courses.[49]

The vocational element rose increasingly to the fore during the later 1930s, and the Board of Education acquiesced in this trend. It was not politically expedient for the Board to be suspected of subordinating educational aspirations to agricultural requirements, and therefore the Board's signals to LEAs and schools were glimpsed between clouds of progressive-sounding dialogue. In 1934 the Board's new pamphlet *Education in the Countryside* made much of the change of title from *Rural Education* published in 1926, and publicly distanced itself from the vocationally minded Ministry of Agriculture. Nevertheless it asserted that:

> neither cultural nor utilitarian needs can be met by an education which does not freely derive its content and its inspiration from the environment of the pupils,

and then argued that:

> schools, and particularly those in country districts, should be regarded ... as social institutions evolved by the community for the preservation of its distinctive life and for the satisfaction of its cultural and other needs.[50]

The best teachers, said the pamphlet, used the local environment as an educational stimulus, and if this included imparting 'some knowledge of the principles underlying the future work of the majority of the children', so much the better.[51] It justified this argument with a survey of southern counties which revealed that 63 per cent of boys left village schools to work on farms or in rural trades, and 70 per cent of girls took up domestic work. For isolated villages the figures were much higher – 87 per cent and 88 per cent respectively.[52]

Hertfordshire county council welcomed the increasingly obvious shift in government policy. In 1935 members recorded their satisfaction at the statement made by Herwald Ramsbotham, a senior Conservative MP, in the House of Commons that the aim of rural schools was 'to create a vital interest in country life, and not to make the education of the children just a stepping stone to life in towns and cities'.[53] In 1936 the education committee took immediate advantage of the Board's revised regulations, which encouraged vocational evening classes for school leavers in rural districts. The county's programme specifically targeted villages whose schools had adopted the Rural Syllabus.[54] In 1937 a Board of Education memorandum eulogised the new generation of rural senior schools far more for the potential extremity of their agricultural bias than for their provision of wider educational and social opportunities compared with small all-age village schools. Greater depth, not greater breadth, seemed the objective – more farm visits, more agricultural history, more rural science.[55] In 1938 the Board provided more money for rural teachers' courses in rural subjects, and urged LEAs to promote the Young Farmers' Club movement.[56] In the weeks immediately prior to the outbreak of war the Board and Ministry of Agriculture sought a joint policy openly encouraging 'any necessary reorientation of rural education' to serve the needs of agriculture.'[57] Captain Morris could not have put it more positively.

Alongside the Rural Syllabus there was a huge expansion in school gardening generally. After the Armistice teachers and HMI began the transformation of gardening from a wartime production line to an educational pursuit, but the county council and education committee showed little hesitation in channelling these efforts to their own advantage as sources of vocational training. Indeed, by the 1930s many intensively worked 'ordinary' school gardens were indistinguishable from those in schools following the Rural Syllabus.

In 1921 there were 258 elementary schools in Hertfordshire; 92 of these had recognised grant-aided gardens and another 50 had cultivated plots on a less formal basis. A total of 116 schools were without gardens, but of these 80 were urban, 10 were for infants and juniors only and most of the remainder were so small that even HMI considered the task beyond them.[58] Gardening, with its direct impact on a range of curriculum subjects, was consistently encouraged by LEA grants, HMI reports, Board of Education pamphlets, county competitions, a host of donated cups and shields, and positive newspaper publicity.[59] It became a fashionable pursuit, but it owed its new status to a combination of paradoxical

Gardening class at Letchmore School, Stevenage, c.1923 (Stevenage Museum)

trends. It appealed as much to those who viewed elementary education as a means of social conditioning as it did to those seeking new practical approaches to teaching and those possessing post-war visions of healthy, happy childhoods. It harked back to older concerns for strictly directed activities inculcating utilitarian skills, and virtues such as discipline, perseverance, ordered routines and patient craftsmanship, in the mass of the nation's children. The uneasy but obviously attractive blend of old attitudes and new aspirations characterised the LEA's *Handbook* of 1923, which emphasised the moral qualities inculcated by gardening and its practical relevance to adult life alongside the need for theoretical understanding and individual experimentation.[60]

The *Handbook* guided developments throughout the 1920s. The pre-war practice of using local gardeners as unqualified instructors was abandoned, and headteachers were expected to take personal charge of the subject which, HMI asserted, should be inextricably linked to English, Art, Handwork, Science and Mathematics.[61] Gardening, therefore, increasingly dominated the rural schools' curriculum, and there can be little doubt that county education committee members found the growing number of classes propagating flowers, fruits, vegetables and small livestock, and studying soils, seasons, weather, pests and manures singularly gratifying. In addition, HMI and headteachers happily reported that if

School garden at Applecroft School, Welwyn Garden City, late 1920s (HALS)

'dull' children were given appropriate tasks they became as interested in gardening as brighter ones.[62] In 1926 the LEA confirmed its enthusiasm for the new breadth and depth of gardening by granting funds for an extensive display by twenty-one schools at the prestigious Bath & West Show.[63]

In 1930 HMI bestowed high praise on both the Rural Syllabus and Oaklands for the stimulating influence they had had on all schools, not just those formally adopting the all-embracing Syllabus. A new 'zest and keenness' for the study of the natural environment were seen everywhere.[64] The county's gardening instructors were made subordinate to Oaklands' principal, and throughout the 1930s the institute broadened the concept of gardening across the county. A strong rural influence was promoted through a combination of intensive courses for teachers, the increased involvement of girls, the thorough correlation of gardening with other subjects, the regular inspection of gardens and syllabuses, plenty of practical tips and the regular dissemination of ideas and pamphlets from the Ministry of Agriculture.[65]

During the early 1930s the acute economic depression probably ensured Oaklands kept its paymasters constantly in mind. In 1932 it came under close scrutiny from the county council's Special Expenditure Committee, but by then it was the LEA's indispensable ally after a decade of shrewdly targeted work since the post-

to play the LEA at its own game. Throughout the years from 1927 to 1939 a prolonged series of tortuous negotiations were conducted, resulting in a number of compromises in each of which Board policy, education committee objectives and village aspirations were fulfilled to varying degrees of satisfaction. Overall, though, the education committee triumphed, as few groups of villages were fully reorganised and few villages lost their schools. The crucial point was that increasing portions of rural districts were becoming urbanised, making it increasingly difficult for the LEA to avoid acquiescing in the establishment of new or refurbished senior schools serving a cluster of decapitated village schools, a number of which might well become too small to survive the reduction in roll. Many county councillors and education committee members from rural areas found the thought of village pupils falling under the influence of the children and culture of urban senior schools utterly abhorrent.

On all occasions the LEA sought to assert its own preferences. Sometimes a scheme could be agreed quickly if all parties stood to gain. In 1929–30, for example, the LEA was unusually active in reorganising the neighbouring villages of Ayot St Lawrence, Ayot St Peter and Welwyn. For several years the villages had feared that not all of these three Church of England schools would survive as rolls steadily fell, and the newly established Schools Reorganisation Committee (SRC), acting on behalf of its parent body, the county education committee, negotiated a solution whereby Ayot St Lawrence's school closed, Ayot St Peter's became a junior and infants' school for both villages, and all pupils over the age of eleven joined those at Welwyn, whose school remained all-age but now became sufficiently large to have separate junior and senior departments.[89] The managers were in agreement, as all the schools were Anglican, the most dilapidated building was closed and sold, and all efforts could be directed at improving Welwyn's premises and accentuating its rural bias. From the education committee's perspective, public expenditure was reduced, family inconvenience minimised, the Hadow benefits cheaply acquired, and the county's rural policy upheld. By 1930 the school at Welwyn had such a high reputation for its Rural Syllabus activities that the SRC acceded at once to Bloom's request that two other small Anglican schools in the neighbourhood should be asked to accept decapitation and send their older pupils to Welwyn. Woolmer Green agreed, but Digswell refused and stayed all-age until after the Second World War.[90] The LEA never subjected it to any further pressure as, either way, all the pupils remained country-educated children.

Intransigent managers and antipathetic communities could easily frustrate group reorganisation schemes. Accumulating pressures could also oblige the SRC to take on the unwelcome role of arbiter in heated local disputes, with not only the interests of county councillors and education committee members at stake but also the Board of Education and Bloom making their views clearly felt about the appropriateness of any solution. A striking case occurred in 1929 when the Board finally persuaded the procrastinating SRC to coax some agreement between the neighbouring but warring villages of Offley and Cockernhoe, each possessing particularly decrepit school buildings. In the end Offley stayed all-age and its refurbishment was agreed, but to Cockernhoe's fury its school was decapitated. Villagers were only partly mollified by the LEA's promise of transport to Offley and the provision of facilities for cheap hot dinners.[91] A similar combination of dilapidated buildings and declining rolls had existed for many years in Rushden, Sandon and Wallington, a triangle of villages to the east of Baldock. Once again rivalry between neighbouring communities and jealousies between managers frustrated all hopes of agreement about local reorganisation and school improvements. Finally the Board lost patience and threatened to withdraw its grant because of the state of the buildings, forcing the LEA to propose a single new all-age school and the provision of transport. This was postponed indefinitely during the recession of the early 1930s, and it was not until 1936, after numerous local, county and diocesan meetings, that Rushden and Wallington finally resolved their differences and agreed to refurbish one shared Anglican school. This left Sandon out in the cold until 1938, when the LEA stepped in to agree a new school.[92] In all these villages, though, the children stayed in rural schools.

In 1930 Bloom proposed the reorganisation of ten village schools around a new purpose-built senior school with a rural bias sited in the market town of Buntingford. He played upon the avowed preferences of the LEA and used a little flattery to get his way. He argued that the village schools endured 'generally poor' premises, the practical work they could offer was limited, and their older pupils needed better discipline and greater stimulation. He tempted education committee members with the thought that a model senior school:

> in the heart of agricultural Hertfordshire would afford a fine opportunity for carrying out the County Council's aims in regard to rural education as expressed in the Herts Rural Syllabus.[93]

He added the temptation of national fame to the local investment, as:

> under favourable conditions of staffing and equipment a really high level of attainment might be attained and a senior school with an agricultural bias might be created which would be a model for the country.[94]

The education committee agreed. The scheme promised an intensive rural bias throughout a prime agricultural area suffering severe depopulation. The farming community would appreciate the rural bias being formalised in the facilities and staffing of a brand new senior school which, it was decided, would offer part-time vocational courses for interested pupils up to the age of sixteen before their entry to Oaklands. Rural parents would see that new senior schools were not only an urban phenomenon. Only the village school managers had mixed feelings. No longer would they face mounting expenditure on facilities for their senior pupils, but the reduced rolls would leave four schools with twenty-five pupils or fewer.[95]

The onset of the national depression in 1930 and the government's calls for strict economies in public expenditure called a halt to reorganisation plans. The Buntingford negotiations foundered on the questions of the new building and the future of the decapitated schools, and talks on a scheme involving five independently minded Anglican schools in and around Hunsdon also came to a complete standstill.[96] In January 1932 the education committee was obliged to debate the fate of eighteen schools with twenty-five pupils or fewer on roll. Although members shared the general enthusiasm for cutting costs, and revelled in the investigations of its Special Expenditure Committee, it was clear that any reductions would not be at the expense of rural communities. The committee refused to 'destroy the centre of village life' by closing Great Wymondley and Hinxworth schools, or to overburden other schools by closing Arkley or Shephall, and a combination of the inconvenience it would cause and the cost of transport saved six others. In the end just two very small schools closed and another two amalgamated.[97]

In April 1932 the committee reprieved another four schools newly identified for possible closure with a ringing public affirmation of the principle that modest savings did not compensate for the permanent damage to village life. The vocational aspect of elementary education, with an equally strong element of social conditioning, was uppermost in members' minds in the widely reported statement that they:

> do not consider that the education provided in a town school is necessarily the best education for a country child having regard to his probable future occupation and interests.[98]

The determined education committee reprieved Gilston in 1933 and Therfield in 1935.[99] When it finally agreed Clothall's closure in November 1932, it was in full knowledge that no growth could be expected in the village and that the schools in the nearby agricultural centre of Baldock had spare places.[100] Similar circumstances, with the additional incentive of appalling inspection reports, explain Great Wymondley's demise in 1934 after prolonged agonising.[101]

As the depression faded the Buntingford scheme looked more hopeful. The villages acknowledged the financial difficulties in maintaining their all-age schools, and recognised the educational advantages of the new senior school with its distinctive rural bias.[102] Graveson, too, appreciated and publicised the advantages to the district. Handicraft, he argued, would benefit from the concentration of expensive equipment, group activities would benefit from skilful streaming, and pupils and the whole locality would benefit from the wide range of rurally oriented programmes of study across the curriculum.[103] In 1937 all ten village schools approved the resurrected proposal, and the education committee took obvious pride in providing an officially recognised, fully equipped, rurally biased senior school. It opened in September 1939, and by then fourteen surrounding schools had decided upon decapitation.[104]

The reorganisation at Buntingford was the only complete rural scheme implemented before the outbreak of war, and it was the only district to gain a new rural senior school. The LEA did not accept it as a precedent for action on such a scale elsewhere, despite Bloom's enthusiasm. In vain he incorporated six other rural senior schools, serving a total of forty-five villages, into the comprehensive county reorganisation proposals he drew up in 1936. His accompanying report, made just before the Buntingford agreement, lamented that 'reorganisation of the rural schools of Hertfordshire may be said to have made no headway at all.'[105] Just 12 per cent of them had been reorganised, compared with the national average for rural areas of 27 per cent.[106] Bloom's tone reflected his frustration. He stated that no evidence existed to suggest rural children became 'urbanised' by being concentrated in senior schools. He deprecated the enforced limitations of space, specialist teaching and competition in village schools. He commended another LEA – almost certainly Suffolk – which had negotiated a county-wide agreement with church authorities which enabled an equitable reorganisation into junior and senior schools to take place as swiftly as finances permitted.[107]

Hertfordshire, however, continued to keep its rural children in an exclusively rural atmosphere throughout their formative years. 'There were', Graveson reasserted at the County Teachers' Association annual dinner in 1936, 'two different types of education for the rural and urban children', and no-one disagreed then or after the newspaper report.[108] In the eyes of county councillors the fatal weakness of Bloom's proposals was his division of Hertfordshire into numerous catchment 'circles' comprising a mix of town and country junior schools feeding urban-based senior schools. Suffolk's example of county-wide rural decapitation and the dominance of urban senior schools was anathema to them. In 1937, amid calls for 'agriculture and horticulture in every school', and laments for the future of farming if Bloom's report was accepted, the county council voted unanimously to ensure 'a fair proportion of senior schools in rural areas'.[109]

The intensity of Hertfordshire's rural bias was unusual, and the same forces had not conjoined in the neighbouring counties of Essex and Buckinghamshire. In 1928 W.O. Lester Smith, the influential director of education in Essex, confirmed that rural schools would be reorganised, without delay, alongside urban ones.[110] Different priorities prevailed there. For Essex LEA the problems of rural employers were completely outweighed by the advantages of specialist teachers, greater stimulation and increased employment opportunities for the pupils. Only where rural headteachers 'of rare genius' existed would reorganisation be deferred, and then only until their retirement. A county report in 1934, and a further survey in 1935 examining developments since 1928, confirmed that this policy was implemented – although badly affected, as everywhere, by the depression of the early 1930s.[111]

In Buckinghamshire, too, the LEA forged ahead with rural reorganisation from 1927 onwards and, in marked contrast to Hertfordshire LEA, it had scant sympathy with local objections. There was no attempt to preserve rural isolation, and every attempt to avoid giving an agricultural bias to the new senior schools serving a cluster of surrounding villages.[112] Indeed, after several bruising disagreements with local objectors to rural reorganisation, in 1935 the unabashed Buckinghamshire education committee publicly regretted the 'hesitation on the part of some of those living in those areas to accept the view that this change is an educational gain'.[113]

During the years 1936 to 1939 the struggle between the Board of Education and Hertfordshire LEA over rural reorganisation was played out against the general adoption within many Hertfordshire towns of the Hadow recommendations and the establishment of up-to-date senior schools. For example, in 1936 Bloom urged that rural as well as urban children over eleven should have the opportunity to attend the reorganised senior school in Hitchin. Predictably, the education committee rejected the idea, preferring to persuade the managers of the school in the large village of Offley nearby to reorganise as a small rurally biased senior school accepting pupils from most of the country schools Bloom had in mind.[114]

In July 1936 an Education Act was passed. It was much criticised at the time, and by historians ever since, as a reluctant and mean-spirited Conservative attempt to raise the school leaving age to fifteen while affording pupils every opportunity to avoid it by gaining what was liberally described as 'beneficial employment'. However, the Act also contained relatively generous financial clauses aimed at providing the necessary extra senior school places by 1 September 1939, the date the extra year was to become mandatory. LEAs were permitted to enter into 'special agreements' with managers of voluntary schools, whereby grants of between 50 per cent and 75 per cent of the capital costs could be made towards the enlargement and improvement of existing schools, or the building of new ones, for senior elementary pupils. In addition, the minimum grant to LEAs towards the cost of new council senior school buildings and equipment was raised from 20 per cent to 50 per cent. The government hoped that at least some of the financial difficulties preventing Anglican and Roman Catholic schools agreeing to reorganisation schemes could be overcome. All parties had until only 1 March 1938 to submit proposals to the Board.[115]

Not surprisingly, Hertfordshire education committee welcomed the financial and 'beneficial employment' clauses, and saw the Act as the opportunity to round off the commendable diversity of elementary education provision it had created across the county. In the summer of 1937 the LEA agreed to five rural 'special agreements' with Anglican school managers and the Diocese of St Albans education committee. Buntingford became one, Offley was another, and the existing rurally biased senior departments at Tring, Watton-atte-Stone and Welwyn were to be replaced by new voluntary schools, each serving a larger rural area than before.[116] These were all in small market towns surrounded by village schools which, with varying degrees of willingness, accepted infant and junior status. These schemes contained something for everyone. The Church of England would retain complete control of elementary education. The senior schools would have a marked rural bias, an essential factor for the education committee and local employers. Parents would appreciate the extended facilities, and the Board would see that the LEA was embarking upon a rural reorganisation programme.[117] The county education committee had shown little prior interest in altering the all-age status of the village schools surrounding these small market centres, but in 1936 members were quick to appreciate that the rural 'special agreements' were likely to be comfortably long-term solutions, and would significantly ease everyone's financial headaches.

To the end of the 1930s the LEA retained overwhelming local support for its rural policies. Even Labour county councillors considered some of the benefits worthy of acknowledgement, although they invariably added that depopulation was due to decades of inadequate agricultural wages. At a county council meeting in 1937 Lindgren poured scorn on those who justified village schools primarily as trainers of farm workers and were terrified of letting country children out of their communities. A colleague had no hesitation in asserting that 'many of those present were largely responsible for the shocking conditions in the Hertfordshire villages.'[118] On the other hand, Lindgren believed the village school well worth preserving as a working-class facility, and emphasised the great inconvenience that distant senior schools could cause labouring families. To that extent he concurred with county policy, and that concurrence meant that no-one in Hertfordshire – unlike Essex and Buckinghamshire – gave much thought to providing rural children with a broad and balanced education that would prepare them for living and working in any other type of community.

CHAPTER TEN

The church schools controversy

IN 1918 THE CHURCH OF ENGLAND remained a major stakeholder in education, possessing thousands of elementary schools it had established over the past century. In some areas, such as Hertfordshire, it was *the* major stakeholder. However, the 1920s and 1930s represented a prolonged threat to its continuing influence over children's schooling. From the late 1920s onwards the creation of a definite break in children's education at the age of eleven led to a massive long-term reorganisation of school provision, forcing parishes and dioceses within the Church of England, and indeed within the Roman Catholic Church, to make crucial decisions regarding their future roles in education. In addition, the standards of buildings, facilities and equipment, and therefore costs, were constantly rising, despite the intermittent scares regarding the national economy.

If ecclesiastical parishes possessed sufficient funds, they could secure permanent places in the district reorganisation schemes. If they did not, they had two options. They could risk public odium and delay reorganisation indefinitely by falling back upon their legal rights in the hope of changing fortunes, or they could give up their schools and cease their involvement in education in that area, probably for ever. Relinquishing any church school, however impoverished, was not on the agenda of the Anglican diocese of St Albans, or many Church of England parishes in Hertfordshire. As a result, a series of prolonged, determined and frequently bitter struggles ensued to protect church schools against all schemes posing a threat to their continued existence. The continuing influence of Church of England religious teaching was considered well worth the persistent delays to local reorganisation plans and the consistent hostility of all those who found the numerous dilapidated buildings as intolerable as the partisan religious influences.

In 1920, there were still 189 voluntary elementary schools in Hertfordshire,

St Mary's Church of England School, Welwyn, was typical of the larger Anglican schools built in the nineteenth century (HALS)

180 of them Anglican, 7 Roman Catholic and 2 Nonconformist, with 22,256 pupils in average attendance, compared with 66 council schools and 16,490 pupils.[1] Nineteen years later, the ratio of pupils had more than reversed, with 149 voluntary schools (142 Anglican and 7 Roman Catholic) having 16,310 children, compared with 25,389 in 101 council schools.[2] However, these statistics should not be seen in simple terms of Anglican defeat and LEA victory, as they conceal the significant, if partial, success of Anglican efforts, and the deep regret of many economically minded county councillors and education committee members at their LEA's extra administrative and financial responsibilities. A number of large Church of England senior elementary schools had been built, and many others renovated, to counter the loss of several dozen, mainly far smaller, antiquated buildings. The Church of England had many sympathisers, and indeed worshippers, among county councillors and education committee members, and they had welcomed its successes and lamented the closures.

Nevertheless, as the 1920s shaded into the 1930s the huge influx of population, the urgent demands of urban reorganisation and the determined broadening of the curriculum all combined to test the considerable patience of the LEA with impecunious and dilatory church school managers to breaking point. In 1918 the LEA was generally content to allow Church of England parishes to call the educational tune, especially as neither party wished to incur undue expense, but by 1939 the situation and the relationship were very different. The LEA had been obliged to seize the initiative in numerous controversial urban reorganisation schemes and the Church of England was fighting for its educational survival in many towns. Frequently both the LEA and the parishes, whether in agreement or at loggerheads, were besieged by resurgent Nonconformist congregations, usually in formidable alliance with local Liberal and Labour groups, who saw an opportunity to rid significant parts of the county of Anglican schools. In 1918 the LEA went out of its way to protect Anglican interests, but by 1939 its erstwhile partner had become a liability in its die-hard opposition to many LEA proposals. The change was traumatic for all concerned – Church of England parishes, Nonconformist chapels, county, district and town councillors, local political parties, and parents. Old alliances had been eroded and relationships soured, the fires of sectarian controversy had burned fiercely, and political tensions had heightened dramatically.

Anglican problems were acute nationwide immediately after 1918. Building costs were rising just at the time when many Victorian schools, woefully neglected during the war years, needed substantial renovation. The new Education Act had ended all exemptions from attendance, and obliged the extension of practical and advanced instruction for older pupils. The pattern of nineteenth-century school provision was increasingly ill-matched with twentieth-century demographic trends. While many village schools had spaces to spare as depopulation gathered pace, rapidly proliferating urban housing estates led to the embarrassment of numerous impoverished parishes struggling with overcrowded as well as antiquated buildings. Church attendance was in continual decline, and so was income. Estimated numbers of Church of England and Nonconformist worshippers fell from 35.5 per cent of the population in 1901 to 17.7 per cent in 1935. Each year more crumbling Anglican schools across the country, and the last Nonconformist ones, were handed over to the control of LEAs.[3]

A badly shaken Church of England seriously considered reaching a radical agreement with Lloyd George's Coalition administration soon after the war. In 1920 H.A.L. Fisher proposed that voluntary schools should be transferred to LEAs in return for facilities for giving denominational religious instruction in all publicly aided schools where parents wished it. Many Anglicans concurred, welcoming the financial relief and the broader access to children, but the scheme collapsed under the combined opposition of Nonconformists, who saw it bolstering up ailing Anglican influences, Roman Catholics, who feared the eradication of their schools' distinctive influences, and the National Union of Teachers, who opposed all hints of religious tests for teachers.[4]

The Church of England had little choice but to continue to sacrifice numerous schools to LEAs or to arouse a new missionary zeal in its supporters. In the end Anglican dioceses largely went their different ways during the inter-war years, with their bishops playing a wide variety of roles depending upon their convictions and personalities. In St Albans, as in other dioceses, the bishops remained a spiritual, moral and social force very much to be reckoned with by their clergy, and by school managers, parochial church councils and, indeed, the LEA. In an era when the legally enshrined 'dual system' remained firmly in place, significant legal and political, as well as educational, dimensions were added to episcopal authority.

The Right Reverend Michael Bolton Furse, Lord Bishop of St Albans, had no hesitation in exercising every ounce of his authority, and his enthronement on 22 April 1920 proved to be a decisive moment in diocesan and county affairs. Without doubt Furse believed the times were critical for the nation, and without doubt, too, he believed the Church of England could, and should, show the way forward. His personality, convictions, and style of leadership contributed significantly to the pattern of educational development that evolved in Hertfordshire. Lasting nearly twenty-five years, his episcopate revealed the considerable authority that could be wielded by a diocesan bishop at this time, together with the significant social and political support he could call upon with confidence. It revealed, too, the lingering strength of Nonconformists and Liberals, and the rising power of Labour associations, who challenged his assumptions and limited his success.

In November 1919 the *Hertfordshire Advertiser* hailed the impending arrival of the new bishop. It described Furse in suitably vigorous terms as 'muscular Christianity personified' and 'hating extremes, either up or down'.[5] A tireless pastor rather than a scholarly theologian, Furse's long reign amounted to a relentless campaign to promote parish missions, rejuvenate church-based social life, restore crumbling parish churches, retain church schools, and revive voluntary giving to pay for it all. He never hesitated to encourage, even cajole, incumbents and congregations into greater efforts, and he was a constant parish visitor. His exhortatory autobiography, *Stand Therefore!*, derived its force from his life-long assumption that only the Church of England could save families from moral turpitude, the nation from Bolshevik revolution, and the Empire from disintegration.[6]

The Right Reverend Michael Bolton Furse, Lord Bishop of St Albans

Born in 1870, Furse was the son of a wealthy Devon squire and parson who later became Principal of Cuddesdon Theological College, Oxford, and then Archdeacon of Westminster. He had the secure, earnest and well-connected upbringing characteristic of many late Victorian upper-middle-class children and, as historian Andrew Hastings has said, the majority of early twentieth-century Anglican bishops.[7] He was educated at Eton and Trinity College, Oxford, and then travelled the world prior to returning to Oxford as a Fellow of his college in 1895. He was on familiar terms with important figures since his childhood, such as Charles Gore, successively Bishop of Worcester, Birmingham and Oxford, William Stubbs, Bishop of Chester and Oxford, Edward Lyttelton, headmaster of

Haileybury and Eton, and Arthur Winnington-Ingram, Bishop of London, and no doubt he admired the force of their personalities, their pastoral work and their preaching skills in equal measure. With this family background and connections, his preferment came quickly. Ordained in 1896, he remained at Trinity as chaplain until appointed Archdeacon of Johannesburg in 1903. In 1909 the diocese elected him Bishop of Pretoria, where he stayed until translated to St Albans.[8]

Much of Furse's vigorous and uncompromising style of leadership was powered by deep personal convictions, especially regarding the dire need for nationwide moral regeneration. His adult views can be seen developing from childhood. His father had considered a church school 'as indispensable a part of the necessary equipment of the Church for carrying on its work as the parish church itself'.[9] He had subsidised a village school and encouraged others to do likewise. He had chosen and guided the teachers, and endured the hostility of those who feared the unsettling effect of education upon country children. Furse revered his father, and shared his conviction that religion should pervade every aspect of life, and certainly all aspects of education. Decades later, in 1937, Furse publicly acknowledged that his fight to save church schools was the debt he owed his father.[10]

A lasting impression was made on Furse by the prolonged, if unsuccessful, campaign by a group of Oxford clergy and 'some of the squirearchy' to persuade the diocese to prosecute his father under the Clergy Discipline Act for 'Romish practices and teaching'. Like his father, Furse believed the Church of England to be 'nearer to the mind of Christ' than any other church, and while the campaign wounded them both, it was, therefore, faced and countered with determination.[11] Forty years on, Furse proudly reasserted that the Church of England 'stood for the freedom of man against the autocracy of Rome on the one hand, and against the individualism and fissiparous tendencies of Protestantism on the other'.[12] His upbringing had convinced him of the worldwide mission of the Anglican Church, but it served also to identify for him the sects and parties within it, as well as outside, which threatened its success. Such experiences may well explain his singlemindedness, and some of his more aggressive and uncharitable actions at St Albans.

The bishop's social advantages were many, but in them lay the dangers that would intensify local divisions and undermine his educational aspirations. Over six feet tall and powerfully built, Furse cut an imposing figure in parish churches, schools and halls. Classically educated, wealthy, a good amateur actor and an expert sportsman, he was completely at home in the country houses and public schools of Hertfordshire. He was an unashamed admirer of the socially exclusive public schools, and perceived the main sectors of English education – public, secondary and elementary – as separate entities with few children meriting transfer from one to another. His work as an older schoolboy in the Eton Mission in the slums of Hackney had included regular talks to the recipients of its charity on the enduring frailty of human nature, the need for penitence and the hope of divine grace. More than thirty years later in St Albans, when avidly promoting the centrality of religion and morality in the curriculum, he came near to damning sections of the largely working-class clientele of elementary schools as uniquely prone to fecklessness and debauchery, and almost beyond lasting redemption.[13] Such views helped polarise opinion about the bishop. Many agreed with his class distinctions, but others, especially branches of the Labour Party and trades unions, were outraged.

The patrician element in Hertfordshire local government remained unusually strong throughout the inter-war years, and significantly strengthened the voice of the Church of England. Furse's social and educational aspirations for his diocese, all of them concerned with traditional values of personal responsibility, parental duty, voluntary giving and community regeneration, attracted many leading families to his cause. At least four Conservative MPs for Hertfordshire constituencies were staunch Anglicans: Lord Robert Cecil (Hitchin 1911–23), Major Kindersley (Hitchin 1923–31), Lieutenant Colonel Fremantle (St Albans 1919–43) and Dennis Herbert (Watford 1918–45). All four were members of the St Albans Diocesan Synod, and active supporters of Furse's high-profile campaign to preserve church schools. When they, and other Conservative candidates, mentioned education in speeches or interviews, it was to praise the church–state partnership enshrined in the 'dual system', condemn the baleful influence of Labour and atheist teachers, eulogise the Conservative Presidents of the Board of Education, and resist calls for wider access to secondary education.[14] In short, they adhered to the Party line, and their partisan voices did much to reinforce the reality, as well as sharpen the image, of the traditional Anglican–Conservative alliance, and thereby arouse the deepest suspicions of their disparate Liberal, Labour and Nonconformist opponents.

Lord Salisbury was a devoted Anglican and a member of the Diocesan Synod. Indeed, on the national front, the Cecils of Hatfield House and their equally aristocratic relatives effectively controlled the business of the House of Laity in the Church Assembly, the new governing body of the Church of England. The Earl of Selborne was chairman from its inception in 1919 until his death in 1942, and five of his family were members – his son, Lord Wolmer, his son-in-law, Earl Grey, his brothers-in-law, Lord Salisbury and Lord Hugh Cecil, and his sister-in-law, Lady Florence Cecil. They were very active members, sitting on influential sub-committees, while another brother-in-law, Lord Robert Cecil, chaired the Church–State Commission of 1936. Indeed, for all the moderately radical opinions of a few senior clergy, Andrew Hastings concludes that the Cecil dominance of the Church Assembly, firmly buttressed by the family's extensive political experience and assured social position, helped create a more consistently Conservative Church of England in the period after the First World War than before it.[15]

The diocese of St Albans knew it had a fight on its hands immediately after the war. As Furse saw things, an aggressive and atheistic Socialism was in the ascendant, and this was stoked by the militant Bolshevism that had destroyed Imperial Russia. He saw apathy all around him in those who should have been challenging these alien forces. Throughout England worshippers were far fewer, parishes were often indifferent to the fate of their schools, and Furse was sure that family life was decaying in the void left by the decline in moral influences, religious teaching and charitable support. Yet in this discouraging situation he remained utterly convinced that the church school was one of the essential components, alongside the good home and the well-used parish church, in an effective Christian upbringing. There were, simply, no substitutes.

A head-on campaign to avoid marginalisation formed part of the diocese's response. In several towns branches of the Church Managers' and Teachers' Association were hurriedly set up to protect the interests of church schools.[16] In Cheshunt, the vicar met the Workers' Educational Association for a highly charged, well-publicised but inconclusive debate between those who believed religion to be the essential part of education and those who considered it peripheral.[17] In Buntingford, the clergy resolved to match the 'steadily improving' secular side of education with an intensive programme of school lessons, parish classes and home visits.[18] Furse had no sympathy with the diocesan inspector of schools, the Reverend Basil Reay, whose 1918 report had advocated an end to sectarian controversy, speedy accommodation with Nonconformists over religious instruction, and a joint advance on a broad Christian front in all schools.[19] Coincidence or not, a new inspector was soon appointed.

A series of closures and transfers of ailing church schools soon after the war incensed the new bishop. In Hertford, Hoddesdon, Walkern and Watford the parishes initiated closure with their regret more than a little tinged with relief at

the release from a heavy burden. Few seriously lamented the loss of the superannuated buildings and their Church of England status, and the ensuing LEA reor-
ganisations took place without controversy.[20] The fate of the last Anglican school
left in Watford illustrates the interwoven responsibilities and pressures, and also
the limits of episcopal authority over school managers. In 1920 the Board of Education condemned the building, the managers gave notice to discontinue it, and
the LEA resigned itself to total responsibility for the children.[21] Soon afterwards,
Furse issued his first episcopal *cri de coeur*. Asserting that the spiritual health of a
parish was in direct proportion to the strength of its defence of its school, he
urged all clergy and congregations not to flag in the face of secular attacks. Henceforth, he expected all parishes considering capitulating under the burden of renovation schemes to seek advice and support from the diocesan authorities.[22] A
belated stirring of support in Watford led the surprised but delighted education
committee to defer the expansion and renovation of its alternative premises –
another dilapidated school. Interest proved ephemeral, however, and amid considerable embarrassment the church school closed in July 1922.[23]

By the mid-1920s several towns had been compelled by a combination of overcrowded and superannuated buildings to reorganise their schools. Usually the
LEA played the part it preferred, that of broker negotiating the generally accepted
compromise between, on the one hand, local managers, churches, councils and
education sub-committees, and on the other, HMI and the Board of Education.
Usually, too, the cheapest option prevailed. The LEA could rely on this being the
wish of most of the interested parties, and especially the churches. The Board,
though, was far less consistent in the degree to which it demanded local improvements during these years of fluctuating economic fortunes. On a number of occasions parishes burdened with substantial fund-raising, and facing the loss of their
schools, were reprieved by the Board's sudden change of mind during an adverse
turn in the national economy. Such decisions, delaying improvements and preserving dilapidated Anglican schools, disappointed many others and sharpened
sectarian feeling. In Harpenden the vicar ignored the outcries at the unexpected
respite and resurrected his stuttering campaign to renovate the parish's two
schools and fend off LEA intervention.[24] Conversely, in Hitchin it was the Anglicans who bitterly resented the lingering survival of the antiquated Nonconformist school.[25] In Hoddesdon the situation was different again. In 1921 the
recession halted an unusually amicable agreement whereby both crumbling
Anglican and Nonconformist schools closed within months of each other, has-
tening the construction of a new 800-place council school. The Board obliged the

LEA to negotiate with the churches to keep both buildings open with merely the addition of a couple of huts, and it was another five years before anything further was done. Few Anglicans and Nonconformists complained, and district council-lors welcomed the temporary financial relief.[26]

The greatest controversies occurred, as in Harpenden, when the Anglicans decided not to bow out, as most people expected, but strove to maintain their influence when expansion and reorganisation were in the air. Accusations of ecclesiastical privilege and religious indoctrination were accompanied by ques-tions about the quality of provision and freedom of choice, and issues of public cost and accountability were never far away. The Nonconformist trust that Pank valued so highly broke at the first post-war test, and throughout the 1920s and 1930s the Church of England was frequently condemned as a legally protected educational anachronism by Nonconformists, Liberals and Labour groups alike. It perpetuated, its opponents claimed, outmoded aims, and provided poor build-ings, inadequate facilities and a biased education. To add insult to injury, many local children were compelled to endure these evils irrespective of their families' religious persuasion, as no other schools were accessible.

The more the state raised standards, the harder the Church of England had to fight to maintain its role in public education. The harder it fought, the more obvi-ously partisan became its objectives, the more threatening seemed its chances of success, and the more violent and vociferous became the united political, educa-tional and sectarian opposition. In 1926 in Stevenage, for example, the Anglican school managers faced repeated charges that their ancient buildings were the cause of widespread illness among the children. The defenders of the school soon felt besieged, and when their repeated denials were accompanied by counter-accusations of personal malice and Bolshevik-inspired agitation the combined fires of sectarian and political controversy burned brightly.[27] The clashes of the 1920s were mere opening skirmishes, however, compared with the battles of the 1930s.

Issues of finance often complicated local disputes, and sometimes led to unusual alliances. In the early and mid-1920s the parish of St Michael's, Bishop's Stortford, met a mixed reception as it debated and finally decided to build a new infants' school. For the economically minded majority of district councillors the substantial saving in local rates promised by voluntary efforts consistently out-weighed the resentment of those within the council and outside it who much pre-ferred the LEA to renovate the old ex-Nonconformist school building.[28] In Rickmansworth the two Anglican parishes, the district council and the education sub-committee were united in opposition to the LEA's proposals for a new ele-mentary school in this expanding town. In 1921, as a result of their repeated charges of culpable extravagance, the LEA radically downgraded its plans. Catch-ment areas were rearranged, and a few huts were erected to provide the cheapest possible solution. However, the decision cut dangerously across local social and religious groupings, and dramatically rebounded upon the district council and churches. They became the hostile targets of several deeply aggrieved groups, including families of children transferred between a working-class school and a predominantly lower-middle-class one, families of children transferred between schools attached to churches of very different traditions, and non-Anglican fami-lies whose children were transferred to Anglican schools. The Board withdrew its agreement for the new school, and for the next fifteen years the town and its Church of England parishes endured the unhappy and unresolved consequences of the ill-considered reorganisation.[29]

However, considerations of finance were sometimes pushed into the back-ground. In Baldock in 1924, the Liberal and Nonconformist groups, speaking through their majority on the town council, agitated for a new council school. Everyone had agreed, including the parishes providing them, that the Anglican schools needed either serious renovation and expansion, or replacement. The controversy arose over the Anglican decision to remodel its schools, thereby maintaining its dominance over elementary education in the town. Furse actively promoted the Anglican cause locally, giving it a diocesan dimension which stiff-ened the resolve of the opposition. Both parties, when provoked, as invariably they were at public meetings, revealed that the arguments of sanitation, sites, and even costs, were entirely subordinate to the greater battle for control of the schools and the children's hearts and minds. Not surprisingly, the LEA and the Board preferred the cheaper Anglican option, a relatively modest improvement staggered over several years.[30]

In Hertfordshire, as elsewhere, religious and political groups sensed that these were 'make or break' years for the Church of England regarding education. The Baldock controversy indicates this, as does the bitter dispute which swept through the twin villages of Aldenham and Radlett in 1926. Both ancient com-munities were being overwhelmed by new housing estates, and the parish coun-cils and parents' groups campaigned vigorously, but ultimately unsuccessfully, for new well-equipped council schools to replace the antiquated Anglican ones. Their campaign became all the more intense as the long-term alternative, ardently pursued by Furse, was another relatively cheap refurbishment scheme staggered over several years.[31] An identical situation led to an equally highly charged dispute within Chipperfield a few months later.[32] In these controversies, as elsewhere, both sides resorted to well-publicised public meetings complete with partisan speakers and loud interruptions from the floor, and local newspapers filled many columns with detailed reports and correspondence.

In 1928 the Conservative government's decision to create a clear educational divide at the age of eleven and improve facilities for older pupils accentuated rather than allayed local aspirations and anxieties.[33] Lord Eustace Percy, President of the Board of Education, made it clear that he expected LEAs to make the running in reorganising local schools, and he asserted they had all the powers they required.[34] Almost as an omen, the LEAs' recent involvement in Chipperfield, Aldenham and Radlett confirmed the conflicting educational, religious and political interests that could so easily rage around any proposal. Not surprisingly, the county education committee agreed that caution was the watchword.[35]

Late in 1928 the Schools Reorganisation Committee (SRC) began its consultative and planning work. No-one in authority – Sir Edmund Barnard and Captain Morris, chairmen of the county council and education committee, and Lord Eustace Percy at the Board – thought there should be any hurry. They hoped that existing school buildings could be used to better advantage, minimising the need for new works. They recognised that the church schools would have a powerful voice, and would stand their ground. Percy had upheld the desirability of development through cooperation, and the LEA assumed that, as a result, progress would be very slow, and said so publicly.[36]

Everyone accepted that the LEA was the richer partner in the 'dual system', but Furse consistently denied that this implied any change in the relationship. Early in the 1920s the education committee welcomed voluntary investment in schools, but by the end of the decade impoverished parishes were resorting to every legal wile, with full diocesan support, to stagger costly repairs, counter public protests and delay LEA schemes. Education committee members were particularly incensed by the growing Anglican inclination, openly fostered by Furse himself, to accuse council schools of being virtually Godless institutions.[37] The bishop rode roughshod over all protests, but the education committee's sensitivities grew acute just at the time that the rather *ad hoc* reorganisation schemes were being replaced by larger and more urgent programmes forced by the soaring population and government policy. The LEA began to view its Anglican partner as a useful but minor relief of the rates at best and at worst an acutely frustrating producer of disharmony and delay. As the pressure grew, the Church of England could, and did, look obstructionist as well as obscurantist. These public criticisms, along with the charge of 'godlessness', were the last ones the LEA wished to incur itself, and despite many education committee members' sympathies with church schools, official patience wore increasingly thin and relations soured as the 1930s progressed.

In June 1929 Sir Charles Longmore comfortingly reassured his audience at a Church of England fete that 'the County Council would not be a party to any measures which would not help the church schools.'[38] Nevertheless, the LEA refused Furse's request to be regularly and formally consulted by the SRC, presumably seeing it as an unwanted interference with LEA business and an unnecessary provocation to other churches and their political allies.[39] A diocesan policy statement reminding school managers of their legal rights and spiritual duties appeared at the same time, and could not have endeared Furse to the education committee. It reaffirmed that Church of England schools were bulwarks against 'the growing tendency to a purely secular attitude towards life', and as lasting attitudes were believed to become fixed in adolescence, managers were urged to provide for senior rather than junior children if obliged to make a choice. Parishes were encouraged to draw upon the greater financial, legal and moral resources of the diocese when faced with negotiations with the SRC.[40] They were not expected to capitulate. To hand a school over, Furse vehemently declared, would be 'a disaster' and 'cut at the root of religion and education in this country'.[41] The statement was followed by a strident call to arms for a prolonged campaign to restore not only the fabric of church schools but also their place at the heart of the local community alongside the parish church.[42]

Furse sent further shock waves through the county by announcing early in 1929 that a major revision of the 1904 Hertfordshire Agreed Syllabus was needed. An Agreed Religious Instruction Syllabus was just that – a syllabus of undenominational Religious Instruction agreed between the major Christian churches and accepted by the LEA for use in its schools. A well-publicised diocesan letter to the LEA stated bluntly that the current Syllabus contained 'little more than suggested portions of the Bible to study, and says practically nothing about the Christian principles which should be taught'.[43] Council school managers and teachers were appalled, and challenged his claim.[44] For several weeks the atmosphere was tense, as people recalled the acrimony before and after the 1902 Education Act.[45] Sir Edmund Barnard and Captain Morris demurred, fearful of adding more fuel to the sectarian fires already consuming local reorganisation proposals.[46] Indeed, those fires flared fiercely when the diocese intimated that the

Hertfordshire Congregational Union, a major force in the 1904 debate, had no right of representation on Agreed Syllabus panels as it no longer possessed any schools.[47] Furse applied his contempt of those Anglican parishes he believed to be faint-hearted with equal force to Nonconformist congregations; both merited scant sympathy. With justification, Nonconformists immediately suspected that the Church of England sought the best of both worlds – its own schools where possible and, where these could not be provided, an Agreed Syllabus revised heavily in its favour.[48]

In June 1929 a nervous LEA formally established an Agreed Syllabus standing conference, but avoided all direct association with it.[49] Furse was prominent in the discussions, but to the education committee's openly acknowledged surprise and relief a new agreed scheme was submitted to it six months later with no intervening outbursts of controversy. The new syllabus significantly extended the old one; it highlighted that the gospels should be interpreted in the light of Christ's revelation of God and of the life to come, and emphasised the development of Christian life and character through prayer, worship, obedience and service.[50] For Furse, these were vital components in education, but the syllabus still failed to satisfy him. It did not, for example, include the Reformation, the development of the Church of England, or anything about Anglican missionary work. The very features the press praised – an Agreed Syllabus presenting the 'basic facts ... clearly and simply, without the slightest sectarian bias' – Furse was soon to condemn as meaningless.[51] Neither at this sensitive moment, nor later, was he prepared to make any concessions to ecumenicalism, and Nonconformists felt betrayed. It is difficult to explain the bishop's sudden criticisms of the work with which he had been closely, and apparently harmoniously, involved, but perhaps he sought the best of both worlds again – an Agreed Syllabus which was a little more Anglican in content but still alien enough to condemn in the greater campaign to preserve denominational schools.

The widely reported 1929 St Albans Diocesan Conference set the tone for Anglican involvement in educational affairs for the next decade. It was so uncompromising in tone that the Board itself took note.[52] Furse was the driving force, and played relentlessly on fears of the new Labour government, resurgent Roman Catholicism and a corps of unsympathetic teachers in council schools. A fund-raising campaign was launched with a target of £15,000, later raised to £50,000 and then to £80,000, and for the next decade the bishop and dean repeatedly exhorted parishes to greater efforts on behalf of their threatened schools.[53] Furse continued to invoke moral blackmail, portraying each church school as a sacred trust and its preservation as a tangible sign of local faith.[54]

Mounting urban pressures meant that the SRC could not avoid complex situations, and it displayed persistence in attempting to resolve them. Berkhamsted was an early case, and here every conceivable difficulty and cross-current existed. The Anglican schools educated 800 of the 1,000 elementary pupils, but the town possessed a strong Nonconformist minority that was well-represented on the local council, education sub-committee and council school managing body. The principle of a senior school was not disputed, but everything else was – its site, its ownership and its cost. Berkhamsted was a cramped town straggling for two miles along the bottom of a narrow, steep-sided valley, and objections were easy to make against each of the few available sites. The dispute over Church of England or LEA ownership incorporated the whole range of religious and political beliefs but, fundamentally, ranged Anglicans and Conservatives against Nonconformists, Liberals and Labour groups. Cutting across all these issues was the overall cost, involving interwoven questions of sites, facilities, transport and the combatants' preferences for local rates or voluntary subscriptions. The discussions were prolonged and futile, and in the end the managers patched up their schools and the talks collapsed alongside the economy in 1931.[55]

The SRC had some early successes, but in several cases the solutions merely stored up problems for the future. In Hertford and St Albans it negotiated schemes which satisfied the Anglican parishes, local councils and the LEA, but few others. As we have seen in Chapter Eight, in Hertford the impoverished Church of England schools were allowed to survive through decapitation and the disused grammar school became the senior elementary school. St Albans was deliberately divided into three divisions and the eight Anglican schools were given exclusive control over one of them.[56] Here, too, the survival of so many antiquated buildings and the lack of investment in those becoming senior schools were constant causes of complaint.

In both Hertford and St Albans the Roman Catholic elementary schools were allowed to stay all-age with merely an internal reorganisation of classes and curriculum. The Roman Catholic authorities consistently refused to join any reorganisation scheme that threatened the loss of their senior pupils and the all-age (5–14) status of their schools. In the event, the intransigence of this minority group was not perceived by any other group as a threat worth contesting, and the special treatment incited no opposition. They were quietly incorporated into post-Hadow schemes as anomalies on the understanding that they would gradually reorganise themselves internally into junior and senior departments.

Some Anglican schools were highly regarded across local communities, and changes were deeply regretted. In 1932, after more than four years of discussion and delay, the SRC announced that Barnet's reorganisation was complete. The widespread sorrow expressed at the decapitation of a popular Church of England school was a moving tribute to its fine academic tradition, active involvement in community affairs and flourishing Old Boys' Association. Many people deeply resented the curtailment of its work, and the anger persisted. The County Teachers' Association confirmed the lingering dissatisfaction, its journal lamenting that 'much of proved worth has been wiped out, and old traditions and associations ignored'.[57] In Letchworth, the popular Church of England school at Norton played a full part in the town's unusual educational developments, which centred far more upon parental convenience than adherence to government wishes. Until the late 1930s one school had an internal division at the age of nine, another at ten and another none at all. In 1931, Norton managers considered decapitating their school, but discussions across the town led to universal agreement that ten years' time would be soon enough, when the population growth might merit some general reassessment of the situation.[58]

Furse's declared preference for senior schools made them the great prizes in reorganisation negotiations. Not surprisingly, the diocese's model senior school was in St Albans itself, where, notwithstanding the depression, the bishop and dean ensured their showpiece was planned, funded and completed between 1929 and 1934. It certainly improved the quality of provision in the carefully created Anglican 'district' in the city.[59] Other parishes lacked such status, but a few created their own opportunities. In 1929 the SRC considered the cramped all-age Church of England school at Royston to be unsuitable for incorporation into its reorganisation scheme and proposed a new council one. However, the managers hotly disputed the decision, and gained the Board's support for renovation rather than replacement. The skilfully managed and successful fund-raising campaign based itself upon two key factors – the school's excellent reputation, not least for its broad approach to religious education, which far outshone its dismal buildings; and ensuring residents were aware that a new council school would burden them with a sixpenny rate for the next thirty years.[60] A similar reputation and equally lively campaign gained the parish of Wheathampstead both a new senior and a new junior school. It is indicative of overlapping LEA and Anglican interests that while Furse expressed sectarian satisfaction at this victory, Captain Morris emphasised the financial relief.[61]

An even greater Anglican triumph was achieved in Ware where, unusually, the Church of England controlled all three schools, with over 900 pupils on roll. Between 1929 and 1932 their managers circumvented all jealousies of their monopoly and criticisms of their unsatisfactory buildings to survive reorganisation not only unscathed but with reputations enhanced. Pooling resources, the parishes formulated a scheme to renovate and extend their buildings, reorganise them into infant, junior, senior and selective central schools, and place them all under one joint managing body. They launched a successful fund-raising campaign for £5,000, later raised to over £7,000, and gained extensive press, public and business support through the sheer coherence of the changes, the obvious lack of religious discrimination in the schools, and the equally obvious rate relief. Significantly, Furse toned down his speeches and sermons for this campaign, emphasising the similarities between good council and church schools as well as the advantages of attending the latter. In just over three years the Anglican scheme was in place.[62]

Where the factors that made reorganisation in Royston, Wheathampstead and Ware successful were absent, conflicts could frustrate developments for years at a time. The cause could be Anglican disunity as much as external hostility. When the church school in Baldock considered conversion into a senior school in 1929 Furse gave the parish every encouragement, but internal disagreements over the mounting costs caused the scheme to be abandoned. It represented a failure of will and faith abhorrent to Furse.[63] In nearby Hitchin, one parish quickly accepted the SRC's overall scheme whereby its school acquired senior status, only to find the school in the second parish stubbornly delaying reorganisation by refusing decapitation.[64] Similar disunity ruled in Abbots Langley and Kings Langley, where the river Gade running between them symbolised the deep antipathies between these adjacent parishes. In 1930 the SRC, as a matter of urgency, proposed a new council senior school and the decapitation of all five voluntary schools. Immediate deadlock ensued as each parish fought to have a senior school of its own. For the next seven years the parishes campaigned against the LEA and the diocese, but most fiercely of all against each other, while gradually succumbing to the tide of immigration and the hopeless task of maintaining old overcrowded schools as they tried to raise funds for new ones.[65]

The SRC's grand design for comprehensively reorganising the now contiguous old villages and new estates of Hoddesdon, Broxbourne, Wormley, Rye Common and Rye Park foundered for different reasons of parochial individuality. In 1929 a new centrally sited council senior school was proposed, with all other schools becoming contributory junior and infants' schools. Two impoverished

Church of England schools instantly capitulated, but the parish of Broxbourne successfully delayed large-scale planning for the remaining inter-war years by optimistically yet interminably seeking funds to renovate and reorganise the three schools it controlled.[66] The significant educational opportunities being missed by a generation of children aroused deep hostility towards the parish and its faltering efforts. Here, as elsewhere, Furse's sole objective was the inclusion of church schools in as many schemes as possible through the vigorous action of local clergy, school managers and ordinary parishioners. Current hardships and the arguments of opponents were of little concern.

The early 1930s proved increasingly critical for the diocese as pressures mounted within and outside its fold. Government policy and demographic trends were forcing the reorganisation bit between the LEA's teeth, making it increasingly intolerant of Anglican intransigence. In addition, the rising Labour strength in several towns and the arrival of the first Labour county councillors made any lingering tendency towards overt sympathy with Anglican anxieties and aspirations far less easy to conceal.

On top of this, the diocese's own educational crusade faltered. In 1929 Labour had formed a minority administration, with Sir Charles Trevelyan at the Board of Education. Trevelyan fervently believed that raising the school leaving age was the key to successful Hadow-style reorganisation, but his repeated efforts to force Bills through Parliament collapsed in the face of vigorous opposition, not only from Conservatives but also from many Liberals fearful of financial concessions to the Anglicans and, conversely, a group of Roman Catholic Labour MPs who demanded firm guarantees of adequate funding for their schools. Trevelyan's proposals incorporated enhanced grants for senior school building work, vital for district reorganisation and the accommodation of the extra year, but the *quid pro quo* for voluntary schools was a significantly larger LEA representation on their managing bodies.[67]

Furse welcomed the grants, but abhorred any hint of reducing church school managers to mere advisers of the LEA in the appointment and dismissal of staff. However, the issue widened divisions within the diocese, some clergy asserting that church rights were infinitely preferable to LEA grace, while others considered the financial relief worth the loss of privilege in a fundamentally beneficent county.[68] The momentum of Furse's school fund-raising was seriously threatened. At the 1930 Diocesan Conference several clergy and laity argued that government action and the Anson byelaw (which allowed pupils transferred from church schools to council schools to receive Church of England religious instruction at specified times) were rendering voluntary giving to church schools superfluous. The devotees of church restoration rather than school reorganisation clearly hoped they would have the field to themselves, but Furse, Salisbury and Fremantle eventually carried the day with their dark suspicions of the beliefs of council school teachers and scathing contempt for the Agreed Syllabus. With his rousing battle-cry that Anglicans 'may not fail our country and our God', the bishop rendered saving the schools synonymous with the salvation of the country.[69]

Trevelyan's Bills frustrated reorganisation because LEAs as well as church school managers tended to defer decisions until the outcome of the prolonged parliamentary debates and votes. With Trevelyan's final failure followed by the depression, by the mid-1930s Hertfordshire had a vast backlog of building works, and numerous schemes in disarray. Epitomising the situation at its bleakest was Cheshunt, where SRC plans for the district had foundered in a welter of arguments among individual churches, political groups and local councils. There were six Anglican, one Roman Catholic and six council schools catering for over 2,000 pupils. In 1929 the SRC proposed leaving the all-age Roman Catholic school untouched, creating one Anglican and one council senior school, and phasing out or rebuilding the rest after wholesale decapitation. The ensuing conflict raged for a decade, with three Anglican managing bodies in turn considering and then crying off building a costly senior school. Eventually a fourth delighted Furse with its greater determination, but succeeded in arousing the well-rehearsed Labour, Liberal and Nonconformist groups to new heights of opposition. The constant argument and delays left thirteen schools superannuated in design, inadequate in facilities, archaic in organisation and succumbing to the weight of numbers.[70]

By the mid-1930s Furse was openly disappointed in parochial efforts to refurbish schools or contribute to campaign funds. Caustically, and typically, he asserted that the Bolsheviks would leap at the chance to propagate their beliefs five days a week.[71] Unhesitatingly he condemned parochial apathy, the enemy in their midst, bluntly charging:

> that every Church School surrendered definitely weakened the Christian position in this country, and that every Church School that was neglected spiritually was a weapon in the hands of those who confused what was meant by Scripture instruction with what was meant by religious education.[72]

The diocese, though, was over-extended. It was running two campaigns at once – for church restoration as well as church schools – and well-publicised arguments over its priorities at meetings and conferences gave credence to public suspicions of a deeply divided diocese.[73]

In addition, Furse could seem distinctly uncharitable. He proclaimed that education involved the inculcation of Christian virtues, and this necessitated the acquisition of the Christian faith. Few contested this claim, but his utter lack of faith in undenominational religious instruction, and those who taught it, fitted ill with his signature on the new Agreed Syllabus. His suspicions of council school teachers hit a sensitive public nerve, and gained him praise and obloquy in equal measure. Historian Martin Lawn has shown how the Conservative Party, and many of its local associations, became anxious during the 1920s, sometimes to the point of paranoia, at the teaching profession's move towards the Labour Party.[74] Lord Eustace Percy himself spoke publicly about the dangers of potentially subversive socialist teachers, and Scotland Yard's Special Branch investigated at length many teachers active in the Labour Party, especially if they were professed pacifists or atheists.[75] Furse's regular alarmist comments in this vein were set within this national obsession, and contributed to it. They gained him some support at diocesan conferences, but also repeated reproofs from the County Teachers' Association.[76] Understandably, he had a lukewarm reception at the 1930 CTA conference despite, or maybe because of, his public denial a week earlier that he had castigated council school teachers as atheist.[77]

Dioceses differed. The Church of England's contribution to educational developments varied in direction and degree from one to another. Most were far from apathetic, but most preferred cooperation to confrontation. As early as 1925 the Archbishop of Canterbury, Randall Davidson, had told his diocesan conference that they could not compete with the LEAs, and argued that deliberate obstruction to reorganisation schemes would harm the children's education and erode the Church's reputation. 'In these circumstances', he concluded, 'it is useless to make dramatic declarations as to the savings of the Church schools.'[78] Davidson was in full accord with the Bishop of Wakefield, who saw diocesan authorities becoming the trusted advisers of LEAs on religious education in the increasing percentage of council schools. Indeed, a year earlier Cambridgeshire LEA, the Diocese of Ely's Association of Voluntary Schools and the Cambridge Federation of Free Churches had produced an Agreed Syllabus which attained national renown for the stature of its compilers and their sensitive handling of Christian doctrine. The LEA made a public commitment to its full and careful use in schools and teacher-training colleges, and this significantly allayed many Anglicans' fears about the transfer of schools to LEA control.[79] The Cambridge approach was adopted by several other LEAs, and although known and discussed in Hertford-shire it was anathema to Furse.[80] It was anathema also to the staunchly Noncon-formist borough council of Hemel Hempstead, which vigorously resisted the attempts of local Anglicans to secure its use in all local schools.[81]

Even those bishops sharing Furse's fervent desire to preserve church schools eventually sought alternative approaches. In the mid-1930s the Bishop of Gloucester roundly condemned successive governments for starving church schools, their legal partners in the 'dual system', of adequate funds to match the curriculum and building standards demanded by new policies. Reluctantly, though, he acknowledged that the situation appeared irredeemable, and urged diocesan energies, expertise and funds to be directed towards securing more effective religious teaching in all types of schools.[82] George Bell, the internation-ally renowned Bishop of Chichester, was equally realistic about finance but more generous in spirit. In 1930 he announced that his diocese could afford to mod-ernise only a small proportion of its schools, and it could not, and should not, finance any new senior schools. It should, though, actively encourage reorganisa-tion, and he envisaged a new and vibrant partnership with Sussex LEA which included the transfer of numerous schools and overall improvements in religious teaching. Through reciprocal goodwill he sought, and gained, the LEA's liberal interpretation of the Anson byelaw.[83]

Essex LEA and the diocese of Chelmsford followed suit. The county had grap-pled with steady urban immigration for several decades longer than neighbour-ing Hertfordshire, and a tradition of sound LEA school-building was well-established.[84] The diocese recognised this, the Bishop of Chelmsford acknowledging in 1928 that we 'must see that children did not suffer by being edu-cated in church schools'.[85] Several times during the 1930s he rued the closure of village schools and the failure to build new senior ones, but there were no episco-pal tirades or militant campaigns. 'Unhappily', he admitted in 1933, 'we have let things slide to such an extent that it is doubtful whether the Church could impress the politicians with the weight of their case', and his lingering hope that parishes would 'erect a few Senior Schools in places of strategic importance' was never ful-filled.[86] In due course, the bishop rested content that the LEA had adopted the Chichester proposals, and in the later 1930s he went out of his way, perhaps in deliberate contrast to St Albans, to praise academic standards in council schools and the devoted Anglicans working in them.[87]

In Buckinghamshire, another neighbour of Hertfordshire, a far closer work-ing relationship developed between its diocese and LEA. Soon after *The New*

Prospect became government policy the county education committee and Diocese of Oxford Council of Education established a Joint Conference Committee to consider and implement reorganisation schemes in districts with a mix of church and council schools. It produced and refined schemes, and members discussed them at length with local groups. Dilatory or recalcitrant parishes were visited by senior diocesan figures, usually the suffragan Bishop of Buckingham, to resolve problems quickly.[88] There were no attempts to delay schemes, no support for die-hard incumbents, no moral blackmail of parishes, and remarkably few controversies.

Furse never considered such routes, and consistently damned them as abject surrender to inherently unstable public bodies who could easily renege on earlier agreements. Instead, he raged against parochial apathy, and incited bitter sectarian and political controversy. His aim was openly partisan, as he told the 1935 diocesan conference. 'What was needed', he stated, 'was denominational teaching – instruction which tended to give a child an intelligent appreciation of a body of truth that was held by a body of believers.'[89] By then his extremist views were being contested, and the impact of his speech was severely deflated by a loquacious critic who argued that church schools were fading fast, and that diocesan efforts would be better directed at creating good relations with Nonconformists and revitalising the Agreed Syllabus.[90]

However, a solution to Anglican impoverishment, and to some of the reorganisation schemes locked in controversy, seemed to be offered by the 1936 Education Act. This Act, it may be remembered, raised the leaving age to fifteen with one hand and allowed children who secured 'beneficial employment' to escape its demands with the other, and empowered LEAs to enter into financial 'special agreements' with church school managers to hurry along reorganisation schemes. If the LEA and then Board of Education approved, grants of between 50 per cent and 75 per cent of the capital costs could be made towards the extension of existing schools, or the building of new ones, for senior elementary pupils. In return for the enhanced grants the Act brought church school teachers under the authority of the LEA, although managers had the right to determine the suitability of an agreed number of 'reserved' teachers to take responsibility for religious education in accordance with the school's syllabus. The Board required church schools to reach agreement with the LEA and submit grant applications by 1 March 1938.[91]

The financial clauses were welcomed enthusiastically by Hertfordshire LEA, not least because they altered the balance of negotiating power substantially in its favour.[92] 'This gift from the gods' was how Sir Joseph Priestley, chairman of the county council, described them.[93] Seizing the initiative, the SRC never lost it. It formulated new schemes incorporating both council and church schools, it renewed negotiations where they had collapsed, and it made tempting offers of the maximum capital grant of 75 per cent to selected parishes where three-stream senior schools could be built to avoid creating competition with council senior schools in the same locality. The parishes themselves, though, were given little room for manoeuvre. The building standards had to be high, facilities had to include a central hall, craft workshops, science laboratories, domestic science rooms, a gymnasium and playing fields, and a deadline of 31 March 1937 was imposed for financial guarantees.[94]

Furse had feared the ability of the LEA to exploit the Act. During the passage of the Bill he had envisaged a different partnership to the one espoused by the LEA, arguing that the government should match its moral and financial support of church schools with far greater trust in their teachers and teaching. He had opposed any encroachment of the LEA upon staff appointments, claiming such moves placed the Anglican spirit in schools seriously at risk. He had not missed the opportunity to condemn the apparent lack of Christian fellowship among the young as 'the natural outcome of Undenominational Christian teaching'.[95] In the end, though, 'special agreements' were hurriedly reached for eight new Church of England senior schools across the county – in addition to Buntingford, which also qualified for the grants. Four formed part of belated urban reorganisation schemes in Berkhamsted, Bishop's Stortford, Cheshunt and Radlett, and they were planned as large schools with three or four forms of entry. The other four were the smaller rural schools at Offley, Tring, Watton-atte-Stone and Welwyn mentioned earlier. In addition, agreement was reached to enlarge two Anglican schools at Hatfield and Hitchin and three Roman Catholic schools at Barnet, Puckeridge and Waltham Cross. All the schools were given 75 per cent grants.[96]

The agreements were a triumph of grandiose aspirations over inadequate resources. In August 1937 the Archdeacon of Hertford and the diocesan secretary visited the Board of Education to admit that the establishment of nine new schools was probably beyond parochial and diocesan resources, even with the enhanced grants. They argued that as the LEA originally suggested the construction of so many Anglican schools it should not insist upon such rigid financial guarantees and high building standards. Board officials had scant sympathy with this special pleading, and refused to intervene. The meeting's only achievement was to confirm the Board's suspicion that the LEA should distinguish more carefully between rhetoric and reality in its dealings with such an ambivalent diocese.[97]

A frenzy of diocesan activity ensued. The recently appointed dean, C.C. Thicknesse, was well known throughout the Church of England, and at the Board of Education, as a fervent traditionalist in religious education and an aggressive defender of church school rights.[98] In the highly charged atmosphere of the 1937 diocesan conference Thicknesse and Furse savagely indicted 'the results of sixty-seven years of undenominational religious instruction', and called for concerted action to counter the 'growing disregard of the primary duty of Christian worship', challenge the 'widespread revolt against any form of institutional religion' and stem the 'increasing ignorance ... of the Christian faith among the younger generation of parents and their children'. The Church of England's alternative, warned the dean, was 'suicide within two generations'. Their powers of persuasion overrode all opposition to make the 'special agreements' the primary financial objective, and the intensive fund-raising continued.[99]

The fates of the 'special agreements' reveal the dichotomy in the diocese's position. It possessed undoubted rights, but it claimed far more than its declining strength and influence were perceived to merit by the LEA and many sectors of public opinion. In contrast the LEA, whose religious education Furse openly despised, found itself blessed with high rateable values, enhanced government grants and a large measure of control over the new round of negotiations. In such dramatically changing circumstances, talk by William Graveson, the Quaker chairman of the education committee, of 'mutual co-operation and good fellowship' had much of the confidence of the generous victor about it.[100]

The 'special agreements' proved to be 'curate's eggs' – satisfactory in parts. As we have seen, five of them completed long-standing rural schemes, each involving only Church of England schools, where finance rather than discord had caused delay. Buntingford, Offley, Tring, Watton-atte-Stone and Welwyn were small market towns surrounded by Anglican village schools which, short of funds, were reassured by the prospect of their older pupils attending purpose-built senior schools of the same religious and educational persuasions.

The Act certainly neatly resolved the problems in and around Tring. The town's only senior school was Anglican, and although for several years its managers had wished to take the older pupils from the surrounding small villages they were unable to bear their share of the costs of improvements to the building. The school had a high reputation and when the 1936 Act was invoked the 'special agreement' was quickly secured.[101] Even in Aldenham and Radlett, where bitter controversy had raged, the 'special agreement' went largely unchallenged as it brought a new and well-equipped senior school significantly closer to fruition.[102] Intensive fund-raising locally and the selective targeting of diocesan grants eventually ensured the success of these projects, although Buntingford was the only 'special agreement' school in Hertfordshire to open before the outbreak of war in 1939.[103]

The difficulties experienced elsewhere showed the haste with which some decisions had been reached. The Bishop's Stortford agreement was probably the most ill-judged. It relied on the corporate action of eight parishes and their school managers, and it foundered because local interest and parochial harmony fell far short of diocesan expectations. Local jealousies meant that schools and parishes in nearby Sawbridgeworth were determined not to lose their older pupils to their larger neighbour, Bishop's Stortford. After this very public debacle the three parishes in Bishop's Stortford itself suffered an embarrassing failure to incite interest in an independent fund-raising campaign.[104] Indeed, there was a marked reluctance in both these market towns for any expenditure on a new school of any sort. For once this was not due to overt hostility to the churches but, as the local farmer Captain Morris explained at a district council meeting, because both towns considered themselves part of a wider rural community and were content to do without a large centrally sited senior school of any description.[105] In an acerbic assessment of recent trends a few weeks later, Morris argued that as the facilities and curriculum of the new senior schools now aped those of secondary schools, they were increasingly unsuited to the type of children they were intended to teach.[106] Bishop's Stortford and its environs successfully avoided reorganisation until after the Second World War.

In and around Cheshunt and Berkhamsted, where sectarian and political divides had continually frustrated reorganisation, the 'special agreements' ignited confrontations unprecedented in bitterness. In Cheshunt the Anglican parishes launched a major fund-raising campaign while their Nonconformist, Liberal and Labour opponents united in protest to the LEA. Tempers were frayed, both sides argued violently at public meetings, and no holds were barred. The Nonconformist majority on the district council led the opposition, and enjoyed overwhelming public support, partly because the proposed site for the church school was inconvenient, and partly because of the lingering belief that even new church schools would be inferior in facilities to council ones. When the LEA rejected the petitions, the district council accused it of complicity with the Church of England in preserving inadequate schools and doctrinal teaching against the clearly expressed wishes of the majority of local families. Stung by the dangerous charge of conspiracy, Graveson told the district council that it had overstepped its responsibilities, and the 'special agreement' would stand.[107]

In Berkhamsted Furse and the local clergy adopted different tactics, and sought to allay the Nonconformist fears they had so successfully aroused earlier. In February 1937 the hitherto militant rector of Berkhamsted redefined 'the best in education' as 'definite religious teaching which is given in accordance with parents' wishes, whether they be Church [of England] or Chapel.' He made the *volte face* explicit, asserting:

> I would give Chapel people the fullest opportunity to teach their own children in our schools, but it can't be done in State provided schools. That is why our voluntary schools are worth everything that we can do to keep them in the very forefront of our educational system.[108]

Furse's public conversion was equally dramatic, and in speeches, articles and letters he sought to separate the sectarian and political wings of the opposition through appeals to all Christians to support church schools as bastions of fellowship and faith in an age of hedonism and secularism at home and Nazi and Bolshevik tyranny abroad.[109] In typically bluff but uncharacteristically generous fashion, he stated that 'he would welcome as Bishop of the Diocese any Nonconformist who wanted to go into school and teach the children. He would say good luck to him and give him every facility.'[110] Such rough wooing came far too late to carry conviction, and in 1938 the hostile alliances forced Board of Education inquiries in both Cheshunt and Berkhamsted.[111]

Both public inquiries were heated, even venomous at times. The Anglicans reasserted their traditional claims to continue educating the majority of children in these districts. Their buildings, facilities and secular education, they argued, would be equal in quality to any council school, and children of other denominations would receive religious instruction according to their parents' wishes. Their opponents criticised their sites, scorned their declining numbers, doubted their financial guarantees, and condemned the atmosphere of their schools as insidious indoctrination. Two themes remained constant – the desire of Nonconformist, Liberal and Labour groups to end the Church of England's involvement in elementary education, and the belief held by many more people, most of whom had no strong political or religious affiliations, that the LEA would provide the better facilities, and provide them sooner.[112]

The decisions were made on legalities only. In Berkhamsted the Board agreed that the 'special agreement' represented the broad continuation of Church of England provision, and rejected the protest.[113] In Cheshunt, however, the closure of the senior department in a council school as a direct result of the new church school was deemed unnecessary and illegal, and the 'special agreement' was over-turned.[114] The parish of Cheshunt made immediate and frantic efforts to negoti-ate a compromise solution, but it was the end of a long chapter in LEA and Church of England relations in Hertfordshire. After the prolonged, vigorous and spectac-ularly successful opposition to the Anglicans, the LEA publicly distanced itself from any involvement with this defeated, unpopular, but still militant local force, and without further consultation it began to plan its own senior school.[115]

The Right Reverend Michael Furse inspired both devotion and hostility, and he trod where most other Anglican bishops were not inclined to tread. Through-out the period the Church of England remained a social, moral, political, legal and educational force to be reckoned with, and Furse never hesitated to use all the powers at his disposal. Interested primarily in a wide-ranging Anglican revival that incorporated yet transcended education, he was successful in reinvigorating many parishes and providing them with significant spiritual as well as financial and legal support. The subtitle of his autobiography *Stand Therefore!* is *A Bishop's Testimony of Faith in the Church of England*, and this life-long devotion revealed itself in the open celebration of hard-fought educational successes, the contempt for clergy and parishes who failed to follow his lead, and the often scornful treat-ment of external opponents as misguided and, worse, potential threats to social order and national revival. The accumulative effect was to draw the diocese into a closer alliance with its more fervent adherents, including several Conservative MPs and the landed gentry, while contributing significantly to the mounting hos-tile alliances and the increasing coolness of the LEA. Labour strength was grow-ing on the county council during the 1930s, the party maintained a significant presence on several town councils, and the Liberals retained a majority on a number of local councils. They provided a clear focus for all those opposing Anglican aspirations. Whatever the private feelings of individual members might have been, the county council and education committee became increasingly con-scious of the new political forces and resurgent religious ideologies influencing local affairs and they recognised the need to act circumspectly towards their sur-prisingly intemperate, frequently embarrassing, and sometimes downright abu-sive partner in the 'dual system'.

Between 1918 and 1939 the Church of England's share of the elementary school roll in Hertfordshire fell from 57 per cent to 39 per cent. It had surrendered or closed forty or so schools but many of them were small, and the statistics owe much to the LEA's massive urban building programme in the later 1930s. To Furse's delight, though, the Anglicans had built or planned at least twelve large senior schools in compensation. In addition, many more all-age and junior schools had been renovated and enlarged. The story, therefore, was far from one of failure, especially when the nationwide percentage of pupils in Church of England schools had dropped to 22 per cent in 1938.[116] The effort had been great, but Furse never doubted its worth and certainly thought that there was nothing inevitable about the decline.

CHAPTER ELEVEN

A wider view of children's health and welfare 1919–1939

THE TRAUMAS OF THE FIRST WORLD WAR created a groundswell of support for the provision of publicly subsidised medical treatment for children that had overwhelmed the opposition of the county council. The school medical officers, Dr Fremantle and his successor Dr Hyslop Thomson, had not hesitated to play leading roles in the campaign, and to adopt viewpoints diametrically opposed to the majority of county councillors and education committee members. After the war the nation became increasingly health conscious, and Thomson's influence reached far beyond child inspection and treatment procedures into the heart of school life. By the mid-1920s virtually everyone in Hertfordshire was doing his bidding despite the soaring expense, the serious impact upon the school curriculum and the glaring weaknesses in some of the initiatives he undertook. By 1930 he was the single most influential person in educational affairs in the county, wielding immense authority not only over the development of various treatment services, but also over the quality of school buildings and the provision of special education, physical education, domestic science, health education, nursery schooling, school milk and meals.

In August 1917 H.A.L. Fisher had underpinned all the reforms in his Education Bill with the pressing need to raise 'the general standard of physical health among the children of the poor, if a great part of the money spent on our education system is not to be wasted'.[1] He was well aware, as he steered the Bill through Parliament and the country at large, that many sections, including the health and welfare clauses, centred upon collectivist principles.[2] Hertfordshire County Council epitomised the die-hard hostility to collectivism, with members loudly voicing fears of rising rates, the erosion of parental responsibility and the likelihood of the labouring classes gaining unsettling expectations above their station. Nevertheless, Fisher's health proposals secured overwhelming public and Parliamentary support. The 1918 Education Act significantly advanced the state's guaranteed protection of its future citizens, workers and defenders by obliging LEAs to draw up and implement approved schemes of medical treatment for schoolchildren. The Act also allowed them, but fell short of compelling them, to provide or assist in the provision of nurseries, school camps, swimming baths, physical training centres, playing fields and other facilities for social and physical activities.[3]

Despite Fisher's fears about the apathy of some LEAs, the post-war years saw an expansion of the school medical service's work that was particularly dramatic in counties, such as Hertfordshire, which had previously spurned all thoughts of treatment. When Lieutenant Colonel Fremantle was elected Member of Parliament in December 1919 he maintained strong links with the LEA, supporting local developments through fetes, garden parties and letters to the press, and never failing to stress the need for the closest possible partnership between publicly funded and voluntary activity. It was Thomson, though, who seized the opportunity to make the school medical service a dominant force in local health and education. Throughout the 1920s and 1930s his never-ending proposals for expansion were always supported by an array of statistics, and were rarely questioned by county councillors, education committee members, school managers, teachers' associations or newspaper editors. Fewer and fewer challenged the principle that the state had a vested interest in the good health of succeeding generations. County councillors and education committee members came round to supporting Thomson with increasing enthusiasm. It was not so much that they had been overcome or marginalised by the medical 'expert' in their midst, but more a case of members seizing every opportunity to further their policies of practical and vocational elementary education. After 1918 these policies increasingly embraced the development of sound physical and mental health in children through intensive programmes of physical training, domestic science and hygiene, accompanied by family obedience to the enunciations of the school doctors and nurses. To Thomson and Sir George Newman, the Board of Education's chief medical officer, all of these were vital ingredients for improving national efficiency. Arguments extolling healthy elementary schoolchildren for their future economic output, for their likely military qualities of courage and endurance, and for their preservation of the Imperial race, pervaded not only Thomson's reports but also many speeches by local clergy, county councillors and other dignitaries at the increasingly fashionable school prize-giving and sports days.[4]

Thomson shared and was supported by Newman's own passionate belief in the moral qualities engendered by ingraining a healthy lifestyle in children. In 1918, and in every year until his retirement in 1935, Newman emphasised that the school medical service was 'much more than a convenient dispensary for the sick children of the poor, much more even than the establishment of a school clinic'.[5] He elevated the 1918 Act into a neo-Platonist philosophy of interrelated and mutually supporting health education and citizenship. What was true in sixth-century BC Athens, Newman upheld, was equally true in twentieth-century AD Britain – namely that:

> to be a good citizen and a clear thinker a man ... had to be in sound physical health. The physical culture received was designed to build up the body, to prevent disease, and to be a nurture as well as an equipment for athletic achievement or military capacity.[6]

In 1924 Newman extended the school medical service's role even further. It was to intervene in every aspect of children's lives, and those of their parents and teachers. He took a wide view of health education in particular. In often passionate language, sometimes bordering on the intemperate, he indicted the abominable conditions in many homes, and in numerous 'overcrowded, cold and cheerless schools', and went on to castigate the arid hectoring approach to health education adopted by many teachers. Health education, he argued, 'is almost entirely a personal, individual, concrete affair; that is why doing is everything, talking of no avail'. It touched all subjects of the curriculum, and it included the study of food values and contamination, comparative diets, farming, the habits of different countries, the prevention of accidents, famous medical discoveries, modern town planning and public health. In addition, for girls he recommended personal and domestic hygiene, simple physiology, sick nursing and baby care. For boys there should be handyman courses, involving the study of domestic water, gas and electricity supplies, and the workings and maintenance of drains, cookers and fires.[7] Newman's driving vision of classical cultures led to a virtual deification of the duality of physical and mental well-being as the ancient concept of Harmony. There was a desperate modern need, he argued, for:

> the health culture, self-knowledge and spirit of the Greeks as well as the discipline, order and sense of duty of the Romans, and mothers and teachers should bear this in mind.[8]

Newman proved a powerful and persistent force for change.

Thomson's treatment scheme (discussed in Chapter Six) was eventually launched in 1919, but once launched progress was swift, with a host of temporary and hastily converted buildings opening as clinics and treatment centres. A year later Hertfordshire was one of only ninety-one authorities including all six classes of provision in its treatment programme: 'minor ailments'; enlarged tonsils and adenoids; teeth; ringworm; eyes; and the provision of glasses – although families had access to all six in only a minority of districts in any of these authorities, and Hertfordshire was no exception.[9] The new services were almost overwhelmed from the moment of their inception. As Thomson appreciated, school doctors possessed a new willingness to send doubtful cases for further observation or sub-sidised treatment rather than place them, as previously, 'among the normals' to avoid the risk of unnecessary expense to parents.[10] Newman, of course, welcomed such professional trends and associated pressures, arguing that LEAs must make haste to arrange easily accessible treatment or risk 'a harvest of physical degener-ation'.[11]

Thomson's reports became increasingly optimistic, and the statistics are impressive. The most remarkable are the overall 'defects remedied'. In 1918 it was just 36.6 per cent, but by 1926 it had more than doubled, reaching 77.8 per cent. By 1933 the figure had soared to 89.2 per cent and by 1936 to 99.7 per cent.[12] Wherever possible, Thomson had centralised the work of the nurses around the new clinics and he had given the whole enterprise a high public profile. The nurses, eighty-four of them by 1921, had firm guidelines to ensure no opportunity was lost to promote 'with tact and foresight' the range of treatments becoming available and the benefits of well-practised habits of personal hygiene.[13] Their vig-orous campaign against uncleanness had considerable success. Cases of ver-minous heads dropped from 10.2 per cent of children examined in 1919 to 1.3 per cent in 1926, and body infestation from 5.2 per cent to 1.2 per cent over the same period.[14] During the 1930s the hard core of verminous children was no more than 0.5 per cent of children inspected each year, and often less.[15] Not surprisingly, the workload of dentists soared, as in 1919 90 per cent of Hertfordshire's elementary schoolchildren needed treatment.[16] Gradually, however, the early predominance of extractions gave way to fillings, and by 1938 only 10.9 per cent of pupils required attention.[17] By then Thomson prided himself that regular inspection, and the influence of dental hygiene lessons in schools, were paying dividends.

Nationally, expenditure by local authorities on medical inspections and treat-ment fell by 8 per cent between 1921 and 1924, but Hertfordshire, in common with a number of other LEAs, steadfastly refrained from cutting back on school med-ical service developments during these years of acute depression. In doing so it rejected the recommendations of the Treasury and the Report of the Geddes Committee on National Expenditure. It also withstood a host of accusations of profligacy from local newspapers and a minority of hostile county councillors during heated financial debates.[18] The initiatives revealed a dramatic shift in attitudes among the majority of county councillors and education committee members, who now embraced healthy childhood, and the instillation of healthy childhood habits, as integral parts of their vocational education policies. The same determination was shown during the depression which blighted the early 1930s. As historian Bernard Harris has pointed out, these 'slumps' provided parsimonious local authorities with easy, even welcome, opportunities to postpone health and welfare developments, but public opinion and county policies in Hertfordshire had moved a long way from the minimal conformity with social legislation which had characterised actions before 1914.[19]

Thomson never stopped asking for more from the LEA. He was an enthusiastic advocate of new approaches. Scabies was treated with a sulphur-based ointment, and steadily declined from thirty-three cases in 1919 to twenty-four in 1922, and then to a dozen or so annually.[20] Ringworm declined in a similar manner once X-ray treatment began in 1920, and virtually disappeared in the 1930s.[21] In the early 1920s over 800 adenoids and tonsils operations were carried out annually as the accumulation of cases was tackled. In 1925, however, Thomson began to replace the virtually automatic decision to remove enlarged tonsils by a programme of school-based training in correct breathing and dental and nasal hygiene, on the grounds that the troublesome symptoms could be both temporary and prevented. Several district medical officers disagreed and refused to cooperate, but the LEA welcomed the reduction in medical charges and lost schooldays, and formally instructed all schools to add the training to their curriculum.[22]

Health Education and hygiene training were supposed to pervade every aspect of school life, according to the Board's 1928 *Handbook of Suggestions*, which contained an array of exercises in breathing, eating, first-aid and personal safety, and detailed instructions for the daily care of ears, eyes, teeth, nose and throat.[23] However, when Newman obliged all school medical officers to survey the Health Education practices in a sample 10 per cent of their schools in 1929–30 he was presented with a depressing picture of widespread neglect.[24] Thomson's official returns were at odds with the views of some of his colleagues. Thomson reported that only brief and occasional talks were given in four of the six infants' and junior schools he visited, and in the other two, and in two of the three senior boys' schools, there was one half-hour lesson a week. 'Handkerchief drill and breathing exercises' were cited as examples of activities. In the third boys' school and all three senior girls' schools instruction was incidental to other work, mainly domestic subjects in the girls' schools.[25] However, these lack-lustre efforts were confounded by the high standards reported by the enthusiastic district medical officers in Watford and Letchworth. Through personal observation they believed teachers used both systematic and incidental instruction to sound effect, 'the result of which is seen in the healthier atmosphere of the schools and the growing refinement of the children'.[26] Thomson himself was probably relieved when the Hertfordshire Society, a voluntary association which included the promotion of public health and civic amenities among its interests, formed a Health Education Committee soon afterwards to coordinate 'the considerable amount of educational work in relation to health carried out in the county by various bodies and agencies.'[27] These groups were not named, but the Red Cross and NSPCC had major presences, the School Care Committees and Milk Council were active, and the LEA supported evening classes in a range of domestic subjects.

In 1925 Thomson took immediate advantage of the Board of Education's decision to allow schools to remain open during epidemics unless there was evidence that the infection was being spread through school attendance or the disease continued to spread after every effort had been made to discover its cause. It was increasingly widely recognised that closures did little to prevent the spread of diseases such as influenza, measles and whooping cough, as most children would have been exposed to infection by the time attendances started to fall. Some district medical officers remained unconvinced, but the new regulations were imposed across the county and the incidence of closure rapidly declined from 136 instances in 1924 to 35 in 1928 and 26 in 1936.[28] Thomson trusted teachers to act decisively in close partnership with the medical service.

Thomson did not forget the important role played by voluntary agencies. In 1922 some Hertfordshire children suffering from muscular weaknesses, paralysis, rickets, spinal curvatures, congenital deformities, fractures and spasms were referred to Red Cross orthopaedic and massage clinics, and by 1924 Thomson was sufficiently impressed with the results of the experimental therapy to secure the Board's agreement for its inclusion in the county's treatment scheme.[29] His recommendations, together with his estimates for the local share of the costs, were swiftly approved by the county council.[30] The number of cases referred to the clinics soared from 108 in 1925 to 1,112 in 1938.[31]

In conjunction with the county surveyor, Thomson and his assistants were responsible for inspecting and reporting on school buildings. In 1923 Newman intimated that some school medical officers failed to take this duty seriously, but Thomson and his team were not among them and their reports reveal the contribution they made to the steady improvements in facilities and services.[32] After the war there was much to do, but even during the years of depression in the early 1920s repairs and refurbishment were undertaken in the schools which the medical officers had most severely criticised.[33] In 1925 the Board of Education published its infamous 'Black List' of school buildings in particularly bad condition in each LEA. Seven Hertfordshire schools were among the 664 on List 'A' – those condemned by HMI as 'unsuitable for continued recognition and incapable of further improvement'. Another thirty-five Hertfordshire schools appeared on List 'B' as 'unsuitable but capable of improvement'.[34] It is usual to cite the 'Black List' as evidence of local apathy and parsimony, or both, but county records show that most of the council schools in Hertfordshire on List 'B', although not the Church of England ones, were in the process of replacement, renovation or reorganisation by the time the final lists were published.[35] Indeed, there had been a dozen Hertfordshire schools on HMI's draft List 'A' a year or more earlier, but five were subsequently removed as appropriate rebuilding plans were found to be already in hand. Certainly, Thomson and his team had identified the limitations of the buildings in question.[36] The LEA was not, perhaps, as laggardly as the 'Black List' implied. At the very least, the LEA's awareness of the initial surveys by HMI had encouraged well-targeted action.

The Board's campaign against manifestly inadequate school buildings enhanced Thomson's role in county affairs. In 1925, in tune with Board policy, he instructed his assistants to pay detailed attention to sanitary conditions. Although the fourteen district reports made strident criticisms of particular schools which had not yet received the necessary attention, the overall impression is one of standards sufficiently high and progress sufficiently consistent to satisfy this sizeable group of medical practitioners. In Hertford, Puckeridge and St Albans many necessary improvements had been carried out, although some outstanding work remained. There was only sporadic progress in refurbishing the old rural schools surrounding Hitchin and Rickmansworth, but facilities and services were found to be 'generally satisfactory' or 'all in order and well looked after' in East Barnet, New Barnet, Baldock, Berkhamsted, Bushey and Much Hadham. Letchworth and Welwyn Garden City possessed schools of high quality, and in Watford there was a range of fine new buildings, and the renovation of older schools was well in hand.[37]

The LEA's rebuilding and refurbishment of its elderly schools continued steadily, if not spectacularly, throughout the 1920s and 1930s, faltering only between 1930 and 1932, the years of deep depression. Rapid urban growth demanded the constant expansion of existing facilities as well as the erection of new schools, and the LEA's rural policies ensured that county council schools received their fair share of remedial attention and that voluntary school managers were at least encouraged to invest in their buildings.[38] A detailed survey by Thomson in 1936 of the 98 council schools revealed 65 with completely sound structures, good internal design, modern sanitation, central heating and electric light. Of the others, 25 needed their open fires to be replaced by central heating, or relatively minor improvements to the internal design, to reach a satisfactory modern standard. This left just eight with poor structures and superannuated facilities; here, there were grave doubts about the cost-effectiveness of investing in their improvement.[39]

Thomson was also central to dramatic changes in the elementary school curriculum. He contributed much to the remarkable developments in physical training (PT) which culminated in HMI's lavish praise of local practice in 1938 as an example to the whole nation.

In 1919 the Board of Education issued a new PT syllabus which Newman himself had been instrumental in producing. It rejected military drill, and introduced a wide variety of exercises and games linked closely to the increased attention being given to child health. Since 1917 the Board had offered grants of up to half the salary and travelling expenses of PT 'organisers' appointed by LEAs, but Hertfordshire, in common with most counties, remained unimpressed, despite HMI's criticisms of falling standards across the county.[40] Only in 1920 was Major Upton, a Hertfordshire headteacher returning from war service as an army PT instructor, given temporary leave of absence to arrange a series of demonstration lessons based upon the new syllabus. It was the LEA's grudging response to HMI's persistent but modest proposal for the employment of 'some returned soldier among the teachers who could give a year or two going round helping the teachers and generally stirring up the thing'.[41]

Education committee members had expressed fears that teachers would react unfavourably to the interference and advice of subject organisers.[42] These fears proved unfounded, but if they masked greater fears of the financial implications of the PT organiser identifying future needs, they were indeed justified. Upton's initial survey revealed a virtually unrelieved scene of ignorance in staff and inadequacies in facilities. Most schools had gravel yards, and most urban schools had no fields. Few teachers had heard of the 1919 syllabus, and fewer were using it. Upton eulogised the tiny number of schools where enthusiastic staff were leading daily lessons, arranging football and netball matches, and making the best use of local fields and parks for outdoor games. Occasionally well-wishers were donating balls and shirts to schools, but inter-school matches were plagued by problems of transport and team kit.[43] Gilston School, for example, joined the Hertford and District Sports League in May 1921, only to leave in October when parents refused to buy football jerseys.[44]

In 1921 the Board said Upton was unsuitable for his post. HMI had severely criticised his demonstration lessons, and probably his experience as an army instructor was considered inappropriate. That summer he was replaced by Harold Richardson, who was to work closely with Thomson over the next eighteen years to bring Hertfordshire into the vanguard of national developments. Richardson had left training college in 1912 to teach in elementary schools in Dover and Brighton. He had gained a commission during five years of active service in the army, but he eschewed using the title 'Captain' afterwards. Although the records are unclear as to when and where, he had been awarded a diploma in advanced gymnastics and certificates in swimming and country dancing instruction. Most important of all for the Board, he had just completed a year's course at Sheffield College of Physical Training, where he had obtained the highest results of his year and earned the director's plaudit as 'one of the best students who had passed through the College'.[45]

From dragging its feet Hertfordshire education committee was now to be flattered, cajoled and converted by Thomson and Richardson into encouraging and financing a host of new health initiatives. A Physical Training Sub-Committee was established, and Harold Fern became its chairman, holding office throughout the 1920s and 1930s. Fern was a long-standing member, and office holder, on the national committees of the Amateur Swimming Association and English Olympic Association, and an unusually enthusiastic promoter of all sporting activities at all levels of proficiency. He worked closely with Richardson and Thomson, and his signature added lustre to the Physical Training Sub-Committee's quarterly and annual reports to the education committee, which usually alternated lengthy praise for the worth of the LEA's current initiatives with closely argued recommendations for further expansion.[46] However, it was Richardson's name that appeared on the shorter but similar reports which Thomson invariably incorporated as a distinct section in his own annual report.

Behind Thomson, Richardson and Fern lay the consistent influence of HMI and Newman at the Board of Education. Newman saw the county PT organisers as branches of the health service, dedicated, like the medical officers, to the constructive criticism of their employers and the promotion of the 1919 syllabus with its comprehensive programmes of gymnastics exercises, games, swimming and dance. He argued passionately that PT transcended mere physical fitness, and that every teacher should see it as 'a powerful instrument, supplementary to other influences, for winning self-discipline, loyalty, health and high character in his pupils'.[47] He never wavered in his conviction that PT, and especially organised games, brought extensive moral as well as social benefits in its wake. It inculcated skills and qualities that far outlived schooldays, 'such as healthy rivalry, co-operation, courage, endurance, public spirit, fair play, loyalty, and working together in groups'.[48] Fern, Thomson and Richardson were in complete agreement; for them, PT was the keystone of education, not the make-weight. The moral dimension was consistently alluded to in their reports, which strove to justify and maintain the momentum of expansion, and no doubt it represented an effective way of securing education committee votes.

Secure in his support, Richardson quickly established his priorities. In order, these were the introduction of daily PT lessons in all schools, the securing of more playing fields, the formation of local leagues across the county for a range of organised games, the active involvement of voluntary sporting organisations with school sports outside school hours, and the cooperation of the County Teachers' Association in what he termed his 'propaganda work'.[49] All this was undertaken alongside a relentless programme of school visits, demonstrations and teachers' courses, and the early 1920s witnessed a significant advance on all fronts. PT's association with school health ensured that it had the Board of Education's protection at times of national economic anxiety. In 1922 the Board reminded cost-conscious LEAs that the work of PT organisers 'is so potent an auxiliary in the prevention of disability and disease' that cutbacks in this area should be avoided.[50] By the end of 1922 Richardson had given 500 demonstration lessons, held four long courses, encouraged the creation of football, netball and cricket leagues in several towns, masterminded several district athletics meetings, secured a number of fields for school games, and ensured that 65 per cent of schools held daily PT lessons for every class.[51] A year later he reported the gratifying spread of country dancing, the creation of several volunteer associations to manage the leagues he had initiated, and the increasing use of handwork lessons to make canvas shoes, team shirts and football and netball posts.[52] Significantly, county councillors and education committee members wanted to be associated with these popular and rapidly expanding activities, and began to attend district sports meetings, cup finals and even Richardson's demonstrations.[53]

Richardson had a devotion to the strictures of the 1919 Syllabus that seems to have bordered on fanaticism, and he combined the roles of coach, organiser and inspector in ways that were completely new to Hertfordshire schools. Many schools undoubtedly responded to Richardson's initiatives with enthusiasm, despite their lack of equipment, facilities and expertise. His zeal evoked a strong pioneering spirit in teachers. The LEA contributed only half the cost of equipment, forcing schools to demonstrate their commitment to new initiatives by securing the other half through donations, collections, or the proceeds of sales of work.[54] Inevitably, delays occurred as a result. At Kimpton, for example, the school collected £1 11s 2d for a football just in time for the winter season of 1920–1, but only in July 1923 was a similar amount accumulated to provide half the cost of a girls' netball set.[55]

With obvious pride, Richardson's reports recorded the increasing number of district competitions and leagues he had established. In addition, PT in infant classes became far more formal than hitherto, as though he thought that they were the early training establishments for later contests. 'By the time children leave the infant school', he said in 1924:

> they should have had some definite training in the adoption of a good standing position, be able to keep definite rhythm in such movements as marching, running, and dance steps, able to obey and carry out simple commands quickly, and understand the rudiments of fair play in games.[56]

He received constant assurances that developments were in the right direction, and he prized in particular the comments of a headteacher of an all-age school that 'the discipline, tone and work of my children have improved almost beyond recognition since organised physical training had taken its proper place in the curriculum.'[57] HMI visiting other Hertfordshire schools made similar comments. At Stanstead Abbots, for example, organised games were held to have contributed much to 'the general bracing up in tone' and 'firmer control' of the children.[58]

It was as though an educational elixir had been discovered. Local newspapers reflected the popular mood, with reporters attending sports meetings and editors heaping praise on current trends, as 'recreation brings health, and health keeps the brain bright and clear, making easier the task of both teacher and scholar.'[59] In the mid-1920s the education committee agreed to tar all school playgrounds, and to purchase an additional two acres for each new school and pay the rent for fields where none were otherwise available for existing schools. It became increasingly fashionable for local dignitaries to present neighbourhood schools with team kit in school colours – 'a potent factor', Richardson said, 'in getting a lad to appreciate what is meant by "team work" and "esprit de corps"' – and to donate and inscribe trophies, attend and address sports days, and give rather than merely lend fields.[60] Kimpton, which had struggled to raise the cost of a netball set in the early 1920s, found substantial local donations readily forthcoming a decade later to buy posts, sockets, balls, sticks and plimsolls for hockey, and jumpers, shorts, boots and shin pads for football.[61]

In 1925 the County Schools Athletics Association was formed with Sir Charles Longmore, the Clerk to the County Council, as an influential chairman, and in that year, too, the Countess of Verulam took the lead in urging all Hertfordshire landowners to consider sympathetically the need for land for children's games.[62] The following year a county branch of the National Playing Fields Association was established with the Lord Lieutenant, Viscount Hampden, as president and Richardson as secretary.[63] To Richardson's immense satisfaction, in the summer of 1926 all eight district sports associations held inter-school athletics meetings, and at the county championships Longmore, surrounded by county dignitaries, made the opening address. It became an annual event, and the highlight of the sporting year. Richardson believed that in 1926 PT had 'obtained its rightful place in the curriculum'.[64] By 1929, the mix of public and private action ensured that only fifteen schools were left without regular access to playing fields.[65]

The elementary schools' sports days and athletics meetings imitated, though palely, similar occasions which had adorned the public and grammar school life for decades, but there was no hiding the fact that the local benefactors who encouraged the new competitions and sometimes graced them with their presence considered the aims to be very different. Their speeches drove home the point, if ever it was in doubt. There were no references to training for leadership, heroic sporting battles, gentlemanly conduct, stirring ideals which won the Empire, or setting an example to the lower orders, but many statements closely linking the humbling qualities taught by sport – notably striving and fortitude, teamwork and selflessness, winning and modesty, losing and self-examination – with those very same qualities which henceforth should guide every aspect of the children's lives.[66] The need for continual gratitude and greater efforts back in the classroom was emphasised, and honoured guests had no compunction about exposing character flaws in the competitors. 'I saw a regrettable incident', thundered one speaker at a district sports day, 'which I did not consider sporting. I hope I shall never see anything like that again.'[67] Private benefactors were in a strong position to punish those they thought 'undeserving', as Anstey School found when it lost its playing field after local children chased the owners' cows.[68]

In 1927 HMI Miss E.M. Perry surveyed Hertfordshire's PT provision. It was just at the time when Newman was particularly depressed at the 'relative stagnation and inefficiency' that reigned in the 217 LEAs still without PT organisers.[69] She found much to praise, not least Richardson's energy, enterprise and ability to enthuse teachers. His courses for teachers, the quality of the lessons she had observed, and the fact that 2,400 pupils regularly attended swimming baths all received special mention.[70] She did, however, caution against Hertfordshire's mounting emphasis upon 'the physical fitness and efficiency of the few' and the pressures caused by the avid promotion of leagues and competitions. Certainly, by then many school logbooks were recording sporting victories with pride, and among the numerous reports of prize days in local newspapers were many eulogies of individual and team triumphs. A minority of headteachers came close to making a cult of competitive sport, relishing their annual haul of trophies in much the same way as some of them gloried in the number of pupils who gained scholarships to secondary schools each year.[71] The press coverage of elementary school sports meetings and prize days grew in proportion to their general popularity, and this had the effect of increasing the pressure on the more competitively inclined schools to add to their reputation, not only by securing medals and trophies but also by retaining them in subsequent years.[72] It had been a series of short steps for games to be played for the participants' health, then for the spirit of comradeship, then in friendly rivalry, and then for the very public triumph of the school. Healthy exercise through healthy competition began to be transformed in critics' eyes into an unhealthy obsession with victory, adulation and dominance. To others, however, these were highly laudable objectives for the physical fitness, technical excellence and personal discipline necessary for their achievement.

Occasionally schools proved unwilling to follow the popular path. As early as 1923 one school manager preached against the cult of athleticism he saw pervading Hertfordshire elementary schools, and especially 'the idea that a boy is no good unless he can play cricket or football'.[73] In 1928 a headmaster publicly regretted his previous emphasis on the sporting achievements of the few, and he was at pains to assure his prize-day audience that 'a school is not properly judged by these alone.'[74]

Richardson heeded Miss Perry's criticisms, and although the athletics meetings and leagues continued unabated there was a renewed emphasis upon whole-class activities. 'A really good time' became the keynote for PT, and Richardson started to encourage schools to create a greater variety of events, with some requiring less exalted skills, in swimming galas, athletics meetings and sports days, so that more children could take part. He also renewed his efforts to influence the minority of schools who had failed, through wilful neglect he believed, to develop PT beyond half-hearted exercises in full clothing.[75] During the early 1930s the idea that all children had a right to PT in all its forms took hold, and in accordance with Newman's definition of national wealth as the children's 'health of body, mind and soul', Richardson sought greater proficiency in the daily class lessons. The LEA raised its grants to schools and removed the superannuated requirement that schools raised half the cost of equipment.[76] The pressure exerted on teachers to raise their standards of teaching, and their pupils' acquisition of skills, became relentless.

During the 1930s PT soared in the local educational firmament. As a belated result of the 1926 Hadow Report, during the 1930s many urban all-age elementary schools were decapitated, losing their pupils over the age of eleven to senior schools. The LEA accepted the need for a range of appropriate equipment to be provided for senior schools, and Richardson put on an annual series of advanced training courses for teachers, most of whom were non-specialists in PT.[77] The depression of the 1930s threatened education with savage economies but PT's contribution to child health and character formation ensured local initiatives survived unscathed. Newman, Thomson and Richardson made that contribution explicit in all their reports, and in 1932 Fern's sub-committee considered attack the best form of defence and made the claim that 'some of the time given to verbal instruction could with advantage to the child, and thus to the nation, be replaced by physical activities.'[78]

By 1938 22 of Hertfordshire's 25 senior schools, and 9 large all-age schools, had well-qualified staff and portable gymnastics equipment.[79] The time devoted to PT in these schools dramatically increased, and Thomson duly reported the benefits in terms of health and moral training.[80] The senior schools laid on public galas and sports days, and these became social occasions attended by parents, county councillors and other people of note, giving the seal of approval to the new mix of competitions and demonstrations.[81] In 1936 the Board of Education increased the equipment grant, leading the education committee to agree, amid great publicity, that all new senior schools were to have fully equipped gymnasia, and older schools were to have them added in a rolling programme of extensions.[82] Beaumont School in St Albans, completed in 1938, was the first elementary school to have a gymnasium, and the second opened a year later in Hemel Hempstead.[83]

Throughout the 1930s Richardson was continually hunting out new playing fields, hounding dilatory headteachers, seeking more swimming pools and training yet more teachers, but by 1935 he believed all the major battles had been won. His report that year was prefaced by the claims of two headteachers revealing that the moral qualities associated with intensive PT retained considerable currency. The first was convinced that the experience of team games could reform criminally inclined pupils, and the second attributed his children's excellent attitudes and attendances totally to their rigorous daily exercises.[84] By then the Board's revised 1933 Syllabus, with its host of recommended exercises, activities and games, was in full swing, 1,000 teachers had attended Richardson's courses on the use of specialist apparatus, and lessons in Nutrition and Hygiene were closely linked to those in PT.[85] In 1936 a county survey revealed that all infant and junior schoolchildren had daily Physical Education (PE) lessons, and each week senior pupils had three PE lessons, one organised games lesson and, where facilities were accessible, a swimming lesson. In that year 6,000 children from 105 of the county's 255 schools (excluding infant schools) had swimming in their curriculum, with the admission fees and proficiency certificates paid by the LEA.[86] In a significant broadening of emphasis Newman had changed the title Physical Training to Physical Education in 1935.

Richardson and the LEA took immediate advantage of the 1937 Physical Training & Recreation Act which created the mechanisms whereby sporting facilities could be provided for those over school age. 'Today', he had written in 1935, 'the physical well-being of the children is the concern of some Authority; tomorrow it is the child's own', and he had long believed sensitive encouragement was vital for an effective transition.[87] First he revitalised and expanded the range of adult PE classes offered throughout the county as part of the Evening Institute programme. Next he asked headteachers to form PE clubs a few weeks before pupils left school and encourage them to continue as a group at the local Institute the following autumn.[88] It worked, and 1936–7 saw an ambitious programme of 67 classes running in 35 centres. The numbers of participants nearly doubled from 1,221 men and women between the ages of fifteen and their later twenties in the first year to 2,319 in the second.[89]

Richardson was honoured by his peers. In 1936 he became a member of the

Technical Advisory Committee of the Central Council of Physical Education, and in 1939 he was elected chairman of the National Association of Organisers of Physical Education.[90] Viscount Hampden was chairman of the Central Council, and in 1937 Alderman Harold Fern became a member of Lord Aberdare's Physical Recreation Committee – reminders of the enduring support Richardson and Thomson enjoyed from those in positions of influence.[91] In 1938 HMI held up Hertfordshire as a model for emulation, and at the Board's behest Richardson received visitors 'desirous of obtaining an insight' into local policies and practice. It exemplified Newman's assertion in that year that PE, 'wisely conceived and intelligently directed', made a unique contribution to children's all-round development.[92]

Great changes had taken place in PE in Hertfordshire over twenty years. The county council and education committee had become intensely proud of, rather than reluctantly resigned to, PE's dramatic expansion. A rapidly expanding population had stimulated the constant consideration of new school buildings, teaching approaches and facilities, and public opinion had heightened expectations of the LEA and elementary education, not least to provide well-balanced and well-disciplined workers. In addition, there was the acknowledgement that enjoyment, as well as hard training and high achievement, had its rightful place in PE.

With Thomson's consistent encouragement, Domestic Subjects – broadly defined as the theory and practice of cookery, laundrywork, housewifery, hygiene, first aid and baby care – followed PE in its headlong development and rising demands on school time. Although the war had created an impetus for teaching domestic economy – cheap meals and household hygiene – after 1918 Hertfordshire settled back into the pre-war routine whereby a scattering of urban cookery centres provided weekly lessons for older girls while a few instructors intermittently toured the rural districts. Staff slowly increased, until in 1924 there were 20 full-time instructors serving 9 permanent centres, visiting 13 urban centres which operated in the autumn and spring, and touring 42 villages in the summer. However, the full range of courses in cookery, laundrywork and housewifery were restricted to Watford, Hatfield and Bushey. Laundrywork and cookery were taught in Letchworth and Hitchin, but everywhere else only cookery – plain and economical, and based upon the best family diet that could be gained from the average working man's wages.[93]

In the early 1920s a flurry of activity surrounded Domestic Subjects. Two national reports in 1923, one by the Board of Education's Consultative Committee and the other by the Wood Committee, concluded that girls were receiving

grossly inadequate household training to become either efficient wives or domestic servants. Indeed, the Wood Committee was set up specifically to investigate
the causes of, and solutions to, the increasing unpopularity of domestic service.
The *Times Educational Supplement* paid great attention to its findings, and made
much of incompetent girls rushing into domestic service, finding the job 'repel-
lent' because of their lack of training, and marrying in haste solely to escape the
drudgery. The moral was clear, at least to the editor. All because of the neglect of
Domestic Subjects in schools, the unsuccessful maid became the unsuccessful
wife and 'the source of more than half the miseries and a great deal of the drunkenness of slum life'.[94]

Soon afterwards HMI conducted a vigorous campaign for a Domestic Subjects organiser in Hertfordshire, which included a well-attended county conference and a detailed survey of the hotch-potch provision. Thomson, Hallidie and
several female county councillors lent their support, and their persistent arguments shrewdly combined two factors the education committee eventually found
irresistible – increased utility in elementary education and increased cost-effectiveness in public finance.[95]

The first organiser, Miss M.I. Barnes, took office in September 1927, and
immediately redesigned courses and reinvigorated staff. Like Richardson, she
had much in her favour. She had access to the education committee through regular reports, she enjoyed the support of those who had lobbied for her appointment, and in Harold Fern she had an influential sub-committee chairman. There
was also a discernible change in public opinion. The utilitarian value of teaching
a range of household skills and giving moral training in 'self-reliance, cleanliness
and method' remained unquestioned, but Miss Barnes appreciated the wider
links with personal and public health. In 1929 she organised the first residential
course for her team of instructors in partnership with Thomson and Hallidie,
with Thomson himself lecturing on 'Food and Health'. The links between Domestic Subjects and the school medical service stayed close thereafter, with such factors as diet and digestion, and domestic cleanliness and personal hygiene, being
complementary interests.[96]

Miss Barnes's up-dated syllabuses combined the theory and practice of economical housekeeping with the science of cookery – 'food values, digestion and
the laws of health, the effect of heat on various foods' – and the science of laundrywork – 'the composition of soap, soda, blue etc., and the best means of soft-
ening water etc.' Nevertheless, a continuity of purpose accompanied the
modernisation of content. She paid strict attention to the avoidance of waste, the

recycling of materials and the art of making and mending, and she ensured that the enjoyment which she professed permeated her courses came largely from the satisfaction of achieving healthy lives through absolute frugality.[97]

By 1930 the Domestic Subjects staff numbered 30. They taught in 87 centres, and 140 of their 408 classes involved all three key components of Domestic Subjects. Every senior elementary schoolgirl attended classes for a minimum of one day a week for a year, and most town girls attended for two years.[98] In 1930, too, comprehensive urban centres complete with furnished bedrooms, bathrooms and sitting rooms, as well as kitchens and sculleries, were introduced by the LEA, and even rural centres in larger villages began to be fitted with real laundry rooms and kitchens.[99] In common with PE, Domestic Subjects were specifically excluded from any cuts considered by hawkish county councillors during the depression of the early 1930s. 'We are clearly of opinion', stated the investigation sub-committee, 'that no case has been made out for reduction in respect of such subjects as cookery, handicraft and dressmaking, which may be considered as of great importance amongst the subjects useful in later life.' It asserted that the girls' domestic training must be making a significant contribution to the ability of the working classes to cope with the current crisis.[100] During the depression Miss Barnes's staff had risen, and by 1934 it numbered 39.[101]

The irony was that Hertfordshire remained largely unaffected by the depression, and did not suffer the unemployment and social distress of the Midlands and north of England. In contrast, it was during these years that Miss Barnes gradually moved towards viewing modern suburbia as the domestic environment to be modelled in most of the county's urban schools. In 1933 she defended the heavy investment in Domestic Subjects on the assumption that marriage, motherhood and responsibility for a home were but a few years away, and the facilities had to reflect the rise in suburban prosperity and social expectations.[102] However, she viewed the countryside differently, and bemoaned the lack of housecraft opportunities in the rural centres, primarily because many girls 'become daily maids when they leave school.' With the status of service gradually rising again, and with 'a better type of girl' seeking such employment, Miss Barnes deemed Domestic Subjects training crucial for the rural economy.[103]

The LEA agreed, and new senior elementary schools were designed with their own Domestic Subjects rooms and flats attached to them – well before the Board of Education made it compulsory, in 1936.[104] By the middle of 1934 there were nine housecraft houses and flats. Some were converted houses, but a few were purpose-built. Here girls were taught 'cookery, laundrywork, housewifery, mothercraft, household needlework and everything connected with the home'.[105] 'Everything connected with the home' ranged widely, from the lighting of fires and the care of wooden floors to the mending of chairs, laying of lino and clearing of drains.[106]

'Mothercraft', though, usually fell short of sex education and the birth of the babies the girls were trained so assiduously to look after. However, one incident reveals that the subject was not completely taboo. In 1933 the LEA received a petition from a widely representative pressure group in Welwyn Garden City urging 'suitably graded' biology lessons in all Hertfordshire schools. The objective was compulsory sex education and, as the well-argued case was backed by seventy-two signatories including magistrates, doctors, clergy, district councillors and school managers, it was taken seriously. Various county council committees and advisory groups wrestled with the implications of the petition, each well aware that the Roman Catholic church was vehemently opposed to the idea and that a similar request from the Garden City had been rejected in 1931; but they were also aware that a recent national conference on the subject had voted in favour of sex education's incorporation into the curriculum. Moderation prevailed. The LEA issued a statement refusing to direct teachers in any way but viewing 'with favour' sex education given by experienced headteachers or approved assistants 'to senior pupils as opportunity offers'.[107] It could be argued that the LEA had found a convenient way out of its dilemma, but placing responsibility upon the schools could easily have led to bitter public controversies. It seems reasonable to assume that a few progressive schools took advantage of the LEA's judgement, but no records have come to light to confirm this.

In 1937 Miss Barnes proclaimed that the value of Domestic Subjects 'is now fully recognised. It is gradually raising the standards of living and it is hoped that it will help to produce happy homes.'[108] In the final few years before the next world war Domestic Subjects, and the instructors, finally became fully integrated into the curriculum and staff in some large new senior schools, rather than just attached to them. In these schools a cross-curriculum approach tended to develop, with Nutrition linked to the fashionable 'Keep Fit' movement, Hygiene and Physiology linked to Science and Health Education, Housewifery linked to Mathematics and Craft, and Cookery playing its part in open days and social events. By then, the various facets of Domestic Subjects occupied a significant percentage of the older girls' time – 30 per cent of the week, and perhaps more.[109]

Miss Barnes was at pains to make it clear that the 'happy homes' she mentioned in her 1937 report could be those of the girls' employers rather than the girls themselves. As education committee members appreciated, many girls still went into private domestic service, and many more were employed in the now numerous hotels, restaurants, cafes, clubs and institutions.[110] Demand remained high as the county prospered. In a statement proudly reporting that 75 per cent of the girls leaving school in the market town of Royston entered domestic service, 'many as a direct result of the Domestic Subjects training', Miss Barnes revealed how little ambitions for the pupils had changed throughout her reign. She safely assumed that the readers of her report – county councillors, education committee members, senior officials and county newspaper editors – would be as satisfied as she and the Royston headteacher were with this educational outcome.[111]

There were, though, areas of development that Thomson thought entirely inappropriate for Hertfordshire. The LEA steadfastly resisted petitions for the provision of publicly subsidised school meals in 1914, during the shortages of 1917–18 and during the recessions of the early 1920s and 1930s. It believed that a combination of charitable action and recourse to the Poor Law would resolve all likely cases, and it successfully challenged all protestors to identify families who would qualify for subsidised meals under the 1921 Education Act, which demanded proof that a pupil's education was suffering due to inadequate feeding.[112] Thomson never doubted the rectitude of this policy.

However, times were changing. A number of reorganisation schemes in the wake of the 1926 Hadow Report incited considerable parental protest at the lack of official thought given to the children's health and safety at midday, should they be unable to return home. In 1929 the particularly acrimonious scheme proposed for Cuffley and its environs obliged the LEA to accept greater responsibility and direct Miss Barnes, in conjunction with Thomson, to make arrangements for a daily hot meal to be cooked on the central senior school's premises.[113] Capital and administrative costs were borne by the LEA, with pupils' payments of a shilling a week covering the food, wages and fuel. Thomson supported the LEA, and approved the final plans in terms of the nutritional value of the meals, the opportunity to promote good habits in children and the families' freedom from any taint of charity, the Poor Law or the 1921 Act. The arrangements proved popular with managers, teachers, parents and pupils, and they played a significant role in the smooth resolution of at least nine other reorganisation proposals.[114]

Outside these essential schemes, Thomson maintained his hostility to subsidised feeding. In the early 1930s malnutrition was recorded as marked in only about 0.5 per cent of pupils inspected in the county. In 1935 the criteria changed, and 2.7 per cent – 406 children – were suddenly categorised as suffering badly, with similar numbers returned in subsequent years. Thomson found the new figures hard to credit, and he consistently refused to use them as reliable evidence for rate-assisted feeding. In a significant revelation of professional disharmony he blamed the district officers for interpreting the new definition of 'normal' too narrowly, thereby accentuating abnormalities.[115]

In similar vein, Thomson displayed little sympathy with those who argued for the provision of subsidised daily milk supplies to children. In 1929 the National Farmers' Union, seeking markets for surplus production, urged Hertfordshire to join those LEAs already arranging daily supplies of milk to schools. The scheme involved the creation of school milk clubs and the collection of a penny per member per day.[116] All the ingredients for a successful launch seemed there – Thomson verified the value of milk for children, the county council endorsed the scheme as long as it was self-financing, and the farmers supplied the milk cheaply in sealed third-of-a-pint bottles. However, success was patchy. By late 1930 only 25 per cent of Hertfordshire pupils were members and over 100 schools reported the existence of parents unable to afford membership.[117] District medical officers argued that those most needing milk were those debarred from it but, once again, Thomson was unimpressed and the LEA refused any subsidy. Only in 1934, when the government subsidy allowed the cost to drop to a halfpenny a bottle did the number of Hertfordshire pupils drinking milk in school rise – to 46 per cent in 1935 and 53 per cent by 1938.[118] The national average in 1938 was 55.6 per cent.[119] It proved to be a lengthy campaign, fought mainly by teachers and a few enthusiastic district officers, such as the indefatigable Dr Macfadyen in health-conscious Letchworth, to make milk popular with children, to associate it firmly with improvements in health, and to free its supply at cheap rates from the taint of charitable relief. Thomson and the LEA did little to help win the campaign.

Thomson also opposed rate-supported nursery education. In 1929 the government asked all LEAs 'to consider the provision of Nursery Schools for children between the ages of two and five years of age' and to target those areas of greatest poverty where 'the home is squalid, where food is bad and insufficient, and where ill-health passes unnoticed'.[120] It justified the initiative on the grounds that it was 'grossly uneconomic' to allow these deprived children to regress in health between the time they left the supervision of the maternity and child welfare clinics and arrived at school. The county education committee showed little interest, but its belated survey resulted in St Albans, Letchworth and Welwyn Garden City arguing in favour of nursery schools. The City of St Albans only reluctantly conceded that its notorious slum districts merited any special attention, but the two

Garden Cities were far more positive and submitted detailed educational as well as social arguments.[121]

The LEA seemed trapped and was ready to accede to the best-argued case, that of Welwyn Garden City, which had identified the families in need, an appropriate nursery school programme and a convenient site. It was Thomson who provided the justification for a dramatic official *volte face*. Emphasising that 'one of the most important objects of the nursery school' was to monitor the children's health and inculcate good habits, he argued that this could be achieved as effectively and far more cheaply by extending medical inspection to pre-school children and giving remedial advice to their parents.[122] As the education committee considered the Garden Gities to be disproportionately well-equipped with modern elementary schools already, Thomson's views, promoting a more modest and more equitable distribution of resources, must have fallen on particularly receptive ears. Thomson, of course, was primarily concerned with the expansion of the school medical service's core activities, and to him it seemed ridiculous to create expensive nursery sledgehammers to crack such small medical nuts.

It was not until 1938 that the LEA reluctantly made a small grant, under Board of Education pressure, towards a voluntary-funded nursery school recently established in Oxhey, and agreed to build new nursery schools in Watford and Welwyn Garden City. Well-informed and politically aware local groups had initiated these projects, and run skilful campaigns to secure official recognition and annual grants. Armed with shrewd professional advice, and sharing expertise and experiences, they had bypassed the hostile LEA to convince the Board of Education, through a wealth of detailed statistics and socio-economic arguments, that the combination of low wages and high rents in particular districts had created an appropriately needy clientele for the new facilities. As Board officials acknowledged, these groups had fully satisfied the government's criteria for official recognition and grants.[123] County councillors such as Captain Morris were horrified at the news, and in a spectacularly ill-tempered full council debate he asserted that state-organised eugenics was infinitely preferable to state-subsidised nursery schools, while at the other end of the political spectrum George Lindgren, the militant leader of the minority Labour group, angrily accused the council of culpably perpetuating parsimonious '1914 attitudes' towards the well-being of children in need.[124] The bitterness of the argument outside as well as inside the council chamber was fuelled by the general awareness that it was less about money than about the continuing erosion of old assumptions regarding family responsibilities and the primacy of charitable efforts.

In contrast, the problems of older children categorised as 'dull and backward' and 'mentally defective' absorbed a great deal of professional time and public funds. This field was rife with opportunities for experimentation during the inter-war years, and medical practitioners such as Thomson found them irresistible. Their pioneering work attracted public attention, enhanced their professional reputations, and certainly strengthened their hold over local authority decision-making.[125] County developments met with occasional triumphs and far more frequent tribulations, but overall they reveal an education committee and school medical officers persistently investing money and reputations in identification procedures, educational institutions and remedial programmes which continually failed to clarify the nature of individual children's acute learning problems, let alone lead to their resolution.

'Dull and backward' children were deemed to suffer from delayed development and were therefore considered capable of some improvement, especially in a sympathetic environment. The 'mental defectives' were those whose natural abilities were low and usually further impeded by chronic illnesses, physical infirmities, prolonged absences from school, a particularly pernicious home background, or, as often occurred, a combination of these factors. 'High grade mental defectives' were considered educable and therefore placed in residential or day special schools; 'low grade' cases were deemed ineducable and sent to certified institutions, hospitals and asylums. In 1918 the LEA imagined the problems were simple and the solutions at hand, but by 1939 it had learnt from bitter experience that the problems were infinitely complex and the solutions eternally elusive. Yet during these guinea-pig decades hard lessons were learned and invaluable knowledge was acquired through the various trials and numerous errors.[126]

By 1918 Hertfordshire's practice of dispatching mentally defective children to residential schools, homes, hospitals and asylums outside the county was proving alarmingly costly in terms of the fees levied by the receiving authorities, the lengthy periods of family separation, the travelling expenses for visitors, and the reliance on the admissions criteria and quality of care in institutions over which Thomson, Hallidie and the LEA had no effective control. In addition, places were in such short supply that it took on average two years for a child designated in need of specialist care to be found a place.[127]

The solution adopted by the LEA revealed a total failure to appreciate the implications of its actions or the complexity of the problem. Towards the end of the war the large Union Workhouse in Hertford was being run down, and as the LEA needed a large residential school without delay, the county council

Kingsmead Special Residential School, formerly Hertford Union Workhouse. Built in 1869, the redundant workhouse became Kingsmead School in 1919 (HALS)

conveniently tied up several loose ends at minimal cost by approving a proposal to use the redundant building 'as a special educational institution for educable and improvable mentally defective children, and a number of female defectives over the age of sixteen'. The twenty-two workhouse employees became non-teaching staff at the school, and most of the domestic chores were undertaken by the sixteen or so 'female defectives', who remained as permanent residents. Much of the workhouse furniture remained *in situ*, and the main alterations consisted of the provision of inside toilets and doubling the number of girls' baths to two.[128]

The Board of Education approved the admission of 150 pupils to the new school, an increase of 60 on the average number of paupers accommodated there, and headteachers across the county immediately submitted over 200 names to Thomson for consideration.[129] It was anticipated that the curriculum would differ little from that in ordinary schools, although the classes would be smaller. The 60 to 70 children under eleven years of age would have four specially trained teachers delivering a classroom-dominated programme covering all the usual elementary school subjects. The seniors would spend half their time in classrooms under the headteacher and a fifth assistant, and half their time at practical work under instructors drawn from the ex-workhouse staff, or outside – mainly gardening, woodwork and boot-mending for the boys and gardening, sewing and housework for the girls.[130]

Everything happened swiftly, and the belated complaints from two county councillors who challenged the suitability of workhouse staff 'saturated with the traditions and prohibitions of the Poor Law' for the care of mentally defective children were easily overridden.[131] The Hertford Residential School for Mentally Defective Children opened under the less threatening name of 'Kingsmead' in November 1919, but the building's inauspicious history, the county council's parsimony, and the unfavourable publicity given to its debates caused the parents of 37 out of the first 50 children selected for places to refuse permission for admission.[132] Then, and thereafter, Kingsmead never escaped a punitive image in the eyes and minds of many parents, but Thomson and the LEA had little sympathy with such sensitivities. They equated non-cooperation with ingratitude, and readily resorted to legal compulsion after the initial attempts at persuasion failed. As Thomson believed that a root cause of mental deficiency was the inability or unwillingness of parents to care for their children satisfactorily, he approved the determination with which the LEA prosecuted such cases. It was a short but misdirected step to assume an adverse domestic environment had been the primary cause of dullness and backwardness in children, and significantly accentuated 'mental deficiency', and an even more misleading step to assume that the removal of those home conditions would lead *per se* to an improvement in motivation and performance. No doubt the lowly social class of most families of children selected for Kingsmead served to confirm this connection in Thomson's mind. The vast majority of parents were labourers or semi-skilled factory hands, with a few others on parish relief. In 1919 just two families were able to exercise the option to move their children out of the elementary school system. About half the first group of families refusing places were unable to explain their decision, and the others made vague claims that the assessments were inaccurate, that adequate education and training could be given at home, or that childhood ailments had led to a temporary loss of academic progress. It was all in vain. A few families secured deferred admissions pending further investigations, but sooner or later all protests were overruled, in the last resort by the courts. The same painful procedures were repeated throughout the period.[133]

Once at Kingsmead the children were subject to a carefully structured routine, and were closely monitored by a host of specialists – the medical officers, teachers, the domestic superintendent and the visiting chaplain. They received constant medical attention, and Thomson looked for a rapid improvement in weight, posture and bearing as a direct result of the regular meals, enforced cleanliness, punctual bedtimes and generally ordered life in the school. He cited as clear evidence of the evils of parental neglect the disproportionately high number of new admissions suffering from curable but untreated debilitating ailments such as chilblains and bad teeth, and also the marked regression in health which frequently occurred when the children went home on holiday.[134]

The early reports on Kingsmead give insights into the level of achievement categorised as educable or high grade mental deficiency. One class contained older children who could read and write 'equal to Standard I or II of an ordinary school', but another two comprised those who could only recognise letters and copy some of the shapes. The fourth class held those bordering on the ineducable, low grade category. Although on admission about half the children could count to twenty, very few could tell the time or subtract two or three from a number.[135] To judge from this evidence, the academic criteria for admission seem to have been sub-literacy and bare numeracy – the merest hint that progress might be possible. Anything more than this and the children were left in their ordinary elementary classes; anything less than this and they were labelled ineducable. By law Thomson had to identify pupils within this narrow band of capability for Kingsmead, but even senior officials in the Board of Education were unclear about how this could be achieved, privately acknowledging in 1923 that 'the statutory definitions leave room for wide and natural divergence.'[136] As Thomson soon discovered, accurate assessment could be clouded to a remarkable degree by the varying standards of elementary schools, the varying natural and environmental factors contributing to learning difficulties, and the varying quality of the analysis of individual cases by teachers and doctors.

The failure of many children to respond favourably to Kingmead's regime vexed Thomson, but the overriding fascination persisted throughout the 1920s and 1930s. In the early 1920s admission errors were rectified swiftly and crudely. If, after a few weeks' observation, children were reclassified as low grade defectives they were referred to the Mental Deficiency Committee for a place in certified institutions if the home conditions were considered unsatisfactory. There were twelve such cases in the first eighteen months – 15 per cent of the intake.[137] These were years of severe financial constraints, and Kingsmead's efficiency and cost-effectiveness were already in question. The Board of Education began to argue that residential schools for high grade defectives were expensive luxuries that could not be extended, and HMI encouraged LEAs to make better provision for these pupils in ordinary schools. The harsh fact was that places in residential schools cost an average of £90 a year compared with £12 in normal elementary schools.[138]

The school, though, represented a significant investment of public money and professional expertise, and it survived all the economic panics and doubts about its educational worth unscathed. Indeed, its status among county councillors and education committee members soared during the 1920s. They grew proud of their hasty creation, and its experimental work obviously caught their imagination. It became fashionable to take an interest in its inmates and their activities. Kingsmead became a fixed agenda item at education committee meetings, and it received a never-ending stream of visitors from Hertfordshire and beyond. The visitors' book was full of compliments about the modern teaching approaches, the friendly atmosphere, the good behaviour and the quality of art, craft, singing and dancing.[139] Editorial eulogies of Kingsmead followed the trend, with one local newspaper reminding its readers in 1923 that:

> a comparatively few years ago these children would have been given up by their teachers as impossible, as imbeciles ... Today, these defective children are patiently and systematically studied. Their latent abilities and talents are carefully coached and pandered until they are turned out, at the very least, moderately competent of holding their own in life's battle for existence.[140]

In 1923 Thomson refined the initial identification procedures. In order to reduce diagnostic errors and increase cost-effectiveness all borderline cases were referred to specialists at Hill End Mental Hospital for a second opinion based upon the Stanford Revision of the Binet–Simon tests of mental ability. Soon afterwards the Board decided that all cases should be tested in this way.[141] Thomson retained great faith in the Standford–Binet tests, and the results were used to subdivide Kingsmead pupils for training according to their likelihood of employment. He believed pupils with intelligence quotients over 60 could become wholly self-supporting with supervised employment. Those with quotients between 50 and 60 would require close parental supervision or residence in a training centre or colony. Those below 50 needed transfer to a certified institution. In 1925 Thomson's reputation ensured the LEA agreed without demur to provide a certified institution to complement Kingsmead.[142]

In that year, too, Thomson cast his net wider for suitable cases for detailed analysis. As a result of his recommendations the LEA required teachers to refer to him all pupils whose mental age appeared to be three years behind their chrono-logical age, and attendance officers to report all children who were not attending school due to an apparent but not yet confirmed lack of mental capacity.[143] He had justification for his actions. As a national report confirmed a few years later, many teachers were reluctant to identify pupils who might be certified as men-tally defective because they doubted their own professional judgement, or feared a hostile parental response, or disliked the permanent labelling of a child. Teach-ers were also suspected of a tendency to submit the names of pupils who were troublesome as well as backward, but not those who were backward without being troublesome. To add to the problems, it was believed that the misplaced sympathies of attendance officers led them to think that home care and the dep-rivation of local schooling was a lesser evil than official certification and institu-tional incarceration.[144]

The growing confidence of Kingsmead staff in their carefully structured pro-gramme of education and training led to closer links between the school, the bor-ough of Hertford and county society. The contacts paid a variety of dividends. Well-supported sales of the children's craft work were held. The school estab-lished its own Scout and Guide troops, which were incorporated in the county associations, and praised by senior local figures in the movements. The pupils vis-ited local shops, churches and historic sites, performed concerts in local halls and entered district sports events. In return, letters of appreciation and support, and donations of money and goods, became almost routine, not least from borough and county councillors.[145] The comment made by the specialist HMI Dr Alfred Eicholz in 1922 that 'children of this type do not appeal to the popular imagina-tion' did not relate to Hertford and Kingsmead.[146] Perhaps, though, the support for the ordered routines and disciplined activities of these institutionalised chil-dren had more to do with thoughts such as those voiced by Newman in 1925 that 'unemployability, industrial incapacity, delinquency and crime are found not infrequently to have their origin in neglect of the child who is mentally abnor-mal.'[147] Kingsmead's honorary consulting medical officer, Lieutenant Colonel Fremantle MP, probably summed up local attitudes in 1927 when he wrote in the visitors' book, 'It is a real economy as well as philanthropy.'[148]

In 1928 Thomson published the history of children discharged from Kingsmead to highlight its successes, or at least its containment of potential adult problems. The leavers totalled 130, and of the 110 traced 33 were in other institu-tions, 15 in full-time occupations and 62 in the care of their parents but in partial employment.[149] Not surprisingly, Kingsmead survived the financial stringencies of the early 1930s, and the LEA seems to have ignored the national report of the Mental Deficiency Committee which criticised the high *per capita* costs, the lingering social stigma and the high incidence of epidemics associated with residential schools.

Yet, beneath these developments, Thomson harboured doubts about the real impact of Kingsmead on the children. Years of careful training were successful for some of them, he wrote in the late 1920s, in the sense 'that in their social relationship they may eventually attain what superficially at least may appear to be a fairly normal position', but the school could not impart 'balance, judgement, concentration and resistance'.[150] In the 1930s more limited objectives were set for the school. By 1933 the majority of admissions had intelligence quotients above 60, and in that year Cell Barnes opened – the long-awaited institution for the care of lower grade mental defectives. With relief Thomson immediately sent to it all Kingsmead children deemed incapable of further education, and for the remainder of the decade a steady stream of transfers took place.

A new headmistress, appointed in 1930, modernised the curriculum at Kingsmead. In her own words, she aimed to inculcate the habits of 'self-control, obedience, attention and application'. Word building, word matching and sentence construction games were introduced. A graded arithmetic scheme was compiled, with numbers taught through matching, ball bouncing, skipping and shopping games. The fashionable script writing was taught in sand trays, and the rote learning of simple poems was linked to speech training. Geography and History were introduced, and Nature Study rambles became regular events. There was a heightened emphasis, especially with older pupils, on social and vocational training to equip them with basic skills and habits of perseverance and patience necessary for gainful employment. HMI thoroughly approved.[151]

In 1936, however, Thomson finally conceded that scholastic improvement even in higher grade mental defectives could not be predicted by the current tests, even though he had added performance indicators such as the Adaptation Board, Passalong, Block Design and Cube Construction Tests to the Stanford admission tests. Despite all the efforts, great and puzzling variations remained in the pupils' 'actual educational response'. Possibly, he said, 'the improvement of the children in conduct, social bearing and deportment is the most marked feature in the results obtained in a school of this character.'[152]

In the end it was the social and vocational training which justified Kingsmead's continuing existence as the rising cost of residential care and major repairs to the crumbling fabric provoked calls for its closure in the late 1930s. Self-sufficiency, disciplined routines, useful training and cost-cutting went hand in hand. The boys did much of the gardening, painting and basic repairs, while the girls undertook the laundry, cookery and housework. The sports, dancing and trips provided the pupils with healthy exercise, social activity and basic skills, and these came to be valued far more than academic progress. In 1937 Thomson merely hoped that the regime made 'the higher grade type of mental defective in some measure self-supporting'. During 1938 the utilitarian bias reached new heights, when the boys were set to work demolishing the old outhouses, building a greenhouse, extending the vegetable garden, redecorating the school and level-ling a new football field, and the girls undertook more of the routine kitchen work, cleaning and shopping.[153]

In 1936 Thomson acknowledged the existence of the emotional and behav-ioural factors often associated with backwardness which complicated the han-dling and treatment of such pupils. Although maladjustment was not yet officially recognised as a category of handicap, a Hertfordshire psychiatrist, Dr Kimber, persuaded Thomson, and through him the LEA, to fund further testing and treatment of selected children at his St Albans Nerve Clinic. Priority would be given to pupils causing problems in schools through persistent lying, stealing, truancy and insubordination.[154] Parents responded favourably, possibly because the clinic was supportive and had no powers of coercion.[155] In 1937 25 of the 39 Hertfordshire children officially categorised as dull and backward were referred to Kimber, and in 1938 19 out of 35. Over half of these went on to receive treatment from him.[156]

As the Board of Education had long ago feared, the huge investment in Kingsmead had deflected attention away from the numerous other pupils merit-ing special education across the county. It had certainly overshadowed the strange developments taking place in Beechen Grove, the LEA's Special Day School in Watford. Opening in 1916 in an old Nonconformist Sunday School building, this catered for forty children aged between seven and fifteen recom-mended to it by headteachers and school medical officers.[157] Two sisters, the Misses Schulze, were appointed as head and assistant, and for seventeen years their work with mentally defective, morally vulnerable and generally ill-behaved children received unstinting praise, largely because the results they achieved appeared so spectacular and no-one was moved to examine them closely.

The sisters were unchallenged advocates of an intensely practical approach to education through art, music, games and gardening. The children worked on a local allotment and used the council playing field for games. They cleaned the building, prepared their meals, made and laundered their working overalls, and sold their surplus produce and crafts. Over the years they won numerous art and craft awards at county exhibitions, the prize-winning allotment supplied vegetables to the local hospital, the choir sang on the wireless, and Watford Football Club trained a Beechen Grove team capable of playing, and sometimes beating, other local schools.

It was, though, the Schulzes' devotion to music as a therapeutic and educational device that attracted most praise. To Thomson's undisguised admiration, a succession of Beechen Grove pupils were taught to play the piano. He became convinced that 'aural culture does much to improve the mentality of the children', and parents, too, commented favourably on the calming effect of music upon difficult children. In the later 1920s pupils even passed Trinity College of Music piano examinations, and several were entered in national music festivals with conspicuous success.[158] No opprobrium was attached to attending this unusual school. On the contrary, children were proud of it, and appreciative ex-pupils held annual reunions with the Schulzes. In the mid-1920s inspectors from the Board of Education's Medical Department considered the sisters to be 'capable, enthusiastic and thoroughly sympathetic teachers'.[159]

The school established productive links with local employers and a succession of pupils gained and retained jobs. Many girls became daily maids and shop assistants. Boys became apprentice mechanics and carpenters, and gained posts in dairies, warehouses, chemists and engineering works. The Schulzes took great pains to fit individual pupils to particular occupations, and paid them regular visits to maintain their influence. Not surprisingly, the school gained a high reputation in Watford for its moral training, competitive spirit, vocational bias and employment record. This totally justified its existence in Thomson's eyes, and no doubt Beechen Grove's success intensified his efforts at Kingsmead.[160]

In 1933 the praise came to a dramatic end. HMI Bloom took over responsibility from the Board's Medical Department, and during his first inspection he found little to admire in the school.[161] He appreciated the children's enthusiasm for singing and dancing, and the careful training in manners and habits, but not the 'jumbled' records and the 'unreality of the formal teaching'. Reading consisted of mastering short sentences 'parrot-wise', gardening books contained dictated notes and not the children's own writing or drawing, many handwork items were 'in doubtful taste', and speech training was entirely absent. The massive bias towards intensive music tuition was condemned as utterly inappropriate bearing in mind the pupils' other needs.

Most serious of all were Bloom's grave doubts about the accuracy of the children's recorded intelligence quotients. These ranged from 48 to 88, with more than half above 70. Sixteen were below 70, but considered educable. In a damning indictment of local selection procedures and teaching, he stated that if the quotients were correct the school should be securing far better academic progress from many of the pupils. He added that there must be many more children with similar quotients that had not been noticed among Watford's 6,000 elementary school pupils. If, on the other hand, the children's progress did accurately reflect their abilities, he asserted that local identification and categorisation procedures were hopelessly at fault.[162]

Bloom's startling news that largely the wrong things were being taught to largely the wrong children was anathema to the borough and LEA, whose teachers and school medical officers, local and county councillors, parents and employers, believed that Watford's mentally defective children were being accurately identified and supremely well educated. The Schulzes continued to pursue their idiosyncratic approach, the school remained full, pupils still passed music examinations, gardening continued to win prizes and Thomson confidently asserted in 1936 that 'the school is more than justifying its existence.'[163]

The Board, though, seized an opportune moment to bring about Beechen Grove's closure. In 1937 the Schulzes retired, and the LEA sought to replace the superannuated building with a new special day school in Watford. The Board refused, arguing that such provision was unnecessary in view of the potential for special classes in the new elementary schools and the proximity of Kingsmead and Cell Barnes.[164] Both the borough of Watford and the LEA were outraged, but Bloom and the Board remained firm, and Beechen Grove closed amidst a bitter dispute over its effectiveness. Indeed, when Thomson transferred many Beechen Grove pupils to Kingsmead, and a few to Cell Barnes, Bloom argued hotly but in vain that just two merited residential care. The rest, he said, were likely to prosper much better in the flexibly organised routines of special groups in Watford's ordinary elementary schools.[165]

Thomson's devotion to Kingsmead and admiration of Beechen Grove stemmed from his conviction that children's intelligence could be accurately assessed, their learning difficulties readily identified, and their attitudes and skills improved through the exercise of intensive social and educational regimes. One of his lasting concerns was the debilitating effect of negligent home backgrounds, from which stemmed his avowed preference for residential schooling or, in the case of Beechen Grove, the unusually detailed personal attention given to pupils by the Misses Schulze. Not surprisingly, until the later 1930s there were very few examples of special classes in ordinary schools in Hertfordshire, and these were the result of local, not county council, initiatives. By 1921 Letchworth had established two – one for infants and one for juniors. Both were for children who were backward for physical rather than mental reasons. Some had suffered long absences due to scarlet fever or tuberculosis, others had poor sight or hearing or unremedied speech defects, and a few had been badly treated at home. The classes were run by interested but not specially trained teachers, and the aim, the headteachers told Thomson, was to rekindle in the generally dispirited children a desire to learn, primarily through open-air activities, language training, stories and art, and then return them to mainstream classes. Each class numbered twenty-six – small for the period – and as forty or so had attended each one at some time during the academic year 1920–1 the principle of flexibility seemed to work. Just one more early special class can be traced, which catered for 20 boys aged eight to thirteen in a Hitchin school's garden shed. In 1924 HMI found the atmosphere oppressive and the inexperienced teacher paying no attention to individual differences. Four years later, though, HMI found the class in better premises and prospering – evidence, though slight, that the special needs of some pupils in ordinary schools were being taken more seriously into account. Nevertheless, Thomson gave the classes scant attention in his annual reports, and there is no evidence of his encouragement of similar classes elsewhere, except his monotomous yearly repetition of the Board's estimate that 10 per cent of pupils were 'dull and backward' and that 'half of these would require special attention.'[166]

Further special classes made their appearance later in Watford and Hertford. In Watford the building of large new elementary schools to cope with the growth in population allowed classes to be streamed, and by 1927 the borough had four special classes. Individual attention was paramount, and the children were integrated with normal classes for any subjects in which they showed adequate strength. It was clear, though, that the teachers and children of normal classes welcomed not being held back 'by the presence of subnormal children'.[167] In 1931 two classes, for 'retarded' and 'very retarded' pupils, were established in a large reorganised Hertford school. In contrast to Watford, HMI noted that the school's most inadequate teachers, including one who was partially deaf, were allocated to them.[168]

Most children identified as 'dull and backward' stayed in ordinary classes, but there is no evidence of any courses or conferences for teachers on remedial education. Schools coped as best they could, and logbooks record their frustrations. At Much Hadham, for example, HMI wrote that the standard 'would have been fairly good if there had not been in each section such a large percentage of backward scholars', and at Rushden the headmistress had to cope with three 'mentally retarded' older pupils. Reorganisation did not always resolve matters satisfactorily. At Harpenden, when the children over the age of eleven were promoted to the new senior school they left their backward colleagues of the same age behind in the junior school. Similarly, some infants never became juniors. In 1926 and again in 1934 HMI observed totally illiterate boys aged ten in the infants' class at Sacombe. Many of these children were never reported, but even if they were assessed the recommendations could be less than helpful. 'She must pick up at her own pace' was the advice given to the headteacher at Buckland who formally reported a particularly backward girl.[169]

Much was achieved in fostering the physical health and well-being of children during the 1920s and 1930s, and significant experiments had taken place in the treatment of mental deficiency, even if the frustrating results of those experiments meant that solutions remained elusive. Thomson had been central to the vigorous promotion of many initiatives, and also to the deliberate prevention or slowing down of several others. The wartime concern for the resilience of the next generation in its inevitable battles for commercial and Imperial supremacy grew into a national obsession with healthy outdoor activities and competitive sport as prosperity and leisure time increased, especially in the economically buoyant southern counties. The work and responsibilities of the school medical officer expanded, and so did his team of district officers and nurses, in line with the requirements of the 1918 Education Act and the never-ending recommendations for treatment facilities to complement the improvements in inspection and diagnosis. The inter-war years saw the influence of the expert advisers to the county council and education committee rise to levels unimaginable before 1914, but those expert advisers – Richardson in PT, Miss Barnes in Domestic Subjects and Thomson himself – were largely swimming with the tide of events. County councillors and education committee members were equally determined to promote the vocational aspects of elementary education and the physical and moral benefits of disciplined sporting activities. Once education committee members had got over the shock of appointing expert organisers and listening to their advice, they found much of that advice not only in tune with their aspirations but also surprisingly fashionable.

For all the progress, these decades witnessed the continuing bruising encounters between old and new ideas on social reform that had started before the turn of the century, and the controversies had not died away by 1939. Thomson himself epitomised the struggle. On the one hand he fought for widening and easily accessible medical treatment facilities, PT and games opportunities, and Domestic Subjects centres and programmes, and for the effective training and education of mentally defective pupils. Yet he opposed the provision of subsidised school meals, school milk and nursery schools as unnecessary dimensions of child health and drains on the public purse. The conflict between encouraging parental responsibility and family independence through an appropriate degree of support, and destroying them through excessive public aid and state intervention, had not disappeared, and nor, of course, had the perennial desire to slow down the ever-rising local rates. It would need yet another world war to stimulate the creation of the Welfare State.

CHAPTER TWELVE

Conclusion

T HE DEMANDS OF THE 1914–18 war created the momentum for great changes in attitudes towards children. For some it was the moment to revert to Victorian practices, with a minimal schooling in basic literacy, numeracy and Christian values aimed at preparing children to be diligent and dutiful workers in fields, factories and the family homes of their social superiors. For others it was the opportunity to provide children with improved health care and educational opportunities, so that they could exercise a greater degree of personal choice over their later lives. For much of the war the former view prevailed. Immediately hostilities began school buildings were placed at the disposal of the military authorities, male teachers were encouraged to enlist, economies were imposed upon materials and repairs, and, inexorably, children became useful contributors to the war effort as the producers of food and equipment, promoters of patriotism, collectors of funds, and workers in agriculture and commerce. Their efforts were widely praised, partly for raising morale and heightening patriotism at a time of national crisis, and partly for bringing the activities of elementary schools firmly into line with the needs of the local and national economy.

Few in Hertfordshire disagreed with the wartime changes to the curriculum, despite the severe strains on many schools, and county councillors, rural employers and district magistrates remained strongly in favour of children doing their utmost to serve the country in its hour of need, whatever sacrifices this meant in terms of their schooling. Indeed, far from believing that the war jeopardised the children's education, many were convinced that it showed how wrong the prewar trends had been in extending the curriculum at great expense and in ways manifestly inappropriate to the needs of the vast majority of children – and their likely local employers. Hertfordshire provided one of the more extreme instances of this widely held view, and unashamedly so. The irony was that HMI had found so much pre-war teaching dull and counter-productive, while the lessons, collections, concerts and practical activities based upon the war had so much more relevance to pupils' lives and therefore engaged their lively interest.

Nevertheless, the social and political tide was slowly turning, and it had been doing so before 1914. The decade prior to the war had witnessed several major industrial strikes and the mounting strength and aggression of trades unions. The new Labour Party was attracting increasing support, and so were all the groups agitating for more welfare legislation. There was much to worry about. With Ireland in turmoil over Home Rule, with the Suffragette movement resorting to violence as it pursued the vote for women, with mounting evidence of the economic growth of rival nations such as Germany and the USA, and with numerous inquiries revealing the massive extent of squalor and poverty in the nation's cities, the country seemed on the verge of crisis. The well-targeted education and training of the next generation as a healthy, skilled and disciplined national asset had never seemed so important.

The war bound children and schools closely to the needs of the local and national economy, but as the slaughter on the battlefields continued unabated the nation began to see the rising generation as one that should be qualitatively different to its predecessors in terms of its health and the welfare provision it received. Prime Minister Lloyd George recognised the need to bolster the nation's faltering morale with hope of a better future as the war entered its darkest period, and the 1918 Education Act seemed to achieve this by offering extended elementary schooling and greater health care.

After the Armistice the more intensive elements of war-related teaching faded away, but so did any enthusiasm for the provision, via 'continuation schools', of compulsory part-time schooling up to the age of sixteen, let alone the extension of education to the age of eighteen, as originally envisaged. The depression which struck the country in the early 1920s proved significant in ending any thoughts of investment in this direction. Instead, it accentuated the desire for a strong practical and vocational element in elementary education to perpetuate its links with local employment needs during a period of extended national crisis. Inextricably tied up with these arguments were fears of the collapse of the social order, as Bolshevism flourished abroad and seemed to flourish at home. The rabid propaganda circulating during the general elections, the recurrent depressions and the 1926 General Strike made it clear that the distrust, misunderstanding and downright hostility between the social classes was as great as ever, and perhaps, as many people feared, getting greater. Across a deeply divided nation hopes and fears about the future abounded in about equal proportion as the Labour Party attracted more voters, mass strikes occurred in several key industries, and the agitation for greater state provision of welfare services grew in strength.

In Hertfordshire the county council and education committee were dominated to an unusual degree by influential members determined to maintain the prevailing social hierarchy, and schools were key players in its preservation. With the notable exception of Sir Charles Longmore, council officials had little, if any, say in the formulation of policy. During the 1920s and 1930s the elementary schools across Hertfordshire adopted syllabuses significantly influenced by the perceived needs of employers and a lowly view of the future occupations of the vast majority of pupils. The LEA intensified its investment in Domestic Subjects, with jobs in the catering trade and domestic service as much in mind as the girls' likely roles as housewives. The relentless decay of agriculture and rural depopulation led to the intensive promotion of school gardening, local surveys, and the prestigious Rural Syllabus. Country schools were avidly defended against closure, and every effort was made to isolate rural children from urban influences. HMI and the Board of Education failed dismally to persuade the LEA to turn many of its rural schools into junior and infants' schools and send the older pupils to centrally sited senior schools in the nearest town. Such thoughts were anathema to most county councillors.

Conversely, in Hertfordshire's burgeoning towns the growing number of industries and housing estates led to never-ending pressures for heightened attention to practical instruction and technical education. After a slow start in the early 1920s, centres multiplied and courses proliferated. By the later 1930s Hertfordshire was in the vanguard of developments in technical education, with plans for several purpose-built technical colleges. County councillors and education committee members might have ignored government initiatives that did not suit their purpose, but those that did were pursued with a determination that transcended the financial panics frequently blighting national affairs.

The religious influence in education remained strong, and in Hertfordshire the Church of England fought hard to maintain its hold on as many schools as possible. Bishop Furse's aggressively partisan campaign rent asunder old alliances and set ablaze old controversies as he sought to rekindle parochial enthusiasm for church schools and religious education founded exclusively upon Anglican doctrine. His crusade for children's hearts and minds, and his accusations against council school teachers, represented a dramatic but rare throwback by the Church of England to the religious antagonisms of previous generations. He was fortunate that the education committee retained a determination to preserve village schools, most of which were Anglican, and remained largely tolerant of the inadequacies of their premises and facilities. He was less fortunate in the 1930s, when the appalling overcrowding in manifestly superannuated buildings blighted the effective schooling of thousands of children in urban schools. Here Anglican intransigence, coupled with a chronic lack of funds, engendered a bitter polarisation of views. Most Conservatives rallied to the Church of England, while the Liberals, the Nonconformists and the Labour associations united in opposition to the Victorian legacy of a significant sector of education remaining under the authority of a sectarian body to which only a minority of people owed firm allegiance. The stories of Church of England successes and failures reveal the value most parents placed upon sound buildings, modern facilities and sensitive teaching, irrespective of whether the school was in ecclesiastical or lay ownership.

The 1920s and 1930s witnessed the unprecedented rise of various 'experts' in child health and the curriculum. The county organisers for Physical Training, Domestic Subjects, Handicraft and Gardening increasingly guided the detailed investment of the county council in these essentially utilitarian areas of the curriculum. Their work undoubtedly possessed significant educational value, but their reports recognised that their continuing success was perceived far more in terms of fitting children of the lower classes to their preordained roles in life through the patient acquisition of basic skills and the character-forming virtues long associated with such training. Some of the organisers' ideas were innovative, but these early experts always worked within the policies determined by the education committee and county council. Aldermen and county councillors, forever critical of the centralising tendencies of the national government, certainly eschewed relinquishing authority to their own employees.

Dr Hyslop Thomson, the school medical officer, was the expert wielding by far the greatest influence. He was responsible for broadening the range of treatment for elementary schoolchildren, and encouraging the development of Physical Training and Domestic Subjects. During two decades of persistent experimentation he was responsible, too, for the selection, treatment and training given to children with severe learning difficulties living in Kingsmead School. He also bore much responsibility for the regime at Beechen Grove, the neglect of nursery schooling, the half-hearted promotion of school milk, and the failure to support ordinary schools struggling to cope with children with marked learning problems.

During the 1930s a number of extremely well-constructed and equipped senior elementary schools appeared across the county. As several commentators said, they seemed indistinguishable in appearance to secondary schools. It was, though, a false and probably deliberate impression. In practice the two sectors were diverging, not converging. The literary and humanities bias within the secondary schools was far removed from the manual activities increasingly dominating the elementary schools. There were few moves within Hertfordshire to increase the small percentage of elementary school pupils who were deemed suitable candidates for secondary education. Indeed, several secondary school headteachers viewed such children entering their portals with barely concealed contempt. Employers, too, emphasised at numerous trade and association meetings that they sought young people well-prepared in terms of basic literacy and numeracy, practical skills, physical health and moral character for posts in their factories, offices and farms, and not an excessive output of secondary school leavers educated to a high degree in inappropriate subjects. The education committee agreed, and the LEA's determined preservation of an exclusive area of education for largely fee-paying middle-class parents was a cause of constant lament by HMI. In their eyes, the avid development of elementary education never compensated for the denial of other opportunities to the county's children.

In 1939 the county possessed a wide range of ancient and modern communities and a wide range of ancient and modern elementary schools. A host of renovated, patched-up or neglected infant and junior or all-age village schools served diverse farming communities, and a number of new church or council senior schools with a rural bias had been built or were planned for several smaller market towns. The larger urban areas revealed an even more dramatic variety of institutions. Many towns and boroughs, especially the older ones, were making do with cramped and ill-serviced buildings while, not far away, new estates were enjoying new schools with their own playing fields and extensive workshops. A scattering of steadily growing art, science and technical institutes offered further opportunities for advancement, and so did a few selective central schools. The secondary schools remained small, few and far between, and out of reach of the vast majority of families.

Hertfordshire had received high praise from HMI for its Rural Syllabus, Physical Training initiatives, and planned Technical Colleges, and consistent criticism for its failure to reorganise most of its rural schools and broaden admission to secondary schools. Nevertheless, the county's educational priorities had met with widespread public approval because they were calculated to meet the needs of employers and families in an era plagued with economic uncertainty, financial panic, high unemployment and deep fears of social unrest. Despite the pressures of urban expansion and rural decay, the eruptions of religious controversy, and the growth of overt party politics in local government, as the ominous year 1939 dawned county councillors and education committee members remained convinced of the wisdom of their policies. In fact, when it came to matching local educational provision with families' expectations, children's abilities, employers' needs, and the nation's priorities, they thought Hertfordshire had got everything just about right.

On 6 November 1939, soon after the outbreak of another world war, Sir David Rutherford, chairman of the county council, welcomed members to their first meeting in the new neo-Georgian county hall overlooking Hertford. It was in 1936, as the population, prosperity and rateable value of Hertfordshire soared, that the decision had been made to bring under one modern roof all the staff who worked, and committees which met, in cramped and scattered offices in Hertford, Hatfield, St Albans and London.[1] The legacy of Victorian times, when numerous individual bodies had been responsible for aspects of local affairs, was finally broken.

The new purpose-built debating chamber was semi-circular in form, symbolising the corporate rather than confrontational nature of county affairs, and it was adorned with a Brussels tapestry and a massive silver inkstand, the gifts of County Alderman Sir Lionel Faudel-Phillips of nearby Balls Park, designed to emphasise the authority of the council and its chairman. There was, however, a touch of irony about such symbols. Rutherford's address hinted at the dichotomy in Hertfordshire's local government, where patrician interest and a strong vein of paternalism combined uneasily with an ever-increasing burden of mandatory responsibilities, dwindling local autonomy and growing signs of party politics in county affairs. While, he asserted, the imposing surroundings 'will serve to remind us of the dignity of the work of the County Council' and also 'the great generosity of one of its distinguished members', he reassured councillors and ratepayers that the building had been erected primarily in the cause of 'greater economy and efficiency'.[2]

Even as Rutherford was speaking, a dramatic new era was about to start. The Second World War touched every family in the land, and once again the nation's trauma brought to the fore a desire for massive social reconstruction – in health, housing, welfare and education. In the summer of 1945, to many people's surprise, the Conservatives, led by the towering figure of Winston Churchill, were firmly rejected by the war-weary nation at the polls. Clement Atlee became Prime Minister of the first Labour government, with an absolute majority and a mandate for sweeping welfare reforms. As *The Economist* asserted, 'beyond any possibility of mistake, the country wants a Labour Government and a Socialist programme.'[3]

Endnotes

References HALS HEd1 and HALS HEd2 are to school logbooks, except where stated otherwise.

References HALS HEd4 and HALS HCC2 are to papers of the county council and its committees. HEd4 references are laid out as follows – HALS HEd4/26, pp.190–2 HEC 9.4.1920 – with the page number referring to the large numerals in the top right-hand corner of the page, added after each volume was bound. HCC2 volumes do not have this easy referencing system, and therefore the individual CP (County Paper) numbers identifying each set of papers within each volume have been given – for example, HALS HCC2/105 CP39 HEC 31.3.1924.

Chapter 1: Introduction

1.   C.F.G. Masterman (1909) p. 58.

Chapter 2: Hertfordshire in 1914

1.   T. Rook (1984) pp.109–11.
2.   F.G. Cockman (1978) pp.3–7; W. Page (1971 edn) pp.239–40.
3.   Page (1971) pp.134–5, 272–4.
4.   Cockman (1978) pp.5–7; G. Robinson (1980) p.123.
5.   Hertfordshire Archives and Local Studies (HALS) Hertfordshire County Council (HCC) *Survey Report and Analysis of County Development Plan* (1951) pp.102–3; Cockman (1978) pp.8–10; Page (1971) pp.240–1.
6.   Watford Borough Council (1972) *Watford Official Guide*.
7.   British Library, Newspaper Library (BL) *West Hertfordshire and Watford Observer (WH Observer)* 7.4.1923, 29.12.1923, 19.4.1924; *Hertfordshire Express (Express)* 16.10.1920, 24.7.1920; *Hertfordshire Advertiser and St Albans Times (Advertiser)* 21.2.1920; 1.3.1924, 10.5.1924, 8.11.1924, 12.9.1925.
8.   BL *Express* 16.10.1920, 24.7.1920; *Advertiser* 8.11.1924, 12.9.1925.
9.   First Garden City Heritage Museum *The Garden City*, New Series, Vol. II No.14 March 1907.
10. BL *Letchworth Citizen (Citizen)* 14.7.1933, article entitled *Garden City Thirty Years Ago – And Now*; L. Munby (1977) pp.237–40; M. Swenarton (1981) pp.10–12.
11. C.B. Purdom (1913) p.169.
12. Purdom (1913) p.170; HALS HEd2 23/1 Pixmore County Council (CC), His Majesty's Inspec-

tor's (HMI) reports received 26.4.1923, 2.3.1926.

13.   BL *Citizen* 4.3.1932, article entitled *Reginald Hine's Confessions*.

14.   Page (1971) pp.247–64.

15.   HALS Government Papers (GP) Census of England and Wales: Hertfordshire (Census) 1911, General Report, p.116 and Volume X Part 2, pp.179–80.

16.   HALS HCC (1951) *Survey Report*, p.41.

17.   Page (1971) pp.257–8, 262–4; J. Evans (1955).

18.   Page (1971) pp.232, 243–7, 262–4; Robinson (1978) pp.120–2.

19.   HALS GP Census 1911, Volume X Part 2, p.180.

20.   HALS GP Census 1911, General Report, p.47 and Volume I, p.154.

21.   HALS GP Census 1911, General Report, pp.206–7.

22.   HALS GP Census 1911, Volume I, pp.155–8.

23.   The 1911 figures are from the Census 1911, Volume I, pp.155–8, the earlier figures from Page (1971) pp.235–8.

24.   HALS GP Census 1911, General Report – Diagram VI.

25.   Page (1971) pp.134, 232.

26.   W. Carr and A. Hartnett (1996) p.90.

27.   ibid.

28.   Hertfordshire local directories, and newspaper advertisements and reports of events, reveal the numerous private schools, some long-lasting, others short-lived, that catered for children of families seeking fee-paying schools with modest charges.

29.   See Chapter Eight for further discussion.

30.   GP Board of Education (BEd) Statistics of Public Education in England and Wales 1913–14, pp.37–41.

31.   ibid.

32.   viz BL *Hertfordshire, Hemel Hempstead Gazette (Gazette)* 27.6.1914, 4.7.1914.

33.   ibid.

34.   HALS HEd4/20, p.185 Sixth Annual Report on School Health in Public Elementary Schools in Hertfordshire (AR SH) 1913.

35.   ibid.

36.   ibid.

37.   HALS HEd4/20, p.45 Attendance Returns: Autumn Term 1913, and p.652 Attendance Returns: Summer Term 1914.

38.   HALS HEd4/20, p.193 AR SH 1913.

39.   ibid, pp.224, 237, 239–42.

40.   HALS HEd1 103/5 Bishop's Stortford, St Michael's Church of England (CE) Infants 31.10.1913; HEd1 78/1 Puckeridge CE Mixed 3.6.1913.

41.   HALS HEd2 6/7 Hitchin, St Andrew's CE Mixed 11.12.1913, 12.12.1913, 1.4.1914.

42.   HALS HEd1 20/1 Eastwick CE Mixed 27.3.1913, 6.5.1914.

43.   HALS HEd1 113/5 Wareside CE Mixed 10.4.1913.

44.   HALS HEd1 72/1 Wallington CE Mixed 22.7.1913.

45.   BL *Advertiser* 23.1.1915.

46.   BL *Hertfordshire Mercury (Mercury)* 16.10.1915.

47.   BL *Advertiser* 23.1.1915.

48.   BL *Gazette* 27.6.1914, 4.7.1914; *Mercury* 17.4.1915.

49.   Useful works describing and analysing national attitudes and policies in the second half of

the nineteenth century and the early twentieth century from different perspectives, and informing this and other chapters, are N. Daglish, *Education Policy-making in England and Wales: The Crucible Years, 1895–1911* (London, 1996); P. Gordon, R. Aldrich and D. Dean, *Education and Policy in England in the Twentieth Century* (London, 1991); P.H.J.H. Gosden, *The Development of Educational Administration in England and Wales* (Oxford, 1966); J. Harris, *Private Lives, Public Spirit: Britain 1870–1914* (Oxford, 1993); J.S. Hurt, *Elementary Schooling and the Working Classes 1860–1918* (London, 1979); D.K. Jones, *The Making of the Education System 1851–1881* (London, 1977); E.R. Norman, *Church and Society in England 1770–1970* (Oxford, 1976); B. Simon, *The Two Nations and the Educational Structure 1780–1870* (London, 1974 edn) and *Education and the Labour Movement 1870–1920* (London, 1965); J.S. Maclure (ed.), *Educational Documents: England and Wales, 1816 to the present day* (London, 1979); J. Murphy, *Church, State and Schools in Britain 1800–1971* (London, 1971); E.E. Rich, *The Education Act 1870* (Harlow, 1970); H. Roper, *Administering the Elementary Education Acts 1870–1885* (Leeds, 1976); M. Sanderson, *Education and Economic Decline in Britain 1870 to the 1990s* (Cambridge, 1999).

50. HALS HEd1 catalogue, Introduction: Notes and list of British and Foreign Schools Society schools, including a copy of the Hertfordshire page of the 1897 BFSS Annual Report; HEd4/26, pp.406–19 Elementary Education Statistics 1920.

51. In the context of the 1902 Act see B. Simon 'The 1902 Education Act – A Wrong Turning', *History of Education Society Bulletin*, 19 (1977), pp.2–9 and M. Cruikshank 'A Defence of the 1902 Act', *History of Education Society Bulletin*, 19 (1977), pp.9–14, and Daglish (1996) pp.vii–xii, 142–68.

52. BL *Advertiser* 24.1.1920.

53. G. Sheldrick (1989) pp.13–18.

54. *Who Was Who* (1929); BL *Advertiser* 7.2.1920.

55. BL *Advertiser* 24.1.1920.

56. *Who's Who in Hertfordshire 1936* (1936); HALS Kelly's Directories for Hertfordshire, lists of aldermen and county councillors appearing in the minutes of county council meetings.

57. BL *Advertiser* 6.3.1920.

58. D. Cecil (1973) p.271; see also K. Rose (1975).

59. H.C.G. Matthew and B. Harrison (eds) (2004); E. Gaskell (1908) pp.16–17.

60. *Who Was Who* (1941); W.T. Pike (1907) p.87.

61. F.C. Roberts (1979) pp.146–7.

62. Pike (1907); Gaskell (1908); *Who's Who in Hertfordshire* (1936); HALS Kelly's Directory for Hertfordshire 1914.

63. BL *Advertiser* 24.1.1920; *National Farmers' Union Record (NFU) (Herts Edition)* February 1930 p.117.

64. Johann Herbart (1776–1834) believed that a well-balanced adult stemmed from a well-balanced education with 'many sided interests'. Children must be presented with activities and ideas calculated to form their characters that are carefully linked to their previous learning and yet provide new and relevant challenges. His teaching methods embraced four detailed steps – Preparation, Presentation, Association and Systematisation – and these found great favour as structured guidelines with teachers in England.

Friedrich Froebal (1782–1852) sought a pedagogy which reconciled individual interests with the activities of others as children grew up, and therefore cooperative work and play were vitally important to him. His KinderGarten sought to arrange a wide variety of activities and materials through which young children might express and develop their natural abilities. From the late nineteenth century onwards his ideas were enthusiastically promoted in England.

Maria Montessori (1870–1952) saw the teacher primarily as a guide and organiser of young children's carefully planned activities which helped them in the key task of adapting to their environment. She created a graded sequence of didactic material through which children acquired both physical and mental skills. She differed from Froebal in rejecting storytelling in preference to the children's own stimulation of their imagination in using her materials and apparatus. Her ideas were reaching England in the early twentieth century. After visiting Dr Montessori in Rome in 1913, the Rev. Cecil Grant started a Montessori School attached to St George's School in Harpenden.

65. GP Board of Education (GP BEd) Annual Report (AR) for 1910–11 p.25; GP BEd Circular 807: Suggestions on Arithmetic 1912.

66. HALS HEd1 88/2 Hertford, Cowper Testimonial Boys' 13.6.1913; HEd1 94/9 Royston, Queen's Road CC Mixed 7.7.1913; HALS HEd2 28/1 St Albans, Priory Park CC Mixed 18.3.1913; HEd1 72/1 Wallington CE Mixed 22.7.1913.

67. HALS HEd1 7/3 Barkway CE Senior Mixed 24.7.1914.

68. GP BEd AR 1910–11 pp.23–5; GP BEd Circular 808: *Suggestions on English* 1912, pp.3–8.

69. HALS HEd1 67/1 Great Wymondley CE Mixed 9.1.1914.

70. HALS HEd1 78/1 Puckeridge CE Mixed 3.6.1913; HEd1 66/1 Wyddial CE Mixed 1.5.1914; HEd1 18/1 Clothall CE Mixed 14/15.4.1913.

71. J. Adams (1907 edn).

72. GP BEd Circular 833: *Suggestions on History* 1914, p.6.

73. ibid, pp.3–12.

74. HALS HEd1 94/9 Royston, Queen's Road CC Mixed 7.7.1913; HEd1 17/2 Buckland CE Mixed 13.9.1913.

75. HALS HEd1 1/2 Anstey CE Mixed 11.7.1913; HEd1 113/5 Wareside CE Mixed 25.5.1914.

76. viz HALS HEd1 66/1 Wyddial CE Mixed 1.5.1914; HEd1 83/3 Pirton CC Mixed 3.4.1914.

77. GP BEd AR 1910–11 pp.31–3; GP BEd Circular 834: *Suggestions on Geography* 1914, pp.4–9.

78. As a direct result of the rejections the Inter-Departmental Committee on Physical Deterioration was set up. Its report in 1904 confirmed the need to improve the level of national health, and recommended the extension of state welfare aid to children. See Chapter Six.

79. HALS HEd4/20, p.240 AR SH 1913.

80. HALS HEd4/20, pp.642–3 Report of His Majesty's Inspectors (HMI) on the Teaching of Physical Exercises in the County July 1914.

81. BL *Advertiser* 14.2.1920.

82. ibid, p.241. A Board of Education syllabus on Temperance had been issued in 1909 and a Board memorandum on Hygiene had been sent to LEAs in 1910.

83. P.A. Gregg (1965) pp.367–77; Harris (1993) pp.182–3; Jones (1977) pp.51–4.

84. R.B. Haldane (1902) p.86.

85. H. Spencer (1949).

86. P. Magnus (1910) pp.17, 133. Many observers, including John Adams, had vigorously attacked the self-defeating tediousness of much contemporary teaching.

87. BL *Gazette* 27.6.1914; HALS HEd1 83/3 Pirton CC Mixed 3.4.1913.

88. GP BEd Statistics of Public Education in England and Wales 1913–14, pp.64–5.

89. HALS HEd4/20, p.241 AR SH 1913.

90.   BL *Express* 1.8.1914.

91.   HALS HEd2 7/16 Hitchin, St Mary's CE Boys 31.7.1914.

92.   GP BEd *Suggestions on Rural Education* 1908, and Memorandum: The Principles and Methods of Rural Education 1911.

93.   HALS HEd4/20, p.18 Hertford Divisional Subcommittee 2.3.1914.

94.   Stevenage Museum: Stevenage Oral Interview Heritage Project (SOIHP) 1985 – A006/1 (Mr JF born 1910), A010/1 (Mr WN born 1909), A032/1 (Mr JT born 1919), A069/2 (Mr FN born 1907), A111/2 (Mr GB born 1893).

95.   HALS HEd1 94/9 Royston, Queen's Road Council Mixed 9.7.1913.

Chapter 3: The direct effects of military conflict

1.   BL *Advertiser* 2.1.1915.

2.   ibid, 2.1.15, 8.8.1914.

3.   BL *Mercury* 8.8.1914.

4.   ibid, 8.8.1914, 22.8.1914.

5.   ibid, 22.8.1914; *Advertiser* 22.8.1914.

6.   *Mercury* 29.8.1914, 5.9.1914, 14.11.1914.

7.   BL *Mercury* 8.8.1914, 6.2.1915; *Advertiser* 22.8.14, 2.1.1915.

8.   BL *Advertiser* 22.8.1914.

9.   C. Davies (1974) p.165.

10.   HALS HEd1 98/6 Sawbridgeworth, Fawbert and Barnard CC Boys 26.11.1914.

11.   BL *Gazette* 22.1.1916, 29.1.1916.

12.   ibid, 22.1.1916.

13.   ibid, 29.1.1916.

14.   ibid.

15.   ibid.

16.   HALS HEd1 102/2 Much Hadham CE Boys 20.11.1914.

17.   HALS HEd1 113/5 Wareside CE Mixed 17.11.1914.

18.   HALS R.G. Auckland (1998) *Sandridge School Logbook 1894–1928* – transcript of entry dated 6.10.1914.

19.   HALS HEd1 98/6 Sawbridgeworth, Fawbert and Barnard CC Boys 11.1.1916.

20.   HALS HEd1 100/5 High Wych CE Mixed 11.1.1916.

21.   HALS HEd1 102/2 Much Hadham CE Boys 19.2.1915.

22.   ibid, numerous entries, usually weekly, between 1914 and 1919.

23.   HALS HEd1 6/3 Barkway CE Infants 19.4.1915, 8.6.1915; HEd1 7/3 Barkway CE Senior 8.6.1915.

24.   HALS HEd1 4/2 Ayot St Peter CE Mixed 16.11.1914; HEd1 17/2 Buckland CE Mixed 8.6.1915.

25.   HALS HEd1 113/5 Wareside CE Mixed 11.1.1916.

26.   ibid, 12.3.1918.

27.   HALS HEd1 22/1 Gilston, St Mary's CE Mixed 14.9.1917.

28.   HALS HEd1 113/5 Wareside CE Mixed 24.10.1918; HEd1 102/2 Much Hadham CE Boys 26.4.1918.

29.   HALS HEd1 93/4 Hoddesdon CE Boys 6.7.1916.

30.   BL *Express* 12.5.1917.

31.   HALS HEd1 94/9 Royston, Queen's Road CC Mixed 31.7.1916; HEd1 6/3 Barkway CE Infants 26.11.1914; BL *Mercury* 3.11.1917.
32.   BL *Express* 9.11.1918.
33.   ibid, 8.1.1916.
34.   HALS HEd1 12/6 Hertford, Bengeo, Christ Church CE Infants 17.11.1914.
35.   BL *Hertfordshire and Cambridgeshire Reporter and Royston Crow (Reporter)* 4.6.1915; HALS HEd1 3/3 Ashwell, Merchant Taylors' Boys School 4.6.1915.
36.   HALS HEd1 85/7 Bishop's Stortford, Northgate CC Mixed 30.11.1914.
37.   ibid, 20.11.1914.
38.   HALS HEd1 112/3 Braughing, Jenyn's CC Mixed 30.11.1914.
39.   HALS HEd1 98/2 Sawbridgeworth, Fawbert and Barnard CC Girls 2.12.1914; HEd1 98/6 Sawbridgeworth, Fawbert and Barnard CC Boys 21.1.1916, 18.1.1918.
40.   BL *Advertiser* 22.8.1914.
41.   ibid.
42.   HALS HEd2 28/1 St Albans, Priory Park CC Mixed 21.12.1914.
43.   ibid, 14.4.1915, 27.10.1915.
44.   BL *Gazette* 22.8.1914.
45.   ibid, 22.8.1914, 29.8.1914.
46.   ibid.
47.   ibid, 19.9.1914.
48.   ibid.
49.   ibid, 21.11.1914.
50.   ibid, 23.1.1915.
51.   GP BEd AR 1913–14, p.3.
52.   ibid, p.4.
53.   GP BEd Circular 892 20.2.1915.
54.   HALS HEd2 33/4 Watford Union Urban Managers' Minute Book – meetings on 14.10.1915, 18.10.1915; BL *Mercury* 12.2.1916. The dispossessed schools were Chater Boys and Girls, Callow Land Boys and Parkgate Road Boys; the host schools were Victoria Senior Boys and Girls, Alexandra Mixed and Parkgate Road Girls.
55.   HALS HEd4/22, p.425 Hertfordshire Education Committee (HEC) 15.1.1917.
56.   HALS HEd2 33/4 Watford Union Urban Managers' Minute Book 17.1.1916. The newly dispossessed schools were Beechen Grove, Holyrood and Chater Infants' Schools; their hosts were St Andrew's and Victoria Infants' Schools, and also Victoria Senior Boys' School, which was already a host.
57   HALS HEd2 33/5 Watford Union Urban Managers' Minute Book – report by the Special Committee as to School Staffing, February 1916.
58.   ibid, 18.9.1916.
59.   ibid.
60.   GP BEd AR 1914–15, p.17.
61.   HALS HEd2 33/5 Watford Union Urban Managers' Minute Book – HMI report on Alexandra CC Mixed 4.2.1918, 8.2.1918.
62.   ibid, HMI report on Parkgate Road CC Boys 12.10.1917.
63.   ibid, HMI report on Callow Land CC Boys 14.12.1917.
64.   BL *Times Educational Supplement (TES)* 2.5.1916.
65.   GP BEd AR 1914–15, p.16.

66. ibid.

67. BL *TES* 2.5.1916.

68. viz BL *TES* 12.10.1916, 28.12.1916, 13.12.1917, 4.4.1918, and see Chapter Five.

69. BL *Mercury* 5.5.1915.

70. HALS HEd1 94/9 Royston, Queen's Road CC Mixed 19.3.1915, 20.3.1915, 22.3.1915, 13.4.1915, 28.9.1915, 9.2.1916, 29.6.1916, 19.7.1916, 10.11.1916, 4.5.1917, 13.3.1918; BL *Reporter* 26.3.1915; *Express* 2.11.1918.

71. HALS HEd1 94/9 Royston, Queen's Road CC Mixed 20.3.1915, 22.3.1915; BL *Reporter* 26.3.1915.

72. BL *Express* 22.1.1916, 5.2.1916; *Mercury* 12.2.1916; *Reporter* 18.2.1916.

73. BL *TES* 5.11.1912; *Advertiser* 3.12.1912; HALS HEd4/20, pp.137–40 Report of special sub-committee appointed to consider desirability of revising the elementary schoolteachers' scale of salaries 13.3.1914, and p.374 HCC Scale of salaries 4.5.1914.

74. BL *Mercury* 24.10.1914; *Reporter* 23.10.1914; HALS HEd1 17/2 Buckland CE Mixed 27.10.1914.

75. BL *Gazette* 3.7.1915.

76. BL *Mercury* 12.5.1917.

77. HALS HEd1 93/4 Hoddesdon CE Boys, numerous entries June 1914 to February 1919.

78. Numerous entries 1914–18 in HRO HEd2 28/1 St Albans, Priory Park CC Mixed and HEd1 98/6 Sawbridgeworth, Fawbert and Barnard CC Boys.

79. BL *Express* 10.4.1915.

80. BL *Mercury* 8.5.1915.

81. BL *Mercury* 15.5.1915.

82. HALS HEd1 4/2 Ayot St Peter CE Mixed 11.5.1916, 19.1.1917, 26.1.1917; HEd1 6/3 Barkway CE Infants 29.10.1915, HEd1 7/3 Barkway CE Senior 28.10.1915; HEd1 98/6 Sawbridgeworth, Fawbert and Barnard CC Boys 20.10.1915, 25.10.1915, 30.11.1915, HEd1 102/2 Much Hadham CE Boys 17.3.1916; HEd1 112/3 Braughing, Jenyn's CC Mixed 26.2.1915; HEd4/22, pp.34–5 Finance and General Purpose Subcommittee (FGPSC) 17.3.1916; BL *Gazette* 18.3.1916, 22.4.1916, 24.2.1917; Stevenage Musuem SOIHP A071/1 (Mrs LF born 1905). In 1916, when the LEA purchased several thousand slates, the price of paper was 150% higher than before the war, and as the government had restricted the importation of wood pulp to two-thirds of the pre-war total, wholesalers had reduced supplies to customers by the same proportion. Slates were the only alternative to ordering a marked reduction in writing and drawing. When slates were first used at Ayot St Peter on 11 May 1916 the headteacher thought it apposite to record that 'we have been most careful in the use of paper, every Exercise Book being examined by special monitors before being discarded.'

83. BL *Mercury* 16.10.1915.

84. BL *Mercury* 3.4.1915; *Advertiser* 3.7.1915; HALS HEd4/21, p.90 HEC Plans Sub-Committee 12.3.1915 and pp.313–15 Liberty of St Albans Divisional Sub-Committee 31.5.1915.

85. BL *Mercury* 3.4.1915.

86. HALS HEd4/21, pp.644–6 FGPSC 17.12.1915.

87. BL *Gazette* 22.1.1916; *Mercury* 22.1.1916; *WH Observer* 22.1.1916.

88. BL *Weekly Telegraph for Waltham Abbey, Cheshunt and District (Telegraph)* 28.1.1916; *Advertiser* 12.2.1916.

89. HALS HEd4/22, pp.31–2 FGPSC 17.3.1916; BL *Mercury* 1.4.1916.

90. BL *Express* 26.2.1916; *Mercury* 26.2.1916.

91. HALS HEd2 43/2 Barnet Grouped School Managers' minute book 20.12.1915, 28.2.1916,

26.7.1916.

92. HALS HEd2 33/4 Watford Union Urban Managers' Minute Book 20.12.1915, 20.3.1916, 11.7.1916, 18.9.1916, special staffing sub-committee meeting February 1916; BL *WH Observer* 25.12.1915, 26.2.1916; *Advertiser* 22.1.1916.

93. BL *Gazette* 12.8.1916.

94. HALS HEd1 17/2 Buckland CE Mixed 27.10.1914, 18.2.1916, 23.2.1916, 25.1.1917, 19.3.1917, 23.3.1917, 27.3.1917, 16.4.1917, 4.5.1917, 11.6.1917, 17.10.1917.

95. HALS HEd1 98/6 Sawbridgeworth, Fawbert and Barnard CC Boys 16.3.1915, 30.4.1915, 7.5.1915, 8.7.1915, 31.1.1916, 2.8.1916, 11.9.1916, 4.12.1917, 9.1.1918, 29.5.1918.

96. HALS HEd1 113/5 Wareside CE Mixed 11.1.1915, 1.2.1915, 17.3.1915, 3.5.1915, 22.12.1915, 11.1.1916, 14.3.1916, 1.5.1916.

97. GP BEd AR 1916–17, pp.4–5.

98. HALS HEd1 96/1 Watford Callow Land CC Boys' 22.6.1917. See Chapter Five for a more detailed analysis of absenteeism.

99. The schools identified include St Albans Priory Park CC School, Hoddesdon CE Boys' School, Hitchen, St Andrew's CE Mixed School and Sawbridgeworth, Fawbert and Barnard CC Boys' School.

100. See Chapter Four.

101. BL *Hertfordshire and Essex Observer (HandE Observer)* 4.6.1915.

102. BL *Mercury* 29.1.1916, 5.2.1916, 22.7.1916, 21.10.1916, 18.11.1916, 25.11.1916, 23.12.1916. One cannot be sure all cases were recorded in the press, but reporters attended courts as a matter of course and editors delighted in cases likely to shock readers and allow the newspaper to adopt a high moral tone.

103. BL *Express* 2.12.1916.

104. BL *Mercury* 30.12.16, 20.1.1917.

105. BL *Express* 18.3.1916.

106. ibid, 20.5.1916.

107. ibid, 20.5.1916, and see also 12.2.1916.

108. ibid, 27.1.1917. On 20.1.1917 the *Advertiser* published a similar column.

109. ibid.

110. GP BEd Circular 975, containing the Home Office letter entitled *Juvenile Offenders*, December 1916; GP BEd AR 1916–17, pp.4–5.

111. BL *Mercury* 20.1.1917, 10.3.1917, 17.3.1917, 31.3.1917, 21.4.1917, 5.5.1917, 9.6.1917, 21.7.1917, 25.8.1917, 1.9.1917, 3.11.1917, 24.11.1917, 15.12.1917.

112. BL *Express* 3.3.1917.

113. ibid, 30.6.1917.

114. ibid.

115. BL *Mercury* 16.2.1918, 2.3.1918, 9.3.1918, 6.4.1918, 18.5.1918, 22.6.1918, 29.6.1918, 20.7.1918, 17.8.1918, 31.8.1918, 12.10.1918, 26.10.1918.

116. ibid, 29.6.1918.

117. BL *Express* 27.4.1918.

118. ibid.

119. HALS HEd1 85/7 Bishop's Stortford, Northgate CC Mixed 4.1.1915.

120. HALS HEd4/20, pp.893–4 Liberty of St Albans Education Sub-Committee 14.12.1914; BL *Advertiser* 16.1.1915.

121. HALS HEd4/22, p.425 HEC 15.1.1917.

122. HALS HEd1 102/2 Much Hadham CE Boys 14.12.1914, 12.2.1915, 19.2.1915, 5.3.1915, 9.1.1915.

123. ibid, 2.3.1917, 21.5.1917.

124. HALS HEd2 7/16 Hitchin, St Mary's CE Boys 8.10.1917; HEd1 67/1 Great Wymondley CE Mixed 25.1.1918; HEd1 4/2 Ayot St Peter CE Mixed 1.11.1917.

125. BL *WH Observer* 6.2.1915; *Mercury* 17.10.1914; HALS HEd1 6/3 Barkway CE Infants 26.10.1914; HEd1 98/6 Sawbridgeworth, Fawbert and Barnard CC Boys 11.1.1915; GP BEd AR 1914–15, p.17; A. Marwick (1965) pp.43–4. The exact figure is uncertain – the Board stated that there were 30,000 Belgian refugees originally, but Marwick estimates there were eventually about 100,000.

126. HALS HEd1 102/2 Much Hadham CE Boys 15.3.1915.

127. BL *Express* 27.1.1917, and for examples of advertisements 2.12.1916, 26.2.1916, 18.3.1916.

128. GP BEd AR 1914–15, p.17, and see also GP BEd AR 1913–14, p.4.

129. BL *Express* 3.3.1917.

130. ibid.

131. D.H. Robinson (1980) pp.107–9.

132. T. Fegan (2002) p.128.

133. ibid, p.130.

134. Davies (1974) p.175.

135. Stevenage Musuem SOIHP – A078/2 (Mrs MT born 1892).

136. Davies (1974) p.175. See also Fegan (2002) pp.130–1; Robinson (1980) p.116.

137. HALS HEd1 98/6 Sawbridgeworth, Fawbert and Barnard CC Boys 14.10.1915.

138. Fegan (2002) pp.128–9. Technically speaking, the Cuffley airship, like many others, was not a Zeppelin as it was designed and manufactured by the firm of Schutte Lanz – M. Gilbert (1994) p. 289.

139. BL *Mercury* 7.10.1916. In 1985 three Stevenage residents recalled being woken up as children to view Zeppelins caught in searchlights and then lighting up the sky as they burst into flames – Stevenage Museum SOIHP A020/1 (Mrs S born 1908), A057/1 (Miss B F born 1906), A078/2 (Mrs M T born 1892).

140. ibid.

141. HALS HEd1 98/6 Sawbridgeworth, Fawbert and Barnard CC Boys 2.10.1916.

142. HALS HEd1 206/3 Goffs Oak CE Mixed 2.10.1916; HEd1 12/6 Hertford, Bengeo Christ Church CE Infants 2.10.1916; HEd1 88/2 Hertford, Cowper Testimonial Senior Boys 2.10.1916.

143. HALS HEd2 7/17 Hitchin, St Mary's CE Girls 26.10.1915.

144. BL *Telegraph* 22.9.1916.

145. Robinson (1980) pp.107–19.

146. HALS HEd1 88/2 Hertford, Cowper Testimonial Senior Boys 13.6.1917, 14.6.1917; HEd1 93/4 Hoddesdon CE Boys 12.6.1917, 2.10.1917.

147. HALS HEd1 12/6 Hertford, Bengeo Christ Church CE Infants 13.6.1917; HEd1 103/5 Bishop's Stortford, St Michael's CE Infants 2.10.1917.

148. HALS HEd1 98/6 Sawbridgeworth, Fawbert and Barnard CC Boys 13.6.1917; HEd1 22/1 Gilston CE Mixed 1.10.1917.

149. HALS HEd1 12/6 Hertford, Bengeo Christ Church CE Infants 23.9.1917, 1.11.1917.

150. BL *Advertiser* 23.6.1917.

151. ibid.

152. BL *Mercury* 29.9.1918.

153. ibid.

154. BL *Advertiser* 30.6.1917.

155. ibid.

156. HALS HEd1 22/1 Gilston CE Mixed 1.2.1918; HEd1 93/4 Hoddesdon CE Boys 29.1.1918, 30.1.1918; HEd1 98/6 Sawbridgeworth, Fawbert and Barnard CC Boys 18.2.1918; HEd1 100/5 High Wych CE Mixed 18.2.1918, 8.3.1918; HEd1 102/2 Much Hadham CE Boys 1.2.1918; HEd1 113/5 Wareside CE Mixed 1.2.1918.

Chapter 4: Schools at war

1. HALS HEd1 75/2 Sacombe CE Mixed 9.9.1914, 30.9.1914, 30.10.1914.

2. HALS HEd1 85/7 Bishop's Stortford, Northgate CC Mixed 9.10.1914.

3. GP BEd AR 1914–15, p.13.

4. HALS HEd1 102/2 Much Hadham CE Boys 6.11.1914; HEd1 3/3 Ashwell, Merchant Taylors' Boys 2.10.1914.

5. BL *Mercury* 17.10.1914.

6. HALS HEd1 98/6 Sawbridgeworth, Fawbert and Barnard CC Boys 4.5.1915, 11.11.1915, 12.11.1915, 24.7.1917, 6.2.1919, 1.12.1919.

7. HALS HEd1 88/2 Hertford, Cowper Testimonial Senior Boys 11.5.1916.

8. HALS Auckland (1998), entry dated 12.10.1915.

9. HALS HEd1 3/3 Ashwell, Merchant Taylors' Boys 4.12.1914.

10. BL *Reporter* 11.12.1914; *Mercury* 17.10.1915, 26.2.1916, 24.2.1917; HALS HEd1 98/6 Sawbridgeworth, Fawbert and Barnard CC Boys 30.4.1915.

11. HALS HEd1 3/3 Ashwell, Merchant Taylors' Boys 23.7.1915.

12. HALS HEd1 3/3 and 3/4 Ashwell, Merchant Taylors' Boys numerous entries 1914–18.

13. BL *Reporter* 27.10.1916.

14. HEd1 67/1 Great Wymondley CE Mixed 4.3.1918.

15. HALS HEd1 3/3 Ashwell, Merchant Taylors' Boys 15.1.1915.

16. ibid, 12.3.1915, 16.4.1915, 4.6.1915, 18.12.1914.

17. BL *Express* 18.3.1916.

18. HALS HEd1 3/3 Ashwell, Merchant Taylors' Boys 10.12.1915.

19. ibid, 17.12.1915; HEd1 98/6 Sawbridgeworth, Fawbert and Barnard CC Boys 10.9.1918; BL *Reporter* 16.1.1917.

20. HALS HEd1 94/9 Royston, Queen's Road CC Mixed 18.12.1914.

21. BL *Advertiser* 3.10.1914.

22. GP BEd AR 1913–14, p.3; BL *Reporter* 11.12.1914; and *inter alia* HALS HEd1 22/1 Gilston CE Mixed 6.11.1914, 26.2.1915, 23.7.1915, 4.11.1915, 9.11.1915, 4.12.1915, 13.9.1916.

23. HALS HEd1 94/9 Royston, Queen's Road CC Mixed 30.10.1914; HEd1 6/3 Barkway CE Infants 12.11.1915; HEd1 7/3 Barkway CE Senior 12.11.1915.

24. HALS HEd1 1/2 Anstey CE Mixed 6.5.1916; HEd1 22/1 Gilston CE Mixed 23.7.1915, 4.12.1915, 13.9.1916, 20.9.1916; HEd1 24/2 Harpenden, Kinsbourne Green CE Mixed 8.5.1918.

25. HALS HEd1 24/2 Harpenden, Kinsbourne Green CE Mixed 29.3.1916.

26. HALS HEd1 85/7 Bishop's Stortford, Northgate CC Mixed 25.10.1916, 21.12.1916.

27. BL *Mercury* 10.10.1914; *Reporter* 11.12.1914; HALS HEd1 85/7 Bishop's Stortford, Northgate CC Mixed 16.10.1914, 13.11.1914.

28. BL *Reporter* 21.7.1916, 11.12.1914; HALS HEd1 3/3 Ashwell, Merchant Taylors' Boys 4.12.1914; HEd1 85/7 Bishop's Stortford, Northgate CC Mixed 16.10.1914 and 13.11.1914; Auckland (1998), entry dated 20.7.1916 recording a fund-raising concert for Belgian refugees held on Lady Saltmarsh's lawn at Sandridge.

29. HALS HEd1 85/7 Bishop's Stortford, Northgate CC Mixed 14.7.1915; HEd1 20/1 Eastwick CE Mixed 6.7.1915.

30. BL *Mercury* 10.10.1914.

31. BL *Reporter* 21.7.1916, 4.1.1918; *Mercury* 8.4.1916.

32. BL *Reporter* 5.3.1915, 21.7.1916.

33. ibid, 5.3.1915, 21.7.1916.

34. ibid, 21.7.1916.

35. BL *Mercury* 10.4.1915, 17.4.1915; HALS HEd1 85/7 Bishop's Stortford, Northgate CC Mixed 26.3.1915, 18.5.1916; HEd1 112/3 Braughing, Jenyn's CC Mixed 6.3.1916.

36. BL *Mercury* 8.4.1916; *Reporter* 4.1.1918, 18.1.1918; HALS HEd1 7/3 Barkway CE Senior 1.1.1918; HEd2 7/16 Hitchin, St Mary's CE Boys 24.5.1917, 14.12.1917.

37. HALS HEd1 3/3 Ashwell, Merchant Taylors' Boys 20.11.1914; HEd1 96/1 Watford, Callow Land CC Boys 19.11.1914; HEd1 108/2 Stanstead Abbots CE Mixed 25.5.1916. Lord Roberts died in France shortly after his visit to inspect troops in east Hertfordshire.

38. BL *Reporter* 27.10.1916; *Gazette* 18.11.1916; HALS HEd1 85/7 Bishop's Stortford, Northgate CC Mixed 22.9.1916; HEd1 100/5 High Wych CE Mixed 21.9.1916; HEd2 7/16 Hitchin, St Mary's CE Boys 25.9.1916.

39. BL *Mercury* 1.4.1916; HALS HEd1 13/2 Waterford CE Mixed 21.10.15, HEd1 20/1 Eastwick CE Mixed 6.7.1915; HEd1 22/1 Gilston CE Mixed 23.7.1915, 4.11.1915, 9.11.1915, 4.12.1915, 13.9.1916; HEd1 112/3 Braughing, Jenyn's CC Mixed 26.11.1915, 21.1.1916, 28.1.1916; HEd2 7/17 Hitchin, St Mary's CE Girls' 3.11.1915, 2.12.1915, 13.12.1915, 14.12.1915, 8.3.1916.

40. BL *Reporter* 31.3.1916; *Mercury* 1.4.1916.

41. BL *Reporter* 27.10.1916; *Gazette* 18.11.1916; *Advertiser* 27.10.1917, 26.10.1918; HALS HEd1 13/2 Waterford CE Mixed 21.10.1915; HEd1 72/1 Wallington CE Mixed 21.10.1915.

42. BL *Advertiser* 26.10.1918.

43. BL *Express* 30.10.1915, 26.10.1918.

44. BL *Reporter* 27.10.1916.

45. ibid.

46. BL *Gazette* 24.4.1915.

47. ibid, 18.12.1915, 18.11.1916.

48. ibid, 18.11.1916.

49. BL *Mercury* 3.7.1915.

50. HALS HEd4/21, p.279 Central School Attendance Sub-Committee (CSASC) 21.5.1915.

51. HALS HEd1 93/4 Hoddesdon CE Boys 28.9.1915.

52. HALS HEd1 22/1 Gilston CE Mixed 7.6.1916.

53. HALS HEd1 83/3 Pirton CC Mixed 3.6.1918.

54. HALS HEd1 4/2 Ayot St Peter CE Mixed 23.4.1915.

55. HALS HEd1 98/6 Sawbridgeworth, Fawbert and Barnard CC Boys 18.6.1915.

56. HALS HEd1 6/3 Barkway CE Infants 26.3.1915; HEd1 7/3 Barkway CE Senior 23.10.1914 (where most Allied national anthems were played daily); HEd1 75/2 Sacombe CE Mixed 9.9.1914; HEd1 100/5 High Wych CE Mixed 11.9.1915.

57. BL *Reporter* 11.9.1914.

58. BL *Gazette* 16.1.1915.
59. HALS HEd1 7/3 Barkway CE Senior 23.10.1914; HEd1 98/6 Sawbridgeworth, Fawbert and Barnard Boys 21.10.1914.
60. HALS HEd1 96/1 Watford Callow Land CC Boys 21.10.1914.
61. HALS HEd2 7/16 Hitchin, St Mary's CE Boys 21.10.1915.
62. ibid.
63. HALS HEd1 7/5 Barkway CE Junior 21.10.1915; HEd2 7/16 Hitchin, St Mary's CE Boys 21.10.1915.
64. HALS HEd1 85/7 Bishop's Stortford, Northgate CC Mixed 21.10.1915.
65. HALS HEd1 94/9 Royston, Queen's Road CC Mixed 21.10.1915; HEd1 75/2 Sacombe CE Mixed 21.10.1915, 22.10.1915.
66. HALS HEd1 22/1 Gilston CE Mixed 21.10.1915; HEd1 76/1 Sandon CE Mixed 21.10.1915.
67. HALS HEd4/22, p.171 Finance, School Attendance and General Purposes Sub-Committee (FSAGPSC) 2.6.1916.
68. BL *Reporter* 27.10.1916.
69. ibid.
70. BL *WH Observer* 28.10.1916; *Advertiser* 23.2.1918.
71. BL *Advertiser* 23.2.1918.
72. ibid.
73. HALS HEd1 7/3 Barkway CE Senior 24.5.1914; HEd1 98/6 Sawbridgeworth, Fawbert and Barnard CC Boys 22.5.1914.
74. BL *Advertiser* 29.5.1915.
75. ibid.
76. ibid.
77. BL *Express* 29.5.1915.
78. ibid.
79. ibid.
80. HALS HEd1 24/2 Harpenden, Kinsbourne Green CE Mixed 21.5.1915.
81. BL *TES* 24.5.1917.
82. ibid.
83. ibid.
84. HALS HEd1 6/3 Barkway CE Infants 24.5.1917; HEd1 12/6 Hertford, Bengeo Christ Church CE Infants 24.5.1917; HEd1 13/2 Waterford CE Mixed 24.5.1917; HEd1 66/1 Wyddial CE Mixed 24.5.1917; HEd1 83/3 Pirton CC Mixed 24.5.1917; HEd1 85/7 Bishop's Stortford, Northgate CC Mixed 24.5.1916; HEd1 100/5 High Wych CE Mixed 24.5.1917; HEd1 102/2 Much Hadham CE Boys 24.5.1916, 24.5.1917; BL *Express* 2.6.1917; *Mercury* 2.6.1917.
85. BL *Mercury* 2.6.1917; HALS HEd1 102/2 Much Hadham CE Boys 25.5.1917.
86. HALS HEd2 28/1 St Albans, Priory Park CC Mixed 21.5.1915, 2.5.1916, 24.5.1917.
87. HALS HEd1 7/3 Barkway CE Senior 24.5.1918.
88. HALS HEd2 7/16 Hitchin, St Mary's CE Boys 24.5.1917.
89. BL *HandE Observer* 27.5.1916.
90. BL *TES* 24.5.1917.
91. BL *Gazette* 26.5.1917.
92. ibid.
93. ibid.
94. ibid, 22.4.1916.

95. BL *TES* 2.2.1915.

96. BL *WH Observer* 26.8.1916.

97. ibid.

98. BL *Reporter* 26.3.1915.

99. BL *WH Observer* 26.12.1914.

100. HALS HEd1 93/4 Hoddesdon CE Boys 23.9.1914.

101. HALS HEd1 7/3 Barkway CE Senior 18.9.1914, 6.11.1914, 27.7.1917.

102. HALS HEd1 112/3 Braughing, Jenyn's CC Mixed 11.11.1915, 22.12.1915.

103. HRO HEd2 7/16 Hitchin, St Mary's CE Boys 6.9.1915, 15.10.1915, 14.9.1916.

104. GP BEd AR 1914–15, pp.11–14.

105. BL *Express* 9.1.1915.

106. ibid, 16.1.1915.

107. ibid. If any letters defending the essays were written they were not published, and the editor made no further comment.

108. The National Archives: Public Record Office (TNA:PRO) ED 10/81 *The Teacher's World* 10.1.1917.

109. HALS HEd1 7/3 Barkway CE Senior 12.1.1917; HEd2 7/16 Hitchin, St Mary's CE Boys 19.1.1917.

110. BL *WH Observer* 6.2.1915.

111. ibid.

112. TNA:PRO ED 10/81 *The Teacher's World* 10.1.1917.

113. HALS HEd4/20, pp.642–3 Report of HMI on the Teaching of Physical Exercises in the County: July 1914.

114. BL *Mercury* 1.7.1916; *Gazette* 1.7.1916.

115. ibid. At Gilston, for example, drill was undertaken daily, and at Barkway the senior school had the voluntary services of an army lieutenant – HALS HEd1 22/1 Gilston CE Mixed 19.10.1917; HEd1 7/3 Barkway CE Senior 2.10.1917.

116. GP BEd *Elementary Science, including Nature Study* April 1915, p.4.

117. HALS HEd1 12/6 Hertford, Bengeo Christ Church CE Infants September 1915. Further lists appear in September 1916, 1917 and 1918.

118. GP BEd *Elementary Science, including Nature Study* April 1915, pp.4–6.

119. HALS HEd2 7/16 Hitchin, St Mary's CE Boys 9.7.1915.

120. HALS HEd1 6/3 Barkway CE Infants 7.5.1915, 21.9.1915.

121. GP BEd AR 1917–18, p.5

122. *Reporter* 28.5.1915; *Express* 2.6.1917. The children struck by the aeroplane at Norton had been digging up dandelion roots – see Chapter Three.

123. BL *Advertiser* 3.11.1917; *Reporter* 28.6.1918.

124. GP BEd AR 1916–17, p.4; TNA:PRO ED 10/73; GP BEd Circular 1009 15.8.1917.

125. Imperial War Museum DBN/ES/478 *The Collection of Horse Chestnuts* 1917.

126. HALS HEd1 113/5 Wareside CE Mixed 4.10.1917.

127. HALS HEd1 20/1 Eastwick CE Mixed 26.9.1917; HEd2 7/16 Hitchin, St Mary's CE Boys 16.11.1917.

128. HALS HEd1 7/3 Barkway CE Senior 5.10.1917, 16.11.1917; BL *Reporter* 16.11.1917.

129. BL *Mercury* 29.9.1917.

130. ibid.

131. Soft fruit collections had taken place in some LEAs in 1917, but Hertfordshire schools had

concentrated upon horse chestnuts.

132. TNA:PRO ED 10/73 Letter from the Ministry of Food to the Secretary, BEd, 24.7.1918; GP BEd Circular 1056 30.7.1918.

133. BL *Express* 24.8.1918; GP BEd AR 1917–18, p.5.

134. HALS HEd1 102/2 Much Hadham CE Boys 27.9.1918, 18.10.1918.

135. BL *Express* 24.8.1918, 31.8.1918.

136. ibid, 26.10.1918; HALS HEd1 98/6 Sawbridgeworth, Fawbert and Barnard CC Boys 16.9.1918; HEd1 112/3 Braughing, Jenyn's CC Mixed 27.9.1918.

137. HALS HEd1 4/2 Ayot St Peter CE Mixed 11.9.1918, 20.9.1918, 27.9.1918; HEd1 76/1 Sandon CE Mixed 27.9.1918, 4.10.1918, 18.10.1918; HEd1 83/3 Pirton CC Mixed 27.9.1918, 4.10.1918; HEd1 66/1 Wyddial CE Mixed 4.10.1918, 11.10.1918, 18.10.1918.

138. BL *Mercury* 2.11.1918.

139. HALS HEd1 88/2 Hertford Cowper Testimonial Senior Boys 9, 11, 12, 13, 16, 18, 20, 23, 24 and 27.9.1918, 3, 4, 8, 10 and 11.10.1918 and 13.11.1918.

140. It was an impressive amount, but paled beside several counties averaging 60 tons, the 130 tons from neighbouring Buckinghamshire and 313 tons from Gloucestershire – GP BEd AR 1917–18, p.5. Some schools, including some in Hertfordshire, sold their fruit direct to local factories as they paid more than the 3d a pound offered by the Local Food Committees, and these amounts would not be officially recorded – HALS HEd4/25, p.145 HEC 14.4.1919.

141. Quotation from Samuel Smiles' *Self-Help* contained in H. Perkins (1969) p.278.

142. R.J.W. Selleck (1968) pp.44–50.

143. GP BEd Circular 915 1.7.1915.

144. Imperial War Museum: The National War Savings Committee Leaflet 13 *War Savings*, May 1916.

145. BL *Reporter* 3.3.1916.

146. HALS HEd1 7/5 Barkway CE Junior 9.7.1915; HEd1 22/1 Gilston CE Mixed 9.7.1915; HEd2 7/16 Hitchin, St Mary's CE Boys 16.7.1915, 22.6.1916, 2.8.1916.

147. HALS HEd1 13/2 Waterford CE Mixed 18.7.1916.

148. HALS HEd1 112/3 Braughing, Jenyn's CC Mixed 26.7.1918.

149. HALS HEd1 44/3 Norton CE Mixed 13.3.1918.

150. HALS HEd1 83/3 Pirton CC Mixed 1.6.1916.

151. HALS HEd1 75/2 Sacombe CE Mixed 30.10.1918.

152. HALS HEd1 98/6 Sawbridgeworth, Fawbert and Barnard CC Boys 31.1.1918.

153. HALS HEd2 7/16 Hitchin St Mary's CE Boys 20.12.1917.

154. HALS HEd1 96/1 Watford, Callow Land CC Boys 9.5.1918.

155. BL *Gazette* 23.11.1918.

156. ibid, 24.2.1917.

157. BL *WH Observer* 16.10.1915.

158. ibid; *Advertiser* 16.10.1915.

159. BL *WH Observer* 16.10.1915.

160. BL *Mercury* 20.11.1915.

161. ibid.

162. BL *TES* 4.1.1916.

163. GP BEd Circular 944: Public Elementary Schools and Food Supply in Wartime 1916.

164. HALS HEd1 6/3 Barkway CE Infants 24.7.1917, 30.4.1917; HEd1 22/1 Gilston CE Mixed 27.4.1917; HEd1 102/4 Much Hadham CE Girls 1.5.1918; HEd2 7/16 Hitchin, St Mary's CE

Boys 13.6.1917.

165. HALS HEd1 13/2 Waterford CE Mixed 23, 24, 25.7.1917.

166. ibid, 18.3.1918.

167. HALS HEd4/20, pp.884–5 Hertford Divisional Sub-Committee 4.12.1914.

168. BL *Mercury* 16.1.1915.

169. BL *Reporter* 26.3.1915, 31.3.1915, 30.4.1915, 4.6.1915, 3.3.1916, 16.11.1917; HALS HEd1 83/3
Pirton CC Mixed 14.5.1915; HEd1 85/7 Bishop's Stortford, Northgate CC Mixed 12.5.1916;
HEd1 112/3 Braughing, Jenyn's CC Mixed 20.3.1916; HEd2 7/17 Hitchin, St Mary's CE Girls
19.9.1915, 2.8.1916.

170. GP BEd Circular 944: Public Elementary Schools and Food Supply in Wartime 1916.

171. ibid.

172. HALS HEd1 24/2 Harpenden, Kinsbourne Green CE Mixed 1.5.1917; HEd1 76/1 Sandon CE
Mixed 12.12.1917; HEd1 83/3 Pirton CC Mixed 2.7.1917.

173. BL *Express* 17.2.1917.

174. GP BEd AR 1916–17, p.3.

175. BL *TES* 8.3.1917, 28.2.1918; *Mercury* 20.1.1917.

176. HALS HEd4/23, p.247 FSAGPSC 1.10.1917.

177. BL *TES* 28.2.1918.

178. HALS HEd4/24, p.10 FSAGPSC 11.3.1918; HEd4/25, p.145 HEC 14.4.1919.

179. HALS HEd4/24, p.271 FSAGPSC 30.9.1918.

180. BL *Mercury* 22.6.1918.

181. BL *Express* 25.8.1917; *Gazette* 12.8.1916.

182. BL *Express* 25.8.1917.

183. HALS HEd1 83/3 Pirton CC Mixed 8.11.1917, 15.5.1918.

184. HALS HEd1 7/3 Barkway CE Senior 8.3.1917; HEd1 67/1 Great Wymondley CE Mixed
12.12.1918.

185. BL *Reporter* 16.11.1917; HALS HEd4/24, p.271 FSAGPSC 30.9.1918.

186. HALS HEd1 76/1 Sandon CE Mixed 12.12.1917, 21.12.1917, 1.3.1918.

187. HALS HEd1 100/5 High Wych CE Mixed 14.10.1914, 20.4.1917, 1.5.1917, 15.5.1917, 27.6.1917.

188. BL *Mercury* 21.4.1917; HALS HEd1 24/2 Harpenden, Kinsbourne Green CE Mixed 1.5.1917,
8.5.1917.

189. BL *Gazette* 24.2.1917, 23.6.1917.

190. HALS HEd1 102/2 Much Hadham CE Boys 16.5.1917, 20.7.1917, 26.9.1917, 25.3.1918, 5.7.1918.

191. HALS HEd1 13/2 Waterford CE Mixed 13.3.1917, 23.7.1917, 18.3.1918, 3.5.1918, 31.5.1918,
25.6.1919.

192. HALS HEd4/20, p.241 AR SH 1913; BL *Gazette* 27.6.1914.

193. BL *Mercury* 12.12.1914; *Reporter* 31.3.1916; HALS HEd1 75/2 Sacombe CE Mixed 18.10.1915;
HEd1 85/7 Bishop's Stortford, Northgate CC Mixed 9.10.1914, 13.11.1914; HEd2 7/17 Hitchin,
St Mary's CE Girls 16.11.1915, 3.11.1915, 2.12.1915, 13.12.1915, 14.12.1915, 8.3.1916, 18.4.1916.

194. HALS HEd1 6/3 Barkway CE Infants 12.11.1915; HEd1 85/7 Bishop's Stortford, Northgate CC
Mixed 21.10.1915; HEd1 94/9 Royston, Queen's Road CC Mixed 4.11.195, 23.10.1916; HEd2
7/17 Hitchin, St Mary's CE Girls 3.11.1915.

195. BL *Mercury* 12.12.1914.

196. BL *Reporter* 30.4.1915.

197. BL *WH Observer* 16.10.1915; *Advertiser* 16.10.1915, 1.4.1916.

198. HALS HEd1 94/9 Royston, Queen's Road CC Mixed 4.11.1915; HEd2 7/17 Hitchin, St Mary's

CE Girls 3.11.1915.

199. BL *WH Observer* 16.10.1915; *Advertiser* 16.10.1915; HALS HEd1 1/2 Anstey CE Mixed 25.6.1915, 29.10.1915; HEd1 6/3 Barkway CE Infants 12.11.1915; HEd1 7/3 Barkway CE Senior 12.11.1915.

200. HALS HEd2 7/16 Hitchin, St Mary's CE Boys 29.10.1915, HEd2 7/17 Hitchin, St Mary's CE Girls 16.11.1915, 2.12.1915, 13.12.1915, 14.12.1915, 8.3.1916, 18.4.1916.

201. HALS HEd1 112/3 Braughing, Jenyn's CC Mixed 12.11.1915, 26.11.1915.

202. HALS HEd1 75/2 Sacombe CE Mixed 18.10.1915, 22.11.1915.

203. HALS HEd4/21, p.477 Hertford Divisional Sub-Committee 17.9.1915.

204. BL *Advertiser* 22.1.1916.

205. ibid, 1.4.1916; *TES* 23.11.1916.

206. HALS HEd1 7/3 Barkway CE Senior 4.12.1916; HEd4/23, p.137 FSAGPSC 1.6.1917.

207. BL *Advertiser* 1.4.1916; HALS HEd1 1/2 Anstey CE Mixed 12.11.1915, 19.11.1915; HEd1 102/4 Much Hadham CE Girls 24.11.1916; HEd2 7/17 Hitchin, St Mary's CE Girls 2.12.1915, 13.12.1915.

208. BL *Advertiser* 1.4.1916; *TES* 23.11.1916.

209. BL *Advertiser* 1.4.1916.

210. ibid; *WH Observer* 28.10.1916; *TES* 23.11.1916; HALS HEd4/22, p.174 FSAGPSC 2.6.1916.

211. BL *Mercury* 1.7.1916; HALS HEd4/22, p.174 FSAGPSC 2.6.1916.

212. HALS HEd4/22, p.174 FSAGPSC 2.6.1916.

213. HALS HEd1 102/2 Much Hadham CE Boys 26.3.1915.

214. BL *Mercury* 1.7.1916, 28.10.1916; *Gazette* 1.7.1916, 28.10.1916; *HandE Observer* 1.7.1916.

215. BL *Mercury* 1.7.1916.

216. BL *Mercury* 28.10.1916.

217. HALS HEd4/23, p.137 FSAGPSC 1.6.1917; BL *Advertiser* 30.6.1917.

218. HALS HEd4/24, p.197 HEC 14.6.1918.

219. BL *TES* 9.8.1917.

220. ibid; HALS HEd4/23, p.137 FSAGPAC 1.6.1917.

221. HALS HEd1 4/2 Ayot St Peter CE Mixed 6.7.1916; HEd1 6/3 Barkway CE Infants 21.9.1915, 1.8.1916; HEd1 12/6 Hertford, Bengeo Christ Church CE Infants 14.11.1917; HEd1 18/1 Clothall CE Mixed 25.9.1918; HEd1 22/1 Gilston CE Mixed 20.5.1917; HEd1 66/1 Wyddial CE Mixed 19.9.1917; HEd1 72/1 Wallington CE Mixed 21.2.1918; HEd1 75/2 Sacombe CE Mixed 5.12.1917; HEd1 83/3 Pirton CC Mixed 12.12.1917; HEd1 100/5 High Wych CE Mixed 14.10.1914, 4.10.1917; HEd1 103/5 Bishop's Stortford, St Michael's CE Infants 24.3.1914, 14.6.1918; HEd1 108/2 Stanstead Abbots CE Mixed 13.10.1914; HEd1 112/3 Braughing, Jenyn's CC Mixed 27.5.1914; –.1.1917, 17.4.1917, 19.10.1917; HEd1 113/5 Wareside CE Mixed 16.10.1917; HEd2 6/7 Hitchin, St Andrew's CE Mixed 29.1.1914, 1.4.1914, 20.9.1917; HEd2 33/5 Watford Union Urban Managers' Minute Book 12.10.1917, 14.12.1917.

Chapter 5: Children at work

1. In Hertfordshire the ratepayers' share of the total cost of elementary education was nearly the highest in the country. In 1909–10 Hertfordshire ratepayers were bearing 58% of the total cost of elementary education, a figure only exceeded by Surrey's 62.8%. The average was 41.7%. See BL *TES* 5.11.1912.

2. HALS HEd4/21, p.462 CSASC 13.9.1915.

3.   HALS HEd4/20, p.243 AR SH 1913.
4.   HALS HEd4/21, p.152 AR SH 1914.
5.   HALS HEd4/21, pp.462–3 CSASC 13.9.1915.
6.   ibid.
7.   ibid.
8.   ibid.
9.   ibid; Hurt (1979) pp.191–3, 200–13.
10. HALS HEd1 83/3 Pirton CC Mixed 7.7.1916, 6.7.1917.
11. HALS HEd4/22, pp.167–8 FSAGPSC 2.6.1916.
12. HALS HEd4/22, p.292 FSAGPSC 2.10.1916.
13. HALS HEd4/22, p.323 HEC 23.10.1916.
14. BL *Gazette* 28.10.1916.
15. HALS HEd4/23, pp.132–3 FSAGPSC 1.6.1917.
16. BL *Mercury* 7.7.1917; HALS HEd4/23, p.213 AR SH 1916. Fremantle believed, however, that
     full-time work out of doors was largely beneficial in terms of children's health.
17. HALS HEd4/23, p.239 FSAGPSC 1.10.1917. They were superseded in 1919 by the new Educa-
     tion Act's clauses limiting work to children over the age of twelve and to the time between
     the close of school and 8pm on schooldays. The Act allowed LEAs to make a byelaw allowing
     children to work for an hour before school but despite a short but bitter local controversy
     Hertfordshire education committee decided against this – HALS HEd4/25, p.152 HEC
     14.4.1919, p.229 CSASC 30.5.1919 and pp.531–2 HEC 20.10.1919.
18. BL *Mercury* 8.8.1914.
19. ibid.
20. BL *Advertiser* 28.11.1914.
21. ibid.
22. TNA:PRO ED 19/88 Letter from HCC Education Department to the Secretary, BEd
     24.9.1914.
23. TNA:PRO ED 19/88 BEd internal memoranda signed by E. Phipps and G.N. Richardson,
     undated but referring to HCC letter, and letter from BEd signed by G.N. Richardson,
     30.9.1914, to HCC Education Department.
24. BL *Advertiser* 28.11.1914.
25. ibid.
26. BL *Gazette* 4.12.1915.
27. ibid; *Reporter* 27.10.1916; *WH Observer* 31.8.1918; *Advertiser* 28.11.1914, 2.1.1915, 29.5.1915,
     25.9.1915, 23.6.1917, 30.6.1917, 3.11.1917.
28. BL *Gazette* 8.12.1917.
29. HALS HEd4/20, p.727 HEC 12.10.1914; TNA:PRO ED 18/87 The Hertfordshire School Atten-
     dance No3 Byelaws 1910.
30. HALS HEd4/20, p.727 HEC 12.10.1914.
31. BL *Advertiser* 17.10.1914; *Mercury* 17.10.1914; *Gazette* 17.10.1914.
32. ibid.
33. ibid.
34. HALS HEd1 102/2 Much Hadham CE Boys 17.7.1914.
35. HALS HEd1 1/2 Anstey CE Mixed 7.8.1914.
36. HALS HEd1 93/4 Hoddesdon CE Boys 9.11.1914.
37. HALS HEd1 3/3 Ashwell, Merchant Taylors' Boys 30.10.1914.

38. HALS HEd2 7/17 Hitchin, St Mary's CE Girls 3.12.1914.

39. HALS HEd1 100/5 High Wych CE Mixed 26.11.1914.

40. HALS HEd1 108/2 Stanstead Abbots CE Mixed 15.1.1915; HEd1 93/4 Hoddesdon CE Boys 12.2.1915.

41. HALS HEd1 7/3 Barkway CE Senior 5.3.1915.

42. HALS HEd1 76/1 Sandon CE Mixed 24.9.1914, 9.10.1914, 11.1.1915, 19.4.1915, 17.5.1915, 22.6.1915.

43. HALS HEd1 98/6 Sawbridgeworth, Fawbert and Barnard CC Boys 12.2.1915.

44. HALS HEd1 3/3 Ashwell, Merchant Taylors' Boys 5.2.1915, 12.2.1915.

45. BL *WH Observer* 6.2.1915; *Mercury* 6.2.1915.

46. ibid.

47. GP BEd Circular 898 and Enclosure 12.3.1915.

48. ibid.

49. ibid.

50. HALS HEd4/20, p.1 CSASC 22.3.1915.

51. BL *Mercury* 13.2.1915.

52. BL *WH Observer* 20.2.1915.

53. BL *Mercury* 3.4.1915; *WH Observer* 3.4.1915.

54. BL *Mercury* 3.4.1915.

55. ibid.

56. BL *Mercury* 1.5.1915; GP BEd AR 1914–15, p.19; GP BEd School Attendance and Employment in Agriculture – Summary of returns supplied by LEAs for 1.9.1914 to 31.1.1915, p.5. The Board had only released the figures at the end of April.

57. BL *Mercury* 1.5.1915.

58. GP BEd School Attendance and Employment in Agriculture – Summary of returns supplied by LEAs for 1.2.1915 to 30.4.1915.

59. BL *Mercury* 15.5.1915, 16.10.1915.

60. HALS HEd4/21, pp.37–41 Attendance Returns Autumn Term 1914, p.315 Spring Term 1915, pp.455, 459 Summer Term 1915; HEd4/22, p.41 Attendance Returns Autumn Term 1915, p.190 Spring Term 1916.

61. HALS HEd4/21, pp.315–16 Attendance Returns Spring Term 1915, and p.462 CSASC 13.9.1915. Newspapers and school logbooks confirm the adverse weather and illnesses. See, for example, BL *Reporter* 2.7.1915; HALS HEd1 6/3 Barkway CE Infants 19.3.1915; HEd1 67/1 Great Wymondley CE Mixed 19.3.1915; HEd1 75/2 Sacombe CE Mixed 12.2.1915, 31.5.1915, 1.6.1915, 14.6.1915; HEd1 76/1 Sandon CE Mixed 5.2.1915, 19.2.1915; HEd1 98/6 Sawbridgeworth, Fawbert and Barnard CC Boys 9.2.1915; HEd1 100/5 High Wych CE Mixed 14.1.1915; HEd1 102/2 Much Hadham CE Boys 22.1.1915, 23.4.1915, 9.7.1915, 13.7.1915, 16.7.1915; HEd1 112/3 Braughing, Jenyn's CC Mixed 26.2.1915, –.3.1915; HEd2 7/16 and 7/17 Hitchin, St Mary's CE Boys' and Girls' Schools closed during an influenza epidemic from 29.1.1915 until 1.3.1915.

62. HALS HEd4/20, p.45 Attendance Returns Autumn Term 1913; HEd4/21, p.42 Attendance Returns Autumn Term 1914 and p.340 Spring Term 1915; HEd1 75/2 Sacombe CE Mixed 19.2.1915; HEd1 98/6 Sawbridgeworth, Fawbert and Barnard CC Boys 12.2.1915; HEd1 93/4 Hoddesdon CE Boys 12.2.1915; HEd1 100/5 High Wych CE Mixed 15.7.1915; HEd1 108/2 Stanstead Abbots CE Mixed 15.1.1915.

63. HALS HEd4/20, p.45 Attendance Returns Autumn Term 1913; HEd4/21, p.42 Attendance

Returns Autumn Term 1914 and p.340 Spring Term 1915; HEd1 3/3 Ashwell, Merchant Tay-lors' Boys 19.3.1915, 26.3.1915.

64. BL *Mercury* 12.6.1915.

65. BL *Gazette* 3.7.1915; *Mercury* 3.7.1915.

66. BL *Mercury* 5.12.1915.

67. HALS HEd4/21, p.460 Attendance Returns Summer Term 1915; HEd4/22, p.41 Attendance Returns Autumn Term 1915 and p.190 Spring Term 1916.

68. HALS HEd4/21, p.464 CSASC 19.9.1915.

69. HALS HEd4/22, p.41 Attendance Returns Autumn Term 1915.

70. HALS HEd4/22, p.190 Attendance Returns Spring Term 1916.

71. HALS HEd1 100/5 High Wych CE Mixed 13.9.1915, 20.9.1915, 7.10.1915, 11.10.1915, 21.10.1915.

72. HALS HEd1 98/6 Sawbridgeworth, Fawbert and Barnard CC Boys 10.9.1915, 1.10.1915, 5.10.1915, 15.10.1915, 5.11.1915.

73. HALS HEd1 1/2 Anstey CE Mixed 23.10.1914, 22.1.1915, 9.9.1915, 18.5.1916, 29.5.1916, 7.7.1916, 14.7.1916; HEd1 7/3 Barkway CE Senior 18.6.1915, 16.6.1916; HEd1 18/1 Clothall CE Mixed 28.1.1916, 1.11.1916; HEd1 75/2 Sacombe CE Mixed 7.2.1916, 4.5.1916; HEd1 76/1 Sandon CE Mixed 20.9.1915, 7.7.1916; HEd1 83/3 Pirton CC Mixed 29.3.1916, 7.7.1916; HEd1 93/4 Hod-desdon CE Boys 25.6.1915; HEd1 100/5 High Wych CE Mixed 3.8.1916, 10.8.1916; HEd1 112/3 Braughing, Jenyn's CC Mixed 14.4.1916, 25.6.1916; HEd1 113/5 Wareside CE Mixed 5.11.1915, 22.9.1916, 15.11.1916.

74. BL *Gazette* 19.3.1916.

75. HALS HEd1 76/1 Sandon CE Mixed 2.6.1916; HEd1 67/1 Great Wymondley CE Mixed 20.10.1916, 27.10.1916.

76. BL *TES* 2.2.1915.

77. HALS HEd4/21, p.469 HEC: Agricultural Sub-Committee 13.9.1915.

78. HALS HEd4/21, pp.689–91 County War Agricultural Committee 21.1.1916; BL *Mercury* 3.7.1915.

79. GP BEd School Attendance and Employment in Agriculture – Summary of returns supplied by county councils of children excused from school attendance for employment in agricul-ture on 31.1.1916.

80. GP BEd Circular 943: School Attendance and Employment in Agriculture 29.2.1916.

81. TNA:PRO ED 18/87 EB16 BEd internal memorandum signed F.S. Marvin, 1.4.1916.

82. ibid, BEd internal memorandum signed W.R. Barker, –.4.1916.

83. ibid, BEd letter to HCC Education Department, signed W.R. Barker, 9.5.1916.

84. ibid, HCC Education Department letter to Secretary, BEd, 22.6.1916.

85. ibid, BEd internal report by F.S. Marvin, 3.7.1916.

86. ibid, BEd letter to HCC Education Department, signed W.R. Barker, 24.7.1916.

87. ibid, HCC Education Department letter to Secretary, BEd, 8.8.1916.

88. ibid, BEd internal memoranda from W.R. Barker to G.N. Richardson, 10.8.1916, and from F.S. Marvin to G.N. Richardson, 9.10.1916.

89. ibid, BEd internal memorandum from F.S. Marvin to G.N. Richardson, 31.10.1916, enclosing a report from G.F. Wood, 10.10.1916.

90. TNA:PRO ED 11/78 BEd internal memoranda from L.A. Selby-Bigge to W.R. Barker, 7.7.1916, and from W.R. Barker to L.A. Selby-Bigge, 23.9.1916.

91. ibid, quote from paragraph 22 of W.R. Barker's memorandum to L.A. Selby-Bigge.

92. ibid, handwritten footnotes by L.A. Selby-Bigge, 25.9.1916, and by the Marquis of Crewe,

26.9.1916, on W.R. Barker's memorandum to L.A. Selby-Bigge, 23.9.1916.

93. GP BEd School Attendance and Employment in Agriculture – Summary of returns supplied by county LEAs of the numbers of children normally liable to attend school but excused from attendance for the purpose of agricultural employment on 31.1.1916, 31.5.1916 and 16.10.1916.

94. BL *Gazette* 22.1.1916.

95. BL *Express* 20.1.1917; *Advertiser* 20.1.1917.

96. HALS HEd4/21, p.316 CSASC 28.6.1915. Many regular reports were curtailed or abandoned during the war – in this case, highly conveniently.

97. BL *Express* 17.2.1917.

98. HALS HEd1 100/5 High Wych CE Mixed 7.6.1917.

99. BL *Telegraph* 22.9.1916.

100. BL *Mercury* 8.4.1916.

101. BL *Gazette* 21.10.1916; *WH Observer* 30.12.1916.

102. BL *HandC Reporter* 27.10.1916.

103. BL *Mercury* 21.4.1917; *Gazette* 21.4.1917.

104. HALS HEd4/22, p.300 Attendance Returns Summer Term 1916; HEd4/23, p.25 Attendance Returns Autumn Term 1916, p.151 Spring Term 1917 and p.250 Summer Term 1917; HEd4/24, p.28 Attendance Returns Autumn Term 1917 and p.178 Spring Term 1918.

105. HALS HEd4/22, pp.300–1 Exemption Returns April–June 1916 and p.385 July–September 1916; HEd4/23, pp.25–6 Exemption Returns October–December 1916, pp.138–9 January–March 1917, pp.250–1 April–June 1917 and p.359 July–September 1917; HEd4/24, pp.28–9 Exemption Returns October–December 1917 and pp.178–9 January–March 1918.

106. ibid.

107. HALS HEd4/22, p.300 Attendance Returns Summer Term 1916; HEd4/23, p.25 Attendance Returns Autumn Term 1916, p.151 Spring Term 1917 and p.250 Summer Term 1917; HEd4/24, p.28 Attendance Returns Autumn Term 1917 and p.178 Spring Term 1918.

108. BL *Express* 30.6.1917.

109. BL *WH Observer* 30.6.1917.

110. HALS HEd4/22, p.385 FSAGPSC 11.12.1916; HEd4/23, p.132 FSAGPSC 1.6.1917; BL *Mercury* 20.6.1917.

111. HALS HEd4/23, pp.238–9 FSAGPSC 1.10.1917; BL *Advertiser* 13.7.1918.

112. TNA:PRO ED 18/87 letter from Rickmansworth Urban District Education Sub-Committee to BEd 18.7.1917.

113. BL *Advertiser* 27.10.1917.

114. BL *Mercury* 27.10.1917.

115. Marwick (1965) p.117.

116. The Education Reform Council, Workers' Educational Association and the National Union of Teachers, Unionist Social Reform Committee and the Bradford Trades Council were just some of the groups – L. Andrews (1976) pp.12–14.

117. Marwick (1965) pp.243–5.

118. ibid; Andrews (1976) pp.22–34.

119. Marwick (1965) pp.239–46; G.J. DeGroot (1996) pp.210–25.

120. BL *HandE Observer* 26.10.1918; *Advertiser* 26.10.1918.

121. HALS HEd4/24, pp.282–3 Exemption Returns April–June 1918, and p.414 July–September 1918; HEd4/25, pp.65–6 Exemption Returns October–December 1918, pp.236–7

January–March 1919, and p.529 April–June 1919.

122. HALS HEd4/24, p.282 Attendance Returns Summer Term 1918; HEd4/25, p.65 Attendance Returns Autumn Term 1918, p.236 January–March 1919 and pp.523, 527 April–June 1919.

123. Numerous schools record such incidents. See *inter alia* HALS HEd1 7/3 Barkway CE Senior 28.6.1918, 15.7.1918; HEd1 17/2 Buckland CE Mixed 1.7.1918; HEd1 24/2 Harpenden, Kinsbourne Green CE Mixed 9.9.1918, 13.12.1918; HEd1 72/1 Wallington CE Mixed 13.9.1918; HEd1 75/2 Sacombe CE Mixed 11.1.1918; HEd1 76/1 Sandon CE Mixed 14.6.1918, 5.7.1918; HEd1 83/3 Pirton CC Mixed 21.6.1918, 24.6.1918, 8.7.1918, 25.10.1918; HEd1 102/4 Much Hadham CE Girls 11.1.1919; HEd2 6/7 Hitchin, St Andrew's CE Mixed 28.6.1918, 12.7.1918.

124. HALS HEd1 100/5 High Wych CE Mixed 3.5.1918, 13.6.1918.

125. BL *Express* 19.1.1918; HALS HEd1 17/2 Buckland CE Mixed 16 and 17.4.1918; HEd1 22/1 Gilston CE Mixed 25.4.1918, 19.7.1918; HEd1 24/2 Harpenden, Kinsbourne Green CE Mixed 19.4.1918; HEd1 76/1 Sandon CE Mixed 18.1.1918; HEd1 98/2 Sawbridgeworth, Fawbert and Barnard CC Girls and Infants 11.1.1918; HEd1 102/2 Much Hadham CE Boys 18.1.1918, 8.2.1918, 19.4.1918, 30.9.1918; HEd1 113/5 Wareside CE Mixed 16, 17 and 18.1.1918, –.7.1918; HEd2 7/17 Hitchin, St Mary's CE Boys 16.4.1918.

126. HALS HEd1 102/2 Much Hadham CE Boys 1.2.1918; HEd2 6/7 Hitchin, St Andrew's CE Mixed 22.1.1918.

127. HEd2 7/16 Hitchin, St Mary's CE Boys 22.1.1918; HEd1 96/1 Watford, Callow Land CC Boys 1.2.1918.

128. BL *Advertiser* 26.10.1918; *HandE Observer* 26.10.1918; *Express* 2.11.1918; *Mercury* 26.10.1918; HALS HEd4/25, p.282 AR SH 1918 and p.151 HEC 14.4.1919. The ravages of the epidemics and the closures are recorded in the vast majority of school logbooks in 1918–19.

129. HALS HEd2 7/16 Hitchin, St Mary's CE Boys 5.7.1918.

130. BL *Advertiser* 26.10.1918.

Chapter 6: The war and health

1. The range of evidence included the reports of the Royal Commission on the State of Education in England 1861 and the Royal Commission on the Housing of the Working Classes 1885, and the detailed investigations of humanitarians such as Charles Booth's *Life and Labour of the People of London* (1891–1903) and Benjamin Rowntree's *Poverty: A Study of Town Life* (1902).

2. Simon (1965) p.278.

3. Hurt (1979) pp.128–52.

4. ibid, pp.129–30.

5. ibid, pp.130–3.

6. Harris (1993) p.55.

7. ibid, pp.56–7.

8. ibid, p.6.

9. GP BEd Annual Report of the Chief Medical Officer (AR CMO) 1913, p.46.

10. C. Dyhouse, 'Working Class Mothers and Infant Mortality in England, 1895–1914' in C. Webster (ed.) *Biology, Medicine and Society 1840–1940* (Cambridge, 1981), p.89.

11. M. Hyndman (1978) p.231.

12. HALS HEd4/20, p.66 HCC *Elementary Education Handbook* 1914, Chapter VII *School Health*.

13.   ibid.
14.   HALS HEd4/20, p.187 AR SH 1913.
15.   GP BEd AR CMO 1914, pp.244–5.
16.   HALS HEd4/20, p.185 AR SH 1913.
17.   ibid, p.187.
18.   ibid, p.192.
19.   ibid.
20.   ibid.
21.   ibid.
22.   ibid.
23.   ibid, p.208.
24.   ibid.
25.   ibid.
26.   ibid, p.210.
27.   ibid.
28.   ibid, p.212.
29.   ibid, pp.236–40.
30.   ibid, p.217.
31.   ibid, pp.242–3.
32.   ibid, p.217.
33.   ibid.
34.   BL *Gazette* 27.6.1914.
35.   ibid, 4.7.1914.
36.   BL *Advertiser* 8.8.1914.
37.   BL *WH Observer* 22.8.1914.
38.   ibid; HALS HEd4/20, p.654 CSASC 14.9.1914.
39.   HALS HEd4/20, p.654 CSASC 14.9.1914.
40.   HALS HEd4/20, pp.725–6 CSASC – report to HEC 12.10.1914.
41.   ibid.
42.   BL *Mercury* 17.10.1914.
43.   ibid; *Advertiser* 17.10.1914; *Express* 17.10.1914; *Gazette* 17.10.1914.
44.   HALS HEd4/21, p.30 CSASC 22.3.1915.
45.   ibid.
46.   BL *Mercury* 20.2.1915.
47.   HALS HEd4/21, p.486 FGPSC 24.9.1915, p.553 HEC 11.10.1915 and p.565 HCC 8.11.1915.
48.   HALS HEd4/21, p.131 AR SH 1914.
49.   ibid.
50.   ibid, p.152.
51.   GP BEd AR CMO 1914, p.6.
52.   HALS HEd4/21, p.148 AR SH 1914.
53.   ibid, pp.256–7.
54.   ibid.
55.   BL *Mercury* 17.4.1915.
56.   ibid, 8.5.1915.
57.   HALS HEd4/21, pp.484–5 FGPSC 24.9.1915 and p.564 HEC 8.11.1915; BL *Mercury* 12.2.1916.
58.   HALS HEd4/24, p.97 AR SH 1917.

59. ibid.
60. BL *Express* 17.4.1915.
61. BL *Mercury* 20.4.1918; *Express* 2.11.1918.
62. HALS HEd4/20, pp.656–7 CSASC 14.9.1914 and pp.728–30 CSASC report to HEC October 1914. The specialist's fee was one guinea plus expenses for each examination.
63. ibid. The Board paid half the costs.
64. ibid.
65. ibid.
66. HALS HEd4/21, pp.91–2 CSASC 22.3.1915, pp.279–80 CSASC 21.5.1915, p.316 HEC 28.6.1915 and pp.464–5 CSASC 13.9.1915; HEd4/22, pp.169–70 FSAGPSC 2.6.1916; HEd4/23, pp.212–13 AR SH 1916, pp.133–4 FSAGPSC 1.6.1917, pp.239–42 FSAGPSC 1.10.1917 and pp.351–2 FSAGPSC 14.12.1917.
67. HALS HEd4/23, pp.351–2 FSAGPSC 14.12.1917.
68. BL *Express* 22.7.1916.
69. BL *Gazette* 23.1.1915, 18.12.1915, 19.2.1916, 18.3.1916, 22.7.1916.
70. HALS HEd4/23, pp.211–12 AR SH 1916.
71. HALS HEd4/24, p.94 AR SH 1917.
72. ibid.
73. DeGroot (1996) pp.201–4; Marwick (1965) pp.194–5.
74. HALS HEd4/22, p.214 AR SH 1915.
75. HALS HEd4/21, p.476 Hertford Divisional Subcommittee 17.9.1915.
76. ibid.
77. HALS HEd4/23, pp.208–9 AR SH 1916.
78. HALS HEd4/24, p.89 AR SH 1917.
79. BL *Reporter* 11.5.1917.
80. ibid.
81. ibid.
82. DeGroot (1996) pp.201–6; Marwick (1965) pp.191–5.
83. HALS HEd4/25, p.278 AR SH 1918.
84. HALS HEd4/22, p.215 AR SH 1915.
85. HALS HEd4/23, p.209 AR SH 1916.
86. HALS HEd4/25, p.278 AR SH 1918.
87. HALS HEd4/24, p.89 AR SH 1917.
88. HALS HEd4/25, p.278 AR SH 1918.
89. HALS HEd4/22, pp.215–16 AR SH 1915; HEd4/23, p.209 AR SH 1916.
90. BL *WH Observer* 12.6.1915.
91. BL *Gazette* 12.8.1916.
92. BL *WH Observer* 23.6.1917.
93. viz BL *Express* 30.6.1917, 14.7.1917.
94. BL *WH Observer* 23.6.1917.
95. ibid, and 14.7.1917.
96. ibid, 23.6.1917.
97. *Who Was Who* (1952).
98. BL *Mercury* 12.2.1916, 15.11.1919.
99. BL *Express* 7.7.1917.
100. BL *Express* 22.9.1917.

101. ibid, 14.7.1917.
102. ibid.
103. BL *Express* 30.6.1917, 25.8.1917; *WH Observer* 23.6.1917.
104. BL *Express* 7.7.1917.
105. ibid.
106. ibid.
107. GP BEd AR CMO 1919, p.42.
108. BL *Advertiser* 30.6.1917; *Mercury* 30.6.1917.
109. ibid.
110. BL *WH Observer* 30.6.1917.
111. BL *Advertiser* 24.1.1920.
112. HALS HEd4/24, pp.91–4 AR SH 1917; BL *Mercury* 20.4.1918.
113. BL *Express* 26.10.1918.
114. BL *Mercury* 26.10.1918.
115. ibid; *Advertiser* 26.10.1918.
116. HALS HEd4/24, pp.91–4 AR SH 1917; BL *Mercury* 20.4.1918.
117. HALS HEd4/25, p.315 HEC 23.6.1919.

Chapter 7: Continuity and change: Hertfordshire 1914–1939

1. The discussion on the First World War and its aftermath has been informed by S. Constantine, M.W. Kirby and M.B. Rose (eds), *The First World War in British History* (London, 1995); G.J. DeGroot, *Blighty: British Society in the Era of the Great War* (London, 1996); R. van Emden and S. Humphries, *All Quiet on the Home Front* (London, 2003); M. Gilbert, *First World War* (London, 1994); J. Harris, *Private Lives, Public Spirit: Britain 1870–1914* (Oxford, 1993); M. Macmillan, *Peacemakers: The Paris Peace Conference of 1919 and Its Attempt to End War* (London, 2001); A. Marwick, *The Deluge: British Society and the First World War* (London, 1965); J. Stevenson, *British Society 1914–45* (Harmondsworth, 1984); A.J.P. Taylor, *English History 1914–45* (Harmondsworth, 1970 edn); J. Winter and B. Baggett, *The Great War and the Shaping of the 20th Century* (London, 1996).

2. In addition to the sources listed in n.1 above, the discussion on the 1920s and 1930s has been informed by P. Dewey, *War and Progress: Britain 1914–1945* (London, 1997); P. Johnson (ed.), *Twentieth Century Britain: Economic, Social and Cultural Change* (London, 1994); K. Laybourn, *Britain on the Breadline: A Social and Economic History of Britain 1918–39* (Gloucester, 1990); T.O. Lloyd, *Empire to Welfare State: English History 1906–1985* (Oxford, 1986); R. Skidelsky, *Politicians and the Slump: The Labour Government of 1929–31* (London, 1994 edn); J. Stevenson and C. Cook, *The Slump: Society and Politics during the Depression* (London, 1977).

3. The teachers were initially threatened with 15% salary cuts, but vigorous protests led to a reduction to 10%. The full salaries were not restored until 1935. See A. Tropp (1957) pp.222–6.

4. HALS GP Census 1951 County Report for Hertfordshire p.1 Table 1 *Population 1801–1951 and Intercensal Variations.*

5. HALS GP Census 1931 Volume 1 Part 2 County of Hertford p.vii.

6. HALS GP Census 1951 County Report for Hertfordshire p.xiii.

7. ibid.

8. HALS GP Census 1931 Volume 1 Part 2 County of Hertford pp.vii–viii.

9. ibid, Table 2 *Population 1911–1931 and Intercensal Variations*. Not all the names tally with the 1939 map as districts were realigned and renamed after 1931 but Hadham and Buntingford rural districts are roughly conterminous with Braughing rural district, and Ashwell rural district was carved out of the north-eastern half of Hitchin rural district.

10. HALS GP Census 1911 Vol. IX Hertfordshire pp.192–3; Census 1921 Hertfordshire p.32; Census 1931 Vol. II County of Hertford pp.218–19.

11. J. Thirsk (1978) pp.142–8.

12. Economic Survey of Hertfordshire: Farm Economics Branch Report 18, Cambridge 1931, quoted in Thirsk (1978) pp.184–5.

13. Taylor (1970) pp.423–5.

14. Thirsk (1978) p.154; *NFU Record* (Herts Edition), February 1930 pp.108–9.

15. HALS GP Census 1931 General Report pp.119–20 Table L.

16. J.B. Priestley (1934). There is no description of Hertfordshire in the book. At the end of his largely clockwise tour of England Priestley rushed back to London from East Anglia via Newmarket, Royston and Hitchin and then the Great North Road, where fog reduced his car to a crawl.

17. The statistics in this paragraph and the next are taken from HALS GP Census 1911 Volume X Part 1 Hertfordshire pp.192–5; Census 1921 Hertfordshire pp.33–9; Census 1931 Vol II, County of Hertford pp.218–31.

18. HALS GP Census 1931 Volume 1 Part 2 Hertfordshire p.xi; Census 1951 Hertfordshire County Report pp.xix–xxi.

19. BL *Advertiser* 5.9.1925.

20. BL *WH Observer* 19.5.1934, 15.9.1934, 30.3.1935; D. Edwards and R. Pigram (1979) pp.25–7, 76, 85; A.M. Edwards (1981) pp.127–42.

21. BL *Advertiser* 24.1.1925.

22. Edwards (1981) pp.116–19; HALS HCC2/150 CP49 Highways Committee 24.5.1935; BL *Telegraph* 5.4.1935.

23. BL *Express* 16.10.1920, 24.7.1920, Supplement 4.5.1930.

24. BL *WH Observer* 8.11.1919, 25.12.1920, 7.4.1923, 29.12.1923, 19.4.1924, Supplement 11.5.1935.

25. BL *Advertiser* 21.2.1920, 1.3.1924, 10.5.1924, 8.11.1924 (quote), 12.9.1925, 3.7.1931. The inquiry used the table of minimum standard of fitness of houses required by the Ministry of Health.

26. BL *Mercury* 10.11.1928.

27. ibid, 7.5.1927.

28. BL *Record* 11.5.1923; *Reporter* 31.10.1924; *Express* 9.2.1929 and Supplement 4.5.1935; *Barnet Press, Finchley and Hendon News (Barnet Press)* 3.8.1929; *Advertiser* 13.5.1932.

29. BL *Express*, Supplement 4.5.1935.

30. TNA:PRO ED 19/379 Administrative Reports on Harpenden 21.11.1934, on East Barnet Valley 23.1.1934, on Rickmansworth 28.6.1934, on St Albans no date but almost certainly 1934.

31. HALS HCC2/150 CP49 Highways Committee 24.5.1935; BL *Advertiser* 26.7.1935. The east and north of the county remained untouched except for improvements planned to the winding Hertford to Bishop's Stortford road via Sawbridgeworth, and the link between Stevenage and Hitchin.

32. BL *HandE Observer* 12.2.1927; *Advertiser* 9.10.1931, 13.5.1932, 25.2.1938; *Telegraph* 28.2.1936; HALS HCC2/152 CP173 HCC 17.1.1936; HCC2/164 CP185 HCC 20.1.1939.

33. BL *Express* 21.4.1923, 3.11.1923.
34. BL *Advertiser* 18.8.1923, 13.5.1927; *Mercury* 11.8.1928; *WH Observer* 7.6.1930.
35. BL *Advertiser* 13.5.1927.
36. H. Clunn (2nd edn 1937) p.2.
37. H.P. White (1963) pp.176–7; D.I. Gordon (1977) pp.112–15.
38. Gordon (1977) pp.121–4; BL *Mercury* 27.6.1925; *Hertdordshire Record (Record)* 4.5.1923.
39. Gordon (1977) pp.129–33, 148.
40. White (1963) p.121; TNA:PRO ED 19/379 HMI Administrative Report on St Albans no date but almost certainly 1934, p.102.
41. White (1963) pp.124–5.
42. ibid, pp.137–8, 145; Edwards and Pigram (1979) pp.75–9.
43. White (1963) pp.162–8; TNA:PRO ED 19/379 HMI Administrative Report on East Barnet Valley 23.1.1934.
44. Swenarton (1981) p.10; F.J. Osborn (1946) pp.57–8.
45. Osborn (1946) pp.76–83; BL *Citizen* 3.7.1925.
46. W.R. Hughes (1919).
47. ibid.
48. BL *Citizen* 4.3.1932, article entitled *Reginald Hine's Confessions*.
49. ibid. The corsets refer to Letchworth's famous Spirella Company.
50. ibid; *Express* 12.1.1924.
51. Hughes (1919) p.96.
52. ibid, pp.96–103; BL *Citizen* 26.10.1922.
53. Hughes (1919) p.85.
54. BL *Citizen* 12.6.1925; HALS HEd2 23/1 Pixmore CC Junior Mixed HMI reports received 26.4.1923, 2.3.1926, 25.4.1933, 9.7.1937 – in the late 1930s the school's needlework course was the exemplar used in teachers' training colleges – see log entry 7.9.1936; HCC2/98 CP70 AR SH 1921; HCC2/102 CP74 AR SH 1922; HCC2/106 CP65 AR SH 1923; HCC2/116 CP219 HEC 7.1.1927; HCC2/118 CP118 CP89 AR SH 1926 – Dr Thomson commended the special classes as exemplars of good practice; TNA:PRO ED 11/115 confidential memoranda from Chief HMI H.M. Richard to BEd, 28.12.1921, 11.5.1922.
55. BL *Advertiser* 11.2.1922.
56. BL *Record* 4.5.1923; *Express* 5.5.1923.
57. BL *Record* 4.5.1923.
58. BL *Express* 27.1.1923, 5.5.1923.
59. BL *Citizen* 2.2.1923.
60. BL *HandE Observer* 24.7.1926.
61. HALS HCC2/158 CP93 HEC 21.6.1937; HCC2/159 CP148 HEC 1.10.1937.
62. BL *NFU Record (Herts Edition)* February 1930; *Advertiser* 16.5.1930.
63. BL *Advertiser* 25.2.1938.
64. HALS HCC2/113 CP45 HEC 29.3.1936.
65. Just 5% of chief education officers had no teaching experience, according to V.C. Greenhalgh (1974) p.163.
66. *Who Was Who* (1941); BL *Mercury* 7.1.1928.
67. *Who Was Who* (1952).
68. ibid.
69. BL *Advertiser* 24.1.1920, 31.1.1920.

70. BL *Advertiser* 13.6.1925; M.B. Furse (1953) p.107.

71. BL *NFU Record (Herts Edition)* February 1930, pp.108, 117; *HandE Observer* – obituary 27.9.1968.

72. *Who's Who in Hertfordshire* (1936); BL *Advertiser* 13.3.1920; *Mercury* 4.8.1939.

73. *Who Was Who* (1961).

74. BL *Citizen* 28.10.1932; *WH Observer* 12.3.1937; *Mercury* 19.3.1937.

75. viz BL *Advertiser* 24.2.1933, 21.2.1936; *Mercury* 19.3.1937.

76. BL *Advertiser* 28.10.1932; *Mercury* 6.11.1931.

77. BL *Advertiser* 24.2.1933.

78. BL *Barnet Press* 6.4.1935, 11.4.1936; *Express* 10.4.1937; *Mercury* 8.4.1938.

79. B. Keith-Lucas and P. Richards (1978) pp.98–102; J.M. Lee (1963) pp.72–4, 80.

80. BL *WH Observer* 1.1.1921.

81. BL *WH Observer* 12.3.1937; *Mercury* 12.3.1937, 19.3.1937.

82. BL *Express* 17.10.1931. Lord Knebworth was killed in a flying accident in 1933; Sir Arnold Wilson became an air gunner in the Second World War, and was killed on active service in 1940.

83. HALS HEd1 113/15 Hertingfordbury, Cowper Endowed – numerous entries regarding visits by the Desboroughs; HEd1 19/2 Digswell CE Mixed 18.1.1923, 15.3.1928; HEd1 4/2 Ayot St Peter CE Mixed 27.2.1922, 24.5.1922; BL *Advertiser* 17.1.1920; *HandE Observer* 2.8.1924; Tresham Gilbey – *Who Was Who* (1952); V. Sparrow (1981); F.M. Page (1959).

84. BL *Advertiser* 9.10.1931.

Chapter 8: *Education, social class and employment*

1. Several major manufacturers, notably Tootal Broadhurst, British Westinghouse, Cadbury, Boots, Rowntree, and Crosse & Blackwell, welcomed the step forward – see Andrews (1976) pp.50–2. For many years they had run trades schools, as had John Dickinson and Co., whose factories straddled Hertfordshire's Gade valley.

2. Andrews (1976) pp.36–40.

3. BL *Barnet Press* 17.4.1918, 6.3.1920; *Citizen* 11.7.1919, 24.10.1919.

4. BL *WH Observer* 1.11.1919; HALS HEd4/26 p.460 HEC 21.6.1920.

5. BL *Barnet Press* 3.5.1919.

6. BL *Advertiser* 21.2.1920.

7. ibid, 27.12.1919.

8. BL *Record* 31.10.1919, 21.11.1919.

9. ibid, 16.4.1920, 8.10.1920.

10. HALS HEd4/26, pp.490–9 HEC Education Act Scheme Sub-Committee 21.6.1920.

11. ibid; BL *Mercury* 1.11.1919.

12. BL *Mercury* 13.11.1920; *Reporter* 26.11.1920; *Gazette* 27.11.1920.

13. BL *Express* 12.2.1921.

14. BL *Record* 17.2.1922, 21.4.1922; *HandE Observer* 25.2.1922, 16.9.1922; *Mercury* 15.4.1922.

15. BL *Advertiser* 18.2.1922.

16. BL *Mercury* 8.11.1929.

17. H. Hendrick (1980) pp.159–73.

18. HALS HEd4/25, pp.25–6 *Regulations for County Minor Scholarships* March 1919; HEd4/26,

pp.5–7 *Regulations for County Minor Scholarships* February 1920.

19. HALS HCC2/108 CP218 HEC 9.1.1925.
20. HALS HEd4/26, p.338 Higher Education Sub-Committee (HESC) 4.6.1920.
21. HALS HEd4/26, pp.490–9 HEC 21.6.1921; HEd4/27, pp.1–10 Returns as to Secondary Schools for the quarter ended 31 December 1920, HEC 15.4.1921; Simon (1974) Table 4, p.366.
22. HALS HCC2/108 CP218 HEC 9.1.1925.
23. BL *Telegraph* 13.2.1920.
24. HALS HCC2/99 CP122 Secondary School Sub-Committee 19.9.1922.
25. BL *Barnet Press* 9.2.1924.
26. BL *Telegraph* 9.10.1925.
27. HALS HCC2/108 CP218 HEC 9.1.1925.
28. BL *Barnet Press* 14.2.1925.
29. BL *Express* 14.11.1925.
30. HALS HCC2/108 CP218 HEC 9.1.1925; BL *Barnet Press* 24.1.1925, 14.2.1925, 7.6.1925.
31. HALS HCC2/105 CP39 HEC 31.3.1924.
32. BL *WH Observer* 14.7.1928; *Gazette* 14.7.1928; *Advertiser* 26.10.1928, 2.11.1928; *Express* 23.1.1932; *HandE Observer* 24.12.1932.
33. HALS HEd2 7/16 Hitchin, St Mary's CE Senior numerous entries 1919–39 and articles in the *Hertfordshire Express* – especially prize days reports on 24.12.1927, 29.12.1928, 27.12.1930.
34. HALS HEd4/26, pp.490–9 HEC Education Act Scheme Sub-Committee 21.6.1920.
35. HALS HEd4/24, pp.415–16 HEC 13.1.1919.
36. HALS HCC2/106 CP67 Physical Training and Practical Instruction Sub-Committee (PT&PI SC) 30.5.1924.
37. HALS HCC2/107 CP128 PT&PI SC 12.9.1924.
38. HALS HCC2/116 CP221 Annual Report on Handicraft (ARH) 1926; HCC2/124 CP209 ARH 1928.
39. HALS HCC2/128 CP226 ARH 1929.
40. HALS HCC2/132 CP216 ARH 1930.
41. HALS HCC2/124 CP209 ARH 1928.
42. ibid; HCC2/128 CP236 ARH 1929.
43. TNA:PRO ED 96/38 HMI General Report on the Provision and Teaching of Handicraft in Hertfordshire December 1932; HCC2/155 CP120 ARH 31.7.1936.
44. ibid.
45. HALS HCC2/163 CP121 ARH 31.7.1938.
46. See, for example, HALS HEd1 169/12 Rickmansworth, Croxley Green CE Senior, Time Table Autumn Term 1938, Schemes of Work and Periods per Week Spring Term 1939.
47. TNA:PRO ED 20/42 Watford Higher Elementary School: internal BEd memorandum 27.8.1920; HALS HEd1 79/1 St Albans Central HMI report re visits 3.3.1923, 12–13.6.1923, 11.7.1923.
48. HALS HEd2 35/1 Watford Central 31.8.1920, 16.6.1923, HMI report 18.10.1922.
49. ibid, HMI report 15.7.1925.
50. ibid, 19.11.1920, 19.1.1921.
51. ibid, HMI report re visits 24–27.4.1934.
52. HALS HEd1 79/1 St Albans Central HMI reports re visits 3.3.1923, 12–13.6.1923, 11.7.1923; BL *Advertiser* 11.4.1925.

53. HALS HEd1 79/1 St Albans Central HMI reports re visits 3.3.1923, 12–13.6.1923, 11.7.1923 and
     22–23.6.1926.

54. HALS HCC2/118 CP83 HESC 30.5.1927.

55. ibid.

56. HALS HEd1 79/1 St Albans Central HMI report received 20.3.1933 and report re visits
     13–14.10.1936.

57. Evans (1955) pp.191–2; students' exercise books, copy of *Dickinson News* 1938 and unpub-
     lished article written by school director, 8.12.1942, in author's possession.

58. TNA:PRO ED 75/15A Day Continuation School, Apsley Mills Centre – letter from F. Clark,
     J. Dickinson and Co. to BEd 31.5.1921, and BEd internal memorandum 17.6.1921.

59. BL *Gazette* 14.3.1938. It finally closed in 1952, shortly after Hemel Hempstead Technical
     School opened.

60. TNA:PRO ED 120/36 Hemel Hempstead 1918 Act Scheme 6.8.1920; BL *Gazette* 3.5.1919,
     10.5.1919, 17.5.1919, 21.6.1919, 19.2.1921.

61. BL *Gazette* 20.1.1923, 24.3.1923, 31.3.1923, 14.4.1923, 19.9.1925.

62. TNA:PRO ED 97/126 Hemel Hempstead: Advanced Instruction Questionnaire, 9.4.1921.

63. BL *WH Observer* 21.11.1925; *Gazette* 14.11.1925, 21.11.1925, 2.1.1926, 22.6.1929. 21.9.1929.

64. BL *Gazette* 9.3.1929.

65. HALS HEd3 7/1 Annual Report of the Chief Education Officer (AR CEO) 31.3.1933.

66. BL *Gazette* 21.9.1929.

67. TNA:PRO ED 72/722 Hemel Hempstead Reorganisation Scheme 1938; BL *Gazette* 7.4.1939;
     WH Observer 5.5.1939. In addition, an Anglican selective central school existed in Ware
     during the 1930s but its logbooks and managers' minute books cannot be traced, and entries
     in county council papers and newspapers are too sparse to analyse its development. It
     seemed popular, it incited no controversy and possibly possessed links with the chemical,
     brewing and furniture factories in the Lea valley.

68. BL *Barnet Press* 12.4.1924.

69. TNA:PRO ED 97/111 GP BEd internal memorandum 6.12.1925; GP BEd AR 1925–6 pp.32–4.

70. HALS HEd1 40/1 Knebworth, London Road CC Mixed: managers' minutes 27.1.1927,
     18.3.1927, 8.4.1927, 15.6.1927.

71. Stevenage Museum SOIHP A002/3 (Mrs MS born 1919). Probably she started at the 'top' in
     1930.

72. BL *Citizen* 18.2.1927.

73. J.W. Cole and R.H. Pearsall (n.d., c.1925). The full Consultative Committee included
     Dr B.M. Allen: ex-Education Department, London County Council; Professor C.R. Darling:
     Professor of Physics, Royal Military Academy, Woolwich; Sidney Humphries: Principal, City
     of London School; R.R. Hyde: Director, Industrial Welfare Society; B. Mouat Jones: Princi-
     pal, College of Technology, Manchester; Dr Albert Mansbridge: Chairman, The World Asso-
     ciation for Adult Education; Major R. Mitchell: Vice President, Regent Street Polytechnic; Dr
     C. Grant Robertson: Principal, University of Birmingham; Dr W.A. Scoble: Principal of Engi-
     neering, Woolwich Polytechnic; Dr W. Mansergh Varley: Principal, Brighton Technical Col-
     lege; Major T. Worswick: Director of Education, Regent Street Polytechnic.

74. BL *Citizen* 18.2.1927.

75. Cole and Pearsall (n.d., c.1925) pp.9–13.

76. ibid, pp.7–11.

77. J.W. Cole et al (1926) p.5.

78. ibid, pp.7–8.

79. BL *Citizen* 14.1.1927, 18.2.1927; HALS HCC2/116 CP219 HEC 7.1.1927. The LEA had been willing to sanction a secondary school as early as 1919, only to be overridden by the Board of Education during the depression of the early 1920s – BL *Express* 5.7.1919; HALS HCC2/98 CP96 HEC 12.6.1922.

80. BL *Express* 19.2.1927.

81. ibid, 15.10.1927.

82. HALS HCC2/119 CP141 HESC 23.9.1927.

83. HALS HCC2/121 CP49 HEC 30.3.1928.

84. HALS HCC2/123 CP145 FGPSC 28.9.1928; BL *Express* 13.10.1928.

85. HALS HCC2/155 CP134 HEC 2.10.1936; HCC2/161 CP28 HEC 8.4.1938; HEd3 7/1 AR CEO 31.32.1938

86. BL *Gazette* 15.2.1919, 17.5.1919, 7.6.1919, 21.6.1919, 19.7.1919, 11.10.1919.

87. BL *Citizen* 2.12.1921, 2.2.1923; *Telegraph* 6.5.1921; *Express* 6.6.1925; *Gazette* 20.8.1927.

88. BL *HandE Observer* 25.2.1922.

89. In 1919 Watford had submitted proposals for a Day Continuation School, and an 'umbrella' Technical College embracing a Junior Technical School and senior Schools of Art, Science and Commerce. The LEA had not only rejected this massive expansion, but during the 1920–1 depression it had withdrawn the grants to the part-time Art, Science and Commerce classes struggling to life again after the war. The bitter protest and mutual recriminations lasted over a year, until the LEA partially backed down and granted the borough the use of an additional penny rate as an area of rapid expansion. See BL *WH Observer* 18.1.1919, 6.9.1919, 31.7.1929, 25.12.1920, 22.1.1921, 9.4.1921; HALS HEd4/26 pp.341–2 HESC 4.6.1920.

90. BL *WH Observer* 18.11.1922, 31.5.1924, 10.3.1939; TNA:PRO ED 82/30 Watford School of Art, Science and Commerce Prospectus 1923–4, Report of HMI April 1926.

91. HALS HCC2/115 CP165 HEC 11.10.1926.

92. HALS HCC2/118 CP90 HCC *Higher Education Handbook* June 1927; HCC2/121 CP25 HCC *Evening Schools and Classes* March 1928; HCC/124 CP236 HEC 4.1.1929.

93. HALS HCC2/123 CP144 HESC 24.9.1928; HCC2/125 CP11 HESC 11.3.1929; HCC2/126 CP78 HESC 17.5.1929; HCC2/128 CP261 HEC 13.1.1930; HEd3.7/1 AR CEO 31.3.1929 and 31.3.1932; HCC2/134 CP115 HEC 22.6.1931; BL *WH Observer* 16.4.1931.

94. GP BEd AR 1928, pp.43–6, and Pamphlet 64: Education for Industry and Commerce 1929; BL *TES* 19.2.1927.

95. GP BEd AR 1924–25, pp.24–5, 45–53, 78–81; TNA:PRO ED 23/466 Memorandum on educational policy 1926, signed EP – almost certainly Edward Pelham, the deputy secretary.

96. TNA:PRO ED 114/277 HMI report on the Junior Commercial and Junior Technical Schools at Watford Technical School 31.7.1934; ED 98/34 Watford Junior Technical School: letter from HEC to BEd 8.1.1935.

97. HALS HCC2/122 CP108 HEC 15.6.1928.

98. BL *Barnet Press* 3.8.1929, 23.12.1933, 5.10.1935; HALS HCC2/131 CP155 HESC 19.9.1930; HCC2/139 CP131 HEC 10.10.1932.

99. Maclure (1973) pp.179–88.

100. GP BEd Report of the Consultative Committee on the Education of the Adolescent 1926; R. McKibbon (1998) p.212.

101. Simon (1974) pp.132–47; Lowndes (1969) pp.113–15.

102. ibid; B. Doherty (1964) pp.117–27.

103. BL *Express* 13.10.1928.

104. HALS HCC2/127 CP180 HEC 4.10.1929, and CP181 Programme of Educational Development for the three years commencing 1.4.1930.

105. HALS HCC2/129 CP26 Proposed Reorganisation of Public Elementary School: St Albans 21.3.1930; HCC2/130 CP81 Schools Reorganisation Committee (SRC) 30.5.1930 and CP85 FGPSC 6.6.1930; HCC2/135 CP140 SRC 18.9.1931.

106. TNA:PRO ED 97/125 Watford School Strike; BL *WH Observer* 14.9.1929, 19.10.1929, 2.11.1929, 9.11.1929. Petitions were sent to Sir Charles Trevelyan, Percy's Labour successor as President of the Board of Education, and to the local Conservative MP, Dennis Herbert, but both supported the reorganisation, and the protest eventually ran out of steam, finally collapsing at the threat of court action.

107. HALS HCC2/123 CP145 FGPSC 28.9.1928; HCC2/124 CP195 Proposed Reorganisation of Public Elementary Schools: Barnet Urban 16.11.1928; HCC2/127 CP153 SRC 27.9.1929; HCC2/142 CP75 HEC 23.6.1933; BL *Barnet Press* 5.1.1929, 19.1.1929, 3.8.1929, 2.4.1932, 16.7.1932, 24.9.1932.

108. BL *Mercury* 15.10.1927, 7.3.1930, 26.12.1930, 27.11.1931; HALS HCC2/125 CP2 SRC 22.2.1929; HCC2/127 CP148 FGPSC 16.9.1929; HCC2/129 CP14 FGPSC 24.3.1930; HCC2/131 CP156 FGPSC 22.9.1930; HCC2/135 CP140 SRC 18.9.1931.

109. BL *Citizen* 6.10.1939; *WH Observer* 18.4.1931, 27.1.1934, 15.9.1934, 5.5.1939; *Mercury* 18.6.1937; *Barnet Press* 6.5.1939.

110. TNA:PRO ED19/586 Hertfordshire AC: HMI report on the progress of the reorganisation of Public Elementary Schools on Hadow lines, with suggestions for a comprehensive scheme for the whole county.

111. BL *Mercury* 18.6.1937.

112. BL *Advertiser* 18.3.1932, 29.6.1934; *WH Observer* 16.7.1932; *Mercury* 22.3.1935, 20.3.1936, 18.6.1937; *Gazette* 9.7.1938.

113. HALS HEd1 188/6 Hatfield CE Mixed HMI reports 6.11.1931, 12.2.1936.

114. HALS HCC2/131 CP155 HESC 19.9.1930.

115. HALS HCC2/136 CP186 HESC 30.11.1931 and CP226 HEC 15.1.1932.

116. HALS HEd3 7/1 AR CEO 31.3.1932.

117. HALS HCC2/140 CP180 HEC 20.1.1933.

118. HALS HCC2/122 CP108 HEC 15.6.1928; HCC2/123 CP171 HEC 8.10.1928; HCC2/124 CP236 HEC 4.1.1929; BL *Express* 13.10.1928.

119. TNA:PRO ED 114/278 Report of HMI on the Provision of Post-Primary Education in Watford and District for the period ending 31.7.1934.

120. HALS HCC2/139 CP131 HEC 10.10.1932. The Board's decision represented a small part of the government's overall reductions in public expenditure during the depression, but it played a major political role in reversing the previous Labour government's policy (1929–31) of encouraging the expansion of free places.

121. HALS HCC2/144 CP176 HEC 19.1.1934.

122. HALS HEd3 7/1 AR CEO 31.3.1932, 31.3.1939; HCC2/138 CP84 HEC 24.6.1932; HCC2/162 CP81 HEC 20.6.1938. The national figure for England in 1931 was 9.58%, in 1937 12.86% and in 1938 13.45%. If one includes the figures for Wales, where twice as many elementary school-children transferred to secondary schools than in England, the comparison is even starker. See Simon (1974) Table 4, p.366.

123. HALS HCC2/145 CP39 HEC 13.4.1934.

124. BL *Mercury* 18.8.1933.

125. BL *Advertiser* 14.10.1932; *Citizen* 28.10.1932.

126. HALS HCC2/121 CP49 HEC 30.3.1928; HCC2/131 CP155 HESC 19.9.1930; HCC2/136 CP226 HEC 15.1.1932.

127. HALS HCC2/135 CP143 HESC 18.9.1931; HCC2/145 CP39 HEC 13.4.1934.

128. ibid; BL *Barnet Press* 21.4.1934.

129. HALS HEd3 7/1 AR CEO 31.3.1938, 31.3.1939.

130. HALS HCC2/145 CP39 HEC 13.4.1934; BL *Barnet Press* 13.4.1934; *Advertiser* 20.4.1934, 29.6.1934.

131. BL *Advertiser* 29.6.1934.

132. BL *Barnet Press* 4.4.1936, 19.6.1937; HALS HCC2/151 CP125 HEC 30.9.1935.

133. BL *Barnet Press* 19.11.1938.

134. TNA:PRO ED 114/276 HMI report on the Junior Art Department at Watford Art School, 25–27.4.1934; ED 114/277 HMI report on the Junior Commercial and Junior Technical Schools at Watford Technical School 31.7.1934; ED 114/278 HMI report on the provision of post-primary education in Watford and District July 1934.

135. BL *TES* 2.11.1935; GP BEd Circular 1444: Administrative Programme of Educational Development 1936.

136. TNA:PRO ED 51/38 HMI report on the provision of Technical Education in Hertfordshire 19.12.1935.

137. B. Bailey (1987) pp.57–9.

138. HALS HCC2/155 CP134 HEC 2.10.1936.

139. HALS HCC2/157 CP50 HEC 9.4.1937; HCC2/160 CP205 HEC 17.1.1938; TNA:PRO ED 51/181 HMI report on the provision of further education for women and girls in Hertfordshire 31.7.1937.

140. HALS HCC2/161 CP28 HEC 8.4.1938; HEd3 7/1 AR CEO 31.3.1938.

141. HALS HCC2/163 CP134 7.10.1938; HCC2/164 CP186 HEC 16.1.1939; HCC2/165 CP25 HEC 31.3.1939; HCC2/167 CP131 19.6.1939; BL *Mercury* 6.11.1936, 8.10.1937.

Chapter 9: The countryside

1. GP BEd AR 1922–3, p.22.

2. BL *Record* 21.4.1922.

3. BL *HandE Observer* 25.2.1922.

4. GP BEd AR 1925–6, pp.35–43.

5. BL *Gazette* 12.7.1919.

6. TNA:PRO ED 10/188 House of Commons speech by H.A.L. Fisher on Educational Estimates 19.4.1917.

7. BL *Citizen* 24.10.1919; *Record* 31.10.1919.

8. BL *Gazette* 12.7.1919.

9. BL *HandE Observer* 23.10.1920; HALS HEd4/26, p.655 HEC 15.10.1920.

10. HALS HEd4/26, p.655 HEC 15.10.1920.

11. ibid.

12. BL *Express* 28.6.1919; *WH Observer* 28.6.1919; *Advertiser* 22.11.1919.

13. HALS HEd4/26, p.765 FGPSC 13.12.1920, pp.886–7 HEC 14.1.1921.

14. BL *Express* 12.2.1921; *Advertiser* 11.6.1921; HALS HCC2/98 CP68 FGPSC 29.5.1922.

15. HALS HCC2/101 CP35 HEC 13.4.1923.

16. V. Bell (1950); R.J. Whiteman (ed.) (1936).

17. BL *Express* 12.2.1921; *Record* 6.5.1921.

18. BL *Advertiser* 7.5.1921.

19. HALS HCC2/101 CP8 HESC 16.3.1923; HCC2/104 CP176 FGPSC 17.12.1923.

20. HALS HCC2/107 CP135 HESC 26.9.1924.

21. BL *Express* 26.12.1925; *HandE Observer* 3.4.1926.

22. HALS HCC2/101 CP35 HEC 13.4.1923.

23. HALS HCC2/103 CP166 HCC *Education Handbook: Elementary Education* November 1923, p.24; HCC2/116 CP222 HCC Syllabus of Rural Education Appendix III, p.15; HCC2/129 CP14 FGPSC 24.3.1930; HEd1 39/3 Kimpton CE Mixed 26.4.1926.

24. BL *Record* 23.3.1923; *Mercury* 4.8.1939; HALS HCC2/98 CP68 FGPSC 29.5.1922.

25. BL *Express* 24.11.1923, 11.4.1925; *Mercury* 7.3.1925; *Advertiser* 7.3.1925, 13.5.1927; HALS HCC2/106 CP79 HEC Library Sub-Committee 11.6.1924; HCC2/113 CP45 HEC 29.3.1926; HCC2/119 CP166 HEC 10.10.1927.

26. BL *Advertiser* 13.5.1927; *Mercury* 10.9.1927.

27. HALS HCC2/116 CP222 HCC *Suggested Syllabus of Rural Education* February 1927.

28. BL *Mercury* 10.9.1927.

29. GP BEd Pamphlet 46: *Rural Education* January 1926, pp.9–17.

30. HALS HCC2/116 CP222 HCC *Suggested Syllabus of Rural Education* February 1927, pp.2–3.

31. ibid, pp.5–14.

32. BL *WH Observer* 8.1.1927.

33. HALS HCC2/118 CP83 HESC 30.5.1927; HCC2/122 CP82 FGPSC 1.6.1928; HCC2/123 CP171 HEC 8.10.1928; HEd1 17/2 Buckland CE Senior 14.10.1927, 18.9.1929.

34. HALS HCC2/123 CP171 HEC 8.10.1928; HEd1 112/3 Braughing, Jenyn's CC Mixed 26.4.1927.

35. HALS HEd1 17/2 Buckland CE Senior 27.10.1927, 17.4.1928, 7.10.1930, 6.11.1931, HMI report 28.11.1928; HEd1 19/2 Digswell CE Mixed 20.10.1927, 8.2.1929, 15.4.1929, 17.5.1929, 10.7.1929, 17.7.1929, 1.10.1929, 23.10.1929; HEd1 20/1 Eastwick CE Mixed 11.5.1927, 18.5.1927, 29.6.1927, 13.7.1927, 5.10.1927, 23.11.1927, 16.5.1928, 16.10.1929; HEd1 70/1 Little Berkhamsted CE Mixed 8.7.1927, 3.8.1927, 27.9.1928; HEd1 76/1 Sandon CE Mixed 17.5.1927, HMI report 16.2.1928; HEd1 112/3 Braughing, Jenyn's CC Mixed 22.6.1927, 10.9.1927.

36. HALS HCC2/120 CP226 HEC 9.1.1928.

37. BL *Mercury* 16.6.1928; HALS HCC2/123 CP171 HEC 8.10.1928.

38. BL *Mercury* 21.7.1928.

39. HALS HCC2/128 CP222 HCC *Suggested Syllabus of Rural Education* July 1929.

40. HALS HEd3 7/1 AR CEO 31.3.1929, pp.15–16, 31.3.1930, pp.1–2.

41. HALS HEd1 113/6 Hertingfordbury, Cowper Endowed Mixed 6.7.1927, 26.7.1927, 19.9.1927, 6.10.1927, 30.6.1928, 4.7.1928, 14.11.1928, 3.12.1928, 7.5.1929, 2.12.1929, 9.1.1930, 5.3.1930, 27.3.1930, 5.6.1930, 6.6.1930, 4.12.1930, 4.11.1931, 3.6.1932, 22.6.1932, 15.11.1932, 26.10.1933, 2.4.1936, 3.4.1936. Sir Charles Trevelyan (Labour MP and President of the Board of Education 1929–31), Sir Michael Sadler (director of special inquiries at the Education Department 1895–1903, professor of education, Manchester University 1903–11, vice-chancellor, Leeds University 1911–23, Master of University College, Oxford 1923–34.

42. ibid, 17.5.1933, 20.5.1933, 20.6.1933, 29.6.1933, 19.3.1934, 17.12.1934, 16.7.1935, 8.7.1935.

43. ibid, 12.7.1935, 7.4.1936, 18.1.1939, 10.2.1939, 30.6.1939.

44. HALS HEd1 101/7, 8 and 10 Wilstone CE Mixed files – photographs and articles from *News Chronicle*, *The Weekly News*, *Evening News*, *Reynolds News*, *Daily Telegraph* and *Daily Sketch*, June 1939.

45. HALS HCC2/125 CP19 HMI's Report on the working of the Rural Education Syllabus March 1929.

46. HALS HCC2/139 CP131 HEC 10.10.1932.

47. ibid; HALS HCC2/125 CP19 HMI's Report on the working of the Rural Education Syllabus March 1929; Whiteman (1936); Bell (1950).

48. HALS HEd1 64/15 and 64/16 Watton-atte-Stone CE Mixed: folders of children's work 1936–7.

49. HALS HCC2/118 CP83 HESC 30.5.1927; HCC2/153 CP53 HCC *Higher Education Handbook* 20.7.1936, pp.13–15.

50. GP BEd Pamphlet 99: *Education in the Countryside* 1934, p.7.

51. ibid, p.8.

52. ibid, pp.9–11.

53. BL *Mercury* 26.7.1935.

54. HALS HCC2/153 CP53 HCC *Higher Education Handbook* 20.7.1936, pp.13–15.

55. TNA:PRO ED 11/297 BEd The Place of the Senior School in Agricultural Education 9.11.1937.

56. BL *TES* 25.6.1938; GP BEd AR 1938, pp.4, 54.

57. TNA:PRO ED 11/297 Joint Memorandum to the President of the Board of Education and the Minister of Agriculture and Fisheries by the Parliamentary Secretaries of the two departments August 1939, p.1.

58. HALS HEd4/27, pp.585–7 HEC 21.10.21.

59. HALS HEd4/27, pp.336–7 HEC 13.6.1921, pp.523–5 FGPSC 3.10.1921 and pp.585–7 HEC 21.10.1921; HCC2/97 CP8 FGPSC 10.3.1922; HCC2/103 CP127 FGPSC 8.10.1923; HEd4/28, pp.20–1 PT&PI SC 6.3.1925 and pp.501–3 PT&PI SC 14.9.1925.

60. HALS HCC2/103 CP166 HCC *Education Handbook: Elementary Education* November 1923, pp.32–3. In 1985 two Stevenage residents recalled the pride they took in their plots and produce in local schools in the early 1920s – Stevenage Museum SOIHP A010/1 (Mr WN born 1909), A069/2 (Mr FN born 1907).

61. HALS HCC2/100 CP178 FGPSC 22.12.1922; HEd4/28, pp.723–4 PT&PI SC 27.11.1925; HCC2/113 CP45 HEC 29.3.1926; HCC2/114 CP110 HEC 18.6.1926.

62. BL *Express* 24.11.1923; HALS HEd4/28, p.181 HEC 3.4.1925 and pp.501–3 PT&PI SC 14.9.1925; HEd1 192/5 Holwell, Rand's Charity: HMI report on gardening 30.11.1925.

63. HALS HCC2/114 CP110 HEC 18.6.1926.

64. HALS HCC2/132 CP206 PT&PI SC 8.12.1930; TNA:PRO ED 96/38 HMI Report on School Gardens in Hertfordshire June 1930.

65. HALS HCC2/133 CP41 HCC *Education Handbook: Elementary Education* March 1931, pp.33–5; HCC2/135 CP144 PT&PI SC 21.9.1931; HCC2/139 CP131 HEC 10.10.1932; HCC2/143 CP111 HCC Annual Report on School Gardening (AR SG) July 1933; HCC2/151 CP151 HCC AR SG July 1935; HCC2/155 CP123 HCC AR SG July 1936; HCC2/159 CP136 HCC AR SG July 1937.

66. HALS HCC2/143 CP111 HCC AR SG July 1933, pp.2–3.

67. HALS HEd4/26, pp.190–2 HEC 9.4.1920.

68. ibid; HALS HEd4/26, pp.771–2 FGPSC 13.12.1920, pp.895–6 HEC 14.1.1921 and pp.324–8 HCC *A Three Years' Course of Instruction in Needlework for Pupil-Teachers* May 1920; HEd4/27, pp.232–7 HCC *A Three Years' Course of Instruction for Pupil-Teachers* April 1921.

69. HALS HEd4/26, pp.190–2 HEC 9.4.1920; HEd4/27, pp.501–3 HESC 26.9.1921 and pp.718–20 HESC 23.12.1921.

70. HALS HCC2/103 CP166 HCC *Education Handbook: Elementary Education* November 1923, pp.38–9; HCC2/105 CP12 HESC 17.3.1924.

71. HALS HCC2/113 CP11 HESC 5.3.1926.

72. HALS HEd4/28, p.283 HESC 22.5.1926.

73. BL *TES* 31.7.1926.

74. HALS HCC2/118 CP83 HESC 30.5.1927.

75. HALS HCC2/119 CP141 HESC 23.9.1927; HCC2/125 CP51 HEC 8.4.1929.

76. TNA:PRO ED 77/198 BEd Report on the Preliminary Education and Training of Teachers in Hertfordshire 29.6.1929.

77. ibid.

78. HALS HCC2/127 CP151 HESC 20.9.1929.

79. HALS HCC2/128 CP261 HEC 13.1.1930; BL *Citizen* 22.3.1929; TNA:PRO ED 11/187 National Union of Women Teachers *Memorandum on Rural Education* December 1930.

80. HALS HEd4/26, pp.366–7 FGPSC 11.6.1920.

81. HALS HCC2/97 CP8 FGPSC 10.3.1922.

82. ibid; HCC2/98 CP68 FGPSC 29.5.1922 and CP96 HEC 12.6.1922.

83. BL *Mercury* 22.7.1922; *Advertiser* 22.7.1922.

84. ibid. The ten opposing voters comprised an alliance of extremes. Some believed that larger schools promised a better education, while others were solely concerned with reducing public expenditure by all possible means.

85. HALS HCC2/100 CP178 FGPSC 22.12.1922; HCC2/107 CP165 HEC 17.10.1924; BL *HandE Observer* 17.1.1925.

86. HALS HCC2/103 CP147 HEC 19.10.1923; HCC2/105 CP39 HEC 31.3.1924.

87. BL *HandE Observer* 30.10.1926.

88. BL *Advertiser* 13.5.1927.

89. HALS HCC2/126 CP93 SRC 7.6.1929; HCC2/127 CP153 27.9.1929; HCC2/129 CP50 HEC 11.4.1930.

90. HALS HCC2/130 CP181 SRC 30.5.1930; HCC2/131 CP152 SRC 12.9.1930 and CP178 HEC 3.10.193.

91. HALS HCC2/127 CP153 SRC 27.9.1929; BL *Express* 12.10.1929.

92. HALS HCC2/124 CP204 SRC 16.11.1928; HCC2/126 CP82 FGPSC 3.6.1929; HCC2/146 CP85 HEC 22.6.1934; HCC2/148 CP192 HEC 22.1.1935; HCC2/151 CP125 HEC 30.9.1935; HCC2/155 CP134 HEC 2.10.1936; HCC2/162 CP81 HEC 20.6.1938: BL *Mercury* 17.8.1934; *Reporter* 25.1.1935.

93. HALS HCC2/130 CP85 FGPSC 6.6.1930.

94. ibid.

95. ibid.

96. HALS HCC2/133 CP9 SRC 6.3.1931; HCC2/134 CP78 SRC 15.5.1931; HCC2/135 CP140 SRC 18.9.1931.

97. HALS HCC2/136 CP226 HEC 15.1.1932.

98. HALS HCC2/137 CP36 HEC 8.4.1932.

99. HALS HCC2/142 CP75 HEC 23.6.1933; HCC2/148 CP192 HEC 22.1.1935; HCC2/150 CP76 HEC 21.6.1935; BL *HandE Observer* 25.1.1935.

100. HALS HCC2/139 CP131 HEC 10.10.1932.

101. HALS HCC2/146 CP85 HEC 22.6.1934.

102. HALS HCC2/153 CP30 HEC 30.3.1936.

103. BL *Mercury* 6.11.1936.

104. HALS HCC2/157 CP50 HEC 9.4.1937; HCC2/159 CP148 HEC 1.10.1937; HCC2/164 CP186 HEC 16.1.1939; HEd1 17/2 Buckland CE Mixed 28.6.1939 and HMI report 2.6.1939.

105. TNA:PRO ED 19/586 HMI Hertfordshire County: Report on the progress of reorganisation of Public Elementary Schools on Hadow lines, with suggestions for a comprehensive scheme for the whole County, February 1936.

106. ibid; TNA:PRO ED 11/297 BEd memorandum on reorganisation 1936.

107. TNA:PRO ED 19/586 HMI Hertfordshire County: Report on the progress of reorganisation of Public Elementary Schools on Hadow lines, with suggestions for a comprehensive scheme for the whole County, February 1936. It is probable Bloom had in mind the Board of Education Pamphlet 93: An Experiment in Rural Education, issued in 1933, based upon Suffolk.

108. BL *Mercury* 26.6.1936.

109. ibid, 26.11.1937.

110. Essex Record Office (ERO) 106 Essex Education Committee (EEC) Report on the Organisation of Elementary Schools, December 1928.

111. ERO 106 EEC Reorganisation of Elementary Schools in Rural Areas, 1934; *Education in Essex 1928–1935*, pp.7, 23–33.

112. BL *Buckinghamshire Advertiser* 12.11.1927, 21.6.1929, 19.5.1933, 25.1.1935, 25.10.1935, 22.11.1935, 18.4.1937.

113. Buckinghamshire Record Office, Report of Joint Meeting of the Elementary and Higher Education Sub-Committees 17.1.1935, p.109.

114. HALS HCC2/154 CP84 HEC 22.6.1936; HCC2/157 CP50 HEC 9.4.1937; HCC2/158 CP93 HEC 21.6.1937; BL *Express* 21.5.1938.

115. BL *TES* 1.2.1936, 15.2.1936.

116. HALS HCC2/158 CP93 HEC 21.6.1937.

117. TNA:PRO ED 19/586 HMI Hertfordshire County: Report on the progress of reorganisation of Public Elementary Schools on Hadow lines, February 1936; HALS HCC2/153 CP30 HEC 30.3.1936; HCC2/157 CP50 HEC 9.4.1937; HCC2/160 CP205 HEC 17.1.1938; HCC2/162 CP81 HEC 20.6.1938; HCC2/164 CP186 HEC 16.1.1939; BL *Mercury* 6.11.1936; *WH Observer* 25.2.1938; *Gazette* 26.2.1938; *Express* 18.7.1936, 6.5.1939.

118. BL *Mercury* 26.11.1937.

Chapter 10: The church schools controversy

1. HALS HEd4/26, pp.406–19 HCC Elementary Education statistics 1.4.1920.

2. HALS HEd3 7/1 AR CEO 31.3.1939.

3. B.S. Rowntree and G.R. Lavers (1951) p.343; M. Cruikshank (1963) p.116.

4. Cruikshank (1963) pp.115–20; Murphy (1971) pp.101–2; BL *TES* 1.4.1920, 29.4.1920.

5. BL *Advertiser* 29.11.1919.

6. M.B. Furse (1953).

7. A. Hastings (1986) p.55.

8. Furse (1953) pp.2–11; BL *Advertiser* 29.11.1920.

9. Furse (1953) pp.12–13.

10. BL *Gazette* 27.11.1937.
11. Furse (1953) pp.13–14.
12. ibid, p.15.
13. ibid; BL *Advertiser* 29.11.1919.
14. BL *Gazette* 18.10.1924, 25.5.1929; *Record* 3.11.1922; *Mercury* 15.4.1922, 10.9.1927, 8.11.1929, 20.5.1938; *Advertiser* 28.10.1922, 17.5.1929, 23.5.1930, 17.10.1930, 1.11.1935; *Reporter* 7.12.1923; *Express* 3.6.1933; *WH Observer* 1.4.1922, 2.1.1929; *HandE Observer* 16.10.1926, 12.2.1927.
15. Hastings (1986) pp.55–7, 252–3.
16. BL *Citizen* 4.7.1919; *Express* 11.10.1919; *HandE Observer* 12.6.1920.
17. BL *Telegraph* 27.6.1919.
18. BL *Mercury* 15.4.1922.
19. BL *Record* 18.4.1918; *Gazette* 20.4.1918.
20. BL *Advertiser* 26.6.1920, HALS HEd4/26, pp.368–9 FGPSC 11.6.1920; HCC2/108 CP218 HEC 9.1.1925; HEd4/28, pp.298–9 FGPSC 29.5.1925.
21. HALS HEd4/26, pp.780–2 FGPSC 13.12.1920; BL *WH Observer* 22.1.1921.
22. BL *WH Observer* 9.4.1921.
23. BL *Advertiser* 7.5.1921; *WH Observer* 7.5.1921, 1.4.1922.
24. HALS HEd4/26, p.358 FGPSC 11.6.1929; HCC2/108 CP190 FGPSC 19.12.1924; BL *Advertiser* 22.1.1921, 18.6.1921, 29.10.1921, 25.9.1926, 6.2.1926, 25.12.1926.
25. HALS HCC2/102 CP96 HEC 15.6.1923; HCC2/105 CP39 HEC 31.3.1924; HEd4/28, pp.611–12 HEC 9.10.1925; BL *Express* 16.6.1923; *Advertiser* 5.4.1924, 6.2.1926.
26. BL *HandE Observer* 23.10.1920; *Mercury* 9.4.1921, 5.4.1924, 16.10.1926; HALS HEd4/27, pp.515–16 FGPSC 3.10.1921; HCC2/105 CP39 HEC 31.3.1924; HEd4/28, pp.751–4 FGPSC 7.12.1925.
27. BL *Express* 4.9.1926, 11.9.1926, 18.9.1926, 25.9.1926.
28. HALS HEd4/26, pp.358–9 FGPSC 11.6.1920; HCC2/97 CP8 FGPSC 10.3.1922; HCC2/98 CP96 HEC 12.6.1922; HEd4/28, pp.155–6 HEC 3.4.1925; BL *HandE Observer* 7.2.1925, 6.2.1926, 26.6.1926.
29. BL *WH Observer* 22.1.1921, 18.6.1921, 17.6.1922, 16.4.1932; HALS HCC2/98 CP68 FGPSC 29.5.1922; HCC2/118 CP84 FGPSC 3.6.1927; HCC2/124 CP211 Proposed Reorganisation of Public Elementary Schools: Rickmansworth Urban 16.11.1928; HCC2/129 CP14 FGPSC 24.3.1930; HCC2/151 CP125 HEC 30.9.1935; HCC2/158 CP93 HEC 21.6.1937; TNA:PRO ED 19/379 HMI Administrative Report on Rickmansworth 28.6.1934.
30. BL *Citizen* 14.3.1924, 28.3.1924.
31. BL *Advertiser* 13.2.1926, 3.4.1926, 10.7.1926, 15.5.1926, 16.10.1926; HALS HCC2/113 CP45 HEC 29.3.1926; HCC2/115 CP165 HEC 11.10.1926.
32. BL *Gazette* 13.11.1926, 27.11.1926, 4.12.1926, 3.11.1928; *WH Observer* 19.2.1927, 2.4.1927, 2.11.1927; HALS HCC2/116 CP219 HEC 7.1.1927.
33. GP BEd Circular 1397 18.5.1928 and Pamphlet 60: *The New Prospect in Education* May 1928.
34. ibid; BL *TES* 8.1.1927.
35. BL *Express* 25.6.1927.
36. BL *Express* 13.10.1928; HALS HCC2/124 CP189 SRC 16.11.1928.
37. BL *Mercury* 16.10.1926; *Express* 23.10.1926.
38. BL *Express* 15.6.1929.
39. HALS HCC2/124 CP189 SRC 16.11.1928; HCC2/125 CP51 HEC 8.4.1929.
40. HALS HCC2/125 CP28 A Statement of Diocesan Policy on the Proposed Re-organisation of

Elementary Schools 6.3.1929.

41. BL *Advertiser* 5.4.1929.

42. Despite the sound and fury, however, the policy statement hints that each parish and school were pawns in a larger game as the diocese expected its ultimate sacrifices, in areas where church schools were in a minority, to be matched by LEA concessions where church schools were dominant.

43. BL *HandE Observer* 30.2.1929; *Advertiser* 5.4.1929; *Mercury* 12.4.1929; HALS HCC2/125 CP51 HEC 8.4.1929.

44. ibid.

45. BL *Barnet Press* 18.5.1929.

46. BL *Mercury* 12.4.1929.

47. BL *Advertiser* 19.4.1929; *Mercury* 26.4.1929.

48. BL *Mercury* 26.4.1929; *Barnet Press* 18.5.1929.

49. BL *Advertiser* 10.5.1929.

50. BL *Mercury* 17.1.1930, 7.3.1930; HALS HCC2/128 CP234 *Syllabus of Religious Education* 27.1.1930.

51. BL *Mercury* 17.1.1931.

52. BL *Advertiser* 14.6.1929; *WH Observer* 15.6.1929; *Express* 15.6.1929; *Citizen* 21.6.1929. Newspaper cuttings of the event were circulated among Board officials with the resolutions heavily underlined – TNA:PRO ED 99/39 1929 St Albans Diocesan Conference.

53. *WH Observer* 2.11.1929; *Mercury* 8.11.1929.

54. BL *Advertiser* 5.7.1929; *Barnet Press* 16.11.1929.

55. HALS HCC2/128 CP207 SRC 6.12.1929; HCC2/132 CP205 SRC 28.11.1930 and CP209 FGPSC 15.12.1930; HCC2/149 CP29 HEC 5.4.1935.

56. BL *Advertiser* 20.12.1929; HALS HCC2/127 CP167 Proposed Reorganisation of Public Elementary Schools: St Albans 27.9.1929; HCC2/129 CP26 Proposed Reorganisation of Public Elementary Schools: St Albans 21.3.1930; HCC2/130 CP81 SRC 30.5.1930 and CP85 FGPSC 6.6.1930; HCC2/135 CP140 SRC 18.9.1931.

57. BL *Barnet Press* 5.1.1929, 19.1.1929, 3.8.1929, 2.4.1932, 16.7.1932 (quotation), 24.9.1932, 14.1.1933, 9.1.1937; HALS HCC2/123 CP145 FGPSC 28.9.1928; HCC2/124 CP195 Proposed Reorganisation of Public Elementary Schools: Barnet Urban 16.11.1928; HCC2/127 CP153 SRC 27.9.1929; HCC2/142 CP 75 HEC 23.6.1933.

58. HALS HCC2/131 CP152 SRC 12.9.1930; HCC2/135 CP140 SRC 18.9.1931; HCC2/153 CP30 HEC 30.3.1936; BL *Citizen* 25.6.1937.

59. BL *Advertiser* 20.12.1929, 7.11.1930, 24.2.1933, 18.5.1934.

60. HALS HCC2/125 CP2 SRC 22.2.1929; BL *Reporter* 24.10.1930.

61. HALS HCC2/116 CP219 HEC 7.1.1927; HCC2/119 CP140 FGPSC 19.9.1927; HCC2/133 CP13 FGPSC 13.3.1931; BL *Advertiser* 13.12.1929, 6.5.1932.

62. HALS HCC2/125 CP2 SRC 22.2.1929; HCC2/130 CP81 SRC 30.5.1930; BL *Mercury* 7.3.1930, 26.2.1932, 8.7.1932.

63. HALS HCC2/125 CP2 SRC 22.2.1929; BL *Citizen* 16.8.1929, 20.9.1929, 1.11.1929, 29.11.1929, 10.1.1930.

64. HALS HCC2/125 CP2 SRC 22.2.1929; HCC2/126 CP93 SRC 7.6.1929; HCC2/130 CP81 SRC 30.5.1930; HCC2/131 CP152 SRC 12.9.1930; BL *Express* 21.11.1931.

65. HALS HCC2/132 CP205 SRC 28.9.1930; HCC2/135 CP140 SRC 18.9.1931; HCC2/137 CP36 HEC 8.4.1932; HCC2/146 CP85 HEC 22.6.1934; HCC2/152 CP175 HEC 17.1.1936; BL *WH*

Observer 1.8.1931.

66. HALS HCC2/125 CP2 SRC 22.2.1929; HCC2/126 CP93 SRC 7.6.1929; HCC2/130 CP81 SRC 30.5.1930; HCC2/131 CP152 SRC 12.9.1930; HCC2/132 CP209 FGPSC 15.12.1930; BL *Mercury* 17.1.1930; *Express* 21.11.1931.

67. McKibbin (1998) pp.213–14; Simon (1974) pp.149–67; D.W. Dean (1969) pp.286–300.

68. BL *Advertiser* 16.5.1930.

69. BL *Advertiser* 23.5.1930; *Citizen* 30.5.1930.

70. HALS HCC2/127 CP166 HEC Proposed Reorganisation of Public Elementary Schools: Cheshunt Urban 27.9.1929; HCC2/143 CP128 HEC 6.10.1933; HCC2/149 CP29 HEC 5.4.1935; HCC2/150 CP76 HEC 21.6.1935; HCC2/152 CP175 HEC 17.1.1936; TNA:PRO ED 97/114 BEd internal memorandum 22.6.1934; BL *Telegraph* 30.10.1931, 29.3.1933, 28.12.1934, 26.4.1935, 29.11.1935; *Mercury* 20.5.1938.

71. BL *HandE Observer* 2.11.1935; *Gazette* 27.11.1937.

72. BL *Advertiser* 1.11.1935.

73. BL *Mercury* 8.11.1929, 16.1.1931; *Advertiser* 23.5.1930.

74. M. Lawn (1987) pp.118–25.

75. ibid.

76. BL *Advertiser* 5.7.1929; *Express* 6.7.1929; *Gazette* 26.10.1929; *Citizen* 1.11.1929.

77. BL *Mercury* 7.3.1930; *Advertiser* 14.3.1930. Teachers in other LEAs endured similar charges. Writing in 1943, an ex-education officer in Norfolk poured scorn on the critics, largely clerical and military, who saw 'the red hand of Bolshevism in the spread of elementary education, especially in Council schools' – H.M. Burton (1943) p.61.

78. BL *TES* 11.7.1925.

79. BL *Education* 11.1.1924.

80. ibid, 24.1.1930; *Gazette* 26.10.1929

81. TNA:PRO ED 97/126 Hemel Hempstead file: letter from mayor to Sir Charles Trevelyan, 1.7.1929 and BEd reply, 4.7.1929. The Board refused to interfere in the dispute.

82. BL *TES* 7.9.1935.

83. BL *Education* 24.1.1930.

84. ERO 106 EEC Report of the Director of Education for the three years ended 31 March 1928.

85. BL *Essex Chronicle* 3.2.1928.

86. BL *HandE Observer* 10.6.1933, 9.6.1934; *Essex Chronicle* 21.2.1936. Four Anglican senior schools were considered in the 1930s but none materialised – V.R. Rust (1971) p.34.

87. ERO 106 EEC Reorganisation of Elementary Education in Rural Areas 1934 and *Education in Essex 1928–1935*.

88. Buckinghamshire Record Office, Buckinghamshire Education Committee Files 1/246 and 1/219, Joint Conference Committee 23.9.1929, 24.10.1930, 5.11.1934, 1.5.1936, 5.6.1936.

89. BL *Advertiser* 1.11.1935.

90. ibid.

91. BL *TES* 1.2.1936, 8.2.1936, 26.12.1936.

92. HALS HCC2/153 CP30 HEC 30.3.1936; HCC2/155 CP134 HEC 2.10.1936.

93. BL *Mercury* 26.11.1937.

94. HALS HCC2/155 CP134 HEC 2.10.1936.

95. BL *HandE Observer* 28.3.1936.

96. HALS HCC2/158 CP93 HEC 21.6.1937; BL *Mercury* 25.6.1937.

97. TNA:PRO ED 16/671 BEd interview minutes and memoranda 26.8.1937.

98. BL *HandE Observer* 28.3.1936; Simon (1974) p.206.

99. BL *Advertiser* 12.11.1937; *WH Observer* 12.11.1937; *HandE Observer* 13.11.1937.

100. BL *Mercury* 25.6.1937.

101. HALS HCC2/130 CP81 SRC 30.5.1930; HCC2/131 CP152 SRC 12.9.1930; HCC2/135 CP140 SRC 18.9.1931; HCC2/153 CP30 HEC 30.3.1936; HCC2/157 CP50 HEC 9.4.1937; HCC2/160 CP205 HEC 17.1.1938; HCC2/162 CP81 HEC 20.6.1938; HCC2/164 CP186 HEC 16.1.1939; BL *Mercury* 6.11.1936; *Express* 18.7.1936, 6.5.1939; *WH Observer* 25.2.1938; *Gazette* 26.2.1938; TNA:PRO ED 19/586 HMI Hertfordshire County: Report on the progress of reorganisation of Public Elementary Schools on Hadow lines, February 1936.

102. HALS HCC2/158 CP93 HEC 21.6.1937; HCC2/159 CP148 HEC 1.10.1937; HCC2/163 CP134 HEC 7.10.1938.

103. The 'special agreements' were allowed to proceed after the war.

104. HALS HCC2/155 CP134 HEC 2.10.1936; HCC2/161 CP28 HEC 8.4.1938.

105. BL *HandE Observer* 8.4.1939.

106. BL *Mercury* 12.5.1939.

107. BL *Mercury* 25.6.1937, 15.4.1938; *Telegraph* 2.7.1937, 17.9.1937, 15.10.1937, 29.10.1937, 25.2.1938, 15.4.1938.

108. BL *Gazette* 20.2.1937. See also *Gazette* 26.2.1938; *HandE Observer* 14.5.1938.

109. BL *Advertiser* 12.11.1937; *Gazette* 27.11.1937, 26.2.1938; *WH Observer* 21.1.1938; *HandE Observer* 14.5.1938.

110. BL *WH Observer* 25.2.1938.

111. BL *Mercury* 15.4.1938.

112. BL *Telegraph* 16.9.1938; *Mercury* 16.9.1938; *Gazette* 9.12.1938; *WH Observer* 9.12.1938.

113. HALS HEd3 7/1 AR CEO 1938–9.

114. HALS HCC2/165 CP25 HEC 31.3.1939; *Telegraph* 24.3.1939.

115. HALS HCC2/164 CP186 HEC 16.1.1939; HCC2/165 CP25 HEC 31.3.1939; HCC2/166 CP83 HEC 19.6.1939; BL *Telegraph* 24.3.1939, 18.9.1939, 10.11.1939.

116. Murphy (1971) pp.124–5.

Chapter 11: A wider view of children's health and welfare 1919–1939

1. Maclure (1973) pp.173–5.

2. ibid; BL *Education* 28.3.1919.

3. HALS HEd4/24, pp.315–42 HEC 21.10.1918.

4. From numerous examples, BL *Express* 24.12.1927, 16.2.1929, 11.10.1930, 8.12.1934; *HandE Observer* 31.10.1931; *WH Observer* 27.7.1929.

5. GP BEd AR CMO 1918 pp.40–1; AR CMO 1925 p.144.

6. GP BEd AR CMO 1918 pp.40–1.

7. GP BEd AR CMO 1924 pp.108–16, 153.

8. GP BEd AR CMO 1925 p.144.

9. GP BEd AR CMO 1920 p.65.

10. HALS HEd4/26, pp.371–83 AR SH 1919.

11. GP BEd AR CMO 1920 p.2.

12. HALS HCC2/98 CP70 AR SH 1921; HCC2/118 CP89 AR SH 1926; HCC2/146 CP70 AR SH 1933; HCC2/158 CP78 AR SH 1936.

13. HALS HEd4/27, pp.319–32 AR SH 1920.
14. HALS HEd4/26, pp.371–83 AR SH 1919; HCC2/118 CP89 AR SH 1926.
15. HALS HCC2/146 CP70 AR SH 1933; HCC2/158 CP78 AR SH 1936; HCC2/166 CP62 AR SH 1938.
16. HALS HEd4/26, pp.371–83 AR SH 1919.
17. HCC2/166 CP62 AR SH 1938.
18. B. Harris (1995) pp.94–7; BL *Mercury* 13.11.1920; 6.2.1926; *Express* 12.2.1921; *Record* 17.2.1922, 21.4.1922; *Advertiser* 1.4.1922; *WH Observer* 21.4.1923.
19. Harris (1995) p.98.
20. HALS HCC2/102 CP74 AR SH 1922; HCC2/114 CP80 AR SH 1925; HCC2/126 CP92 AR SH 1928; HCC2/138 CP70 AR SH 1931; HCC2/154 CP66 AR SH 1935; HCC2/166 CP62 AR SH 1938.
21. ibid.
22. HALS HEd4/26, pp.371–83 AR SH 1919; HEd4/27, pp.319–22 AR SH 1920; HEd4/28, pp.280–94 AR SH 1921; HCC2/114 CP80 AR SH 1925; HCC2/118 CP89 AR SH 1926; HCC2/162 CP63 AR SH 1937.
23. GP BEd AR CMO 1927 pp.78–80; AR CMO 1929 pp.39–43.
24. GP BEd AR CMO 1927 pp.78–80 and 1929 pp.39–43. 296 out of 568 junior schools, 271 out of 627 senior boys' schools and even 127 out of 628 senior girls' schools had no time allocated to the teaching of hygiene, and 790 out of 1,414 infants', junior and rural all-age schools surveyed admitted they ignored or only partially adopted ideas in the *Handbook of Suggestions on Health Education*. Newman received a number of vehement protests from chief education officers, although not Howe, that he was far exceeding his authority when he initiated the school Health Education survey. In an ill-tempered letter, James Graham, the influential chief education officer of Leeds, told the Board of Education that 'it was about time he was pulled up with an unmistakable jerk and made to feel he is not the Napoleon he thinks he is' – TNA:PRO ED 24/1366 letter from J. Graham to H.M. Richards, Board of Education 24.2.1930.
25. HALS HCC2/130 CP99 AR SH 1929 pp.43–4.
26. HALS HCC2/122 CP93 AR SH 1927; HCC2/126 CP92 AR SH 1928; HCC2/134 CP89 AR SH 1930.
27. HALS HCC2/142 CP61 AR SH 1932.
28. HALS HCC2/108 CP76 AR SH 1924; HCC2/126 CP92 AR SH 1928; HCC2/158 CP78 AR SH 1936.
29. HALS HCC2/108 CP76 AR SH 1924.
30. HALS HCC2/105 CP10 CSASC 7.3.1924.
31. HALS HCC2/114 CP80 AR SH 1925; HCC2/166 CP62 AR SH 1938.
32. GP BEd AR CMO 1923 p.145.
33. HALS HEd4/26, pp.490–9 HEC 21.6.1920; HCC2/98 CP68 FGPSC 29.5.1922; HCC2/102 CP74 AR SH 1922; HCC2/105 CP39 HEC 31.3.1924.
34. TNA:PRO ED 99/39 BEd Black List: Hertfordshire.
35. HALS HCC2/108 CP190 FGPSC 19.12.1924.
36. HALS HCC2/104 CP205 HEC 7.1.1924; HCC2/105 CP39 HEC 31.3.1924; HCC2/126 CP92 AR SH 1928.
37. HALS HCC2/114 CP80 AR SH 1925.
38. BL *TES* 31.3.1928; HALS HCC2/126 CP92 AR SH 1928; HCC2/146 CP70 AR SH 1933;

HCC2/150 CP56 AR SH 1934; HCC2/154 CP66 AR SH 1935.

39.   HALS HCC2/158 CP78 AR SH 1936.

40.   GP BEd AR 1916–17 p.6; HALS HEd4/25, pp.5–6 FGPSC 29.9.1919.

41.   HALS HEd4/25, pp.5–6 FGPSC 29.9.1919 and pp.4–5 FGPSC 12.12.1919.

42.   ibid.

43.   HALS HEd4/26, pp.1–5 Physical Training Sub-Committee (PTSC) 10.12.1920; HEd1 4/2 Ayot St Peter CE Mixed 10.12.1920; HEd1 33/2 Hinxworth CC Mixed 21.5.1920, 4.6.1920.

44.   HALS HEd1 22/1 Gilston CE Mixed 19.10.1921.

45.   HALS HEd4/27, pp.2–3 HEC 3.10.1921; HCC2/104 CP205 HEC 7.1.1924.

46.   BL *Education* 19.2.1937; *Who's Who in Hertfordshire* (1936) pp.72–3.

47.   GP BEd AR CMO 1921 p.21.

48.   ibid.

49.   HALS HCC2/98 CP70 AR SH 1921.

50.   HALS HCC2/99 CP123 PTSC 22.9.1922.

51.   ibid; HCC2/100 CP170 PTSC 1.12.1922.

52.   HALS HCC2/101 CP6 PTSC 12.3.1923; HCC2/104 CP173 Annual Report on Physical Training (AR PT) 1923.

53.   ibid.

54.   HALS HCC2/106 CP67 PT&PI SC 30.5.1924.

55.   HALS HEd1 39/3 Kimpton CE Mixed 18.11.1920, 2.7.1923.

56.   HALS HCC2/106 CP98 HEC 23.6.1924.

57.   HALS HCC2/108 CP193 AR PT 1924.

58.   HALS HEd1 108/2 Stanstead Abbots CE Mixed 21.2.1927. See also HEd1 188/5 Hatfield CE Boys 9.2.1923.

59.   BL *WH Observer* 20.10.1923.

60.   HALS HCC2/108 CP193 AR PT 1924; HCC2/116 CP220 AR PT 1926; HEd1 24/2 Harpenden, Kinsbourne Green CE Mixed 30.4.1925, 23.12.1925.

61.   HALS HEd1 39/3 Kimpton CE Mixed 18.1.1935, 30.10.1935.

62.   BL *Advertiser* 24.1.1925.

63.   HALS HCC2/113 CP45 HEC 29.3.1926.

64.   HALS HCC2/115 CP165 HEC 11.10.1926; HCC2/116 CP220 AR PT 1926.

65.   HALS HEd3 7/1 AR CEO 1928–9, pp.4–5.

66.   BL *Gazette* 26.4.1924; *Citizen* 5.6.1931; *Mercury* 3.5.1924; *Advertiser* 12.5.1923, 21.7.1923.

67.   BL *Reporter* 11.6.1937.

68.   HALS HEd1 1/2 Anstey CE Mixed 14.12.1926.

69.   GP BEd AR CMO 1928 p.42.

70.   HALS HCC2/117 CP3 PT&PI SC 11.3.1927.

71.   See numerous entries in HALS HEd1 45/2 Brent Pelham CE Mixed 1929–38; HEd1 83/3 Pirton CC Mixed 1925–31; HEd1 94/9 Royston, Queen's Road CC Mixed 1922–33; HEd1 96/1 Watford, Callow Land CC Boys 1929–34; HEd1 100/5 High Wych CE Mixed 1926–32; HEd1 112/3 Braughing, Jenyn's CC Mixed 1923–37; HEd2 7/16 Hitchin, St Mary's CE Senior Mixed 1919–39.

72.   For example, BL *Barnet Press* 8.1.1927; *Gazette* 25.12.1926, 17.12.1927, 11.10.1930; *Express* 16.2.1929; *HandE Observer* 16.10.1926, 3.11.1928, 24.12.1932, 22.12.1934.

73.   BL *Telegraph* 17.8.1923.

74.   BL *Gazette* 1.10.1928.

75. HALS HCC2/128 CP225 AR PT 1929.

76. GP BEd AR CMO 1929 p.54; HALS HCC2/128 CP225 AR PT 1929; HCC2/130 CP122 HEC 16.6.1930.

77. HALS HCC2/129 CP9 PT&PI SC 10.3.1930.

78. GP BEd AR CMO 1932 pp.78–9; HALS HCC2/136 CP204 AR PT 1931; HCC2/138 CP70 AR SMO 1931.

79. HALS HCC2/142 CP75 HEC 26.3.1933; HCC2/159 CP133 AR PT 1936–7; HCC2/163 CP120 AR PT 1937–8.

80. HALS HCC2/142 CP61 AR SH 1932; HCC2/156 CP189 HEC 15.1.1937.

81. BL *Express* 31.12.1932; HALS HEd1 88/2 Hertford, Cowper Testimonial Senior Boys 27.7.1932, 18.7.1933, 25.7.1934, 10.6.1936.

82. HALS HCC2/154 CP84 HEC 22.6.1936; BL *Mercury* 26.6.1936.

83. BL *Advertiser* 3.6.1938; *WH Observer* 5.5.1939.

84. HALS HCC2/151 CP109 AR PT 1934–5.

85. ibid; HCC2/145 CP39 HEC 13.4.1934.

86. HALS HCC2/153 CP30 HEC 30.3.1936; HCC2/155 CP121 AR PT 1935–6.

87. HALS HCC2/151 CP109 AR PT 1934–5.

88. HALS HCC2/154 CP84 HEC 22.6.1936.

89. HALS HCC2/160 CP205 HEC 17.1.1938; HCC2/164 CP186 HEC 16.1.1939.

90. HALS HCC2/155 CP121 AR PT 1936; BL *Education* 1.4.1938; HCC2/162 CP81 HEC 20.6.1938.

91. BL *Education* 19.2.1937.

92. HALS HCC2/163 CP129 AR PT 1937–8; HCC2/164 CP186 HEC 16.1.1939; GP BEd AR CMO 1938 p.29.

93. HALS HCC2/103 CP166 HCC *Education Handbook: Elementary Education* 1923, pp.27–31; HCC2/106 CP67 PT&PI SC 30.5.1924.

94. BL *TES* 3.11.1923.

95. HALS HEd4/28, pp.500–1 PT&PI SC 14.9.1925; HCC2/117 CP3 PT&PI SC 11.3.1927.

96. HALS HCC2/127 CP151 HESC 20.9.1929.

97. HALS HCC2/128 CP224 Annual Report on Domestic Subjects (AR DS) 1929, pp.1–3; HCC2/132 CP217 AR DS 1930, pp.1–7; HCC2/137 CP36 HEC 8.4.1932.

98. HALS HCC2/132 CP217 AR DS 1930. In 1985 several Stevenage residents recalled walking in crocodile fashion to the town's Domestic Subjects 'hut' in the 1920s and 1930s – Stevenage Museum SOIHP A084/1 (Miss MH born 1923), A088/2 (Mrs EP born 1913), A099/1 (Miss JH born 1925), (Miss BG born 1927).

99. HALS HCC2/129 CP9 PT&PI SC 10.3.1930; HCC2/130 CP122 HEC 16.6.1930; HCC2/133 CP10 PT&PI SC 6.3.1931; HCC2/135 CP144 PT&PI SC 21.9.1931; HCC2/136 CP206 AR DS 1931.

100. HALS HCC2/140 HCC Report of the Special Expenditure Committee 22.12.1932; HCC2/135 CP168 HEC 2.10.1931.

101. HALS HCC2/147 CP124 AR DS 1934.

102. HALS HCC2/141 CP24 HEC 7.4.1933.

103. HALS HCC2/143 CP110 AR DS 1933; HCC2/144 CP176 HEC 19.1.1934.

104. HALS HCC2/155 CP122 AR DS 1936; HCC2/156 CP189 HEC 15.1.1937; HCC2/157 CP50 HEC 9.4.1937.

105. HALS HCC2/147 CP124 AR DS 1934; HCC2/144 CP176 HEC 19.1.1934.

106. HALS HEd1 10/1 Barnet, Wood Street Housecraft Centre – Autumn and Spring Terms 1934.

107. BL *Advertiser* 27.1.1933; HALS HCC2/142 CP75 HEC 23.6.1933.

108. HALS HCC2/157 CP50 HEC 9.4.1937.
109. HALS HCC2/163 CP122 AR Housecraft 1938; HCC2/164 CP186 HEC 16.1.1939.
110. ibid; HALS HCC2/155 CP122 AR DS 1936.
111. HALS HCC2/157 CP50 HEC 9.4.1937.
112. HALS HEd4/27, p.313 FGPSC 31.5.1921; *WH Observer* 25.2.1933, 1.7.1933, 16.9.1933.
113. HALS HCC2/128 CP224 AR DS 1929.
114. HALS HCC2/130 CP122 HEC 16.6.1930; HCC2/132 CP217 AR DS 1930; HEd3 7/1 AR CEO 31.3.1935; BL *Gazette* 7.2.1931.
115. HALS HCC2/146 CP70 AR SH 1933; HCC2/154 CP66 AR SH 1935; HCC2/158 CP78 AR SH 1936; HCC2/162 CP63 AR SH 1937; HCC2/166 CP62 AR SH 1938.
116. HALS HCC2/127 CP180 HEC 4.10.1929.
117. HALS HCC2/131 CP156 FGPSC 22.9.1930.
118. GP BEd AR CMO 1934 pp.23–5; HALS HCC2/150 CP76 HEC 21.6.1935; HCC2/166 CP83 HEC 19.6.1939.
119. GP BEd AR CMO 1938–9 pp.23–4.
120. HALS HCC2/129 CP14 FGPSC 24.3.1930.
121. HALS HCC2/131 CP156 FGPSC 22.9.1930.
122. HALS HCC2/132 CP209 FGPSC 15.12.1930.
123. TNA:PRO ED 66/10 letter and statement from Welwyn Nursery School Group to BEd 21.4.1937, letter from BEd to Hertfordshire LEA 19.6.1937; ED 69/106 BEd internal memorandum from Miss K. Elliott to G. Maudsley 11.6.1938 and letter from Oxhey Guild to BEd 15.2.1938; HALS HCC2/159 CP148 HEC 1.10.1937, HCC2/162 CP81 HEC 20.6.1938, HCC2/163 CP134 HEC 7.10.1938. The war prevented the new nurseries being built.
124. BL *Mercury* 26.11.1937.
125. See R. Cooter 'Introduction', L. Bryder 'Wonderlands of buttercups, clover and daisies' and H. Hendrick 'Child labour, medical capital and the school medical service c.1890–1918', in R. Cooter (ed.) (1992); GP BEd AR CMO 1922 p.1.
126. Even historian Brian Simon, usually highly critical of the lost educational opportunities of the inter-war years, acknowledges the significant expenditure and attention given to child health and special education in the inter-war years – Simon (1974) p.287.
127. HALS HEd4/23, pp.380–8 FSAGPSC 14.12.1917.
128. HALS HEd4/24, pp.315–42 HEC 21.10.1918; HEd4/27, pp.110–15 Annual Report on Kingsmead Special Residential School (AR KSRS) 1919–20.
129. ibid.
130. ibid; BL *Mercury* 19.4.1919.
131. BL *Mercury* 19.4.1919, 10.5.1919.
132. HALS HEd4/25, pp.654–63 CSASC 19.12.1919; BL *WH Observer* 17.1.1920.
133. See, for example, HALS HCC2/141 CP24 HEC 7.4.1933; HCC2/145 CP39 HEC 13.4.1934; HCC2/155 CP134 HEC 2.10.1936.
134. HALS HEd4/27, pp.110–15 AR KSRS 1919–20.
135. ibid.
136. TNA:PRO ED 50/150b BEd internal memorandum on policy towards Special Schools, June 1923.
137. HALS HEd4/27, pp.110–15 AR KSRS 1919–20
138. GP BEd AR CMO 1922 p.7; TNA:PRO ED 11/115 BEd memorandum to HMI 28.12.1921, 11.5.1922.

139. HALS HCC2/113 CP25 AR KSRS 1925; HCC2/117 CP20 AR KSRS 1926; HCC2/121 CP27 AR KSRS 1927.

140. BL *Record* 18.5.1923.

141. HALS HCC2/101 CP35 HEC 13.4.1923; HCC2/103 CP147 HEC 19.10.1923; HCC2/106 CP65 AR SH 1923.

142. HALS HCC2/113 CP25 AR KSRS 1925.

143. HALS HCC2/114 CP80 AR SH 1925; HCC2/118 CP89 AR SH 1926.

144. GP Report of the Mental Deficiency Committee, being a joint committee of the Board of Education and Board of Control January 1929, pp.42–3; D.G. Pritchard (1963) p.191.

145. HALS HCC2/113 CP25 AR KSRS 1925; HCC2/125 CP18 AR KSRS 1928; HCC2/129 CP28 AR KSRS 1929; HCC2/133 CP32 AR KSRS 1930.

146. Cited in J. Hurt (1988) p.155.

147. GP BEd AR CMO 1925 p.79.

148. HALS HCC2/121 CP27 AR KSRS 1927.

149. HALS HCC2/125 CP18 AR KSRS 1928.

150. HALS HCC2/126 CP92 AR SH 1928.

151. HALS HCC2/133 CP32 AR KSRS 1930; HCC2/137 CP11 AR KSRS 1931; HEd3 7/1 AR CEO 1934.

152. HALS HCC2/157 CP29 AR KSRS 1936.

153. ibid; HCC2/161 CP8 AR KSRS 1937; HCC2/166 CP52 AR KSRS Jan–March 1939.

154. HALS HCC2/158 CP93 AR SH 1936.

155. D. Thom, 'Wishes, anxieties, play and gestures: child guidance in inter-war England' in Cooter (1992).

156. HALS HCC2/162 CP63 AR SH 1937; HCC2/166 CP62 AR SH 1938.

157. TNA:PRO ED 32/371 HMI report on Watford Special Day School 20.2.1924.

158. HALS HCC2/118 CP89 AR SH 1926; HCC2/122 CP93 AR SH 1927; HCC2/126 CP92 AR SH 1928.

159. TNA:PRO ED 32/371 HMI report on Watford Special Day School 20.2.1924.

160. HALS HCC2/118 CP89 AR SH 1926; HCC2/122 CP93 AR SH 1927; HCC2/126 CP92 AR SH 1928; HCC2/134 CP89 AR SH 1930.

161. TNA:PRO ED 32/371 HMI report on Watford Special Day School 7.11.1933. There appears to be some doubt about the status of Bloom's report as the Medical Department did not formally relinquish responsibility for inspecting the educational side of special school work until September 1934. There was no doubt, though, about its devastating effect. See also GP BEd AR CMO 1933 pp.143–5.

162. ibid.

163. HALS HCC2/158 CP93 AR SH 1936.

164. HALS HCC2/157 CP50 HEC 9.4.1937; HCC2/158 CP93 HEC 21.6.1937.

165. TNA:PRO ED 32/371 GP BEd internal memoranda 26.4.1937, 29.4.1937; HALS HCC2/158 CP93 HEC 21.6.1937.

166. HALS HCC2/98 CP70 AR SH 1921; HCC2/102 CP74 AR SH 1922; HCC2/106 CP65 AR SH 1923; HCC2/105 CP39 HEC 31.3.1924; HEd2 7/13 Hitchin, St Mary's CE Senior Mixed: HMI reports 27.6.1924, 28.3.1928.

167. HALS HCC2/116 CP219 HEC 7.1.1927; HCC2/118 CP89 AR SH 1926.

168. HALS HEd1 88/2 Hertford, Cowper Testimonial Senior Boys 30.7.1931, 8.9.1931, HMI report 8.2.1933

169. HALS HEd 102/2 Much Hadham CE Boys HMI report 18.10.1928; HEd1 48/1 Rushden CE Mixed HMI report 24.9.1933; HEd1 24/2 Harpenden Kinsbourne Green CE Mixed HMI report 11.3.1929; HEd1 75/2 Sacombe CE Mixed HMI reports 5.5.1926, 8.3.1934; HEd1 17/2 Buckland CE Mixed HMI report 8.3.1938.

Chapter 12: Conclusion

1.   BL *Advertiser* 21.2.1936.
2.   HALS HCC2/168 CP150 HCC 6.11.1939.
3.   D. Childs (2nd edn 1986) p.12.

References

British Library: Newspaper Library

Barnet Press, Finchley & Hendon News
Buckinghamshire Advertiser
Education
Essex Chronicle
Hertfordshire Advertiser and St Albans Times
Hertfordshire & Cambridgeshire Reporter and Royston Crow
Hertfordshire & Essex Observer
Hertfordshire Express
Hertfordshire, Hemel Hempstead Gazette
Hertfordshire Mercury
Hertfordshire Record
Letchworth Citizen
National Farmers' Union Record
Times Educational Supplement
Weekly Telegraph for Waltham Abbey, Cheshunt & District
West Hertfordshire & Watford Observer

Buckinghamshire Record Office

Buckinghamshire Education Committee (BEC) Files
BEC 1/30-1/44 Reports of Joint Meetings of the Elementary and Higher Education Sub-Committees 1929–39
BEC 1/219 and 1/246 Joint Conference Committee 1929–39

Essex Record Office

Essex Education Committee File
ERO 106 Report on the Organisation of Elementary Schools 1928
ERO 106 Report of the Director of Education for the three years ended 31 March 1928

ERO 106 Reorganisation of Elementary Schools in Rural Areas 1934
ERO 106 *Education in Essex 1928–1935*

Hertfordshire Archives & Local Studies

School Files
HEd1 1/2 Anstey Church of England Mixed School Logbook
HEd1 3/3, 3/4 Ashwell, Merchant Taylors' Boys' School Logbook
HEd1 4/2 Ayot St Peter Church of England Mixed School Logbook
HEd1 6/3 Barkway Church of England Infants' School Logbook
HEd1 7/3 Barkway Church of England Senior Mixed School Logbook
HEd1 7/5 Barkway Church of England Junior Mixed School Logbook
HEd1 10/1 Barnet, Wood Street Housecraft Centre Syllabus 1934
HEd1 12/6 Hertford, Bengeo, Christ Church Church of England Infants' School Logbook
HEd1 13/2 Waterford Church of England Mixed School Logbook
HEd1 17/2 Buckland Church of England Mixed School Logbook
HEd1 18/1 Clothall Church of England Mixed School Logbook
HEd1 19/2 Digswell Church of England Mixed School Logbook
HEd1 20/1 Eastwick Church of England Mixed School Logbook
HEd1 22/1 Gilston Church of England Mixed School Logbook
HEd1 24/2 Harpenden, Kinsbourne Green Church of England Mixed School Logbook
HEd1 33/2 Hinxworth County Council Mixed School Logbook
HEd1 39/3 Kimpton Church of England Mixed School Logbook
HEd1 40/1 Knebworth, London Road County Council Mixed School Managers' Minute Book
HEd1 44/3 Norton Church of England Mixed School Logbook
HEd1 45/2 Brent Pelham Church of England Mixed School Logbook
HEd1 48/1 Rushden Church of England Mixed School Logbook
HEd1 64/15, 64/16 Watton-atte-Stone Church of England Mixed School Folders of Children's Work 1936–7
HEd1 66/1 Wyddial Church of England Mixed School Logbook
HEd1 67/1 Great Wymondley Church of England Mixed School Logbook
HEd1 70/1 Little Berkhamsted Church of England Mixed School Logbook
HEd1 72/1 Wallington Church of England Mixed School Logbook
HEd1 75/2 Sacombe Church of England Mixed School Logbook
HEd1 76/1 Sandon Church of England Mixed School Logbook
HEd1 78/1 Puckeridge Church of England Mixed School Logbook
HEd1 79/1 St Albans County Council Central School Logbook
HEd1 83/3 Pirton County Council Mixed School Logbook
HEd1 85/7 Bishop's Stortford, Northgate County Council Mixed School Logbook
HEd1 88/2 Hertford, Cowper Testimonial Senior Boys' School Logbook
HEd1 93/4 Hoddesdon Church of England Boys' School Logbook

HEd1 94/9 Royston, Queen's Road County Council Mixed School Logbook

HEd1 96/1 Watford, Callow Land County Council Boys' School Logbook

HEd1 98/2 Sawbridgeworth, Fawbert & Barnard County Council Girls' and Infants' School Logbook

HEd1 98/6 Sawbridgeworth, Fawbert & Barnard County Council Boys' School Logbook

HEd1 100/5 High Wych Church of England Mixed School Logbook

HEd1 101/7, 101/8 and 101/10 Wilstone Church of England Mixed School Logbook and Files

HEd1 102/2 Much Hadham Church of England Boys' School Logbook

HEd1 102/4 Much Hadham Church of England Girls' School Logbook

HEd1 103/5 Bishop's Stortford, St Michael's Church of England Infants' School Logbook

HEd1 108/2 Stanstead Abbotts Church of England Mixed School Logbook

HEd1 112/3 Braughing, Jenyn's County Council Mixed School Logbook

HEd1 113/5 Wareside Church of England Mixed School Logbook

HEd1 133/15, 133/16 Hertingfordbury, Cowper Endowed School Logbook

HEd1 169/12 Rickmansworth, Croxley Green Church of England Senior School, Time Table Autumn Term 1938, Schemes of Work and Periods per Week Spring Term 1939

HEd1 188/5, 188/6 Hatfield Church of England Mixed School Logbook

HEd1 192/5 Holwell, Rand's Charity Mixed School Logbook

HEd1 206/3 Goffs Oak Church of England Mixed School Logbook

HEd2 6/7 Hitchin, St Andrew's Church of England Mixed School Logbook

HEd2 7/13 Hitchin, St Mary's Church of England Senior Mixed School Logbook

HEd2 7/16 Hitchin, St Mary's Church of England Boys' School Logbook

HEd2 7/17 Hitchin, St Mary's Church of England Girls' School Logbook

HEd2 23/1 Letchworth, Pixmore County Council Junior Mixed School Logbook

HEd2 28/1 St Albans, Priory Park County Council Mixed School Logbook

HEd2 33/4, 33/5 Watford Union Urban Managers' Minute Book

HEd2 35/1 Watford County Council Central School Logbook

HEd2 43/2 Barnet Grouped School Managers' Minute Book

Hertfordshire County Council and County Education Committee Papers
HEd3 7/1 Annual Reports of the Chief Education Officer 1933–40

HEd4/20 to HEd4/28 County Education Committee Papers 1914–26

HCC2/97 to HCC2/168 County Council, Committee and Sub-Committee Papers 1922–40

Hertfordshire Local Studies Library
R.G. Auckland (1998) *Sandridge School Logbook 1894–1928* – Transcript

Census 1911, 1921, 1931, 1951

Hertfordshire County Council: *Survey Report & Analysis of County Development Plan, 1951*

Kelly's Directories for Hertfordshire

Imperial War Museum Files

DBN/ES/478 *The Collection of Horse Chestnuts* 1917
The National War Savings Committee Leaflet 13 *War Savings* May 1916

Letchworth First Garden City Heritage Museum

Magazine: *The Garden City (New Series) 1907*

The National Archives: Public Record Office Education Files

ED 10/73, /81, /188
ED 11/78, /115, /187, /279, /297
ED 16/671
ED 18/87
ED 19/88, /379, /586
ED 20/42
ED 23/466
ED 24/1366
ED 32/371
ED 50/150b
ED 51/38, /181
ED 66/10
ED 69/106
ED 72/722
ED 75/15A
ED 77/198
ED 83/30
ED 96/38
ED 97/111, /114, /125, /126
ED 98/34
ED 99/39
ED 114/276, /277, /278
ED 120/36

Stevenage Museum Files

Stevenage 1985 Oral Interview Heritage Project tapes and files

Department for Education and Skills Library

Government Papers

Board of Education: Annual Reports 1913–39

Board of Education: Annual Reports of the Chief Medical Officer 1913–39

Board of Education: Statistics of Public Education in England and Wales 1913–14, 1914–15

Board of Education: Circulars 807, 808, 833, 834, 892, 898, 915, 943, 944, 975, 1009, 1056, 1397, 1444

Board of Education: Pamphlets 46, 60, 64, 99

Board of Education: Suggestions on Rural Education 1908

Board of Education: Memorandum – The Principles and Methods of Rural Education 1911

Board of Education: Elementary Science, including Nature Study 1915

Board of Education: School Attendance and Employment in Agriculture – Summary of returns supplied by LEAs for 1 September 1914 to 31 January 1915

Board of Education: School Attendance and Employment in Agriculture – Summary of returns supplied by LEAs for 1 February 1915 to 30 April 1915

Board of Education: School Attendance and Employment in Agriculture – Summary of returns supplied by county councils of children excused from school attendance for employment in agriculture on 31 January 1916

Board of Education: School Attendance and Employment in Agriculture – Summary of returns supplied by county LEAs of the number of children normally liable to attend school but excused from attendance for the purpose of agricultural employment on 31 January 1916, 31 May 1916 and 16 October 1916

Board of Education: Report of the Consultative Committee on the Education of the Adolescent December 1926 (The Hadow Report)

Board of Education and Board of Control: Report of the Mental Deficiency Committee being a joint committee of the Board of Education and Board of Control January 1929

Books, articles and dissertations

J. Adams (1907 edn) *The Herbartian Psychology Applied to Education*, Heath

L. Andrews (1976) *The Education Act, 1918*, Routledge and Kegan Paul

B. Bailey (1987) 'The development of technical education 1934–39' in *History of Education*, 16

V. Bell (1950) *The Dodo: The Story of a Village Schoolmaster*, Faber

H.M. Burton (1943) *The Education of the Countryman*, Kegan Paul

W. Carr and A. Hartnett (1996) *Education and the Struggle for Democracy*, Open University

D. Cecil (1973) *The Cecils of Hatfield House*, Constable

D. Childs (2nd edn 1986) *Britain since 1945: A Political History*, Routledge

H. Clunn (2nd edn 1937) *The Face of the Home Counties*, Simpkin Marshall

F.G. Cockman (1978) *The Railways of Hertfordshire,* Hertfordshire Library Service and Hertfordshire Local History Council

J.W. Cole and R.H. Pearsall (n.d., but probably late 1925) *Letchworth Civic College: A co-ordinated system of education for a small town* (n.p., but probably the Civic College Committee)

J.W. Cole et al (1926) *Education: methods and ideals in Letchworth* (n.p., but probably Civic College Committee)

S. Constantine, M.W. Kirby and M.B. Rose (eds) (1995) *The First World War in British History*, Edward Arnold

R. Cooter (ed.) (1992) *In the Name of the Child: Health and Welfare 1880–1940*, Routledge

M. Cruikshank (1963) *Church and State in English Education*, Macmillan

M. Cruikshank (1977) 'A Defence of the 1902 Act' in *History of Education Society Bulletin*, 19

N. Daglish (1996) *Education Policy-making in England and Wales: The Crucible Years, 1895–1911*, Woburn Press

C. Davies (1974) *Clean Clothes on Sunday*, Terence Dalton

D.W. Dean (1969) 'The Difficulties of a Labour Educational Policy: The Failure of the Trevelyan Bill, 1929–31' in *British Journal of Educational Studies*, 17

G.J. DeGroot (1996) *Blighty: British Society in the Era of the Great War*, Longman

P. Dewey (1997) *War and Progress: Britain 1914–1945*, Longman

B. Doherty (1964) 'The Hadow Report 1926' in *Durham Research Review*, 15

C. Dyhouse (1981) 'Working Class Mothers and Infant Mortality in England, 1895–1914' in C. Webster (ed.) *Biology, Medicine and Society 1840–1940*, Cambridge University Press

A.M. Edwards (1981) *The Design of Suburbia: A Critical Study in Environmental History*, Pembridge

D. Edwards and R. Pigram (1979) *The Romance of Metroland*, Midas

R. van Emden and S. Humphries (2003) *All Quiet on the Home Front*, Hodder Headline

J. Evans (1955) *The Endless Web: John Dickinson and Co. Ltd. 1804–1954*, Jonathan Cape

T. Fegan (2002) *The Baby Killers: German Air Raids on Britain in the First World War*, Leo Cooper

M.B. Furse (1953) *Stand Therefore! A Bishop's Testimony of Faith in the Church of England*, SPCK

E. Gaskell (1908) *Hertfordshire Leaders*, Queenhithe

M. Gilbert (1994) *First World War*, Weidenfeld and Nicolson

D.I. Gordon (1977) *A Regional History of the Railways of Great Britain, Vol.5, The Eastern Counties*, David and Charles

P. Gordon, R. Aldrich and D. Dean (1991) *Education and Policy in England in the Twentieth Century*, Woburn Press

P.H.J.H. Gosden (1966) *The Development of Educational Administration in England and Wales*, Blackwell

V.C. Greenhalgh (1974) *Local Government Administrators 1870–1974: The Emergence and Growth of a Profession*, PhD University of Leeds

P.A. Gregg (1965) *Social and Economic History of Britain 1760–1965*, Harrap

R.B. Haldane (1902) *Education and Empire*, Murray

B. Harris (1995) *The Health of the Schoolchild: A History of the School Medical Service in England and Wales*, Open University

J. Harris (1993) *Private Lives, Public Spirit: Britain 1870–1914*, Oxford University Press

A. Hastings (1986) *A History of English Christianity 1920–1985*, Collins

H. Hendrick (1980) 'A Race of Intelligent Unskilled Labourers: the Adolescent Worker and the Debate on Compulsory Part-Time Day Continuation Schools, 1900–1922' in *History of Education*, 9

W.R. Hughes (1919) *New Town: A Proposal in Agricultural, Industrial, Educational, Civic and Social Reconstruction*, J.M. Dent

J. Hurt (1979) *Elementary Schooling and the Working Classes 1860–1918*, Routledge and Kegan Paul

J. Hurt (1988) *Outside the Mainstream: A History of Special Education*, Batsford

M. Hyndman (1978) *Schools and Schooling in England and Wales: A Documentary History*, Harper and Row

P. Johnson (ed.) (1994) *Twentieth Century Britain: Economic, Social and Cultural Change*, Longman

D.K. Jones (1977) *The Making of the Education System 1851–1881*, Routledge and Kegan Paul

B. Keith-Lucas and P. Richards (1978) *A History of Local Government in the Twentieth Century*, Allen and Unwin

M. Lawn (1987) *Servants of the State: The Contested Control of Teaching 1900–1930*, Falmer

K. Laybourn (1990) *Britain on the Breadline: A Social and Economic History of Britain 1918–39*, Sutton

J.M. Lee (1963) *Social Leaders and Public Persons: A Study of Local Government in Cheshire since 1888*, Oxford

T.O. Lloyd (1986) *Empire to Welfare State: English History 1906–1985*, Oxford University Press

G.A.N. Lowndes (1969) *The Silent Social Revolution: an account of the expansion of public education in England and Wales, 1895-1965*, Oxford University Press

J.S. Maclure (ed.) (3rd edn 1973) *Educational Documents: England and Wales, 1816 to the present day*, Methuen

M. Macmillan (2001) *Peacemakers: The Paris Peace Conference of 1919 and Its Attempt to End War*, John Murray

P. Magnus (1910) *Educational Aims and Efforts 1880–1910*, Longmans, Green and Co.

A. Marwick (1965) *The Deluge: British Society and the First World War*, The Bodley Head

C.F.G. Masterman (1909) *The Condition of England*, Methuen

H.C.G. Matthew and B. Harrison (2004) *Oxford Dictionary of National Biography*, Oxford University Press

R. McKibbon (1998) *Classes and Cultures: England 1918–51*, Clarendon Press

L. Munby (1977) *The Hertfordshire Landscape*, Hodder and Stoughton

J. Murphy (1971) *Church, State and Schools in Britain 1800–1971*, Routledge and Kegan Paul

E.R. Norman (1976) *Church and Society in England 1770–1970*, Clarendon Press

F.J. Osborn (1946) *Green Belt Cities: The British Contribution*, Evelyn Adams and Mackay

F.M. Page (1959) *History of Hertford*, Spriggs

W. Page (ed.) (1971 edn) *Victoria County History of Hertfordshire*, vol. 4, University of London, Institute of Historical Research

H. Perkins (1969) *The Origins of Modern English Society 1780–1880*, Routledge and Kegan Paul

W.T. Pike (1907) *Bucks, Beds and Herts in the 20th Century: Contemporary Biographies*, W.T. Pike Publishing

J.B. Priestley (1934) *English Journey: Being a rambling but truthful account of what one man saw and heard and felt and thought during a journey through England during the autumn of the year 1933*, Mandarin

D.G. Pritchard (1963) *Education and the Handicapped*, Routledge

C.B. Purdom (1913) *The Garden City – a study in the development of a modern town*, Dent

E.E. Rich (1970) *The Education Act 1870*, Longman

F.C. Roberts (1979) *Obituaries from The Times 1951–60*, Newspaper Archives Developments Ltd

D.H. Robinson (1980) *The Zeppelin in Combat*, University of Washington Press

G. Robinson (1978) *Hertfordshire*, Barracuda

T. Rook (1984) *A History of Hertfordshire*, Phillimore

H. Roper (1976) *Administering the Education Acts 1870–1885*, University of Leeds Museum of Education

K. Rose (1975) *The Later Cecils*, Weidenfeld and Nicolson

B.S. Rowntree and G.R. Lavers (1951) *English Life and Leisure*, Longmans, Green

V.R. Rust (1971) *The Development of Primary and Secondary Education in Essex 1902–57*, MA University of Kent

M. Sanderson (1999) *Education and Economic Decline in Britain 1870 to the 1990s*, Cambridge University Press

R.J.W. Selleck (1968) *The New Education 1870–1914*, Pitman

G. Sheldrick (1989) *The Hart Reguardant: Hertfordshire County Council 1889–1898*, Hertfordshire Publications

B. Simon (1965) *Education and the Labour Movement 1870–1920*, Lawrence and Wishart

B. Simon (1974 edn) *The Two Nations and the Educational Structure 1780–1870*, Lawrence and Wishart

B. Simon (1977) 'The 1902 Education Act – A Wrong Turning' in *History of Education Society Bulletin*, 19

R. Skidelsky (1994 edn) *Politicians and the Slump: The Labour Government of 1929–31*, Macmillan Papermac

V. Sparrow (1981) *Yesterday's Stortford*, Barracuda

H. Spencer (1949) *Essays on Education*, Dent

J. Stevenson and C. Cook (1977) *The Slump: Society and Politics during the Depression*, Jonathan Cape

J. Stevenson (1984) *British Society 1914–45*, Penguin

M. Swenarton (1981) *Homes Fit For Heroes: the politics and architecture of early state housing in Britain*, Heinemann

A.J.P. Taylor (1970 edn) *English History 1914–45*, Penguin

J. Thirsk (1978) *The Agrarian History of England and Wales 1914–1939*, Cambridge University Press

A. Tropp (1957) *The School Teachers: the growth of the teaching profession in England and Wales from 1800 to the present day*, Heinemann

Watford Borough Council (1972) *Watford Official Guide*

H.P. White (1963) *A Regional History of the Railways of Great Britain, Vol.3, Greater London*, David and Charles, Newton Abbot

R.J. Whiteman (1936) *Hexton: A Parish Survey*, Hexton (privately printed)

Who's Who in Hertfordshire (1936) Who's Who in the County Series

Who Was Who Vol. 2 1916–1928 (1929) A. & C. Black

Who Was Who Vol. 3 1929–1940 (1941) A. & C. Black

Who Was Who Vol. 4 1941–1950 (1952) A. & C. Black

Who Was Who Vol. 7 1961–1970 (1972) A. & C. Black

J. Winter and B. Baggett (1996) *The Great War and the Shaping of the 20th Century*, Penguin Studio

Index